Lecture Notes in Artificial Intelligence 7249

Subseries of Lecture Notes in Computer Science

Luc Steels (Ed.)

Computational Issues in Fluid Construction Grammar

A New Formalism for the Representation of Lexicons and Grammars

Volume Editor

Luc Steels
Universitat Pompeu Fabra - CSIC
ICREA - Institute for Evolutionary Biology
PRBB Building
Doctor Aiguader 88
08003 Barcelona, Spain
E-mail: steels@arti.vub.ac.be

ISSN 0302-9743 e-ISSN 1611-3349
ISBN 978-3-642-34119-9 e-ISBN 978-3-642-34120-5
DOI 10.1007/978-3-642-34120-5
Springer Heidelberg Dordrecht London New York

Library of Congress Control Number: 2012950906

CR Subject Classification (1998): I.2.7, I.2, F.4.2-3, F.3, D.2-3

LNCS Sublibrary: SL 7 – Artificial Intelligence

Typesetting: Camera-ready by author, data conversion by Scientific Publishing Services, Chennai, India

Printed on acid-free paper

Springer is part of Springer Science+Business Media (www.springer.com)

Preface

Fluid construction grammar (FCG) is a new formalism for the representation of lexicons and grammars. It is fully operational and has been used in a wide range of case studies for different languages, both for studying specific grammatical phenomena and design patterns [2] and for investigating language learning and language evolution [3]. It is available for download at http://www.fcg-net.org/. FCG builds further on decades of research in formal and computational linguistics but applies these insights toward capturing the core ideas of a constructional approach to language [1]. This means that lexico-grammar takes the form of bi-directional associations between a semantic pole and a syntactic pole that capture, respectively, aspects of the meaning and the form of an utterance. In the case of FCG, these associations can be used unchanged either for parsing or for production.

This book is not a tutorial nor an introductory text on FCG. The reader is referred to [2] as well as the FCG website for such materials. Instead, it focuses on the many complex computational issues that arise when writing challenging real-world grammars. The book emphasizes depth of analysis rather than broad scope. It starts with Part I, Basics, which contains two papers. The first paper "Design Methods for Fluid Construction Grammar" by Luc Steels introduces some design methods that are currently used to write FCG grammars, emphasizing the use of templates that are computational abstractions over the intricate details that are needed to get operational reversible constructions. The second paper "Tools for Grammar Engineering" by Martin Loetzsch focuses on how grammar writers interface with the FCG system. This happens either through a Web-based graphical interface where both constructions and transient structures become active objects that can be inspected or through a text-based editor.

Part II, Implementation, discusses some of the aspects of the current implementation. The first contribution by Remi van Trijp entitled "A Reflective Architecture for Robust Language Processing and Learning" explores how the same representations and procedures for routine language processing can be reused for meta-level processing in order to handle problems or novelty in linguistic interactions, such as unknown words, ungrammatical utterances, or incomplete fragments. The second contribution by Kevin Stadler "Chunking Constructions" considers the problem of how a chain of constructions can be chunked together and stored as such in memory in order to avoid search and speed-up processing.

Part III, Case Studies, looks at a range of linguistic phenomena and shows each time how they can be handled in fluid construction grammar. Each contribution focuses on a particular human natural language which is representative for the phenomenon being studied. "Expressing Grammatical Meaning with Morphology: A Case Study for Russian Aspect" by Kateryna Gerasymova focuses on the complete system of expression of aspect in Russian. The contribution "Handling Scope in Fluid Construction Grammar: A Case Study for Spanish Modals" by Katrien Beuls studies various typical challenges for grammars, such as syncretism (one form has multiple functions), scoping, sequencing of constructions, and handling of discourse context using Spanish modals as case study. Polish is the target language for a contribution by Sebastian Hoefer entitled "Complex Declension Systems and Morphology in Fluid Construction Grammar: A Case Study of Polish." Polish is notorious for a complex system of nominal declensions and this contribution shows that the design pattern of feature matrices can be extended to deal with them. The final case study entitled "Field Topology and Information Structure: A Case Study for German Constituent Order" by Vanessa Micelli studies a design pattern based on field topology. She shows how this pattern can be implemented in FCG and used to handle constituent ordering in the German main clause.

Part IV, Formal Analysis, looks at the formal foundations of FCG. The first paper by Joachim De Beule entitled "A Formal Deconstruction of Fluid Construction Grammar" defines the basic notions of FCG in a formal way. A companion paper by Josefina Sierra Santibáñez, "A Logic Programming Approach to Parsing and Production in Fluid Construction Grammar," compared FCG matching and merging with the standard unification operators of first order logic, which opens the door to using techniques from logic computation such as satisfiability problem solving to build alternative implementations.

The final part of this book, Part V Comparisons, takes a broader view and compares or seeks other implementations of construction grammar. The first paper by Nancy Chang, Joachim De Beule and Vanessa Micelli, entitled "Computational Construction Grammar: Comparing ECG and FCG," compares fluid construction grammar with another attempt at formalizing and operationalizing construction grammar, namely embodied construction grammar. The second paper, "Fluid Construction Grammar and Feature Constraint Logics," by Liviu Ciortuz and Vlad Saveluc tries to bridge the gap between FCG and mainstream unification grammars using feature constraint logics. Finally, the third paper, "Fluid Construction Grammar in the Brain," by Chrisantha Fernando describes the first efforts to find a neural implementation of FCG.

The papers in this volume attest to the rich research that is building up around fluid construction grammar, both from the viewpoint of linguistic case studies and from the viewpoint of language processing. It shows that deep language processing with precision grammars remains as challenging as ever and that many discoveries are still waiting to be made. This volume is just a stepping stone and much more work needs to be done.

March 2012 Luc Steels

References

1. Goldberg, A.E.: Constructions: A New Theoretical Approach to Language. Trends in Cognitive Science 7(5), 219–224 (May 2003)
2. Steels, L. (ed.): Design Patterns in Fluid Construction Grammar. John Benjamins, Pub., Amsterdam (2011)
3. Steels, L. (ed.): Experiments in Cultural Language Evolution. John Benjamins, Pub., Amsterdam (2012)

Table of Contents

Part I: Basics

Design Methods for Fluid Construction Grammar 3
Luc Steels

Tools for Grammar Engineering 37
Martin Loetzsch

Part II: Implementation

A Reflective Architecture for Robust Language Processing and Learning 51
Remi van Trijp

Chunking Constructions 75
Kevin Stadler

Part III: Case Studies

Expressing Grammatical Meaning with Morphology: A Case Study for Russian Aspect 91
Kateryna Gerasymova

Handling Scope in Fluid Construction Grammar: A Case Study for Spanish Modals 123
Katrien Beuls

Complex Declension Systems and Morphology in Fluid Construction Grammar: A Case Study of Polish 143
Sebastian Höfer

Field Topology and Information Structure: A Case Study for German Constituent Order 178
Vanessa Micelli

Part IV: Formal Analysis

A Formal Deconstruction of Fluid Construction Grammar 215
Joachim De Beule

A Logic Programming Approach to Parsing and Production in Fluid Construction Grammar ... 239
Josefina Sierra-Santibáñez

Part V: Comparisons

Computational Construction Grammar: Comparing ECG and FCG ... 259
Nancy Chang, Joachim De Beule, and Vanessa Micelli

Fluid Construction Grammar and Feature Constraint Logics ... 289
Liviu Ciortuz and Vlad Saveluc

Fluid Construction Grammar in the Brain ... 312
Chrisantha Fernando

Author Index ... 331

Part I
Basics

Design Methods for Fluid Construction Grammar

Luc Steels[1,2]

[1] ICREA-Institut de Biologia Evolutiva (CSIC-UPF), Barcelona, Spain
[2] Sony Computer Science Laboratory Paris, France

Abstract. The paper sketches a methodology for designing and implementing complex lexicons and grammars using Fluid Construction Grammar (FCG). FCG emphasizes a functional viewpoint of language and decomposes grammatical systems based on their semantic domains and communicative functions. Rather than directly specifying all the components of a construction explicitly, which would lead to highly complex definitions, FCG uses abstractions in the form of templates that implement design patterns common across human languages.

1 Introduction

Fluid Construction Grammar (FCG) is a new formalization of many ideas that have been proposed in the recent literature on cognitive linguistics ([20, 21, 46]) and construction grammar ([8, 14, 15, 18, 26]). A *construction* is a regular pattern of usage in a language - such as a word, a combination of words, an idiom, or a syntactic pattern - which has a conventionalized meaning and function. For example, a resultative construction implies a particular syntactic pattern of the form: Subject Verb Direct-Object Predicate, as in "Mary licked her plate clean". It expresses that the referent of the Direct-Object ("her plate") gets into a particular state ("clean") based on the action described in the main verb ("licked") and carried out by the subject ("Mary").

A *construction grammar* catalogs the different constructions in a language, both their semantic (including pragmatic) aspects and their syntactic (including morphological and phonetic) aspects. Although construction grammars are usually described only in verbal terms, particularly when the grammar is intended for second language learning or teaching, it is entirely possible to formalize and operationalize construction grammar in order to model human natural language processing. Such an implementation has the advantage of making it clear what a construction entails, and it makes the use of construction grammars in computational applications possible.

Formalizations of construction grammar differ from generative rewrite grammars in two ways:

1. The definition of constructions takes the form of *bi-directional associations* relating aspects of meaning to aspects of form, so that the same construction can be used unchanged in parsing as well as production *without* compromising efficiency. Production here entails more than randomly generating a

L. Steels (Ed.): Computational Issues in FCG, LNAI 7249, pp. 3–36, 2012.

possible sentence. It is the process whereby the meaning resulting from conceptualization is turned into the best possible sentence respecting as much as possible known conventions of the language.
2. The bi-directional associations potentially have to take into consideration aspects from all levels of language (pragmatics, semantics, syntax, morphology and phonetics), simply because human language is not modularly organized. For example, Hungarian (poly-personal) verbal agreement is based on semantic considerations, because the position of the subject with respect to the deictic center is taken into account, syntactic considerations, because it happens only when a certain case structure is present, morphological considerations, because the form of the verb determines which suffix is used, and phonetic considerations because there has to be vowel harmony between the main vowel in the verb stem and the suffix [3]. Lexicon and grammar can therefore be best organized vertically based on data structures that cut across different levels rather than horizontally in terms of modular autonomous layers where syntax is treated independently from semantics or phonetics.

A construction in formal construction grammar therefore defines not only a particular syntactic pattern but also the semantic structure implied by the pattern, and it may include additional pragmatic, morphological and phonetic aspects, as well as the extra meaning that the construction contributes to the meanings contributed by its constituents.

FCG is one of a growing number of computational construction grammars, which also includes Embodied Construction Grammar [2] and Sign-based Construction Grammar [25]. It has been developed specifically for building deep production and comprehension systems that can act as the core of grounded human-robot or robot-robot interactions, utilizing world models derived from perception and motor activity (see Figure 1) [35]. Deep language processing requires handling rich representations of grammatical structure and an integration of semantics right into the grammar (as opposed to delegating the problem of semantics to another component).

FCG is based on techniques widely used in current computational linguistics, in particular the representation of linguistic structures with feature structures [4, 7], and the use of unification for applying constructions to expand linguistic structures in language parsing and production, as pioneered in Functional Unification Grammar [17], and also used in Lexical Functional Grammar [9], and Head-driven Phrase structure Grammar ([28, 29]). At the same time, FCG introduces a number of innovations, such as a powerful structure-building operator called the J-operator. FCG is implemented on top of a Common LISP environment as most other computational grammars. It is fully operational and made available for free to the research community (http://www.fcg-net.org/). It has already been used in a variety of experiments in (artificial) language evolution and human-robot interaction [38, 39, 43].

Fig. 1. FCG has been developed for experiments in human-robot and robot-robot interaction, which requires that not only lexical and syntactic issues be handled but also semantics and grounded meaning

There are now various introductory texts and papers reporting worked out examples in FCG (see in particular [41] and [43]). The present paper focuses on the design methods that have emerged for coping with the complexity of real world grammars. Complexity is not meant here with respect to the size of the inventory of constructions (although that is also a critical point) but rather with respect to the depth with which the relevant linguistic phenomena are handled. Computer science has a lot of experience in building very complex systems and has proposed various design concepts such as the use of design patterns, computational abstractions, compilation from high level specifications, etc. These same concepts are potentially of great value in grammar design as well.

Typically, constructions in FCG are defined in terms of a layer of abstractions based on *templates*. Templates capture common design patterns relevant for human languages, such as functional structure, agreement, field topology, valence, linking, etc. [41] Different templates together build an operational construction so that a modular design remains possible, even though at the operational level this modularity is no longer explicitly present. Efficiency considerations are separated as much as possible from design considerations. Efficiency is gained by compiling templates, by maintaining dependencies between constructions that can be used for priming [49] and by chunking combinations of constructions [32]. The use of templates also plays an important role in modeling language learning, because they can act as primitive operators for expanding or changing constructions.

The remainder of this paper is structured along the three proposed levels of grammar design and implementation. The first section addresses the linguistic level. It introduces the main linguistic principles of construction grammar in general and the specific linguistic approach that is used in Fluid Construction Grammar in particular. These principles are familiar to linguists but are included to help computer scientists grasp the fundamentals of construction grammar. The next section turns to the design level, explicating the notion of a design pattern and the templates used to implement them. The third section turns to the operational level, introducing some of the main representational mechanisms and processing steps available in FCG. The operational level is defined here only very briefly. It is discussed more formally in a later chapter of this book [10] and the reader is referred to the introductory papers in [41] and the manual and other on-line resources on the FCG distribution website: http://www.fcg-net.org/.

2 Linguistic Level

This section briefly introduces the general approach to language that is advocated in construction grammars, and some of the more specific choices that have been adopted for Fluid Construction Grammar. One of the most principled points is that Fluid Construction Grammar advocates a functionalist rather than formalist perspective on language.

2.1 The Functionalist versus Formalist Perspective on Language

The debate between functionalists and formalists has been raging in linguistics for a long time, although the debate is often more rhetorical than real [27]. Nevertheless, there is a profound difference in point of view, with significant consequences on how one approaches language processing and language learning. From a functionalist point of view, language is primarily seen as a tool for communication. The speaker is influencing the cognitive activities that go on in the mind of the hearer, so that the hearer will pay attention to certain aspects of the world, perform certain actions, store information, start a thinking process, etc. A specific sentence is a way to evoke some of the tools provided by the language and provide specific settings for their usage.

From a formalist perspective, language is not primarily studied as a communicative tool. The focus of analysis is on the perceivable properties of sentences and their structure. It would be like describing a hammer as consisting of a cylinder and a block, attached in a particular way to each other, whereas a functionalist perspective would describe a hammer as consisting of a handle and a head. The handle is for holding the hammer and the head for hitting the object. The handle and the head typically take the form of a cylinder and a block, but the functionalist perspective emphasizes the importance of their function, particularly because the same function can often be achieved by objects with many different kinds of shapes. For example, the two cylinders could be of equal size, the handle could either stick through the head or be attached to it in some other way, the head could take the form of a block instead of a cylinder, etc. More radically, an entirely different object such as a shoe can become a hammer with the sole functioning as head.

In linguistics, those adopting a formalist viewpoint emphasize the syntactic structures of a language, usually by defining a procedure for generating all possible structures judged to be grammatical in a language, whereas those adopting a functionalist viewpoint focus on identifying how forms achieve syntactic and semantic functions. Thus, the distinction between nouns and verbs is not viewed as purely structural, i.e. in terms of which syntactic structures they can be part of, but in terms of possible functions that nouns and verbs can have in communicative activities: Nouns can be used as nominals to introduce classes of objects for forming referring expressions whereas verbs typically introduce classes of events to describe a state of affairs.

Generally speaking, taking a functional stance for dealing with tools has a number of clear advantages. The better you understand the function of each component of a tool the more you can use it properly. A functional perspective also helps to select the right variant of a tool for a particular context, for recognizing a tool even if it does not have a classical shape, and for improving it. Of course, often people use tools without understanding them fully and just imitate how they have seen others using the tool. This stage is often the first step towards acquiring full mastery which unavoidably requires a functionalist perspective.

The same advantages can be seen when language is treated as a tool. A functional analysis leads to a better understanding of why language is the way it is and to parsing and production systems that are more flexible and robust [44]. It suggests also an alternative to purely statistical language learning techniques, one which uses *functional inference* instead of inductive inference. Concretely, the learner figures out the meaning and the function of unknown words or constructions by reconstructing which unknown forms were introduced to achieve them [34].

2.2 Semantic Functions and Cognitive Operations

Once we adopt a functionalist view on language, it becomes clear quite quickly that every element in a sentence has both a meaning and a semantic function. The *meaning* or semantic content of a word is the concept it introduces, and the *semantic function* is what is to be done with this building block during interpretation. For example, the word "slow" in "the slow train" evokes the concept 'slow', which concerns the relative speed of moving objects. Its semantic function, at least in this phrase, is to restrict the set of possible referents of the noun, specifically to restrict the set of trains in the context to those that have a slow speed.

The same meaning can have a variety of semantic functions, as illustrated in the following sentences:

1. The *slow* train.
2. They *slow* down.
3. The *slow* go first.
4. The train was *slow*.
5. They ran *slowly*.

All these sentences make use of the concept of 'slow', but they differ in what they require the hearer to do with this concept: (in 1.) to use it to further restrict the class of possible referents, (in 2.) to circumscribe the movement of the subject of the sentence, (in 3.) to identify a class of objects based on their speed, (in 4.) to assert a property of the subject, and (in 5.) to provide an additional attribute of the movement introduced by the verb.

The notion of semantic function is often only vaguely defined. When we want to formalize and operationalize grammar we need a more precise definition. FCG assumes the perspective of procedural semantics, which proposes that the interpretation of a sentence requires executing a set of cognitive operations over a perceptually grounded world model and discourse model [50, 51]. Each operation yields a particular result (for example it delineates a set of objects in the context) which can then again be used by other operations. The operations include set operations, selection of elements out of sets, filtering operations, the computation of perceptual features of specific entities, geometric transformations of positions of objects to achieve perspective reversal, etc.

Here are some concrete examples of cognitive operations:

1. `get-context`, which gets the objects in the present context and stores them in a discourse model.
2. `filter-set-class`, which takes a set of objects in the discourse model and filters out those which belong to a certain identified class.
3. `count-elements-set`, which takes a set of objects in the discourse model and counts how many elements it contains.
4. `select-unique-element`, which selects the unique element out of a singleton set.
5. `set-union`, which forms the union of two sets.
6. `describe-event`, which asserts that a particular event takes place in the current context

Our group has developed a meaning representation system called Incremental Recruitment Language (IRL) that can be used for grounded procedural semantics [33]. Each cognitive operation in IRL takes a number of arguments, one of which (usually called the target argument) is considered to be the result of the cognitive operation. Cognitive operations can be combined together in a network with one operation providing or using results produced by another one, as shown for example in Figure 2 from [31], which represents the procedural semantics of the German phrase "der vordere Block" (the front block). When such a network is executed, each cognitive operation computes specific values for its arguments as fitting with the present world model and discourse context. These values propagate in the network until no more computation can be done. IRL is not further discussed in the present book because its details are not directly relevant to grammatical processing. See reference [30] for an introduction and more examples.

We can now be more precise about what a semantic function is. It specifies the *role* of a conceptual building block, such as 'slow', in a particular cognitive operation. For example, the semantic function of "slow" in "the slow train" is

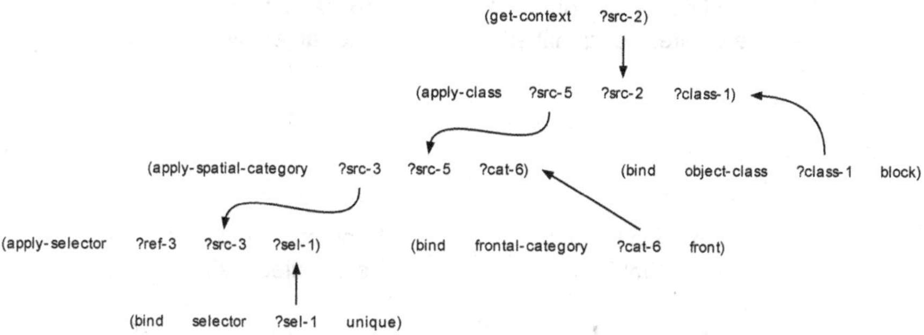

Fig. 2. Example of a network of cognitive operations as needed for interpreting the German sentence "der vordere Block" (the front block). Each cognitive operation has a number of arguments (indicated with a question mark in front of them) which are to be filled by specific values. The arrows indicate that there are data flow relations between the different cognitive operations.

called a *qualifier* because the concept 'slow' is used in this case as the qualifier of a `filter-set-qualifier` operation. This operation filters a set of objects in the discourse model with respect to whether they satisfy a given attribute. The target outcome of this filtering operation is to further restrict a set of possible referents.

With each semantic function corresponds also a *syntactic function* which is associated with a *lexical category*, also known as a part of speech or a word class. For example, the semantic function of "slowly" is to modify the movement concept introduced by the verb "ran". This syntactic function is usually called adverbial. The adverbial function is signalled by the affix "-ly", which turns "slow", by default an adjective, into an adverb.

The same lexical category is associated with many potential syntactic functions and the same syntactic function with many potential semantic functions. For example, an adjective may be used as a qualifier (as in "the slow train") but also as a predicate (as in "the train is slow"). The same word "light" may be used in an adjectival function as a qualifier (as in "the light block") or in an adverbial function as a modifier of another color concept (as in "the light green block").

In parsing, the choice of which syntactic or semantic function is actually the case is based on the syntactic and semantic context. In production, the choice is based on what cognitive operations the speaker wants the hearer to perform. For example, if the speaker wants the hearer to perform a `filter-set-qualifier` operation using 'slow', this will require a word that can act in an adjectival function. Many human languages (including English) are quite flexible with respect to which lexical category can satisfy which syntactic function because a word which by default belongs to one category can often be coerced into another category, and this coercion can then become conventionally accepted in the language. For example, in "The slow go first", the adjective "slow" has been coerced

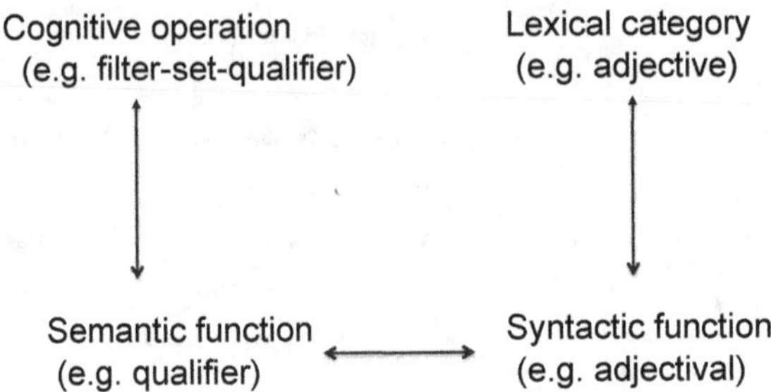

Fig. 3. From a functional point of view, lexical category are associated with possible syntactic functions, which are associated with possible semantic functions. A semantic functions specifies the role of a concept in a cognitive operation.

into a nominal function so that it can be used semantically to identify a class of objects.

The associations between lexical categories, syntactic functions and semantic functions are bi-directional (see figure 3). Information about the lexical category of a word is used during parsing to hypothesize a possible syntactic function, which is then used to hypothesize a possible semantic function. During production, the mappings are used in the reverse order. A particular semantic function is potentially actualized with a particular syntactic function, which is then expressed using words with specific lexical categories. The table in Figure 4 contains some more examples of such associations, all involving the word "slow" as illustrated in the sentences given earlier.

lex-cat	syntactic fnct	semantic fnct	cognitive oper
1. adjective	adjectival	qualifier	filter-set-qualifier
2. verb	verbal	event	describe-event
3. noun	nominal	identifier	filter-set-identifier
4. adjective	predicate	predicate	describe-predicate
5. adverb	adverbial	modifier	apply-modifier

Fig. 4. Examples of associations between lexical categories (parts of speech), syntactic functions, and semantic functions. The relevant cognitive operation is given in the last column.

2.3 Phrasal Structures

One of the key characteristics of human languages is their hierarchical or compositional nature. A sentence does not only consist of individual words which each have their own syntactic and semantic functions, but of phrases that group several words or phrases together so that they can function as units in their own right. Phrases belong to a particular syntactic type (for example nominal phrase) and have the potential to take on syntactic or semantic functions within larger phrases, just like individual words. The meaning of a phrase consists of a network of cognitive operations whose arguments are interlinked. These operations and some of the bindings for their arguments are provided by the individual words, but the phrase may add additional cognitive operations and linkings of its own.

From a functionalist perspective, phrases are primarily defined in terms of the functions of their constituents, just as a hammer is primarily defined from a functional point of view in terms of the functions of its components. For example, a nominal phrase like "the train" consists of a determiner and a nominal. The semantic function of the nominal is to identify a set of objects in the present context, and the determiner then specifies which element or elements needs to be selected out of this set.

The constraints that allow a constituent (word or phrase) to play a particular role within a phrase depend on the language. They typically include the following:

1. *Syntactic Categorizations*: Constituents of a phrase typically have to belong to certain lexical categories (if they are individual words) or phrase types (if they are phrases themselves), or they need to have at least the potential to take on certain syntactic functions, possibly after coercion. For example, a constituent can normally only be the determiner of a nominal phrase if it is an article or numeral.
2. *Semantic Categorizations*: The referent of a constituent typically has to be of a certain semantic type. For example, the meaning of a nominal has to produce a set, and this set is often restricted based on the kind of nominal phrase it occurs in. For example, a plural definite article implies that the set of objects from which the determiner selects one or more elements has to be a countable set.
3. *Ordering*: Often the constituents of a phrase are constrained in terms of the order in which they appear inside the phrase. For example, a compositional color description such as "light blue" requires that the constituent introducing the non-hue category acting as modifier appears before the hue category acting as the qualifier.
4. *Agreement*: Often there are syntactic and semantic agreement relations between the constituents of a phrase. For example, the constituents functioning as the determiner, adjectival, and nominal of the same nominal phrase have to agree with respect to number and gender in French.

The primary function of a phrasal construction is to define all these characteristics and to specify also properties of the phrase as a whole, such as which features percolate up from constituents to the phrase (for example, if the noun in a nominal phrase is feminine then the phrase as a whole will be feminine in French), what additional syntactic and semantic properties hold for the phrase, and how the meaning of the phrase is composed by combining the meanings of the parts [40].

2.4 The Grammar Square

Lexical items and phrase structure form the backbone of a sentence because they signal the main conceptual building blocks that the speaker wants to convey and how these building blocks are to be used when interpreting a sentence. It turns out that human languages often convey various additional meanings (usually called *grammatical meanings*) by modulating and extending the basic skeletal structure or by adding morphological or phonetic variations on the words already used. This is similar to the way in which a (classical) figurative painting introduces a basic structure for the scene, such as the different figures against the background, and then superimposes additional aspects. For example, the painter may use a particular color palette to give the scene an emotional quality, or add contrast in terms of lighter and shaded areas to highlight some of the elements in the scene, or depict strong facial expressions and postures to add drama.

Grammatical meanings expressed in many human languages can be classified in terms of the different semantic and functional domains they are concerned with. Here are some examples:

- *Argument-structure*: Most languages have ways in which the roles of participants in events can be made clearer by specifying who does what to whom, overlaid on the basic phrase structure, for example, by using cases and morphological affixes or by exploiting the sequential ordering of constituents in the sentence and using specific prepositions.
- *Tense-Aspect*: Many languages have ways to be more precise about the relation of an event with respect to the time of discourse (present/past/future) or to highlight the internal structure of events (ongoing, terminated, repetitive, etc.).
- *Modality*: Many languages have ways to express the epistemic attitudes of the speaker with respect to the information that is provided in the sentence. For example, they may specify whether the state of affairs described by the main verb is true or only hypothesized, what evidence was available and how this was acquired, whether the source is reliable, etc.
- *Determination*: Many languages have ways to be more precise about how the referent of a nominal phrase can be accessed, usually in terms of different articles such as "the", "some", or "every", or in terms of marking morphologically the distinction between mass or count nouns or definite and indefinite referents.
- *Social status*: Many languages express the social attitude of the speaker or the relation between speaker and hearer by adding morphological markers or particles, or by choosing other lexical items. A very simple example is the use of "tu" versus "vous" for the second person pronoun in French.
- *Information structure*: Many languages are able to provide information related to discourse, such as what object is assumed to be known from earlier conversation, what information addresses a question posed in the dialog, what the main highlighted topic is, etc. For example, German marks a constituent as being the focal topic of a sentence by moving it into first sentence position (fronting) or by stressing it.

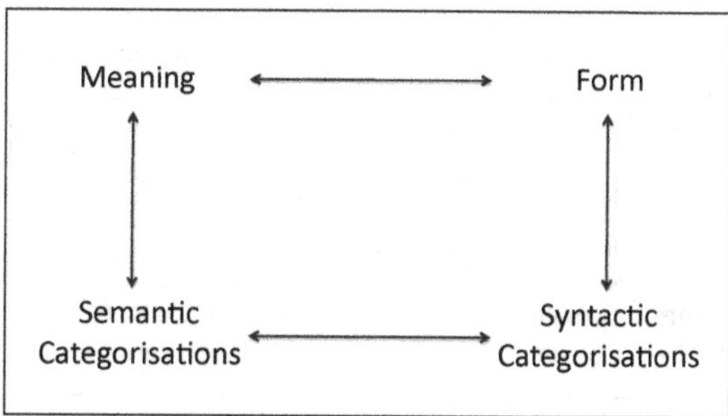

Fig. 5. The grammar square depicts the different associations between meaning and form. Meaning is directly related to a specific form in the case of lexical constructions. But in the case of grammatical meanings it goes through the intermediary of semantic and syntactic categorizations.

Not all grammatical meanings are explicitly expressible in all languages, and for each language there are significant differences in the semantic distinctions they express and how they do it. What is common, however, is that grammatical meanings are mapped to syntactic forms through the intermediary of semantic and syntactic categorizations that are language-specific (Figure 5).

This multi-layered character of the mapping from meaning to form is characteristic for grammar, in opposition to the lexicon, which immediately maps aspects of meaning to aspects of form. Grammatical mappings are always bi-directional. In production, they are traversed from meaning to form and in production from form to meaning. The reason why languages use indirect mappings for grammar, rather than going directly from meaning to form, is that this allows the definition of more abstract relations between meaning and form and because other factors may play a role in the mapping so that more information can be packed into the same material.

Here is a concrete example of this multi-layered mapping for the domain of argument structure (illustrated in more detail in [47]). Specific participant roles such as the pusher of a push-event are not directly mapped onto syntactic markers, because that would require a large set of markers, specific to each verb. Instead, participant roles are semantically categorized in terms of abstract semantic roles such as agent, patient, beneficiary, instrument, location, etc., and these semantic roles are first mapped onto syntactic cases such as nominative, accusative, dative, genitive (or in language without a case system onto grammatical relations such as subject, direct object, indirect object, oblique object), before they are mapped to surface markers such as morphological affixes or constituent orderings. At each step, context, and hence additional meaning, can play a role. For example, the semantic role of agent can be mapped to subject (or nominative) in active sentences only. When the speaker wants to highlight the patient, he can make it the subject, as in "the block was pushed to the edge of the table".

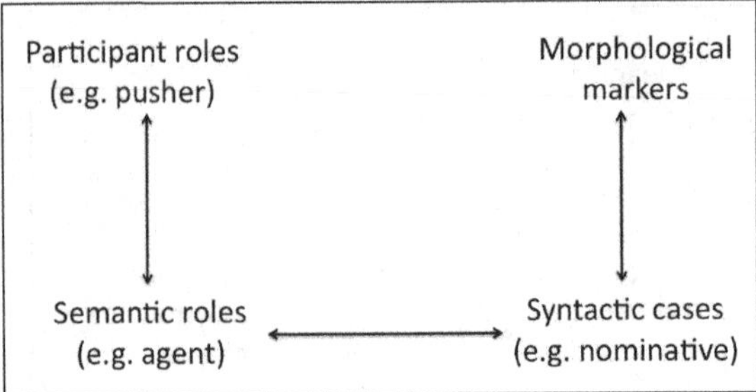

Fig. 6. Instantiation of the grammar square for argument structure. Participant roles in events are not directly mapped to specific markers but through the intermediary of abstract semantic categorizations in the form of semantic roles, such as agent or instrument, and abstract syntactic categorizations in the form of grammatical relations or cases, such as subject or nominative.

Semantic and syntactic categorizations cannot always be so neatly distinguished. For example, in the case of tense, many languages use a more direct mapping from semantic categorizations of the time moment of an event (present - past - future) to surface realizations based on auxiliaries or morphological markers (as in: come - came - will come). Nevertheless, in analyzing the grammar of a language it is extremely useful to keep the distinction in mind between the four layers of the grammar square and to study what contextual factors influence the mapping from one layer to another.

2.5 Analysis Steps

The various insights into the nature and functioning of human language briefly discussed in the previous subsections, translate into a series of steps for analyzing a fragment of language.

1. The first step is to delineate the primary semantic domain of interest and the communicative functions that will be investigated. For example, a study might focus on the domain of spatial language, which uses spatial relations and perspective to identify objects in a scene, as in "the ball left of the box" [22]. Another study might focus on the description of events, using sentences such as "the ball rolled off the table", which would imply a classification of event types and aspects of events that are to be made explicit [45]. Next, the kind of world model that will be derivable from perceptual and motor processing and the information that needs to be stored in the discourse model has to be determined as well as the concepts that are available in this semantic domain, such as spatial categories, event types, or image schemas for objects. Finally, the cognitive operations that will make use of these building blocks need to be identified as well as the networks that are needed to achieve the communicative functions in the chosen domain (as shown in Figure 2).

2. The next step is to survey which meanings can be directly covered by words in the lexicon. Typically, words will introduce certain concepts, and each word

will have a particular potential for expressing semantic functions. The potential comes from the lexical categories to which the word belongs, which allow it to have certain possible syntactic functions.

3. The third step focuses on phrases, identifying what kind of phrases are available in the language fragment under investigation, how each phrase combines the networks contributed by its constituents, and what additional meanings are to be added. This step also investigates what syntactic and semantic constraints have to be present, for example, what ordering constraints have to be imposed among the constituents, whether there are agreement relations between constituents, which features should percolate from constituents to the phrase as a whole, and so on.

4. In addition to the primary semantic domains which determine the basic skeleton and vocabulary of a language fragment, there may be secondary semantic domains that are overlaid on top of the primary domains, expressing grammatical meanings such as modality, tense, aspect, determination, or information structure. For each of these domains, the analyst needs to pin down what has to be represented in the world model or the discourse model as well as how this information can be derived through sensory-motor processing or inference. The domains will also introduce additional cognitive operations and subnetworks. Secondary domains usually do not introduce new syntactic functions, but they operate through syntactic and semantic features that translate into morphological markers, grammatical function words, modulations of constituent ordering or phonetic markings (intonation, stress). The grammar square mappings from meanings to semantic categorizations, syntactic categorizations, and finally to markers must be worked out and in particular the contextual constraints that determine each of the steps in the mapping.

3 The Design Level

In the previous section, the basic linguistic outlook used in Fluid Construction Grammar was briefly presented, and a set of methodological steps was introduced that help to structure the investigation of some fragment of a language. However, it remains an enormous challenge to turn this kind of analysis into a formal system that is effective in parsing and producing utterances, particularly because language is to a large extent non-modular and multi-functional. The same element (for example, the same word) can have multiple functions and play a role in expressing different semantic domains, and constraints from many different levels (pragmatic, semantic, syntactic, morphological and phonetic) often interact strongly. This multi-functional nature of linguistic components introduces enormous challenges for grammar design, both to master the complexity of defining constructions that capture all constraints, but also to avoid combinatorial explosions in the search space built up during parsing or production.

FCG uses several techniques from computer science for handling complexity. The first one is to make a distinction between a design level and an operational level, in the same way computer programming makes a distinction between a high level programming language and a low level machine-oriented language. In the case of FCG, the operational level is based on the detailed definition of operational constructions that are applied through a process of matching and merging. At the design level, these constructions are defined more abstractly using a series of templates. Each template deals with a particular aspect of a construction and helps to implement a certain design pattern.

3.1 Design Patterns

The notion of a *design pattern* was originally introduced by architects [1]. A design pattern captures a particular solution to a design problem that can be reused, after adaptation to local circumstances. For example, a dome structure can be used for spanning large spaces, but many different types of domes are built depending on the materials used or the aesthetic qualities the architect is after. Design patterns are also very common in software engineering where they refer to reusable approaches for tackling a class of software design problems [12]. They are also an important concept in biology, where they refer to a particular class of physiological and metabolic solutions for recurrent problems like maintaining body temperature, extracting oxygen, building a basic body plan [5].

In human languages, we also find common design patterns across language families. The most obvious one is to build *phrases* by grouping words (or phrases) in order to express compositional meanings. The nature and complexity of phrases, and which mechanisms are used to indicate which constituents can be grouped together, differs significantly from one language to another. Nevertheless, there are a lot of common mechanisms.

Another design pattern commonly used in human languages is that of *agreement systems*. Agreement means that some syntactic or semantic features of one constituent are shared with other constituents. Agreement is used to indicate that there is some sort of linking between constituents, for example, because they are components of the same phrase or because they share the same referent. Thus, the subject and the verb of a sentence agree with respect to number and person in English. In German, articles and nouns which belong to the same nominal phrase agree for number, gender, and case. In Spanish, pronouns agree with respect to gender and number with the referring expression that introduces their referent. The features entering in agreement relations are typically derived based on semantic categorizations (for example the distinction between singular and plural number) or on the syntactic context (for example the case distinction between nominative and dative).

Features are either associated with words themselves, or they are explicitly marked through morphology or phonetic variations of the word stem. Within phrases, they often percolate up from one constituent (usually the so called head of the phrase) to the phrase as a whole. For example, definiteness percolates from the determiner to the determiner-nominal phrase. Individual languages differ in terms of when they use agreement relations, which features are supposed to agree with each other, and which features percolate. But again, we find some common fundamental mechanisms. For example, features usually come in feature bundles , and often a particular word or phrase has multiple alternative feature bundles so that special processing techniques are needed to avoid combinatorial explosions [48]. A concrete example for Polish agreement is discussed in a later chapter of this book [16].

Another example of a design pattern is *field topology*. Field topology is a way to introduce more flexibility and sophistication in the use of word order within a phrase. In most languages, it is sufficient to express ordering constraints among the constituents of a phrase with the `meets`-relation, which is valid between two constituents X and Y if X immediately precedes Y. But sometimes this kind of representation is too weak because the ordering relations are exploited to express many different grammatical meanings. This is the case, for example, in German sentences, where almost any constituent can be put in front of the sentence in order to emphasize that it is the topic, for example the answer to a recently asked question.

Field topology associates with each phrase a set of fields. A field can capture one or more constituents, depending on a number of interacting constraints, and the final ordering of the sentence is then derived by sequentially retrieving the fillers of each field. For example, in German, five fields are typically hypothesized. There is the so called *Vorfeld*, or front field, which may capture constituents that express the topic of the sentence. The finite verb always comes into the second field (the *linke Klammer*, or left bracket), followed by three fields for other constituents: the *Mittelfeld*, or middle field, the *rechte Klammer*, or right bracket and the *Nachfeld*, or end field. The *rechte Klammer* contains the non-finite verb. Most implementations of German constituent order use a field topology approach by postulating these five fields. A worked out example in FCG is discussed in [24].

Although field topology has been primarily used for German (and Dutch) sentence constituent ordering, there are many other ordering phenomena that can potentially be handled using this design pattern. For example, the ordering of multiple adjectives in French follows a particular sequence, with some adjectives appearing before and some after the noun [19]. The ordering is mostly based on the semantic categories to which these adjectives refer. For example, size adjectives appear before the noun whereas color adjectives come after, as in "un grand ballon rouge" (literally: "a big ball red", to mean "a big red ball") We can handle this phenomenon as well by postulating a set of fields for each type of adjective. During production, these fields capture the adjectives that satisfy the constraints of the field, and the nominal phrase is then constructed by collecting the fillers of these fields sequentially, which are non-empty.

Agreement and field topology are design patterns oriented towards the syntactic structuring and morphological markings of sentences. There are other design patterns that are oriented towards semantic aspects. For example, the networks contributed by individual words need to be linked together in phrases, and networks from different phrases need to be linked together into networks defining the meaning of larger phrases [37]. A design pattern for handling this kind of issue is known as a linking pattern.

A *linking pattern* relies on the definition of the external arguments of subnetworks supplied by words or constituents. These arguments can be linked to the external arguments supplied by other subnetworks. For example, the cognitive operation `filter-set-class`, which filters a set of objects based on a class, has two external arguments: one for the class and the other for the filtered set. The cognitive operation `select-unique-element` selecting the unique element out of a singleton has two external arguments as well: one for the set from which an element has to be selected and the other for the chosen element. When these two cognitive operations are combined in a single network (as in the phrase "the mouse", where "mouse" introduces the class identifier), the new network has only two external arguments: One for the selected element and another for the original source set as used by the filter operation. Internally, the non-external arguments are linked together in the combined network so that the set derived by `filter-set-class` on the basis of the class 'mouse' is the set from which the element is selected by `select-unique-element`.

3.2 Constructions

A *construction* is the basic computational unit at the operational level in FCG. It contains a *semantic pole* that captures aspects of pragmatics, meaning, semantic structure and semantic categorization, and *a syntactic pole* that captures aspects of syntactic structure, syntactic categorization, as well as phonetic and morphological marking. Constructions typically have a set of units for the different constituents. Information is represented in terms of features associated with each of the units.

The data structure built during the parsing and production of a particular sentence is called a *transient structure*. It has the same division into units and features as a construction, as well as a semantic and a syntactic pole. Initially the transient structure contains only one unit (usually called the *top-unit*), which contains everything that is known when processing starts. In parsing, it contains a feature `form` that contains a description of all the form characteristics of the utterance. In production, the top-unit contains a feature `meaning` that contains the complete meaning which the speaker wants to express.

A construction is viewed as a bi-directional association between meaning (the semantic pole) and form (the syntactic pole). In production the semantic pole of the construction is matched against the semantic pole of the transient structure in order to check whether the construction is applicable, and then the information contained in the syntactic pole of the construction is added by merging it with the syntactic pole of the transient structure. In parsing, the syntactic pole of the construction is matched against the transient structure to see whether the construction is applicable, and if this is the case then information from the semantic pole is merged with the transient structure so as to progressively reconstruct the semantic structure and meaning of the sentence. One construction thus prepares the ground for the application of the next construction, so that we get a chain of construction applications (see Figure 7). Usually there is more than one construction that can apply at any point in time, and we therefore get

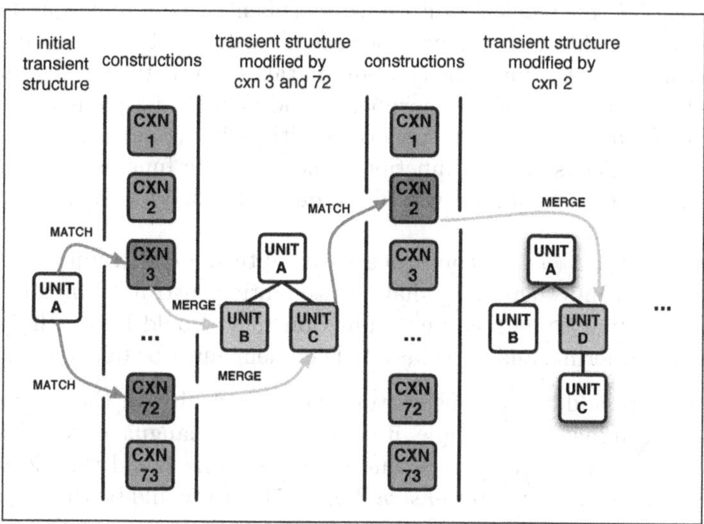

Fig. 7. Constructions are applied in a chain starting from an initial transient structure. Application either fails in mid-stream or continues until a complete sentence can be produced (in language production) or the meaning could be completely reconstructed.

a search space in which different search paths have to be tried out to find the best possible solution.

Constructions are complicated because of their bi-directional nature. It is not enough to say, for example, that a determiner-nominal phrase consists of a determiner and a nominal, we also need to say when such a determiner-nominal phrase should be used (in production) and how the meaning of the determiner and nominal is to be combined (in parsing). We also need to specify the agreement relations, percolations, and linkings of subnetworks. An additional factor that makes constructions complicated is that both syntactic *and* semantic issues need to be considered at the same time. This leads to much greater efficiency compared to a separation of the grammar into different layers or a decomposition of linguistic decisions into small steps. A construction should take as many constraints as possible into account before building more structure, so that search gets maximally avoided. On the other hand, it makes it much harder to write grammars.

To make the analysis and implementation of grammars nevertheless doable, FCG divides constructions up into different *construction sets*. This helps also to streamline the processing of constructions because all constructions in one set can be considered before the next set in the sequence is tried. Here are some example construction sets that are typically found for most applications:

1. *Lexical constructions* introduce lexical items, i.e. word stems. They specify the meaning, external arguments, phonetic, syntactic and semantic categories, and form of a word.

2. *Morphological constructions* introduce morphemes, i.e. prefixes and suffixes that are attached to word stems. They specify with what word the morpheme can be combined, the form the combintion takes, syntactic and semantic categorizations, the form of the morpheme, and possibly its phonetic features.
3. *Functional constructions* are concerned with defining associations between lexical categories, syntactic functions, and semantic functions. They define potential values. The actual values are decided based on the syntactic and semantic context.
4. *Phrasal constructions* are concerned with capturing constraints on phrases: What constituents there are, what the semantic constraints on constituents are, which semantic and syntactic function they should have, what kind of agreement, ordering, and percolation phenomena must be taken into account.

There are usually additional construction sets that deal with the expression of grammatical meaning. For example, it could be that a language expresses argument structure using semantic roles and cases, and this would then lead to the inclusion of *argument-structure constructions* [47]. Or it could be that a language has an elaborate system of aspect which would require constructions that handle the semantic and syntactic features related to aspect so that morphological constructions can mark them with external forms [13].

3.3 Templates

A design pattern does not directly translate into a particular construction because one construction will integrate aspects of many different design patterns, and a single design pattern has an impact on many different constructions. For example, to implement agreement requires that lexical constructions, morphological constructions, and phrasal constructions introduce syntactic and semantic features and that agreement relations are defined within the context of the relevant phrasal constructions. It is nevertheless possible to capture some of the basic aspects of design patterns into abstractions that hide a lot of the implementation details. FCG does this using templates.

A *template* determines some of the aspects of a construction. It has a number of slots which act as parameters for how exactly the template should be instantiated. When a template is applied to a construction it extends the construction as a side effect (Figure 8). Each construction has a unique name so that templates can retrieve the construction they want to have an impact on. Moreover, the units in a construction are associated with variable-names so that they can be used by different templates to add more information.

The general syntax for using a template takes the following form:

(*template-name* *construction-name* *optional-parameters*
:slot-name-1 *value-name-1*
...
:slot-name-n *value-name-n*)

The set of possible templates is open, and a grammar designer implements the specific templates required for the language phenomena that he or she is

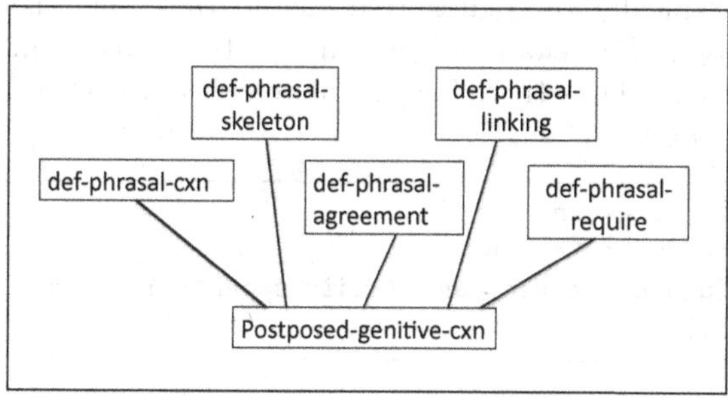

Fig. 8. Different templates progressively add more structure to a construction. Each template adds information relevant to a particular design pattern. For example, the **def-phrasal-agreement** template adds mechanisms to implement the relevant agreement relations to the **postposed-genitive-cxn**.

interested in and from then on uses these templates. There are libraries of templates made available with each FCG release. The more specific templates are, the easier it is to focus on the specific linguistic aspects of the language being studied because computational issues are hidden as much as possible. But the less they will be relevant for other languages.

The values of slots can either be symbols, lists of symbols, or expressions using the same special operators as used at the operational level. FCG uses logic variables as commonly used in logic programming languages. They are denoted by putting a question mark in front of the name of the variable. Variables get bound as a side effect of the matching and merging process, either to constants or to other variables. (Details of FCG-variables, special operators, and the basic unification operations that use them are discussed in a follow up chapter [10].)

Here are a few examples of templates. There are first of all some 'shell templates' that create a shell for a construction with a given name. The template also puts the construction in a particular construction set. Shell templates are of the form

(**def** *-construction-type construction-name*
 ... *invocation of other templates* ...)

Typical names for shell templates are **def-lex-cxn**, **def-morph-cxn**, **def-fun-cxn**, **def-phrasal-cxn**, etc., to build lexical, morphological, functional or phrasal constructions respectively.

For example, let us initialize the definition of a lexical construction called **mine-cxn** for defining the word "mine", as it may appear in possessive constructions, such as "this house of mine". The process of building this construction starts with the creation of a shell using the **def-lex-cxn** template. Only the name of the construction has to be supplied:

```
(def-lex-cxn mine-cxn)
```

Next, there are typically templates that define the basic skeletal structure of each construction. For example, lexical constructions primarily associate meaning with a string. Thus there is a template called `def-lex-skeleton` with slots for `:meaning` and `:string`.

```
(def-lex-skeleton mine-cxn
  :meaning (== (context ?context)
               (dialog-participant ?indiv speaker ?context))
  :string "mine"))
```

The linking design pattern requires defining the external arguments of the subnetwork introduced by this lexical item, which is usually done with an extra slot called `:args` in the `def-lex-skeleton` template:

```
(def-lex-skeleton mine-cxn
  :meaning (== (context ?context)
               (dialog-participant ?indiv speaker ?context))
  :args (?indiv)
  :string "mine"))
```

Syntactic and semantic categorizations are associated with lexical items by another template, called `def-lex-cat`. It has a slot `:sem-cat` for the semantic categorizations and a slot `:syn-cat` for the syntactic categorizations:

```
(def-lex-cat mine-cxn
  :sem-cat (==1 (sem-function possessive))
  :syn-cat (==1 (lex-cat pronoun)
                (person 1st)
                (number singular)
                (case genitive)))
```

The semantic function of "mine" is that of possessive. From a syntactic side, it is a 1st person, singular pronoun in the genitive case. All of this is of course meant to be an example. FCG allows the grammar designer to use any kind of feature deemed necessary. Templates can also incorporate more information or less, depending on preferred implementation style. For example the syntactic and semantic categorizations could also be put in a single lexical template together with the meaning and string.

Here is another more elaborate example to illustrate the use of templates for building constructions (discussed at length in [40]). It defines a possessive phrasal construction, underlying a phrase such as "this house of mine". The possessive phrasal construction involves two constituents: a nominal phrase ("this house") and a possessive pronominal "mine". The construction itself is called `postposed-genitive-cxn`. It starts with the creation of a shell that makes this construction a member of the set of phrasal constructions:

```
(def-phrasal-cxn postposed-genitive-cxn)
```

Next, the **def-phrasal-skeleton** template is used to introduce units both for the phrase as a whole, with a slot called **:phrase**, and for the different constituents, with a slot called **:constituents**. The constituents are defined in terms of their semantic functions, syntactic functions, lexical categories, phrase types, or syntactic and semantic categorizations. Information is provided on the phrase-type of the parent and its possible syntactic and semantic functions:

```
(def-phrasal-skeleton postposed-genitive-cxn
  :phrase
  (?possessive-nominal-phrase
    :sem-function referring
    :phrase-type nominal-phrase)
  :constituents
  ((?nominal-unit
     :sem-function referring
     :phrase-type nominal-phrase)
   (?pronominal-unit
     :sem-function possessive
     :lex-cat pronoun
     :syn-cat (==1 (case genitive)))))
```

The variables that are used for the constituents (i.e. **?nominal-unit**, **?pronominal-unit**) and for the parent phrase (i.e. **?possessive-nominal-phrase**) can be used by other templates to address these units and add more information. Other variables used in feature values can also be used across templates.

Other templates implement other design patterns. For example, the postposed genitive construction requires that the number of the nominal unit percolates to the possessive nominal phrase as a whole. This is specified with a template called **def-phrasal-agreement**. For all constituents that share features and for the parent phrase in which features percolate up from the constituents, the def-phrasal-agreement lists the following:

```
(def-phrasal-agreement postposed-genitive-cxn
  (?possessive-nominal-phrase
    :syn-cat (==1 (number ?number)
                  (is-definite ?definiteness)))
  (?nominal-unit
    :syn-cat  (==1 (is-definite ?definiteness)
                   (number ?number))))
```

The variables **?possessive-nominal-phrase** and **?nominal-unit** are used to retrieve which units are involved, and the slot-values specify which syntactic and/or semantic categories have to agree. Use of the same variable name indicates that this indicates that an agreement relation is established. For example, **?number** of the possessive nominal phrase is shared with **?number** of the

`?nominal-unit`. Thanks to the unification operation, bindings can flow in both directions: It is not only possible that the number value propagates up from the nominal-unit to the phrase but also that it propagates down from the nominal phrase to the nominal unit.

Phrasal constructions may add some meaning of their own, and they may add form constraints over and above the form constraints supplied by individual constituents, which is usually specified with another template called `def-phrasal-require`. It has a slot for constructional meaning, called `:cxn-meaning`, and a slot for constructional form, called `:cxn-form`. The `postposed-genitive-cxn` illustrates how the construction adds a possessive relation as part of the meaning, a grammatical function word, namely "of", and ordering relations between these components:

```
(def-phrasal-require postposed-genitive-cxn
  (?possessive-nominal-phrase
    :cxn-meaning (== (possessive ?referent-nominal
                                 ?referent-pronominal))
    :cxn-form (== (meets ?nominal-unit ?word-of)
                  (string ?word-of "of")
                  (meets ?word-of ?pronominal-unit))))
```

As a final example, we use a template called `def-phrasal-linking`, to establish the linking between the external arguments of the constituents and the parent phrase [36]. The template simply lists for each constituent which external arguments are involved and if the same variable-name is used they are assumed to be linked. The unification operation takes care of the binding of the relevant variables.

```
(def-phrasal-linking postposed-genitive-cxn
  (?possessive-nominal-phrase
    :args (?referent-nominal))
  (?nominal-unit
    :args (?referent-nominal))
  (?pronominal-unit
    :args (?referent-pronominal)))
```

4 The Operational Level

This paper advocates that the design of a lexicon and grammar for a particular language fragment should proceed in a top-down manner, starting from an analysis at the *linguistic level*, identifying the semantic domains and functions, and the representations and communications functions that need to be expressed in the language and how they are expressed. It then moves to the *design level* with the identification of design patterns and the templates that actualize them. For example, to implement agreement requires templates that add syntactic and semantic categorizations to units and templates that specify what agreement and percolation relations need to be established for a particular phrase.

We now arrive at the *operational level*, which is the level at which constructions with all their details have to be defined. Although constructions can be defined by hand, it is much easier to do so using templates. Nevertheless it is import to understand the operational level also, partly to be able to follow in detail what changes a construction has made and why it does (or does not) trigger, and partly to be able to extend or adapt the set of available templates. The remainder of this section provides a brief introduction to the main structures and operations at the operational level. The reader is referred to a later chapter [10] for more details, and to the examples further discussed in this book or in other publications [41].

4.1 Representing Transient Structures

FCG uses feature structures for representing the information that is built up during parsing and production, thus following generally accepted practices in contemporary computational linguistics, The so called *transient structure* starts in parsing with all the information that can be extracted from the utterance (strings, ordering, possibly phonetic information) and progressively reconstructs semantic and syntactic structures and meanings. In production, the transient structure contains initially only the meaning that needs to be expressed. Different constructions cover parts of this meaning, progressively building up phrasal structures and constraining the form of the sentence until a concrete sentence can be derived.

The feature structures used in FCG compose the linguistic structure in terms of units with features and values. Units have names, and these names can be bound to variables for reference inside constructions. Consequently, hierarchical structure is represented explicitly by a feature called *subunits* filled by names of all subunits.

The transient structure is decomposed into a semantic pole and a syntactic pole to improve readability and efficiency. The graphical representation in Figure 9 provides an example of a simple determiner-nominal phrase in (taken from [42], which explains this example in detail). There is a list notation which reflects the internal LISP-based implementation of feature structures. Graphical representations are constructed automatically by the FCG-system and there is a browser for interactive and selective display (see [23]).

The same feature structure is shown in list notation in Figure 9. The unit names are in bold and the unit features in italics. In the semantic pole, there is a unit for `top`, which has one semantic subunit called `nominal-phrase-12`. `nominal-phrase-12` has two semantic subunits: `mouse-12` and `the-11`. The same unit-names are found on the syntactic pole with pending syntactic features. Indices like 12 or 11 are there to distinguish between instances of a symbol but do not carry meaning.

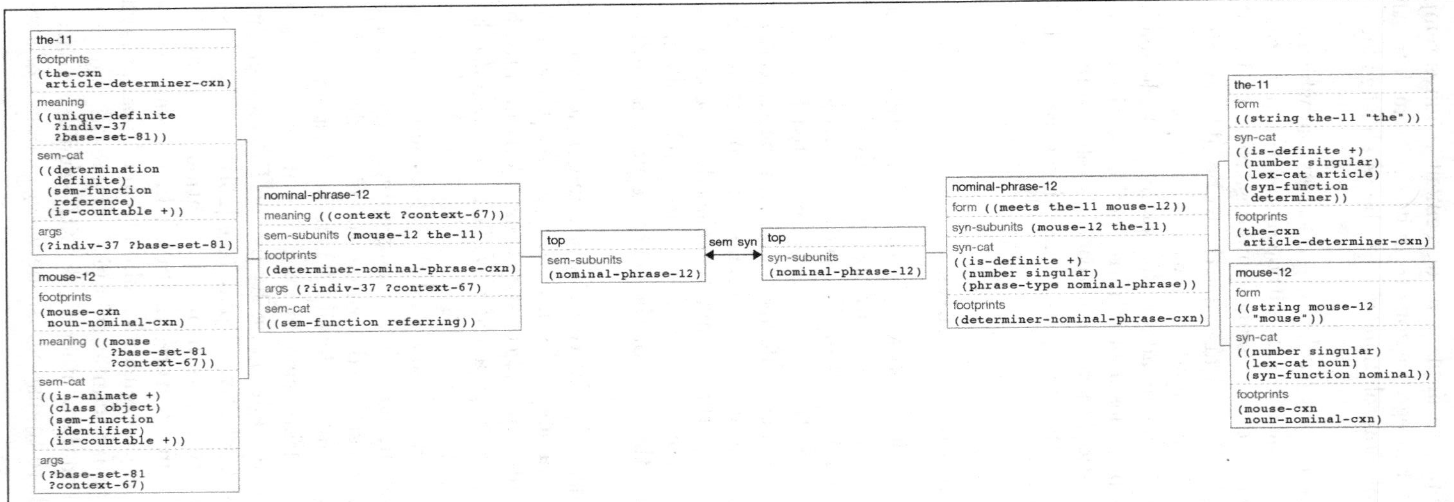

Fig. 9. Graphical display of a transient structure when parsing or producing "the mouse". Each box represents a unit with its name and feature values. All features of the semantic poles are displayed on the left side and all features of the syntactic poles on the right side. Both poles are shown in more detail in Figure 10.

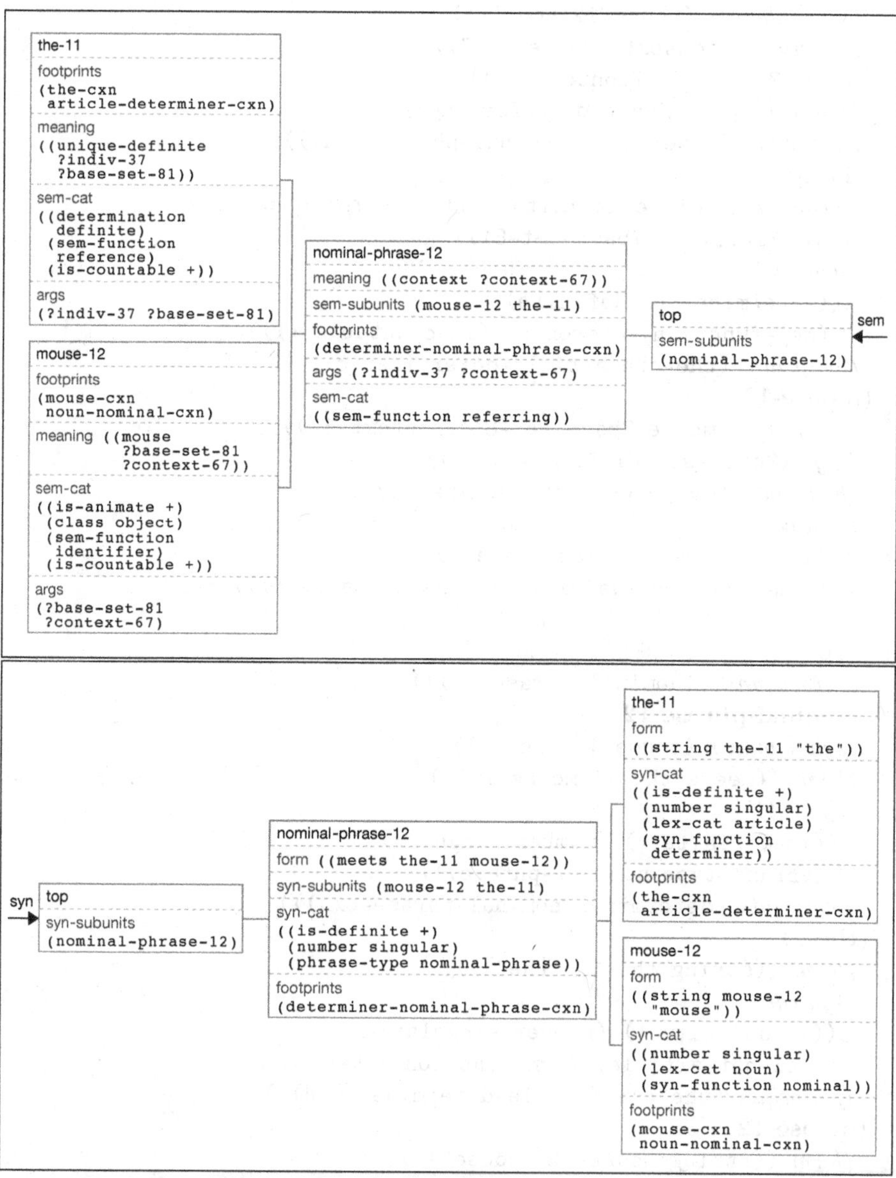

Fig. 10. Zooming in on the semantic (top) and syntactic (bottom) poles of the transient structure shown in Figure 9

```
( (top
   (sem-subunits (nominal-phrase-12)))
  (nominal-phrase-12
   (sem-subunits (mouse-12 the-11))
   (meaning ((context ?context-67)))
   (args (?indiv-37 ?context-67))
   (sem-cat ((sem-function referring)))
   (footprints (determiner-nominal-phrase-cxn)))
  (the-11
   (meaning ((unique-definite ?indiv-37 ?base-set-81)))
   (args (?indiv-37 ?base-set-81))
   (sem-cat
    ((determination definite)
     (sem-function reference) (is-countable +)))
   (footprints (the-cxn article-determiner-cxn)))
  (mouse-12
   (meaning ((mouse ?base-set-81 ?context-67)))
   (args (?base-set-81 ?context-67))
   (footprints (mouse-cxn noun-nominal-cxn))
   (sem-cat
    ((is-animate +) (class object)
     (sem-function identifier) (is-countable +)))))
<-->
( (top
   (syn-subunits (nominal-phrase-12)))
  (nominal-phrase-12
   (syn-subunits (mouse-12 the-11))
   (form ((meets the-11 mouse-12)))
   (syn-cat
    ((is-definite +) (number singular)
     (phrase-type nominal-phrase)))
   (footprints (determiner-nominal-phrase-cxn)))
  (the-11
   (form ((string the-11 "the")))
   (syn-cat
    ((is-definite +) (number singular)
     (lex-cat article) (syn-function determiner)))
   (footprints (the-cxn article-determiner-cxn)))
  (mouse-12
   (form ((string mouse-12 "mouse")))
   (syn-cat
    ((number singular) (lex-cat noun)
     (syn-function nominal)))
   (footprints (mouse-cxn noun-nominal-cxn))))
```

Feature structures in FCG do not fundamentally differ from those used in other feature-structure based formalisms. For example, part of the syntactic pole of the transient structure in Figure 10 would be represented in many other unification-based formalisms as follows:

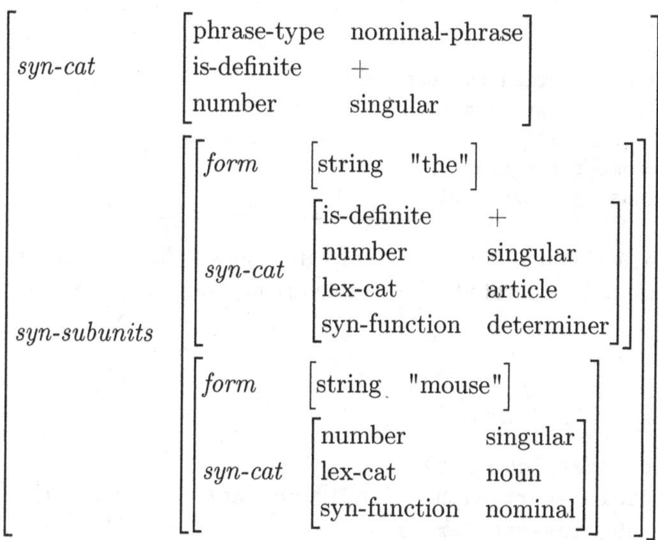

The main difference concerns the use of names for units and the use of logic variables for representing values of features that are unknown.

4.2 Representing Constructions

Constructions use the same representations as transient structures: They consist of units with features and values, which are matched against transient structures and then merged so that information present in the construction, but not yet in the transient structure, gets added. Constructions are more abstract than transient structures. They leave out information so that the construction matches with a wide range of transient structures. They contain variables that can be bound to specific values contained in a transient structure. And they may specify partial values using a set of special operators, such as an includes operator (if only some of the elements have to be present), a uniquely includes operator (if a particular element can appear only once), an excludes operator (if an element should not occur), and so on.

Different templates build up different elements of a construction. For example, the lexical construction for "mine" was defined earlier using the following templates:

```
(def-lex-cxn mine-cxn
  (def-lex-skeleton mine-cxn
    :meaning (== (context ?context)
                 (dialog-participant ?indiv speaker ?context))
    :args (?indiv)
    :string "mine")
  (def-lex-cat mine-cxn
    :sem-cat (==1 (sem-function possessive))
    :syn-cat (==1 (lex-cat pronoun)
                  (person 1st)
                  (number singular)
                  (case genitive))))
```

The operational construction based on these templates looks as follows, with the semantic and syntactic pole separated by a double arrow <->:

```
(def-cxn mine-cxn
  ((?top-unit
    (tag ?meaning
         (meaning
            (== (context ?context)
                (dialog-participant ?indiv speaker ?context))))
    (footprints (==0 mine-cxn lex)))
   ((J ?word-mine ?top-unit)
    ?meaning
    (args (?indiv))
    (footprints (==1 mine-cxn lex))
    (sem-cat (==1 (sem-function possessive)))))
  <-->
  ((?top-unit
    (footprints (==0 mine-cxn lex))
    (tag ?form
         (form (== (string ?word-mine "mine")))))
   ((J ?word-mine ?top-unit)
    ?form
    (footprints (==1 mine-cxn lex))
    (syn-cat
      (==1 (lex-cat pronoun)
           (person 1st)
           (number singular)
           (case genitive))))))
```

In production, the construction is applied from the semantic pole to the syntactic pole. It looks out whether a particular meaning is present in the `?top-unit` (which is the initial top unit of a transient structure). If that meaning is found, the construction creates a new sub-unit (bound to the variable `?word-mine`) and hangs it from the top-unit on the semantic side. It also adds information about the external arguments of the word and its semantic categorizations. On the syntactic side, the construction creates a syntactic subunit and adds information about the word form (the string "mine") as well as syntactic categorizations concerning lexical-class, person, number and case.

In parsing, the construction is applied from the syntactic pole to the semantic pole. It looks out for the presence of a particular string (namely "mine") in the top-unit. If that is the case, the construction builds a new unit bound to `?word-mine` and hangs it from `?top-unit`. The string is moved from the form feature of the top-unit to the form feature of the new unit, and syntactic categorizations are added. On the semantic side, the construction creates a new semantic subunit and adds information about its meaning and its semantic categorization.

Parts of this operational construction are clearly based on the elements supplied by the templates: the `:meaning`, `:string` and `:args` come from the `def-lex-skeleton` template, and the `:syn-cat` and `:sem-cat` come from the `def-lex-cat` template. However, more is needed to make a construction fully operational. Choices have to be made as to whether information is put into the semantic pole or the syntactic pole, and if triggering the construction or additive in merging should be conditional. Other issues concern the question of how new units are built and how information is moved to them, and how the recursive application of constructions is regulated. This section briefly discusses some procedural annotations in operational constructions that have been designed for these purposes.

4.3 Procedural Annotations

Procedural annotations consist of extra information supplied with a construction to carry out structure building operations or to avoid that constructions keep applying indefinitely. Structure building requires two operations: a way to create new units and hang them somewhere from an existing unit in the hierarchy, and a way to associate information with the new unit, possibly by moving features or values that were located elsewhere.

The J-operator. The J-operator is the main FCG primitive for building hierarchical structure [11]. It has three arguments: a *daughter-unit*, a *parent-unit*, and possibly a set of *pending-subunits*. These are either specified with concrete names or with variables that have been bound elsewhere in the matching or merging process. When the daughter-unit is an unbound variable at the time of merging, a new unit will be created for it. For example, in the `mine-cxn` above, the following expression evokes the J-operator.

```
(J ?word-mine ?top-unit)
```

It introduces a new daughter-unit bound to `?word-mine` and hangs it as a subunit from a parent-unit bound to `?top-unit`. There are no further pending units, otherwise they would be made subunits of the daughter-unit. The J-operator can associate additional information with the daughter-unit. In the example of the `mine-cxn` construction, the J-operator adds information about the lexical category, person, number, and case.

The TAG-operator. The J-operator is made more versatile by introducing a way to *tag* parts of a feature structure so that they can be moved elsewhere in the transient structure. The tag-operator has two arguments: a variable, known as the *tag-variable*, and a set of features and values that are bound to the tag-variable. The normal matching process is still used to check whether the features and values match. If a tag-variable re-occurs inside a unit governed by a J-operator, then the structure is *moved* from its old position to its new position.

Here is an example. In production, the top-unit initially contains all the meanings that need to be covered , and lexical constructions take those parts that they can cover and encapsulate them in a new unit. This is done with the tag operator, which binds the meaning of the word "mine" and then moves into the `?word-mine` unit created by the J-operator, as illustrated in the semantic pole of the `mine-cxn` construction.

```
(tag ?meaning
     (meaning
       (== (context ?context)
           (dialog-participant ?indiv speaker ?context))))
```

The meaning covered by the word is tagged and then moved from the top-unit to the newly created unit that covers this meaning in production. The form introduced by the word is also tagged and then moved from the top-unit to a newly created unit in parsing.

Footprints. One of the biggest issues in language processing is the management of the search space. This arises unavoidably in parsing because most word forms or syntactic constraints have multiple meanings and functions, and it is often not possible to make a definite choice until more of the sentence has been processed. It also arises in production because there is usually more than one way to express a particular meaning, and it is not always possible to decide fully which choice is the most appropriate until other aspects of the sentence are worked out. Many techniques help to avoid search whenever possible, for example, choices can be left open as variables until enough information is available to choose their bindings, or the value of a particular syntactic feature (such as the lexical-category) can be a list of potential values from which one is then actually chosen to be the actual value.

Adding `footprints` to a transient structure is another technique for avoiding search and particularly the harmful recursive application of constructions. Footprints are represented as one of the features of a unit. They are left behind by constructions, so that other constructions (or the same construction) can see that this construction was involved in building a particular piece of structure and hence can refrain from application. By convention, the name of the footprint left behind by a construction is the name of the construction itself. A construction may also leave behind other footprints. For example, if the construction is a member of a family of constructions, each construction leaves behind a family footprint so that more general constructions of the same family will no longer trigger. Another example concerns the handling of defaults. Constructions that deal with overt cases leave behind footprints so that default construction dealing with an unmarked case does not need to trigger anymore (see examples in [3]).

In the example given earlier, the `mine-cxn` construction first checks whether it has not yet already applied on the `?top-unit`, so that recursive application is avoided. Once it has applied, it leaves behind a footprint that it was involved in building the new unit bound to `?word-mine` so that there can be no recursive application where the unit `?word-mine` becomes bound to `?top-unit`. Footprints are not only useful for controlling the application of constructions. They are also useful for a grammar designer who is inspecting transient structures in order to figure out which construction did what.

5 Conclusions

This paper introduced some of the design principles that are currently used in Fluid Construction Grammar. We distinguished three levels of analysis: a linguistic level, a design level and an operational level. The linguistic level starts from an analysis of which semantic domains and communicative functions are relevant for the language fragment being studied. It then investigates first the functional structure underlying sentences: which semantic functions are involved, how do they map to syntactic functions, and how are syntactic functions expressed in the language. Next it investigates the expression of grammatical meanings, such as tense and aspect, using the grammar square as guidance.

The design level starts from an analysis of the major design patterns that are used in the language fragment and then seeks to find out which templates could be used to implement them. A template emphasises linguistic content, hiding computational details as much as possible. Templates are translated automatically to the operational level by a compilation process so that we obtain the 'real' constructions that drive parsing and production processes. Constructions can be written by hand, but it is much more efficient to do so with templates, as later chapters with case studies show.

FCG is an attempt to capture many ideas that have been floating around in the construction grammar literature. But there are certainly still many ideas which are not yet incorporated. For example, inheritance plays an important role in many construction grammars but it is not a core component of FCG, and the same phenomena are captured in other ways. FCG uses many of the same techniques found in other unification-based grammars, but there are also profound differences. For example, FCG constructions are split into two poles which are used differently in parsing and production, whereas HPSG would put everything together in a single structure. Deeper comparisons with other attempts for formalizing construction grammar and the relation to other unification-based grammars are discussed in later chapters of this book (see particularly [6]). FCG is still a very new formalism and many issues remain to be explored. In some cases, solutions developed in other unification-based grammars can be nicely translated into FCG. In other cases, FCG suggests new venues that might be translatable to other formalisms, but this needs to be examined.

Acknowledgements. FCG has been under development for a decade with teams at the University of Brussels (VUB AI Lab) and the Sony Computer Science Laboratory in Paris. The primary source of funding has come from the Sony Computer Science Laboratory with additional funding provided by the EU-FP6 ECagents project and the EU-FP7 ALEAR project.

References

[1] Alexander, C.: The Timeless Way of Building. Oxford University Press, Oxford (1979)

[2] Bergen, B.K., Chang, N.: Embodied Construction Grammar. In: Östman, J.O., Fried, M. (eds.) Construction Grammars: Cognitive Grounding and Theoretical Extensions. John Benjamins, Amsterdam (2005)

[3] Beuls, K.: Construction sets and unmarked forms: A case study for Hungarian verbal agreement. In: Steels, L. (ed.) Design Patterns in Fluid Construction Grammar. John Benjamins, Amsterdam (2011)

[4] Carpenter, B.: The Logic of Typed Feature Structures. Cambridge University Press, Cambridge (1992)

[5] Carroll, S., Grenier, J., Weatherbee, S.: From DNA to Diversity. Molecular Genetics and the Evolution of Animal Design. Blackwell Science, Oxford (2001)

[6] Ciortuz, L., Saveluc, V.: Fluid Construction Grammar and Feature Constraint Logics. In: Steels, L. (ed.) Computational Issues in FCG. LNCS (LNAI), vol. 7249, pp. 289–311. Springer, Heidelberg (2012)

[7] Copestake, A.: Implementing Typed Feature Structure Grammars. CSLI Publications, Stanford (2002)

[8] Croft, W.: Radical Construction Grammar. Oxford University Press, Oxford (2001)

[9] Dalrymple, M., Kaplan, R., Maxwell, J., Zaenen, A.: Formal issues in Lexical-Functional Grammar. CSLI Publications, Stanford (1995)

[10] De Beule, J.: A Formal Deconstruction of Fluid Construction Grammar. In: Steels, L. (ed.) Computational Issues in FCG. LNCS (LNAI), vol. 7249, pp. 215–238. Springer, Heidelberg (2012)

[11] De Beule, J., Steels, L.: Hierarchy in Fluid Construction Grammars. In: Furbach, U. (ed.) KI 2005. LNCS (LNAI), vol. 3698, pp. 1–15. Springer, Heidelberg (2005)

[12] Gamma, E., Helm, R., Johnson, R., Vlissides, J.: Design Patterns: Elements of Reusable Object-Oriented Software. Addison-Wesley Pub. Co., Reading (1995)

[13] Gerasymova, K.: Expressing Grammatical Meaning with Morphology: A Case Study for Russian Aspect. In: Steels, L. (ed.) Computational Issues in FCG. LNCS (LNAI), vol. 7249, pp. 91–122. Springer, Heidelberg (2012)

[14] Goldberg, A.E.: A Construction Grammar Approach to Argument Structure. Chicago UP, Chicago (1995)

[15] Goldberg, A.E.: Constructions: a new theoretical approach to language. Trends in Cognitive Sciences 7(5), 219–224 (2003)
[16] Höfer, S.: Complex Declension Systems and Morphology in Fluid Construction Grammar: A Case Study of Polish. In: Steels, L. (ed.) Computational Issues in FCG. LNCS (LNAI), vol. 7249, pp. 143–177. Springer, Heidelberg (2012)
[17] Kay, M.: Parsing in functional unification grammar. In: Grosz, B., Spark-Jones, K., Webber, B. (eds.) Readings in Natural Language Processing. Morgan Kaufmann, San Francisco (1986)
[18] Kay, P., Fillmore, C.: Grammatical constructions and linguistic generalizations: the what's x doing y? Language 72, 1–33 (1996)
[19] Laenzlinger, C.: French adjective ordering: Perspectives on dp-internal movement types. Lingua 115(5), 645–689 (2000)
[20] Langacker, R.W.: Foundations of Cognitive Grammar, vol. 1. Stanford University Press, Stanford (1987)
[21] Langacker, R.W.: A dynamic usage-based model. In: Barlow, M., Kemmer, S. (eds.) Usage-Based Models of Language, pp. 1–63. Chicago University Press, Chicago (2002)
[22] Levinson, S.C.: Space in Language and Cognition. In: Language, Culture and Cognition, vol. 5. Cambridge University Press, Cambridge (2003)
[23] Loetzsch, M.: Tools for Grammar Engineering. In: Steels, L. (ed.) Computational Issues in FCG. LNCS (LNAI), vol. 7249, pp. 37–47. Springer, Heidelberg (2012)
[24] Micelli, V.: Field Topology and Information Structure: A Case Study for German Constituent Order. In: Steels, L. (ed.) Computational Issues in FCG. LNCS (LNAI), vol. 7249, pp. 178–211. Springer, Heidelberg (2012)
[25] Michaelis, L.: Sign-based construction grammar. In: Heine, B., Narrog, H. (eds.) The Oxford Handbook of Linguistic Analysis. Oxford University Press, Oxford (2009)
[26] Michaelis, L., Lambrecht, K.: Toward a construction-based theory of language function: The case of nominal extraposition. Language 72, 215–247 (1996)
[27] Newmeyer, F. (ed.): Language Form and Language Function. MIT Press, Cambridge (1998)
[28] Pollard, C., Sag, I.A.: Head-Driven Phrase Structure Grammar. Chicago University Press, Chicago (1994)
[29] Sag, I., Wasow, T., Bender, E.: Syntactic Theory. A Formal Introduction. CSLI Publications, Stanford (2003)
[30] Spranger, M., Pauw, S., Loetzsch, M., Steels, L.: Open-ended Procedural Semantics. In: Steels, L., Hild, M. (eds.) Language Grounding in Robots. Springer, New York (2012)
[31] Spranger, M., Loetzsch, M.: Syntactic indeterminacy and semantic ambiguity: A case study for German spatial phrases. In: Steels, L. (ed.) Design Patterns in Fluid Construction Grammar. John Benjamins, Amsterdam (2011)
[32] Stadler, K.: Chunking Constructions. In: Steels, L. (ed.) Computational Issues in FCG. LNCS (LNAI), vol. 7249, pp. 75–88. Springer, Heidelberg (2012)
[33] Steels, L.: Language as a Complex Adaptive System. In: Schoenauer, M., Deb, K., Rudolph, G., Lutton, E., Merelo, J.J., Schwefel, H.-P. (eds.) PPSN 2000. LNCS, vol. 1917, pp. 17–26. Springer, Heidelberg (2000)
[34] Steels, L.: Constructivist development of grounded construction grammars. In: Scott, D., Daelemans, W., Walker, M. (eds.) Proceedings of ACL, pp. 9–16. ACL, Barcelona (2004)
[35] Steels, L.: Grounding Language through Evolutionary Language Games. In: Steels, L., Hild, M. (eds.) Language Grounding in Robots. Springer, New York (2012)

[36] Steels, L., De Beule, J., Neubauer, N.: Linking in Fluid Construction Grammars. In: Proceedings of BNAIC, pp. 11–18. Transactions of the Belgian Royal Society of Arts and Sciences, Brussels (2005)
[37] Steels, L., De Beule, J., Neubauer, N.: Bnaic. Transactions of the Belgian Royal Society for Science and Arts (October 2005)
[38] Steels, L., Kaplan, F.: Spontaneous lexicon change. In: Proceedings of COLING-ACL 1998, pp. 1243–1250. Morgan Kaufmann, San Francisco (1998)
[39] Steels, L.: The emergence of grammar in communicating autonomous robotic agents. In: Horn, W. (ed.) ECAI 2000: Proceedings of the 14th European Conference on Artificial Life, pp. 764–769. IOS Publishing, Amsterdam (2000)
[40] Steels, L.: A design pattern for phrasal constructions. In: Steels, L. (ed.) Design Patterns in Fluid Construction Grammar.John Benjamins, Amsterdam (2011)
[41] Steels, L. (ed.): Design Patterns in Fluid Construction Grammar. John Benjamins, Amsterdam (2011)
[42] Steels, L.: A first encounter with Fluid Construction Grammar. In: Steels, L. (ed.) Design Patterns in Fluid Construction Grammar. John Benjamins, Amsterdam (2011)
[43] Steels, L. (ed.): Experiments in Cultural Language Evolution. John Benjamins, Amsterdam (2012)
[44] Steels, L., van Trijp, R.: How to make construction grammars fluid and robust. In: Steels, L. (ed.) Design Patterns in Fluid Construction Grammar. John Benjamins, Amsterdam (2011)
[45] Talmy, L.: Toward a Cognitive Semantics, Typology and Process in Concept Structuring, vol. 2. MIT Press, Cambridge (2000)
[46] Tomasello, M.: Constructing a Language. A Usage Based Theory of Language Acquisition. Harvard University Press (2003)
[47] van Trijp, R.: A design pattern for argument structure constructions. In: Steels, L. (ed.) Design Patterns in Fluid Construction Grammar. John Benjamins, Amsterdam (2011)
[48] van Trijp, R.: Feature matrices and agreement: A case study for German case. In: Steels, L. (ed.) Design Patterns in Fluid Construction Grammar. John Benjamins, Amsterdam (2011)
[49] Wellens, P.: Organizing constructions in networks. In: Steels, L. (ed.) Design Patterns in Fluid Construction Grammar. John Benjamins, Amsterdam (2011)
[50] Winograd, T.: A procedural model of language understanding. In: Computation & Intelligence, pp. 203–234. American Association for Artificial Intelligence, Menlo Park (1995), http://dl.acm.org/citation.cfm?id=216000.216012
[51] Woods, W.: Problems in procedural semantics. In: Pylyshyn, Z., Demopolous, W. (eds.) Meaning and Cognitive Structure. Ablex Publishing, New York (1986)

Tools for Grammar Engineering

Martin Loetzsch

Artificial Intelligence Laboratory, Vrije Universiteit Brussel, Belgium

Abstract. Developing a FCG grammar can easily become very complex when larger sets of interdependent constructions are involved and when consequently tracking down mistakes in single constructions or analyzing the overall behavior of the system becomes difficult. FCG supports users in this task by providing interfaces for accessing most of its internal representations together with powerful debugging and visualization tools. This paper will outline some of these interfaces and explain its visualization components in detail.

1 Introduction

Fluid Construction Grammar is a formalism for defining grammars along the lines advocated by construction grammarians and a theory and implementation on how sentences are parsed and produced using construction grammar [4]. Unlike many other implementations of grammar formalisms, FCG does not come with a standalone program that is started once and then provides a (possibly graphical) user interface for editing and testing grammars – FCG is rather a software framework that users directly interact with. FCG is written in the programming language Common Lisp [3], which is commonly used in artificial intelligence and computational linguistics. The choice of Lisp makes it very easy to adapt FCG to a variety of usage scenarios because Lisp allows for powerful yet simple abstractions that flexibly wrap core mechanisms for specific uses. Lisp makes it also easy to write *macros* that allow the definition of constructions by specifying only their relevant features (and thus avoid writing redundant code).

In addition to the increased flexibility of use, the choice of Lisp as a programming language means that the traditional time consuming "edit - compile - test cycle" (i.e. changing code, then compiling the program and then testing it) does not exist. Instead, users load the FCG framework into a Lisp programming environment and then on top of that develop and test their grammar or multi-agent experiment. During that, the "Lisp image" (i.e. the "program") is constantly running and changes (e.g. adding constructions or changing functions) have immediate effect on the state of the system.

A minimal example of a typical interaction with FCG is shown in Figure 1 (see [5] for a first introduction to FCG). The GNU Emacs text editor (shown on the right) serves here as a Lisp environment, but any other Lisp IDE can be used. The Emacs window contains a Lisp file with a variety of Lisp expressions that each are manually evaluated by the user to change the state of the Lisp image (but such a file can also be loaded and evaluated automatically as

L. Steels (Ed.): Computational Issues in FCG, LNAI 7249, pp. 37–47, 2012.

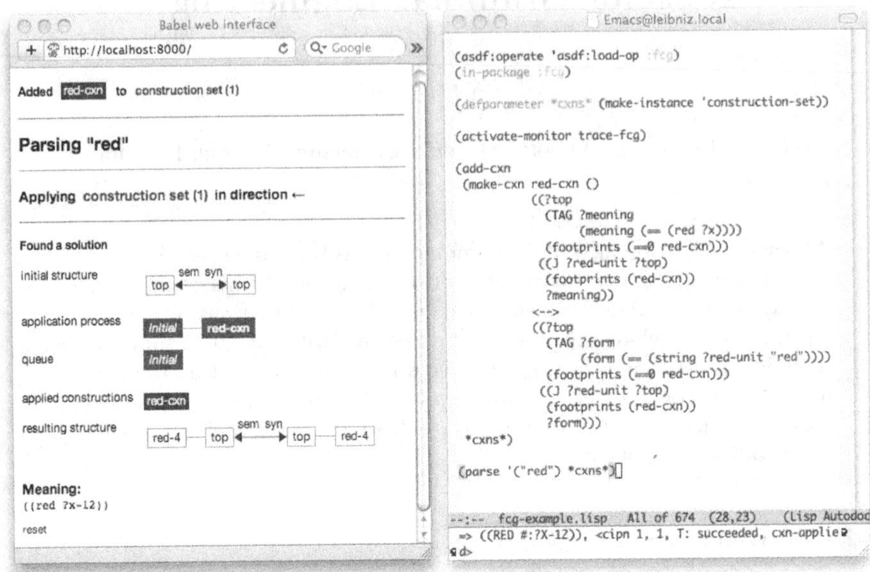

Fig. 1. Interacting with FCG. On the right, a Lisp development environment (here GNU Emacs) containing a minimal example of using FCG is shown. The result of evaluating some of the expressions in the example (such as adding a construction to a set and parsing an utterance) is then visualized in real-time through a standard web browser (here Safari, on the left).

a part of a larger application). The first two expressions `(asdf:operate ..)` and `(in-package ..)` load the FCG framework into the current Lisp image so that from then on it can be used by the user. Then an empty construction set is created `(defparameter ..)` and a monitor for visualizations is activated. The fifth expression `(add-cxn ...)` adds a new construction to the previously created construction set and the notification "Added red-cxn to construction-set (1)" appears in the web browser window. Finally, the utterance "red" is parsed and some graphical output of FCGs processing appears in the web browser. Changing the previously defined construction or adding new constructions does not require to repeat all the steps above because the Lisp image is still running and thus developing a grammar is a continuous process of adding or replacing constructions and then trying them out.

The learning curve for new users of FCG is quite high because they have to learn how to work with a Lisp environment. However, there are detailed instructions for getting FCG running on all major platforms / Lisp implementations and once this initial hurdle is taken, interacting with FCG becomes an inspiring experience. Part of this experience is an extensive visualization and debugging component, which we will introduce in Section 2 and explain in a bit more in Section 3.

2 Understanding FCG Processing

Producing or parsing utterances in FCG involves complex processes that depend on the interplay of the involved constructions as well as often unpredictable external systems for discourse, semantics and learning. Consequently, understanding the behavior of such processes may become quite a challenge. For example it can be very difficult to track down which construction needs to be changed when a production or parsing process fails, or to analyze which construction is responsible for an undesired utterance or meaning. Even when the behaviour is as expected it might be far from trivial to understand or show why this is the case, or for example how a grammar could be further refined. Furthermore, when FCG is applied in multi-agent learning scenarios where constructions are continuously created, adapted or removed by agents or where systems for embodied semantics provide open-ended streams of conceptual structures, the behavior of FCG grammars can not be tested in isolation because it tightly interacts with all these other subsystems. These sorts of difficulties in understanding the underlying dynamics of complex software systems are a common problem in many areas of computer science such as robotics, artificial intelligence and distributed systems.

The probably most common approach to tackle this problem is *tracing*, i.e. by printing information about what is going on to to the Lisp listener (either by directly adding print statements to the code or by using built-in trace facilities or other custom mechanisms). The advantages of this technique are that (1) it is very easy to do and (2) it allows to monitor program execution at almost any level of detail (i.e. from only the result of applying a construction set to near-complete information including all intermediate processing steps). When the level of detail is high however, the output rapidly becomes unmanageable: complete traces of FCG search processes can reach hundreds of text pages. Furthermore, plain text in a Lisp listener is not easy to read and can only be presented linearly which makes it impractical for getting an overview of, or a 'feeling' for, particular dynamics of FCG.

A second method is to retrospectively analyse a search process by *inspecting* Lisp objects – either using inspector tools of Lisp environments or by directly calling chains of accessor functions on an object. As we will explain further below, FCG allows users to access detailed data representations of most of its internal processing steps so that the complete chain of operations can be reconstructed. Inspection has the advantage that it does not require to change or write any code but on the other hand does not provide any overview of a process whatsoever. Furthermore, accessing for example a node deep in a search process requires a high number of manual steps and often it is unclear which one of the many objects to inspect, which prevents inspection to be useful in many cases.

Third, many Lisp implementations and development environments provide mechanisms for manually *stepping* through code either by using the built in step facilities or by invoking the stepper directly from the code. This technique can be very helpful for finding logical mistakes in small pieces of code, but in order to make use of stepping one has to know which part of the code to look at. Stepping through a large construction set application just for exploring its dynamics would take hours and is thus impracticable.

A last technique is to create *visualisations*: they are great to get an intuition of an algorithm's dynamics because our mind understands graphical representations much better than text output, which is why in areas such as for example robotics it is exceptional to even write programs without having graphical means to verify that the system behaves as expected (ideally even for each intermediate step). Visualisations are costly, because it takes time to implement them, but they often pay off in the long run when they become an invaluable eye into the system's internals. A clear disadvantage is that visual representations only allow for a low to medium level of detail: complex data structures have to be transformed into two-dimensional (or sometimes 3D) representations, involving constraints such as available window size and a required visual clarity so that the representation remains readable. Furthermore, despite many recent developments in cross-platform libraries for graphical user interfaces, there is none that easily works in all major Common Lisp implementations and there is a lot of overhead in dealing with windows, menus and other user interface elements, event handling and the interaction with the actual code to monitor. Finally, FCG processing relies on many textual (i.e. semantic structures) and hierarchical (e.g. feature structures, search processes) data structures, which in turn are hard to visualise. Although virtually every graphic library has means to display text on the screen, the responsibility for arranging text blocks (estimating widths an heights of text areas depending on available space, avoiding overlap, re-flowing multi-line text) is usually in the hand of the programmer.

The implementation of the FCG formalism comes with an extensive user interface (called *web interface*) that combines many of the advantages of the previously introduced techniques, while at the same time removing most of their respective disadvantages. The main idea (we will go into some of the details in the next section) is to use a normal web browser as a terminal for tracing internals of FCG. That is, information is "printed" in real time to the web browser window instead of to the Lisp listener. This already has the advantage that different colors, text styles, backgrounds and many other graphical means can be used to make representations more readable than if there were printed as plain text. Second, recent advances in HTML rendering engines have made it possible to create tree-like representations (for feature structures, search trees, etc.) that are automatically laid out by the client browsers so the available screen space is used as economically as possible. And third, scripting mechanisms of contemporary web browsers allow to create expandable and collapsible elements so that details of a structure or a process can be initially hidden but then be recursively revealed if the user clicks on them, thus enabling to display the most important information of a structure or process in a single browser window, while still providing access to the smallest details. Forth and finally, current web technologies enable to interact with FCG grammars through the browser window (e.g. applying constructions to previously selected transient feature structures with a mouse click).

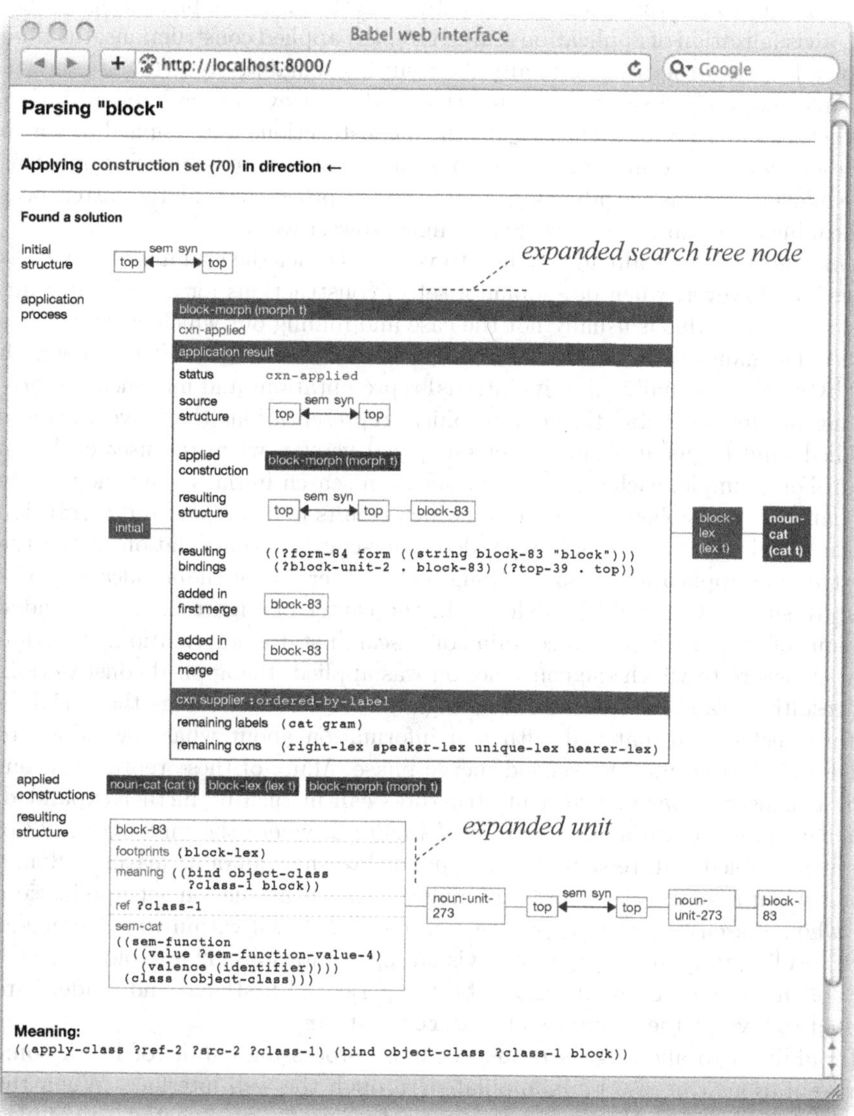

Fig. 2. Example output produced by the web interface. The search tree node (`block-morph`) and unit (`block-83`) of the resulting structure have been manually expanded.

An example for such interactive visualizations is shown in Figure 2. The utterance "block" is parsed and as a side effect, a condensed visualization of the involved processes and representations is sent to the web browser. This high-level summary shows the utterance, the applied construction set, the initial coupled feature structure, a visualization of application search tree, the applied constructions, the final coupled feature structure and finally the resulting semantic structure are shown. This information is already enough to get a good overview of what happened, that is, whether the processing succeeded, which constructions were applied in which order and what the resulting utterance or semantic structure is. Showing only this little information has the advantage that even the processing of larger utterances or meanings can still be visualized in a single browser window.

This information is already enough to verify whether the grammar behaves as expected. However, when developing a set of constructions for a particular linguistic example, this is usually not the case and finding out which constructions need to be changed to yield the desired result is far from trivial. FCG helps with this by making virtually all of its internal representations and intermediate processing results accessible through graphical representations that reveal a more detailed (and bigger in terms of screen space) version when the user clicks on them. For example, each node in a application search initially only shows only the name of the applied construction (which results in a compact representation of the search tree), but when expanded, near-complete information about the construction application, goal tests and other internals of the application process are shown. Concretely, as shown in the center of Figure 2, the expanded versions of search tree nodes contain some search status information, the transient structure to which the construction was applied, the applied construction, the resulting transient structure, bindings that show what things the variables in the construction matched with and information about what was added to which unit in the first and second merge phase. Many of these representations such as constructions or transient structures can in turn be further expanded, as for example shown at the bottom of Figure 2, where the unit `block-83` of the final coupled feature structure is expanded to show all of its features. Sometimes, when a goal test requires running another construction set application, the whole search tree of that process will be also shown within that particular node, leading to quite deeply nested visual representations. This exploratory aspect of the interaction with FCG is best experienced firsthand and readers are invited to try out the examples at `www.fcg-net.org`.

In addition to allowing users inspect most processing details of FCG, some representations can also be manipulated through the web interface. When the mouse is moved over the graphical representation of a construction, a coupled feature structure, or a search node, a small menu appears that offers a set of operations on the structure:

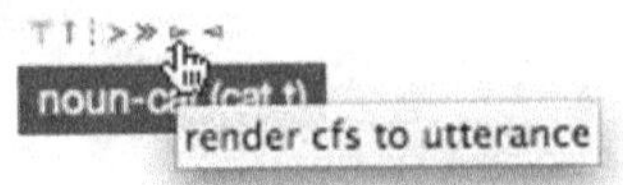

For search nodes, these operations include rendering the transient structure of the node into an utterance or extracting its meaning, saving the actual node or its transient structure to a global variable so that it can be accessed from within Lisp, and restarting the search process below the node. Furthermore, the pop-up menu of constructions contains operations for saving and printing the construction as well as for applying the construction to a previously saved transient structure in parsing or production. Finally, coupled feature structures also can be saved, printed, rendered, etc. – additionally there are operations for applying all constructions of the construction inventory to the structure in order to see which constructions apply and which not.

All these mechanisms help FCG users to quickly find and fix problems in their grammars. For example, in order to find out why a construction that should have been applied did not apply, the expandable graphical representations of construction application search trees make it easy to find the last "correct" transient structure, which can be saved through its menu to a global variable and then can be compared to the construction in question side by side. The changes to the construction are made in the Lisp editor, but as soon as the construction is added to a construction inventory, a graphical representation of the changed construction will appear in the web browser, where it can be applied to the saved transient structure through its popup menu. This isolated application test is continued until the construction behaves as expected and can be tried out again within a complete production or parsing process.

3 The Web Interface and Monitoring System

FCG shares its visualization and monitoring mechanisms with other systems for discourse, semantics and learning under the umbrella of the Babel2 framework [2, 6]. The web interface is described in detail in [1] and the monitoring system in [2, Chapter 3], but we will nevertheless outline some basic design choices and components in this section.

The web interface is based on the HUNCHENTOOT web server that runs in the same Lisp image as FCG/ Babel2 and is loaded automatically with FCG. Web browsers connect to the web interface by loading an empty client page and then content can be *pushed* to that page from within Lisp through an AJAX-based client-side event loop that frequently polls the web server for new elements to display. Creating HTML elements in Lisp is a straightforward transformation of s-expressions such as `((p :style "color:red") "hi!")` into `<p style="color:red">hi!</p>"` and with these basic mechanisms it is already possible to create program traces that are much more readable and informative than plain text because different colors, a multitude of font styles, sizes, backgrounds or borders can be used.

Contemporary HTML rendering engines are extremely good in distributing the available browser window width among recursively nested child elements, and in re-flowing the layout when the window size changes or when more data

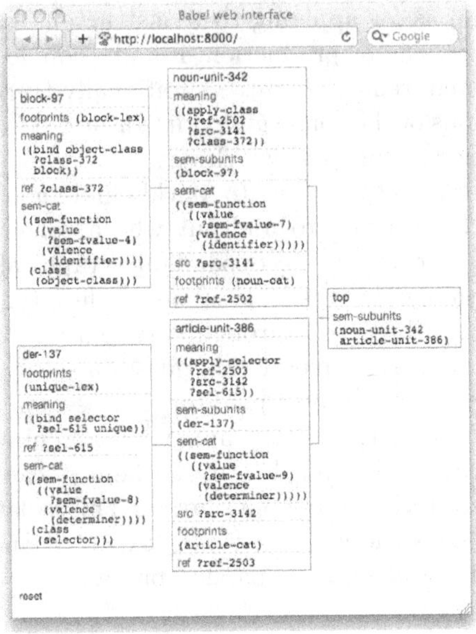

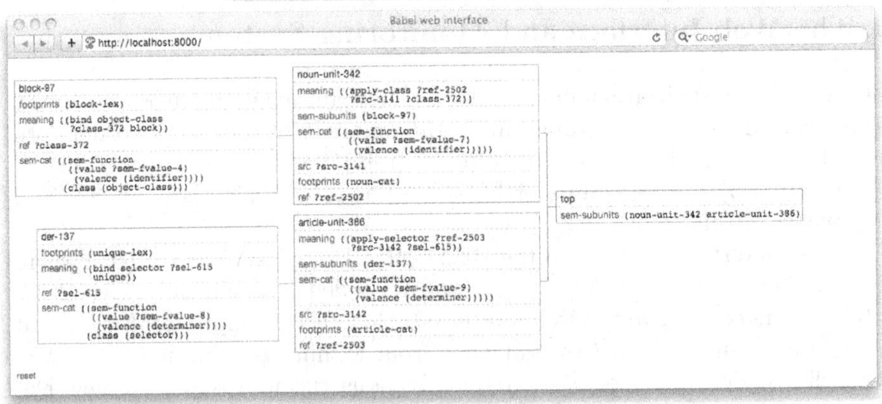

Fig. 3. Example for a resizing HTML representation of a feature structure. The same semantic pole of a transient structure is automatically rendered by the Safari web browser to fit into a horizontally constrained space (top) or a more wide browser window (bottom).

is added to the page). FCGs web interface heavily exploits these abilities by providing general mechanisms for drawing tree-like structures (such as search trees, feature structures, constructions) in HTML. Tree nodes and horizontal and vertical lines connecting them are created as recursively nested tables and the web browser then takes care of fitting the tree in the available space and of adjusting the width of the nodes accordingly. Furthermore, as many of FCGs representations are Lisp s-expressions (e.g. semantic structures, feature values of coupled feature structures), and experienced Lisp users strongly rely on proper indentation of parentheses, the web interface can create HTML representations of s-expressions that automatically adopt their width to the available space, while remaining properly indented. As shown in Figure 3, this flexible layout of feature structures (and other tree-like representations) results in a very efficient use of (precious) browser window space.

A second key feature of the web interface is the way in which complex data and control structures can be displayed: the level of detail of what is visualised is not restricted by the size of the web browser window. The trick is to create simplified visual representations of data that *expand* into a detailed version when the user clicks on them and that *collapse* to their original state when clicked a second time. As for example explained above in Section 2, for a production or parsing process the user initially is presented with the main results of the application process and the search tree and then can get to almost any intermediate representation by clicking through the HTML elements in the client page. Technically, the web interface internally stores for each of expandable elements both a collapsed and expanded version (actually anonymous functions are stored to avoid computing HTML code that never gets requested). The collapsed version is initially sent to the client page, and when the user clicks on the element the expanded version is requested from the Lisp side using Ajax communication.

The use of lexical closures makes the web interface very fast and responsive, but users may not always want the visualizations to be computed (or switch between alternative visualizations). The *monitoring* system of FCG/ Babel2 solves this issue (for details see chapter 3 of [2]). The main idea is to not clutter the source code of FCGs implementation with code that produces debug traces, but rather to have a event/ notification/ event handler system that separates actual code from debugging and visualization mechanisms. For example, after each application of a construction set, an event is triggered that notifies a list of *monitors* of the finished application. Those monitors that are *active* can then *handle* this event, for example by adding visualizations to the web interface. Consequently, FCG users can switch different visualizations on and off by activating/ deactivating monitors.

Finally, advanced users of FCG and Lisp can easily create their own visualizations and monitors for their specific experiments. The web interface provides mechanisms for defining client side Javascript and CSS code fragments, for replacing and appending the content of existing HTML elements, and so on.

When the basic graphical capabilities of HTML are not sufficient for certain visualisation purposes, SVG graphics or Flash animations can of course be also sent to the client page.

4 Conclusions

The tools for grammar engineering introduced in this chapter have changed the way users of FCG interact with the system, not only making the experience richer, but also more trouble-free. Meaningful processing traces allow FCG developers to debug and make sense of the formalism itself and they help FCG users to see the effects of their linguistic rules by having access to all details of the parsing process without losing a general overview. Some dynamics that were previously mystifying and impenetrable have cleared up and as a welcome side-effect newcomers to FCG grasp the material at a considerably faster speed because of the way they can interact with and gradually investigate the dynamics. Furthermore, having detailed visualizations is very helpful explaining the working of FCG to other audiences – in fact most of the graphics in this book are visualizations created by the web interface.

Using a web server and web browsers as the main technology for designing a user interface might seem as an unusual choice and indeed only a few years ago it would not have been feasible to implement a system such as described here. Although our present-day web standards are much older, they were only poorly supported making it strenuous for web developers to ensure the interoperability of their web sites in different browsers. Fortunately, things have improved. Today valid XHTML+CSS code is properly interpreted by a variety of browsers and AJAX has become an ubiquitous technology that just works. Particularly impressive is the way contemporary HTML rendering engines are able to layout (and re-flow) heavily nested HTML constructs with incredible speed and perfectly looking in almost all cases. Furthermore, not needing to rely on other external libraries for user interfaces than (readily available) web browsers makes the visualization component of FCG/ Babel2 very lightweight and easily employable on a wide variety of Lisp implementations and platforms.

Acknowledgements. The research in this paper was conducted at the Artificial Intelligence Laboratory at the Vrije Universiteit Brussel (VUB AI lab) and is partly funded through the EU FP7 ALEAR project.

References

[1] Loetzsch, M., Bleys, J., Wellens, P.: Understanding the dynamics of complex lisp programs. In: Proceedings of the 2nd European Lisp Symposium, Milano, Italy, pp. 59–69 (May 2009)

[2] Loetzsch, M., Wellens, P., De Beule, J., Bleys, J., van Trijp, R.: The Babel2 manual. Tech. Rep. AI-Memo 01-08, AI-Lab VUB, Brussels, Belgium (2008)

[3] Steele, G.L.: Common LISP: The Language, 2nd edn. Digital Press, Bedford (1990)

[4] Steels, L. (ed.): Design Patterns in Fluid Construction Grammar. John Benjamins, Amsterdam (2011)
[5] Steels, L.: A first encounter with Fluid Construction Grammar. In: Steels, L. (ed.) Design Patterns in Fluid Construction Grammar. John Benjamins, Amsterdam (2011)
[6] Steels, L., Loetzsch, M.: Babel: a tool for running experiments on the evolution of language. In: Nolfi, S., Mirolli, M. (eds.) Evolution of Communication and Language in Embodied Agents, pp. 307–313. Springer, Heidelberg (2010)

Part II
Implementation

A Reflective Architecture for Robust Language Processing and Learning

Remi van Trijp

Sony Computer Science Laboratory Paris, France

Abstract. Becoming a proficient speaker of a language requires more than just learning a set of words and grammar rules, it also implies mastering the ways in which speakers of that language typically innovate: stretching the meaning of words, introducing new grammatical constructions, introducing a new category, and so on. This paper demonstrates that such meta-knowledge can be represented and applied by reusing similar representations and processing techniques as needed for routine linguistic processing, which makes it possible that language processing makes use of computational reflection.

1 Introduction

When looking at natural language, two striking observations immediately jump to the mind. First, there is an extraordinary amount of diversity among the world's languages [10] and 'almost every newly described language presents us with some "crazy" new category that hardly fits existing taxonomies' [9, p. 119]. Secondly, languages are not static homogeneous entities, but rather complex adaptive systems [24] that dynamically change over time and in which new forms are forever emerging [11]. These observations pose strong requirements on linguistic formalisms, which need to support an enormous amount of variety while at the same time coping with the open-ended nature of language [33].

Both requirements may seem overwhelming for anyone who wants to develop operational explanations for language, but two formalisms within the cognitive linguistics tradition have nevertheless accepted the challenge: Fluid Construction Grammar (FCG; for handling parsing and production; see the remainder of this volume and [26]) and Incremental Recruitment Language (IRL; a constraint language that has been proposed for operationalizing embodied cognitive semantics [20]). Both IRL and FCG have the necessary expressivity for capturing the myriad of conceptual and grammatical structures of language. FCG is based on *feature structures* and *matching and merging* (i.e. unification) [6, 18, 28, 32], whereas IRL is based on *constraints* and *constraint propagation.*[1]

[1] In order to fully appreciate the technical details of this paper, the reader is expected to have a firm grasp of the FCG-system and a basic understanding of IRL. Interested readers are also advised to first check [33] for learning about how problems concerning robustness and fluidity are typically handled in FCG, and [4, 15] for how that approach is implemented.

L. Steels (Ed.): Computational Issues in FCG, LNAI 7249, pp. 51–74, 2012.

Both FCG and IRL are embedded in a double-layered *meta-level architecture* for handling unforeseen problems and inventing novel solutions [4, 33]. This meta-level architecture allows the implementation of *computational reflection* [19], which is commonly defined as "the activity performed by a system when doing computation about (and by that possibly affecting) its own computation" [16, p. 21]. The architecture is illustrated in Figure 1. On the one hand, there is a *routine layer* that handles habitual processing. On top of that, a *meta-layer* tries to detect and solve problems that may occur in routine processing through *diagnostics and repairs* (also called *meta-layer operators*). For instance, a diagnostic may detect that the listener encountered an unknown word, while a repair can ask the language system to perform a top-down prediction on what kind of word it is and what its meaning might be (see [4, 33]; and the remainder of this paper for more concrete examples). Once a repair is made, computation resumes at the routine-layer.

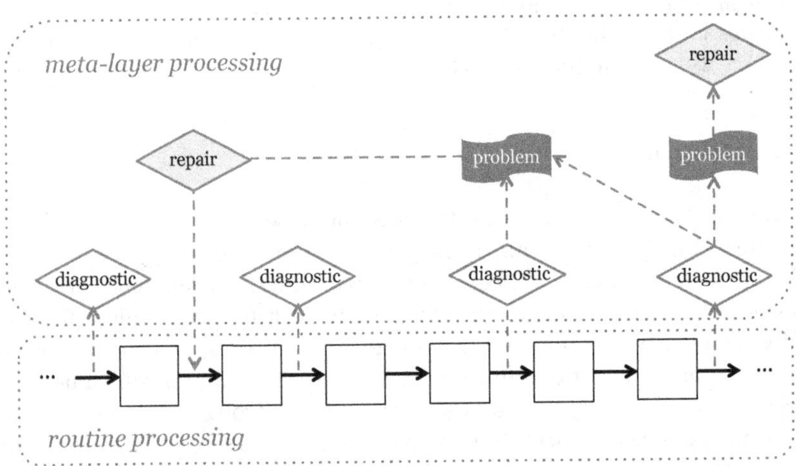

Fig. 1. FCG and IRL feature a double-layered meta-level architecture. Besides a layer for routine processing, a meta-layer diagnoses and repairs problems that may occur in the routine layer [4].

Recent studies on the evolution of language [29, 30] have identified numerous meta-layer operators that operationalize open-ended language processing for specific domains such as agreement [3], tense-aspect [7], event structure [34, 36], space [14, 21], and quantifiers [17]. However, most operationalizations implement the *functions* of the diagnostics and repairs in LISP code, so the language processing system is only reflective in a weak sense. Figure 2 shows a typical example of this approach in pseudo-code. The diagnostic shown in the Figure tries to detect unknown words by looking for unprocessed strings in each last search node (or 'leaf') of linguistic processing. If the set of those strings contains exactly one word, the diagnostic reports an `unknown-word` problem.

diagnostic (detect-unknown-word)

```
when SEARCH-NODE in PARSING is a LEAF
then get the UNPROCESSED-STRINGS from the SEARCH-NODE
     when the UNPROCESSED-STRINGS contain a SINGLE-WORD
     then report UNKNOWN-WORD problem
```

Fig. 2. Most diagnostics and repairs for IRL and FCG are implemented directly as computational functions, whereas full reflection requires that IRL and FCG are their own meta-language

This paper demonstrates that the same representation and application machinery now used at the routine language processing layer can also be used for the meta-layer, which makes the whole system reflective in a strong sense. By doing so, this paper paves the way towards experiments in which novel language strategies emerge and become culturally shared. More specifically, this paper proposes the following approach:

1. Diagnostics can be represented as *feature structures*, which can be processed by the FCG-interpreter. Problems are detected by *matching* these feature structures against other feature structures.
2. Repairs can be represented as *constraint networks*, which can be configured, executed and chunked by IRL.
3. Diagnostics and repairs that exclusively operate on the linguistic level can be associated to each other in the form of *coupled feature structures* and thus become part of the linguistic inventory in their own right.

I use the term *language strategy* for a particular set of diagnostics and repairs (see [31], for a more complete definition of a language strategy). Language strategies are processed in the meta-layer and allow a language user to acquire and expand a *language system*, which are the concrete choices made in a language for producing and comprehending utterances, such as the English word-order system. Language systems are processed in the routine layer.

2 Diagnostics Based on Matching

This section demonstrates through a series of examples how feature structures, which are used for representing linguistic knowledge in FCG [22], can represent diagnostics. When they are able to match with a transient structure they detect a specific problem.

2.1 A First Example: Detecting an Unknown Word

Let's start with one of the most common problems in deep language processing: unknown words [1]. The key to diagnosing this problem through the FCG machinery (rather than by using a tailored LISP function) is to understand how routine processing handles familiar words. As explained in more detail by [27], FCG processing first involves a *transient structure*, which is a temporary data structure that contains all the information of the utterance that a speaker is producing, or that a listener is parsing. The transient structure consists of a semantic and a syntactic pole. Both poles comprise a set of units, which have feature structures associated with them. The following transient structure represents the initial structure of the utterance *the snark* at the beginning of a parsing task:

Example 1

```
((top-unit))
<-->
((top-unit
  (form ((string the-unit "the")
         (string snark-unit "snark")
         (meets the-unit snark-unit)))))
```

As can be seen, both the semantic pole (above the double arrow symbol) and the syntactic pole have a unit called `top-unit`. The top-unit on the semantic pole is still empty because we're at the beginning of a parsing task hence the listener has not analyzed any of the words yet. The top-unit of the right pole has a `form` feature, whose value contains two words and an ordering constraint (`meets`) between the words. During parsing, the FCG-interpreter then tries to apply linguistic constructions to the transient structure and, by doing so, modifying it. For example, the following lexical entry applies for the word *the*:

Example 2

```
((?top-unit
  (tag ?meaning (meaning (== (unique-entity ?entity))))
  (footprints (==0 the-lex)))
 ((J ?the-unit ?top-unit)
  ?meaning
  (args (?entity))
  (footprints (the-lex lex))))
<-->
((?top-unit
  (tag ?form (form (== (string ?the-unit "the"))))
  (footprints (==0 the-lex)))
 ((J ?the-unit ?top-unit)
  ?form
  (footprints (the-lex lex))))
```

The above lexical construction is kept simple for illustration purposes. In parsing, all it does is look for any unit whose `form` feature contains the string "the" in its value. If such a unit is found, the construction builds a new unit for the article and moves the form to this new unit. The construction also leaves a footprint that prevents it from applying a second time. On the semantic pole, the construction builds a corresponding unit for the article and it adds the article's meaning to this new unit. So when applying the lexical construction of example 2 to the transient structure in example 1, the transient structure is modified into the following structure:

Example 3

```
((top-unit
  (sem-subunits (the-unit)))
 (the-unit
  (meaning ((unique-entity ?entity)))
  (args (?entity))
  (footprints (the-lex lex))))
<-->
((top-unit
  (syn-subunits (the-unit))
  (form ((string snark-unit "snark")
         (meets the-unit snark-unit))))
 (the-unit
  (form ((string the-unit "the")))
  (footprints (the-lex lex))))
```

It is common design practice in FCG to consider the `top-unit` as a buffer that temporarily holds all data concerning meaning (on the semantic pole) or form (on the syntactic pole) until they are moved into their proper units by lexical constructions. If all lexical constructions abide by this design rule, all meanings and strings that are left in the top-unit after all constructions have been tried can be considered as unprocessed and therefore problematic. For detecting whether any unknown words are left, we can thus simply define a *meta-level feature structure* that matches on any string in the top-unit:

Example 4

diagnostic (string)

```
((?top-unit
  (form (== (string ?any-unit ?any-string)))
  (footprints (==0 lex))))
```

This diagnostic looks exactly like the 'conditional' features of a lexical construction (i.e. units that need to be 'matched' before the other features are merged by the FCG-interpreter), except for the fact that there is a variable `?any-string` instead of an actual string, and that the feature structure cannot trigger if the footprint `lex` has been left in the unit by a lexical construction.

Assume now that the FCG-system did not have a lexical construction for the word `snark`, which is likely because it is an imaginary word invented by Lewis

Carroll for his 1876 poem *The Hunting of the Snark*, so routine processing gets stuck at the transient structure of example 3. The FCG-interpreter can now *match* the meta-level feature structure of example 4 with the syntactic pole of that transient structure, which yields the following bindings:

```
((?any-string . "snark") (?any-unit . snark-unit) (?top-unit . top-unit))
```

In other words, the meta-level feature structure matches with the `top-unit` and finds the unknown string *snark*. Here, there is only one unknown word, but if there would be multiple unknown strings, matching would yield multiple hypotheses. This example, which is kept simple for illustration purposes, achieves the same result as the diagnostic that was illustrated in Figure 2.

By exploiting the same feature structure representation as FCG uses for transient structures and linguistic constructions, the FCG-interpreter can be reused without resorting to tailor-made functions. Moreover, the diagnostic explicitly uses the design pattern shared by all lexical constructions, namely that strings and meanings are taken from the buffer-like top-unit and put into their own unit, whereas the tailored function keeps this information implicit.

2.2 Internal Agreement

A common feature of language is 'internal agreement', which involves two or more linguistic units that share semantic or syntactic features such as gender or number [3]. For example, in the French noun phrase *la femme* ('the woman'), the singular-feminine definite article *la* is used in agreement with the gender and number of *femme*, as opposed to the singular-masculine article *le* as in *le garçon* ('the boy').

Assume now a grammar of French that uses phrasal constructions for handling agreement between an adjacent determiner and noun, using the design pattern for phrasal constructions as proposed by [25]. The schema in Figure 3 illustrates how a DetNP-construction modifies the transient structure on the left to the resulting transient structure on the right: the construction takes the units for the determiner and the noun and groups them together as subunits of a new NP-unit, which has the same number and gender features as its two subunits.

Just like with lexical constructions, we can exploit the design pattern captured in phrasal constructions for detecting problems. The diagnostic in example 5 detects whether the DetNP-construction applied successfully or not. It looks for any unit that contains at least two subunits, and which does not contain the feature-value pair `(phrase-type nominal-phrase)` (ensuring that the phrasal construction did not apply on this unit). The two specified subunits should 'meet' each other (i.e. be adjacent), and they should be a determiner and a noun. Both the determiner and the noun have a `number` and `gender` feature, but their values are unspecified through unique variables for each unit, which allows the actual values to differ from each other.

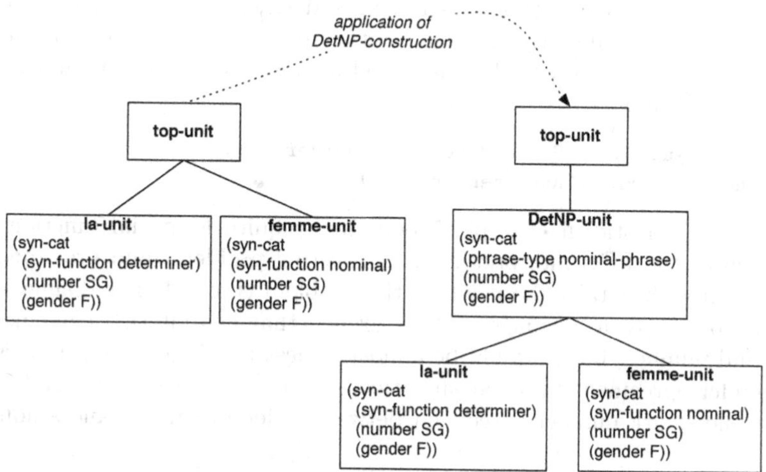

Fig. 3. The DetNP-construction groups a determiner- and noun-unit together as subunits of a phrasal unit

Example 5

diagnostic (internal-agreement)

```
((?top-unit
   (syn-subunits (== ?determiner-unit ?noun-unit))
   (form (== (meets ?determiner-unit ?noun-unit)))
   (syn-cat (==0 (phrase-type nominal-phrase))))
  (?determiner-unit
   (syn-cat
    (==1 (gender ?determiner-gender)
         (number ?determiner-number)
         (syn-function determiner))))
  (?noun-unit
   (syn-cat
    (==1 (gender ?noun-gender)
         (number ?noun-number)
         (syn-function nominal)))))
```

Suppose the FCG-interpreter has to parse the ungrammatical utterance **le femme.* Matching the meta-level feature structure would yield the following bindings for those unique variables:

```
((?determiner-number . SG) (?determiner-gender . M)
 (?noun-number . SG) (?noun-gender . F))
```

From these bindings, we can infer that there is a problem with the **gender** feature, because there are two different values for both units: masculine and feminine. The **number** feature, on the other hand, is singular for both units because the variables `?determiner-number` and `?noun-number` are both bound to the same value. Similarly, the diagnostic can detect a problem of number (but not of gender) if it would be matched against a feature structure for the utterance **la femmes*:

```
((?determiner-number . SG) (?determiner-gender . F)
 (?noun-number . PL) (?noun-gender . F))
```

Again, the diagnostic in example 5 does not require a special function, but simply reuses the FCG-interpreter for discovering problems and providing the FCG-system with details about where the problem is found. The diagnostic is, however, specific to a language such as French that has internal agreement of gender and number, but it would be almost useless for English, which does not mark gender agreement between an article and the adjacent noun, and which also does not mark number agreement between a definite article and a noun.

2.3 Word Order

Another widespread language strategy is based on using word order for marking various kinds of grammatical or pragmatic functions, but there is a wide variety in which word order constraints are applied by particular languages. For example, Dutch is fairly free in its word order constraints but it is a so-called V2 (verb second) language, which means that (with the exception of certain constructions), the inflected verbal unit of a Dutch utterance has to be in second position in the main clause. For example, a Dutch speaker would translate 'Yesterday, I went walking' as *Gisteren ging ik wandelen*, literally 'yesterday went I walk'. The following meta-level feature structure is able to diagnose violations of the Dutch V2-constraint:

Example 6

diagnostic (V2-constraint)

```
((?top-unit
   (syn-subunits
    (== ?unit-a ?unit-b ?verbal-unit))
   (form (== (meets ?unit-a ?unit-b)
             (meets ?unit-b ?verbal-unit))))
 (?verbal-unit
   (syn-cat (==1 (syn-function verbal)
                 (inflected? +)))))
```

The diagnostic uses two adjacency constraints to check whether there is any 'illegal' unit that precedes the verbal unit, which itself is identified through its syntactic function and the inflection constraint. Thus if an English speaker who learns Dutch would say **Gisteren ik ging wandelen*, the diagnostic would find matching variables for `?unit-a` (the adverbial phrase *gisteren* 'yesterday') and `?unit-b` (the subject *ik* 'I'), which means that at least one of these two units is in the wrong position.

2.4 Unexpressed Meanings

Diagnostics can not only be of lexical or morphosyntactic nature, but also target semantic properties. In dialogues it often happens that a language user cannot remember a particular word for the meaning he wishes to express, especially when speaking in a foreign language. This problem is equivalent to detecting unknown words, hence we can use a similar solution on the meaning side. The meta-level feature structure of example 7 triggers on all meanings that have been left unprocessed by lexical constructions.

Example 7

diagnostic (meaning)

```
((?top-unit
   (meaning (== (?predicate . ?args)))
   (footprints (==0 lex))))
```

Suppose that FCG-processing got stuck at a transient structure that includes the following top-unit, which contains an unprocessed temporal meaning that states that one event happened before another one:

```
(top-unit
 (meaning ((before ev-1 ev-2))))
```

Matching the meta-level structure yields the following bindings:

```
((?predicate . before) (?args ev-1 ev-2) (?top-unit . top-unit))
```

The diagnostic finds out that the unexpressed meaning predicate (if one uses a predicate calculus for handling meaning) is `before`. The diagnostic also uses a dot before the variable `?args`, which is a Common Lisp notation that corresponds to 'the rest of the list', so `?args` is bound to the remainder of the meaning element `(ev-1 ev-2)`. For each unexpressed meaning predicate, the diagnostic thus returns a binding for the predicate and its arguments.

2.5 Valence

A major challenge for linguistic formalisms is the distribution of verbs (i.e. which argument structures are compatible with which verbs). Usually, a verbal lexical entry contains a `valence` feature that states which semantic (and syntactic) roles the verb can assign to its arguments. Problems, however, arise when speakers wish to override those constraints, as when for instance using the intransitive verb `sneeze` in a Caused-Motion frame as in *Pat sneezed the napkin off the table* [8, p. 3]. Assume the following meaning and semantic valence for the verb *sneeze*:

```
(meaning
 (== (sneeze ?ev)
     (sneezer ?ev ?sneezer)))
(sem-cat
 (==1 (sem-valence
       (==1 (agent ?ev ?sneezer)))))
```

Using a predicate calculus for meaning, the verb contains one predicate for the event itself and one predicate for the participant who's sneezing (the sneezer). The semantic valence of the verb states that the sneezer can be categorized in terms of the semantic role **agent** by repeating the variable **?sneezer** for its argument, thereby making the verb compatible with the intransitive construction (see [35] for a detailed discussion of valence and argument structure constructions in FCG).

The Caused-Motion construction, however, requires not only an Agent but also a Patient and a Direction, as found in the valence of verbs that typically express caused motion such as *push* and *pull.* There is thus a mismatch between the valence of *sneeze* and the requirements of the Caused-Motion construction, which means that the argument structure construction will not be triggered during routine processing.

According to Goldberg [8], this problem can be solved through *coercion.* Goldberg argues that the Caused-Motion construction only specifies that the Agent is obligatory and that the other roles can be added by the construction itself on the condition that there are no conflicts with the semantics of the verb. If we want to operationalize this hypothesis, an adequate diagnostic thus needs to figure out the following two things. First, it has to detect that the Caused-Motion construction failed to apply, and if so, it has to check whether the verb can be coerced into the Caused-Motion frame if necessary. The meta-level feature structure shown in example 8 achieves both goals.

Example 8

diagnostic (Caused-Motion)

```
((?top-unit
   (sem-subunits
    (== ?agent-unit ?verbal-unit ?patient-unit
         ?direction-unit))
   (meaning
    (== (cause-move ?ev) (causer ?ev ?agent)
         (moved ?ev ?patient)
         (direction ?ev ?direction)))
   (footprints (==0 arg-cxn)))
  (?verbal-unit
   (sem-cat (==1 (sem-valence
                   (==1 (agent ?ev ?agent)))))
   (args (?ev)))
  (?agent-unit
   (args (?agent)))
  (?patient-unit
   (args (?patient)))
  (?direction-unit
   (args (?direction))))
```

The diagnostic in example 8 matches if there is a unit whose **meaning** feature contains a Caused-Motion frame. The **footprints** ensure that no argument-structure construction has applied on this unit. The diagnostic also verifies whether all necessary units are present, and whether the semantic valence of the verb contains at least the obligatory Agent-role. When matched against a transient structure that contains the verb *sneeze*, the diagnostic would thus immediately be capable of linking the sneezer-role to the causer-role in the Caused-Motion frame through the variable `?agent`.

3 Diagnostics Based on Merging

The examples in the previous sections have all used the *matching* facility of the FCG-interpreter. A second way in which meta-level feature structures can be exploited is to use *merging*. The merge-operation is more permissive than matching and hence should only be used as a test for conflicts. In this usage, the meta-level feature structure does not represent a particular problem, but rather captures certain 'felicity conditions' of a language. This means that a failure in merging it with the transient structure reveals a violation of the constraints of that language. Let's take the example of internal agreement in French again. The following meta-level feature structure checks whether the `number` and `gender` features of a determiner and an adjacent noun agree with each other when it is merged with a transient structure:

Example 9

diagnostic (internal-agreement-2)

```
((?top-unit
  (syn-subunits (== ?determiner-unit ?noun-unit))
  (form (== (meets ?determiner-unit ?noun-unit))))
 (?determiner-unit
  (syn-cat
   (==1 (gender ?gender)
        (number ?number)
        (syn-function determiner))))
 (?noun-unit
  (syn-cat
   (==1 (gender ?gender)
        (number ?number)
        (syn-function nominal)))))
```

The meta-level feature structure uses the same variables `?gender` and `?number` for both units, indicating that the determiner and the noun need to have the same value for both features. Merging the meta-level feature structure with the transient structure of *la femme* ('the woman') would thus succeed because both forms are feminine-singular. However, merging would fail for utterances such as **le femme* because the two words have different gender values.

However, using FCG's merging operation for diagnosing problems is less powerful than using the matcher because there is less feedback: merging simply fails without providing more information about what caused the failure. So when the diagnostic of example 9 reports a problem, it cannot say whether the problem is caused by mismatches in gender, number or both.

4 Exploiting Constraint Networks for Repairs

As explained in more detail by [4], *repairs* are powerful operations that try to solve the problems detected by diagnostics. Repairs are able to modify the inventory used in routine processing, and to restart or even repurpose a parsing or production task. As is the case for diagnostics, most currently implemented repairs for FCG are specific functions that look as the repair shown in Figure 4.

repair `(add-meta-level-cxn problem parsing-task)`

```
If there is an UNKNOWN-WORD in PROBLEM
then add a META-LEVEL CONSTRUCTION of UNKNOWN-WORD to GRAMMAR
   and restart PARSING-TASK
else return FAILURE
```

Fig. 4. Most current FCG repairs are implemented as specific LISP functions

The repair handles unknown words by inserting a meta-level construction in the linguistic inventory. Interested readers are kindly referred to [33] to learn more about how the solution works. Roughly speaking, the meta-level construction creates a new unit for the unknown word and makes it compatible with any semantic and syntactic specification, which may trigger the application of other constructions that were previously blocked. Returning to our example of *the snark*, for instance, a DeterminerNominal construction can now treat *snark* as a noun because it is immediately preceded by a determiner. FCG can thus overcome the problem and continue parsing until a final transient structure is found that passes all the 'goal tests' that decide on the adequacy of a parse result [5].

Writing a specific function for each repair is useful for fast prototyping, but soon becomes problematic. First, there is no uniform and coherent way of representing and processing repairs. As a result, it largely depends on the grammar engineer's appreciation of particular problems whether the repair is adequate or not. Secondly, there is no 'safe' way of testing the consequences of a repair: repairs have to 'commit' their changes to the linguistic inventory and then restart a process before any hidden effects may pop up. Needless to say, when complex problems need to be solved, writing adequate repairs soon involves a lot of trial and error, even for experienced grammar engineers.

This paper proposes that the implementation of repairs should be treated as *constraint satisfaction problems*, which allows the grammar engineer to define constraints that need to be satisfied before a repair is allowed to commit its changes to the inventory. For this purpose, repairs can be formulated as *constraint networks* using IRL, a constraint language that has been proposed for handling conceptualization and interpretation [20], and which can be considered as FCG's sister formalism. The next subsection shows a first example of an 'IRL repair'. The subsequent section then goes a step further and shows the full power of IRL for implementing repairs.

4.1 A First Example: Repairing an Unknown Word

Assume that a diagnostic has detected the unknown word *snark* in the utterance *the snark*. We now need to define a network of constraints that performs the same operations as the repair function in Figure 4 and that first tests the solution instead of immediately committing any changes and restarting the parsing task. Every IRL repair network consists of the following elements:

- *An object store*, which contains 'linguistic types' such as transient structures, constructions, meanings and strings. Specific instantiations of each type are called 'linguistic instances'.
- *A component store*, which contains 'linguistic operators', which are the building blocks of each network. These operators perform specific operations on linguistic instances, such as applying a construction, fetching the inventory of constructions, and so on.

A possible repair network is shown in Figure 5. Every node in a repair network evokes a specific linguistic operation, represented by the name of the operator and a list of its arguments, for instance `(get-construction-inventory ?inventory)`. The arguments are variables (indicated by a question mark) that are or will be bound to a linguistic instance. Binding variables to a specific linguistic instance of a certain type is done by the special operator `bind`. For example, the operation `(bind string ?word snark)` binds the word *snark* (which is of type `string`) to the variable `?word`. Different operations in the network are linked to each other through the variables. For example, the variable `?inventory` is shared by two operations. In its list notation, the network looks as follows:

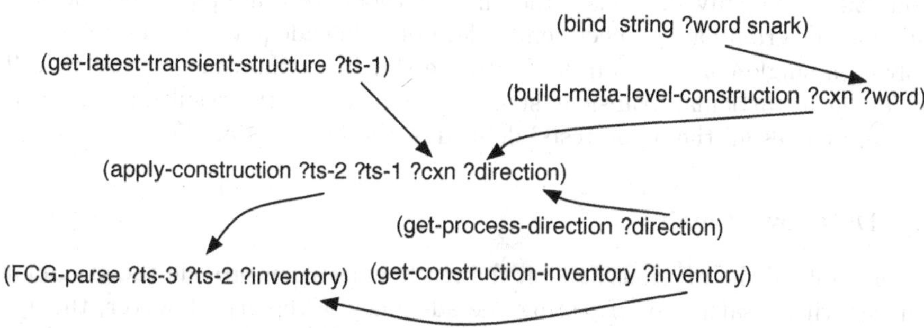

Fig. 5. A possible IRL repair network for handling unknown words. This first example does not yet exploit the full power of IRL and uses a sequential order for the execution of linguistic operations (with precedence relations indicated by the arrows).

```
((bind string ?word snark)
 (get-construction-inventory ?inventory)
 (get-latest-transient-structure ?ts-1)
 (get-process-direction ?direction)
 (build-meta-level-construction ?cxn ?word)
 (apply-construction ?ts-2 ?ts-1 ?cxn ?direction)
 (FCG-parse ?ts-3 ?ts-2 ?inventory))
```

An explanation of how each operator can be implemented in IRL can be found in [20]. When described in words, the network performs the following operations:

1. Take the unknown word *snark* of type `string` (provided by a diagnostic) and bind it to the variable `?word`.
2. Get the construction inventory from the parsing task in which the problem was detected and bind it to the variable `?inventory`.
3. Get the latest transient structure from the parsing task in which the problem was detected and bind it to the variable `?ts-1` (transient structure 1).
4. Get the processing direction (parsing or production) from the task in which the problem was detected and bind it to the variable `?direction`.
5. Build a meta-level construction using the linguistic instance bound to the variable `?word`. Bind the meta-level construction to the variable `?cxn` (construction).
6. Take the linguistic instances bound to the variables `?cxn` (of type 'construction'), `?ts-1` (of type 'transient structure') and `?direction` (of type 'process-direction'). Apply the construction to the transient structure to obtain a new transient structure. Bind this new transient structure to the variable `?ts-2`.
7. Take the linguistic instances bound to `?inventory` (of type 'construction-inventory') and `?ts-2` (of type 'transient structure'). Perform a parsing task with these linguistic instances in order to obtain a new transient structure. Bind the final transient structure to `?ts-3`.

Particular constraints can be defined for each operation. For example, the operation `FCG-parse` only succeeds if the final transient structure passes all the goal tests that the grammar engineer defined for obtaining adequate results. Likewise, applying a single construction is only successful if (a) the construction indeed applies on a particular transient structure, and (b) if the resulting transient structure passes all the 'node tests' defined in the FCG-system [5].

4.2 Dataflow Repairs

The example of the previous section showed how IRL can provide the grammar engineer with a safer way of testing the adequacy of repairs. However, the applied IRL-network still featured a simple sequential control flow in which there is a fixed order in which the network's constraints are executed, which does not necessarily warrant a constraint propagation approach. This section justifies the use of IRL by showing how the formalism allows the operationalization of

Table 1. In a dataflow approach, the operator *apply-construction* can perform different computations depending on the availability of linguistic instances

Available instances	Computation
- Resulting transient structure - Source transient structure	The operator can compute which construction needs to be applied (and in which direction) in order to go from the source to the resulting transient structure.
- Resulting transient structure - Source transient structure - Direction	The operator can compute which construction needs to be applied in order to go from the source to the resulting transient structure.
- Resulting transient structure - Source transient structure - Construction	The operator can compute the direction of application.
- Resulting transient structure - Source transient structure - Construction - Direction	The operator can perform a 'sanity check' to see whether application of the construction on the source structure indeed leads to the resulting structure.

dataflow repairs, in which information can propagate in any direction depending on instance availability [23]. The main advantage of dataflow repairs is that they can be used for both parsing and production at the same time.

Apply-construction. Using dataflow instead of control flow makes it possible to develop more powerful linguistic operators. For instance, in a control flow approach, the operator `apply-construction` (which takes four arguments: a resulting transient structure, a source transient structure, a construction and a process-direction; see Figure 4) requires three available instances (the source transient structure, construction and direction) before it can return a new transient structure. In a dataflow approach, at least the scenarios listed in Table 1 become possible.

In principle, it is also possible to implement a scenario in which the operator has the output transient structure and the construction as available instances in order to compute what the source transient structure was. This scenario however requires the retroactive application of constructions, which is currently not supported in FCG.

In sum, depending on the particular configuration of instance availability, the operators can already perform various computations and pass the results to other operators instead of waiting for other procedures to finish their work. IRL keeps cycling through each operator until no more computation can be achieved.

Build-meta-level-construction. With the power of IRL's dataflow approach comes the possibility of anticipating different scenarios of instance availability depending on the task that the FCG-interpreter needs to perform. For example, when building a meta-level construction for an unknown word during parsing, the FCG-interpreter already has the form of the new construction at its disposal.

Table 2. Different scenarios of instance availability for the linguistic operator *build-meta-level-construction*

Available instances	Computation
- String (parsing)	The operator assumes a meta-level meaning and builds a meta-level construction. The results are bound to the variables `?meaning` and `?cxn`.
- Meaning (production)	The operator assumes a meta-level form and creates a new construction. The results are bound to the variables `?word` and `?cxn`.
- Meaning - String	The operator builds a meta-level construction and binds it to the variable `?cxn`.

The same function, however, would also be useful for a problem in production in which the FCG-interpreter has a novel meaning to express but no corresponding form yet. A new 'call pattern' for the operator that allows the meaning and form to be specified looks as follows:

```
(build-meta-level-construction ?cxn ?meaning ?word)
```

The operator now needs to be implemented in such a way that it can handle at least the situations listed in Table 2. Now that the principle and power of dataflow repairs are clear, it is time to change the IRL repair of Figure 5 into a repair that can be applied in both parsing and production. Such a repair is shown in Figure 6. The linking lines between operations in the figure do not have arrows anymore, which illustrates the dataflow approach. The bind operations are shown in dark grey and italics to indicate that their availability depends on whether FCG is producing or parsing an utterance.

Apart from the new call pattern for `build-meta-level-construction`, the operator `FCG-parse` has been replaced by the more general operator `FCG-apply`. As opposed to `FCG-parse`, this operator takes a fourth argument, which is the direction of processing: from meaning to form, or from form to meaning. The direction is provided by the operator `get-process-direction`, which fetches the direction from the task that the FCG-interpreter is performing. In its list notation, the network looks as follows (the bind operations are left out; these have to be provided by the diagnostics):

```
((get-construction-inventory ?inventory)
 (get-latest-transient-structure ?ts-1)
 (get-process-direction ?direction)
 (build-meta-level-construction ?cxn ?meaning ?word)
 (apply-construction ?ts-2 ?ts-1 ?cxn ?direction)
 (FCG-apply ?ts-3 ?ts-2 ?inventory ?direction))
```

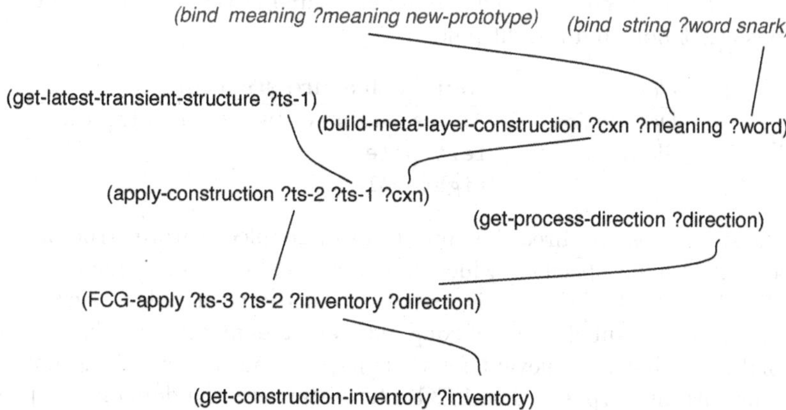

Fig. 6. A dataflow repair. This IRL network implements the solution of a meta-level construction for both parsing and production. The bind operations for meaning and form are shown in grey italic because their availability depends on the direction of processing.

5 Diagnostics and Repairs as Coupled Feature Structures

The previous two sections have shown how FCG and IRL can be exploited for representing and processing meta-level operators. The approach can readily be applied in the current formalisms without needing any extensions. One limitation of the current implementation, however, is that the repair of a problem involves a lot of (computational) red tape: first, a diagnostic needs to be implemented that operates on certain predefined situations. If the diagnostic detects issues in processing, it needs to instantiate a problem, which subsequently triggers one or more repairs [4]. Using problems as 'mediators' between diagnostics and repairs allows for a lot of flexibility, but it would often be much more efficient to implement a 'quick fix' by directly coupling a repair to a diagnostic.

This section explores a way in which meta-level operators can be directly associated to each other in the form of *coupled feature structures*, thereby representing them in the same way as transient structures and constructions. In the remainder of this paper, I will use the term *fix* for the association of a diagnostic and an IRL-repair, because they are meant to be efficient solutions that blend in seamlessly with routine processing. All of the examples presented in this section have been computationally implemented in a proof-of-concept fashion and are therefore not (yet) part of the current FCG implementation.

5.1 Coupled Feature Structures

In FCG, both transient structures and constructions use the same feature structure representation, which is implemented in CLOS (Common Lisp Object

System; see [13]). A `coupled-feature-structure` is the base class for both, which has a left pole and a right pole:

Definition 1.

class	**coupled-feature-structure**
Description	An association of two feature structures.
Slots	`left-pole`
	`right-pole`

Transient structures are direct instantiations of coupled feature structures. For each pole, it can be specified which domain it belongs to: semantic or syntactic. By default, the left pole is semantic and the right pole is syntactic. A `construction` is a subclass of a `coupled-feature-structure` that contains additional slots that are relevant for their application, but which do not matter for our current purposes. The FCG-interpreter uses the domain of a pole of a construction to decide whether it should operate on the semantic or on the syntactic pole of a transient structure.

In order to integrate a meta-level fix into FCG-processing, we need to define another subclass of a `coupled-feature-structure`, which inherits a left pole and a right pole. Diagnostics are contained in the right pole (as they can be considered as the 'form' of a problem) and repairs go in the left pole (as they are the 'meaning' of a problem). In principle, no additional slots are required, but here we include three slots called `name`, `domain` and `score`:

Definition 2.

class	**fix**	subclass of coupled-feature-structure
Description	A coupling of a diagnostic and a repair.	
Slots	`name`	
	`domain`	
	`score`	

The `name` of a fix is a symbol for identifying it. The slot `score` could potentially be exploited to orchestrate a competition between different fixes if there are multiple ways of repairing the same problem, or if there are different problems that try to exploit the same repair. The `domain` slot specifies whether the diagnostic of the fix should operate on the semantic or the syntactic pole of a transient structure.

5.2 Extending FCG-Apply

Let's return to the problem of *Pat sneezed the napkin off the table*, where the speaker wishes to express a Caused-Motion frame using the intransitive verb *sneeze*, whose valence is incompatible with the requirements of the Caused-Motion construction. However, coercing verbs into the Caused-Motion frame is a recurrent and productive pattern in English [8], hence it is worthwhile to implement a `fix` that first decides whether coercion is needed and indeed possible (i.e. whether the verb can be coerced), and if so, immediately performs coercion.

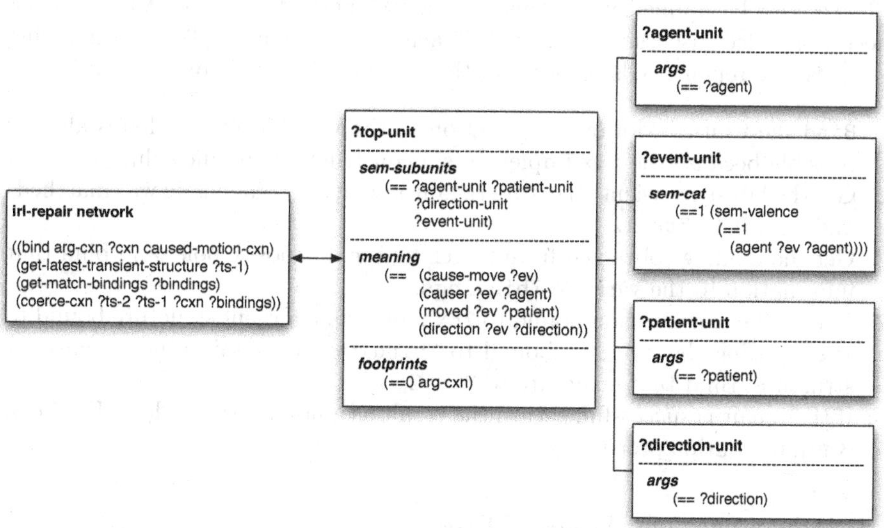

Fig. 7. This 'fix' associates a diagnostic (right pole) with a repair (left pole). The diagnostic first checks the need and opportunity for coercion. The repair then performs coercion, thereby exploiting the bindings obtained by matching the diagnostic.

We have already defined a meta-level feature structure in example 8 that is capable of detecting the need and opportunity for coercion: if no argument structure construction has been applied, the diagnostic checks whether the speaker wishes to express the Caused-Motion frame and whether the verb can at least assign the Agent-role to one of its arguments, which is the only obligatory semantic role. If so, the diagnostic is supposed to report a problem. In a `fix`, however, the repair is immediately triggered. Figure 7 shows how the diagnostic and repair are coupled to each other, with the diagnostic on the right and the repair on the left (both in a graphical representation). In order for the `fix` to be applied, the method `fcg-apply` (which is used for applying constructions) needs to specialize on applying a `fix` to a transient structure. This specialized method looks as follows:

FCG-apply `(fix transient-structure)`

```
if the DOMAIN of FIX is SEMANTIC
then MATCH the DIAGNOSTIC of FIX
      with SEMANTIC-POLE of TRANSIENT-STRUCTURE
else MATCH it with SYNTACTIC-POLE of TRANSIENT-STRUCTURE
if MATCH is found
then EXECUTE the IRL REPAIR NETWORK of FIX and RETURN RESULT
else do nothing
```

All fixes can be applied using this specialized method. Interested readers can check a detailed discussion of how FCG achieves coercion in [33]. Summarizing in words, the repair needs to perform the following linguistic operations:

1. `Bind` the Caused-Motion construction to the variable `?cxn`. This is already possible because the `fix` implements a construction-specific solution.
2. Get the latest transient structure (against which the diagnostic was matched) and bind it to `?ts-1`.
3. Get the bindings obtained from matching the diagnostic pole, and bind that information to the variable `?bindings`.
4. Coerce the construction bound to `?cxn` into the transient structure bound to `?ts-1`, using the bindings bound to `?bindings`, to obtain a new transient-structure. Bind that structure to `?ts-2`.
5. If the repair is successful, return the result as a new search node so FCG can continue routine processing.

5.3 Advantages and Issues of Fixes

Besides efficiency and the blending of fixes with routine processing, one of the main advantages of a `fix` is that the bindings obtained from matching the diagnostic against the transient structure can be passed to other linguistic operators. For example the operator `coerce-cxn` performs a powerful operation that skips FCG's matching phase and tries to merge both poles of a construction with a transient structure [33]. Without the inhibitive constraints of matching, however, there is always the danger of an explosion of the possible merge-results, which is exactly the reason why other precision-grammar formalisms that do not have a matching phase implement additional constraints on the unification of feature structures [12, p. 437]. By passing the match-bindings to `coerce-cxn`, improbable coercions can be ruled out. Moreover, if the IRL-repairs are treated as feature structures, they can be matched and merged as well, which opens up the possibility of enriching the repairs with additional information in the form of feature structures.

The most natural way of applying a meta-level fix is to first detect problems by matching the diagnostic against a transient structure and then solving the problem by executing the IRL repair network. However, just like linguistic constructions are bidirectional, fixes can in principle be applied in the other direction as well. For instance, if a speaker introduces a novelty in conversation, the listener might infer why he did so (i.e. detect what the speaker's problem was) by recognizing which repair was performed by the speaker. The prospects of reasoning over fixes for learning and robust language processing is in itself an exciting new research avenue that needs closer examination in future work.

In sum, it is technically speaking possible to blend meta-level fixes with routine processing: all that is required is an additional class `fix` and an `fcg-apply` method that specializes on this new class. However, blending fixes with routine processing requires more control on *when* a fix is allowed to fire: the fix in Figure 7 should only be applied after routine processing has tried all argument structure constructions, and likewise, a fix that would insert a meta-level construction for handling unknown words should only be executed after the application of 'normal' lexical constructions. Fortunately, FCG already provides various ways in which the application of constructions (and fixes) can be regulated, such as specializing the search algorithm [5], using dependency networks [37], or by treating fixes as 'defaults' using construction sets [2].

6 Discussion and Conclusion

This paper has demonstrated how the same representations and processing techniques that support routine language processing can be reused for implementing diagnostics and repairs, which makes it possible that language processing makes use of strong computational reflection. All of the discussed examples have been fully implemented; most of them without needing any extensions to the existing computational frameworks of FCG and IRL. The approach adopted in this paper has both practical and scientific merits: it offers new ways for grammar engineers to operationalize their hypotheses, and it paves the way to research on how language strategies can be culturally acquired by autonomous agents.

The first set of examples demonstrated how diagnostics can be represented as feature structures, which can be matched against transient structures by the FCG-interpreter. Using feature structures provides a uniform way of representing linguistic knowledge in transient structures, constructions and diagnostics, which potentially allows diagnostics to be directly abstracted from recurrent patterns and structures of a particular language.

Next, I have shown how repairs can be represented as constraint networks using IRL. Such repairs consist of linguistic operators (such as coercion) that perform operations on linguistic instances (such as constructions). There are three main advantages of using this approach. First, the dataflow of IRL constraints allows the same repair to work for both production and parsing. Secondly, IRL provides grammar engineers with a coherent and safer way of implementing and testing adequate repairs. Finally, the use of IRL allows future research to focus on the origins of culturally acquired repairs by letting IRL autonomously compose networks of linguistic operations and chunking successful networks.

The final part has shown how diagnostics and repairs can be coupled to each other and become a meta-level 'fix' for processing problems. Using a small extension to the FCG-system for handling associations of diagnostics and repairs, fixes can blend in with routine processing and efficiently handle problems immediately as they occur. Future research needs to focus on how associations of diagnostics and repairs can marry the strengths of constraint networks (IRL) and feature structures (FCG) in a more powerful way.

Acknowledgements. This research was conducted at and funded by the Sony Computer Science Laboratory Paris, with additional funding from the EU FP7 Alear project. I would like to thank Luc Steels, director of the VUB AI-Lab at the Vrije Universiteit Brussel and Sony CSL Paris, for his invaluable feedback and pioneering ideas. I also thank my colleagues for their support, in particular Katrien Beuls for her courtesy in allowing me to use Figure 1, Kevin Stadler for his comments, and Joachim De Beule (whose earlier work on FCG included a system of 'fixes' that inspired this research). All remaining errors are of course my own.

References

[1] Baldwin, T., Beavers, J., Bender, E.M., Flickinger, D., Kim, A., Oepen, S.: Beauty and the beast: What running a broad-coverage precision grammar over the BNC taught us about the grammar – and the corpus. In: Kepser, S., Reis, M. (eds.) Linguistic Evidence: Empirical, Theoretical, and Computational Perspectives, pp. 49–69. Mouton de Gruyter, Berlin (2005)

[2] Beuls, K.: Construction sets and unmarked forms: A case study for Hungarian verbal agreement. In: Steels, L. (ed.) Design Patterns in Fluid Construction Grammar. John Benjamins, Amsterdam (2011)

[3] Beuls, K., Steels, L., Höfer, S.: The emergence of internal agreement systems. In: Steels, L. (ed.) Experiments in Cultural Language Evolution. John Benjamins, Amsterdam (2012)

[4] Beuls, K., van Trijp, R., Wellens, P.: Diagnostics and Repairs in Fluid Construction Grammar. In: Steels, L., Hild, M. (eds.) Language Grounding in Robots. Springer, New York (2012)

[5] Bleys, J., Stadler, K., De Beule, J.: Search in linguistic processing. In: Steels, L. (ed.) Design Patterns in Fluid Construction Grammar. John Benjamins, Amsterdam (2011)

[6] De Beule, J.: A Formal Deconstruction of Fluid Construction Grammar. In: Steels, L. (ed.) Computational Issues in FCG. LNCS (LNAI), vol. 7249, pp. 215–238. Springer, Heidelberg (2012)

[7] Gerasymova, K., Spranger, M.: An Experiment in Temporal Language Learning. In: Steels, L., Hild, M. (eds.) Language Grounding in Robots. Springer, New York (2012)

[8] Goldberg, A.E.: A Construction Grammar Approach to Argument Structure. Chicago UP, Chicago (1995)

[9] Haspelmath, M.: Pre-established categories don't exist – consequences for language description and typology. Linguistic Typology 11(1), 119–132 (2007)

[10] Haspelmath, M., Dryer, M.S., Gil, D., Comrie, B. (eds.): The World Atlas of Language Structures. Oxford University Press, Oxford (2005)

[11] Hopper, P.: Emergent grammar. BLC 13, 139–157 (1987)

[12] Jurafsky, D., Martin, J.H.: Speech and Language Processing. An Introduction to Natural Language Processing. In: Computational Linguistics, and Speech Recognition. Prentice Hall, New Jersey (2000)

[13] Keene, S.: Object-Oriented Programming in Common Lisp: A Programmar's Guide to CLOS. Addison-Wesley, Boston (1988)

[14] Loetzsch, M., van Trijp, R., Steels, L.: Typological and Computational Investigations of Spatial Perspective. In: Wachsmuth, I., Knoblich, G. (eds.) Modelling Communication 2008. LNCS (LNAI), vol. 4930, pp. 125–142. Springer, Heidelberg (2008)

[15] Loetzsch, M., Wellens, P., De Beule, J., Bleys, J., van Trijp, R.: The babel2 manual. Tech. Rep. AI-Memo 01-08, AI-Lab VUB, Brussels (2008)

[16] Maes, P.: Issues in computational reflection. In: Maes, P., Nardi, D. (eds.) Meta-Level Architectures and Reflection, pp. 21–35. Elsevier, Amsterdam (1988)
[17] Pauw, S., Hilferty, J.: The emergence of quantifiers. In: Steels, L. (ed.) Experiments in Cultural Language Evolution. John Benjamins, Amsterdam (2012)
[18] Santibáñez, J.S.: A Logic Programming Approach to Parsing and Production in Fluid Construction Grammar. In: Steels, L. (ed.) Computational Issues in FCG. LNCS (LNAI), vol. 7249, pp. 239–255. Springer, Heidelberg (2012)
[19] Smith, B.C.: Procedural Reflection in Programming Languages. Ph.D. thesis, Massachusetts Institute of Technology, Cambridge MA (1982)
[20] Spranger, M., Pauw, S., Loetzsch, M., Steels, L.: Open-ended Procedural Semantics. In: Steels, L., Hild, M. (eds.) Language Grounding in Robots. Springer, New York (2012)
[21] Spranger, M., Steels, L.: Emergent functional grammar for space. In: Steels, L. (ed.) Experiments in Cultural Language Evolution. John Benjamins, Amsterdam (2012)
[22] Steels, L., De Beule, J., Wellens, P.: Fluid Construction Grammar on Real Robots. In: Steels, L., Hild, M. (eds.) Language Grounding in Robots. Springer, New York (2012)
[23] Steels, L.: The emergence of grammar in communicating autonomous robotic agents. In: Horn, W. (ed.) Proceedings of the 14th European Conference on Artificial Intelligence (ECAI), pp. 764–769. IOS Press, Berlin (2000)
[24] Steels, L.: Language as a Complex Adaptive System. In: Schoenauer, M., Deb, K., Rudolph, G., Lutton, E., Merelo, J.J., Schwefel, H.-P. (eds.) PPSN 2000. LNCS, vol. 1917, pp. 17–28. Springer, Heidelberg (2000)
[25] Steels, L.: A design pattern for phrasal constructions. In: Steels, L. (ed.) Design Patterns in Fluid Construction Grammar. John Benjamins, Amsterdam (2011)
[26] Steels, L. (ed.): Design Patterns in Fluid Construction Grammar. John Benjamins, Amsterdam (2011)
[27] Steels, L.: A first encounter with Fluid Construction Grammar. In: Steels, L. (ed.) Design Patterns in Fluid Construction Grammar. John Benjamins, Amsterdam (2011)
[28] Steels, L.: Design Methods for Fluid Construction Grammar. In: Steels, L. (ed.) Computational Issues in FCG. LNCS (LNAI), vol. 7249, pp. 3–36. Springer, Heidelberg (2012)
[29] Steels, L. (ed.): Experiments in Cultural Language Evolution. John Benjamins, Amsterdam (2012)
[30] Steels, L.: Modeling the cultural evolution of language. Physics of Life Reviews (2011)
[31] Steels, L.: Self-organization and selection in cultural language evolution. In: Steels, L. (ed.) Experiments in Cultural Language Evolution. John Benjamins, Amsterdam (2012)
[32] Steels, L., De Beule, J.: Unify and Merge in Fluid Construction Grammar. In: Vogt, P., Sugita, Y., Tuci, E., Nehaniv, C.L. (eds.) EELC 2006. LNCS (LNAI), vol. 4211, pp. 197–223. Springer, Heidelberg (2006)
[33] Steels, L., van Trijp, R.: How to make construction grammars fluid and robust. In: Steels, L. (ed.) Design Patterns in Fluid Construction Grammar. John Benjamins, Amsterdam (2011)
[34] van Trijp, R.: Grammaticalization and semantic maps: Evidence from artificial language evolution. Linguistic Discovery 8(1), 310–326 (2010)

[35] van Trijp, R.: A design pattern for argument structure constructions. In: Steels, L. (ed.) Design Patterns in Fluid Construction Grammar. John Benjamins, Amsterdam (2011)
[36] van Trijp, R.: The Emergence of Case Systems for Marking Event Structure. In: Steels, L. (ed.) Experiments in Cultural Language Evolution. John Benjamins, Amsterdam (2012)
[37] Wellens, P.: Organizing constructions in networks. In: Steels, L. (ed.) Design Patterns in Fluid Construction Grammar. John Benjamins, Amsterdam (2011)

Chunking Constructions

Kevin Stadler

Artificial Intelligence Laboratory, Vrije Universiteit Brussel, Belgium

Abstract. Compositionality is a core property of human languages that sets them apart from other communication systems found in the animal world. But psycholinguistic evidence indicates that humans do not always decompose complex expressions in language processing. Redundant representations of compositional structure appear to be necessary to account for human linguistic capacities, a fact that should be reflected in any realistic language processing framework. This chapter presents an algorithm for dynamically combining multiple constructions into a single *chunk* in Fluid Construction Grammar. We further investigate where cases of spontaneous combinations of productive constructions occur in natural language, and discuss the relevance of redundant representations for experiments on artificial language evolution.

1 Introduction

Compositionality is one of the defining properties of human languages. Being able to use productive rules to combine words into complex expressions gives rise to the uniquely human capacity to easily communicate previously unexpressed meanings. Consequently, it is these compositional rules which have been at the center of investigations in mainstream linguistic theory for the last few decades, with idiosyncratic properties of particular expressions or lexical items pushed to the periphery of linguistic theory.

But psycholinguistic evidence indicates that humans make use of a significant amount of direct access to compositional structures, even for perfectly productive and transparent combinations which would be analysed as compositional by a linguist [9]. This intriguing finding, which is at odds with the very formal and fully generalising dogma of generative grammar [8], has sparked interest in the question of what the productive units of language really are, and why. Computational models have helped address this question, with grammar learning reframed as a problem of finding the optimal encoding balance between storage and computation (i.e. a tradeoff between machine-level resources [23]), or the ability to predict future novelty versus future reuse in order to best account for the linguistic data observed [11].

What these models still share with the generative paradigm is their reductive stance in linguistic description, also coined the "rule/list fallacy" [7] – the assumption that any kind of linguistic knowledge would have to be *either* stored in an autonomous lexical entry *or* be derived productively via rule, but not both. In a *usage-based* account on the other hand, knowledge about particular

L. Steels (Ed.): Computational Issues in FCG, LNAI 7249, pp. 75–88, 2012.

instances is never generalised away, specific experiences are stored while at the same time giving rise to more general, productive patterns [1]. Formal and computational models of language should therefore not only require the possibility of having *multiple representations* to account for the same compositional structures [10], but consequently also a theory and mechanisms which can efficiently handle and make use of these 'redundancies'.

In cognitive linguistics, this need for multiple representations has been countered by approaches such as Construction Grammar [5]. Their uniform representation of linguistic knowledge signifies not only that the boundary between pure lexical entries and compositional rules (such as grammatical constructions) is gradual rather than abrupt. The fact that all linguistic items – lexical, idiomatic and syntactic – are stored and retrieved from the same linguistic inventory, the *constructicon*, also lends itself to the idea of co-maintaining representations of the same structure at many different levels of abstraction.

What characterises these multiple representations is that they are not a static immutable representation of our language capacity but that they can be derived and updated dynamically. During interactive dialogue, for example, humans exhibit a strong tendency for *routinisation* [12]: when a compositional phrase is used with a specific meaning in discourse, it is likely to be adopted by the conversation partner and become a *routine*, a strong convention for the duration of a conversation. But such routines are more than just a temporary phenomenon of dialogue. Depending on factors such as frequency or saliency they might also persist beyond the scope of a conversation and leave a permanent trace in a human's linguistic inventory [1].

While such mechanisms have already been proposed in the theoretical literature, we want to bring these models to a next level by describing a computational algorithm of how to dynamically derive holistic routines in Fluid Construction Grammar [17]. The following section presents a formal definition of the algorithm which can be used to *chunk* constructions, with reference to the computational concepts employed by FCG. Section 3 discusses consequences of using multiple representations and handling and exploiting redundant information in the linguistic inventory. Section 4 addresses not only the repercussions of the approach for artificial language evolution experiments but also potential applications in natural language processing tasks, followed by the conclusion.

2 Chunking in Fluid Construction Grammar

For the remainder of this article we will use the simple example phrase "the pretty dog" to illustrate the workings of the algorithm. The example is highly simplified and we make no claim about the best or most realistic linguistic representation of the example phrase. For our purposes, we only require a very simple grammar with the three lexical constructions (`the-cxn`, `pretty-cxn` and `dog-cxn`) as well as two grammatical constructions to link the adjective to the noun (`adjective-noun-cxn`) as well as the article to the noun phrase (`article-np-cxn`).

While we assume familiarity with the basic concepts of Fluid Construction Grammar, we briefly recapitulate the core concepts employed by FCG before presenting the chunking algorithm. For a more detailed account of the construction application process in FCG we kindly refer the interested reader to [17] as well as the individual articles referenced throughout this section.

Figure 1 shows the `adjective-noun-cxn` from the example phrase which represents the coupling of a specific semantic structure on the left with its syntactic representation on the right. The construction expresses the association of two sibling units (an adjective and a noun) under one overarching unit. On the semantic pole, the construction establishes variable equality between the respective referents of the units' semantic predicates by using the same `?ref` variable. On the syntactic pole on the right, this operation is expressed by a `form` feature which specifies that the form content of the adjective-unit has to directly precede the form content of the noun-unit.

Of the units visible in the example construction, we will refer to the first three (above the dashed line) as the *match units* of the construction, since they have to unify with the *transient feature structure* during the matching phase of FCG construction application [18]. The transient feature structure, which captures FCG's intermediate processing structure, has to fulfill the constraints expressed within the match units in order for the construction to apply. In the case of the example construction they assert that the lexical categories (`lex-cat`) of the two units which are combined are `adjective` and `noun`, respectively. They stand in contrast to the *J-units* (below the dashed line) which are the core component of FCG responsible for building hierarchy [3]. Their contents are ignored during the initial matching phase but are merged in during the second phase of construction application, which allows the creation of new units on both poles.

2.1 Terminology

The *chunking* algorithm presented here can be used to combine a collection of co-occurring constructions into one holistic *chunked construction* which has as its main property that its application results in exactly the same changes to the FCG feature structure as if all of its constituent constructions had applied consecutively. To determine which constructions are candidates for such a chunking operation, the algorithm builds on the networks of application dependencies which can be tracked by FCG [22]. An example of such a dependency network for the example phrase "the pretty dog" can be seen in Figure 2. The network captures the dependencies between the constructions, i.e. it shows which constructions could only apply because of material that was merged in by earlier constructions. Note that the conditions are not explicitly expressed in the networks, and usually much more general than visible in the specific examples. The `adjective-noun-cxn` for example can take as its constituents any units with the lexical categories `adjective` and `noun`, respectively.

The relationships captured by the dependency networks provide the basis for the chunking algorithm, since it only makes sense to chunk together constructions which actually interact in construction application, i.e. they merge in or

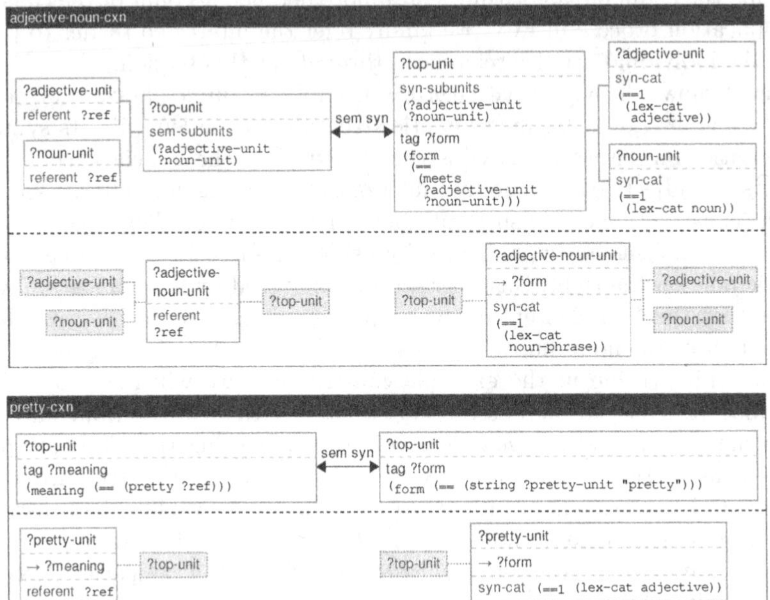

Fig. 1. Two of the original constructions required to parse or produce the example phrase. Above: the phrasal `adjective-noun-cxn` which consists of three match units (above the dotted line) and one J-unit (below) on each pole. The match units match onto the adjective and noun units as well as their parent unit, while the J-unit is used to introduce hierarchy into the transient feature structure. Below: the simple lexical `pretty-cxn` with just one match unit matching on the simple semantic predicate `pretty` and its corresponding string representation, and one J-unit to manipulate the feature structure accordingly.

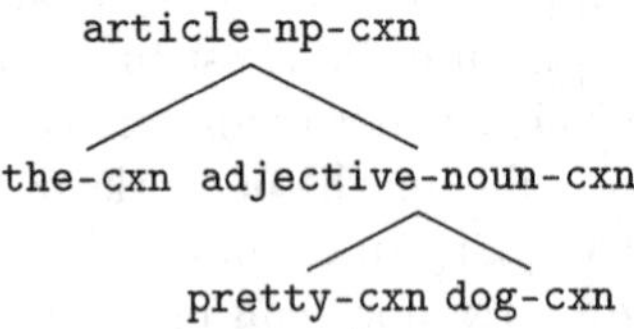

Fig. 2. The construction dependency network [22] for parsing the example phrase "the pretty dog", using three lexical constructions as well as two grammatical ones (`adjective-noun-cxn` and `article-np-cxn`). Note that the ordering of constructions is only for clarification, the exact ordering of constituents is not dependent on the ordering of construction applications. The direction of processing is bottom-up (i.e. the `adjective-noun-cxn` could only apply because both `pretty-cxn` and `dog-cxn` applied before and supplied material for the `adjective-noun-cxn` to match on, although in no particular order). The exact matching conditions are also not shown, but since the model is general they can be arbitrarily complex (or simple).

match on the same material of the transient feature structure. Consequently, it is only possible to chunk together connected subsets of a dependency network. Example chunks from the given network could be `the-cxn` together with `dog-cxn`, `adjective-noun-cxn` and `article-np-cxn`, which would leave an open slot for any adjective and thus represent a general `the-<adjective>-dog-cxn`. The maximal case is when the entirety of the network is chunked together, which would signify a direct representation of the entire phrase "the pretty dog" including linking operations [13]. We call the (sub-)hierarchy of a dependency network that a chunked construction is based on its underlying *construction hierarchy* or also the *chunked hierarchy*, and the constructions which contribute to a chunked construction its *constituent constructions*.

2.2 The Algorithm

In order for a chunked construction to have exactly the same impact on the transient feature structure as if all of its constituent constructions had applied consecutively, this construction has to meet the following requirements:

- it combines all the match conditions expressed by its constituent constructions (it is consequently applicable in exactly the same contexts as its underlying construction hierarchy)
- it merges in all the same units and unit-content as all the constructions of the original hierarchy

Starting from an initially empty construction with no units on either pole, the chunked construction is created through the following steps which are applied to both the semantic and the syntactic poles separately:

- Given a hierarchy of dependent constructions, represented by a subtree of a construction dependency network, go through the constructions bottom-up[1] and, for every construction:
  1. match units which are matched on parts of the feature structure which were already there before the first construction of the chunked hierarchy applied are copied over to the chunked construction as they are or, if the unit is already part of the chunked hierarchy, the match constraints are merged into the already existing unit.
  2. match units which are matched on structure which was only merged in by one of the previous constructions which are part of the chunked hierarchy are added to the chunked construction as J-units. The reasoning behind this is as follows: if the chunked construction applies then all the match conditions for the leaves of the dependency network are met (since the relevant match conditions were taken over as they are). Consequently,

[1] The exact ordering doesn't matter as long as a construction's priming constructions (i.e. its children in the dependency network, which means that they provided some content for the construction to match on) are processed first. This can easily be achieved by processing the constructions in the order of their original application.

the applicability of all inner constructions is met since all conditions of its dependent constructions are met. While the match conditions of all inner constructions of the dependency hierarchy are thus not relevant, the information is still required for merging, making the transformation to J-units an ideal solution.

3. J-units are copied over as they are, or merged with the current unit content if the J-unit is already part of the chunked construction.

- Return the chunked construction

Additional issues have to be taken into account every time a unit is added to the chunked construction:

- *Merging units*: when the same unit is referred to from more than one construction of the hierarchy, the contents of the respective match units have to be merged together into one unit. This operation is not to be confused with the merge applied during construction application, where content from a match pattern is merged into the transient feature structure [2]. Rather, we are talking about merging multiple match patterns into one all-encompassing match pattern. What this means becomes clear when looking at the example of a chunked construction in Figure 3. All five constructions underlying this chunk matched on different subparts of the top unit's `meaning` and `form` features – in the chunked construction all these constraints are brought together in one unit, with all special operators (in this case only ==) being preserved. The example case is trivial since the constraints are non-overlapping, but more complex handling is required when different special operators applying on the same feature have to be combined.
- *Tracking of transitive variable equalities*: during step-wise construction application, variable linking (such as equating the referents of two previously unrelated units) is carried out incrementally [19]. Individual variables are added one by one and get linked during the unification step of construction application. In a chunked construction however there are no intermediate unification steps, therefore all variable equalities have to be expressed explicitly. This can also be seen in Figure 4, where only one variable is introduced on the semantic pole, in contrast to three in the original construction application process which only get equated later on by the two grammatical linking constructions. To take care of this, the variable bindings established during construction application have to be inspected every time a new construction is processed during the build-up of a chunked construction. Whenever a binding between two variables is detected, the algorithm selects one of them to become the new unique representation of that variable, and greedily replaces all occurrences of the other variable. This approach makes the linking of variables explicit and guarantees that all variable equalities are expressed in only one step whenever the chunked construction is applied.

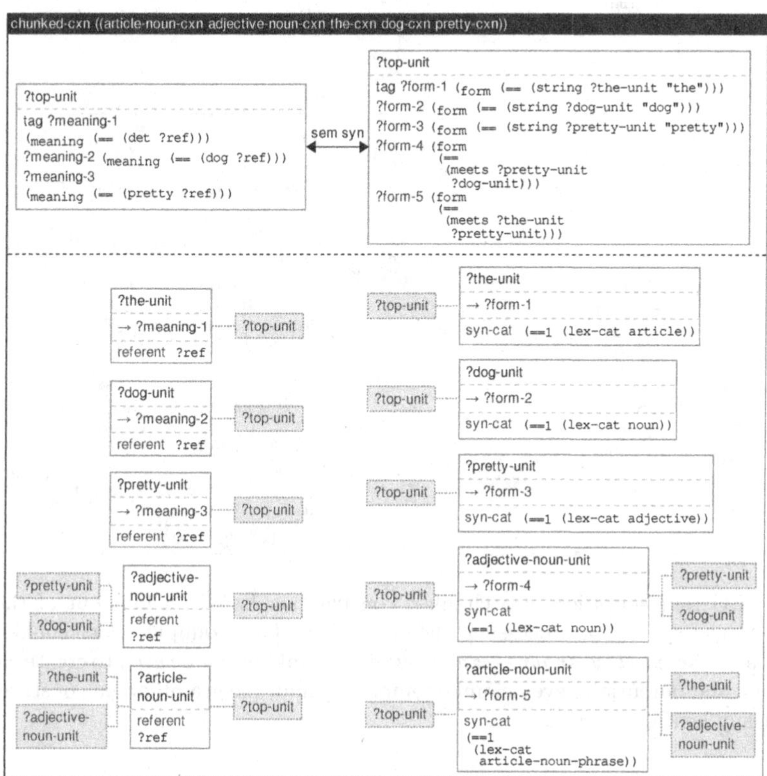

Fig. 3. FCG representation of the chunked construction derived from the full original construction hierarchy for processing "the pretty dog". The construction encompasses the match conditions and operations of all three lexical constructions as well as the two linking constructions.

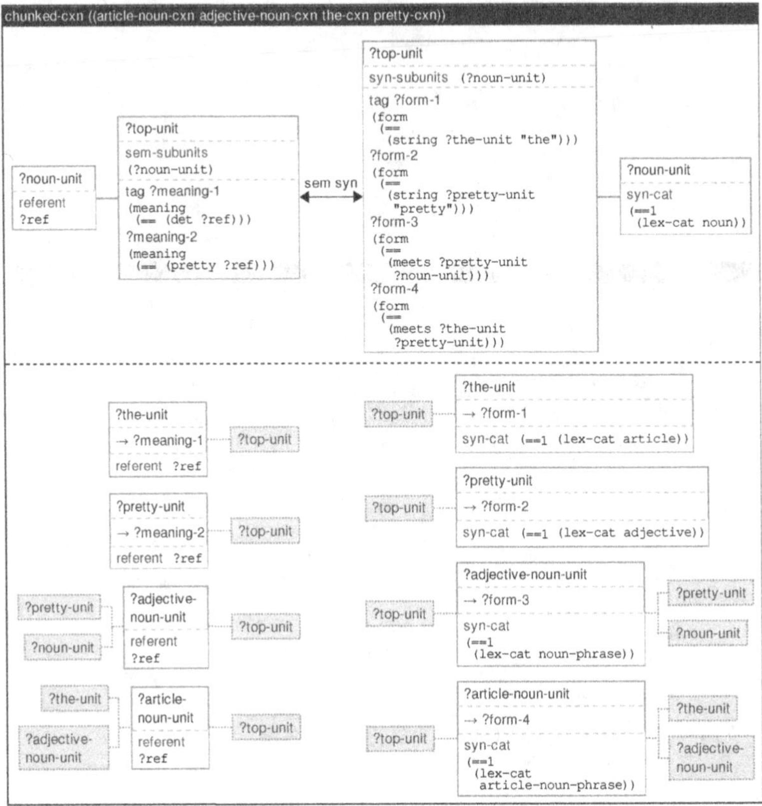

Fig. 4. FCG representation of a chunked construction based on four out of the five constructions required for processing "the pretty dog". This example, which could be rephrased as a ***the-pretty-<noun>-cxn*** shows how chunking can be used to create chunks with slots, and potentially even chunks comprising multiple grammatical constructions without any lexical material.

3 Computational and Conceptual Considerations

The immediate use of chunked constructions is evident: since they apply in the same contexts as their underlying construction hierarchy and affect the feature structure in exactly the same way, they can be used in place of these compositional construction applications. It is useful to look into some of the consequences and challenges of the approach.

– From a processing point of view, chunking introduces the possibility of trade-off between grammar size and complexity of search. The flexibility of full compositionality is sacrificed for a reduction in combinatorial complexity of the search space in combination with a decrease of processing cost for the application of individual constructions. The sacrifice for this is, however, potentially huge: adding all potential subhierarchies of all utterances that are encountered by a speaker in parsing or production to the constructicon would lead to the holistic storage of all compositional (sub-)structures ever encountered, as exemplified in Figure 5. This explosion in grammar size would have to be dampened, retaining only those constructions which are actually relevant and useful to the language user.

- In some ways the optimisations that chunked constructions reproduce functionality of construction dependency networks, particularly the *priming* networks already implemented in FCG [22]. But unlike in dependency networks, chunked constructions are *autonomous* from their original constituent parts. While entrenchment through frequent co-occurrence can lead to a strong preference for co-activation in dependency networks as well, the underlying representations of the constituent constructions do not change, and are individually activated and processed every time the compositional structure is encountered. In the chunking approach, the content of the constructions is copied and the new constructicon entries are not explicitly coupled to their constituent parts. The only connection betweem them is in fact indirect, through direct competition in search. This corresponds nicely to the duality observed in human language processing: while a human might use a chunked version of a construction in active parsing and production, the compositional route is still present and very much accessible to the language user when required. He can potentially be aware of the compositionality of his or her utterance since it is still represented in the linguistic inventory, but in most cases of processing this representation is not regarded due to a preference for the holistic analysis.
- Another important feature which sets the chunking approach apart from optimisations using construction networks is that it is possible to chunk together structures in which a single construction is used *more than once*. This is relevant for any compositional idiomatic expression in which the same construction occurs at least twice, and particularly when a construction can be used recursively, as is the case in natural language. The easiest example for this is a noun phrase which is embedded in another (more complex) noun phrase, such as "the cat on the mat". In a priming network, trying to capture the entrenched and thus preferred parsing of such a phrase will result in a (potentially indirect) circle. Instead of representing a particular instance of chunking, construction networks constitute a separate layer which generalises eagerly to all (co-)occurrences of constructions. The interesting fact that chunked constructions do not introduce an additional layer of representation into the formalism will be discussed in more detail in the next section.

No matter to what extent chunked constructions are used in practice, the approach brings additional challenges for search. Creating redundant representations is only half the job, more importantly this redundancy has to be handled and exploited efficiently during actual parsing and production. The decision of which chunked constructions to retain or even reinforce and which ones to remove from the linguistic inventory are closely coupled to their utility for the

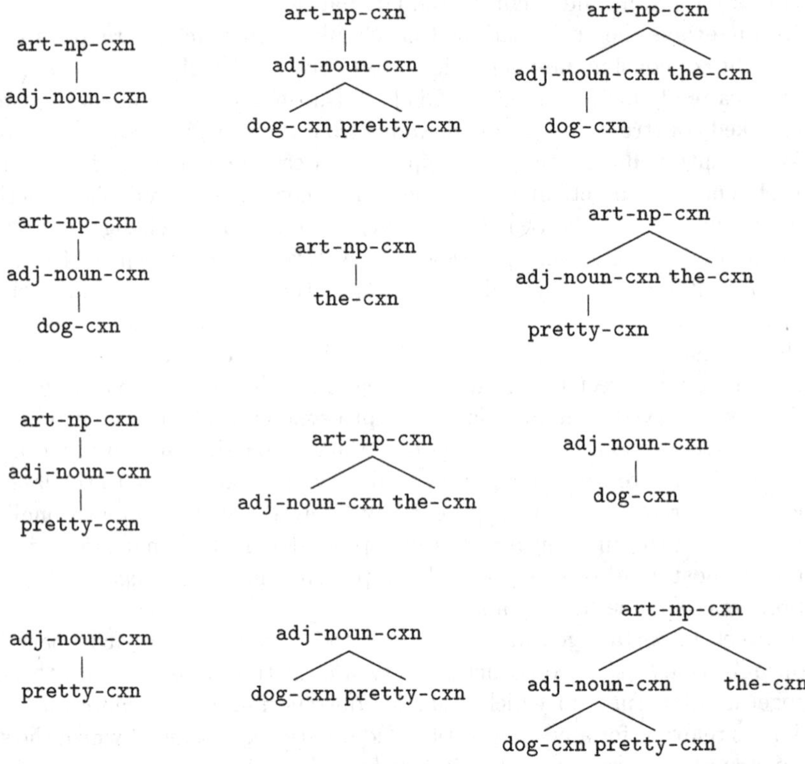

Fig. 5. The twelve different chunkable sub-hierarchies for the dependency network of the example phrase. The minimal case with just two grammatical constructions can be found at the top left, the full hierarchy which also corresponds to the complete dependency network of the parse at the bottom right. The number of possible combinations for a dependency hierarchy is a function of the tree structure of the dependencies. Note that with the exception of the last two, none of these hierarchies can be represented by their surface forms alone, since the resulting collapsed constructions contain both semantic as well as syntactic slots (such as the chunked construction in Figure 4). The hierarchy in the middle of the second line for example could be coined a general `the-<noun-phrase>-cxn`, the one above it a somewhat more specialised `<article>-pretty-dog-cxn`.

language user, which is highly correlated to their frequency of activation during search. Intelligent models of construction inventory self-organisation should not only capture the autonomy of frequently accessed chunked constructions, but also dampen the productivity of its constituent constructions when they are only infrequently activated on their own.

4 Applications

The study of the emergence and self-organisation of linguistic inventories has been at the core of experiments carried out in Fluid Construction Grammar. While the distributed development of a shared lexicon [14] and shared ontologies of perceptually grounded categories [15] have been investigated and successfully characterised early, the extension of these principles to compositional structures is not that straightforward. The additional problem arising with compositional structures is that of *multi-level selection* [21]. For competition on one level (i.e. holistic names) consolidation strategies based on lateral inhibition constitute an adequate model for selecting linguistic conventions. But once such entries are themselves re-used as parts of larger compositional structures it is not clear on which units the lateral inhibition dynamics should apply. So far only the explicit linking of constructions in a separate network layer has been proposed as a solution [20], but a model building on chunked constructions offers an alternative approach to the same problem. Instead of explicitly coupling individual co-occurring constructions together, chunked constructions added to the constructicon could *implicitly* compete with their compositional constituents during search. One of the central tenets of the multiple representation model is that there is more than just one productive unit at play in producing or understanding any compositional structure, as exemplified by dual-route models of lexical access in which direct and compositional access explicitly compete with each other [6]. Given the similarity of the phenomena in these two domains, it is likely that a cognitively plausible computational model of capturing redundancy and productivity in human language will also provide answers to open research questions in the field of self-organising communication systems.

Conversely, a better understanding of language coordination dynamics based on computational models would also lead to improvements in Natural Language Processing systems. The phenomenon of *routinisation* in humans happens automatically and leads to strong lexical and syntactic alignment processes between interlocutors [12]. Such alignment processes and their importance for the emergence of shared communication systems is well-known [16], but they are hardly exploited in natural language applications. For example, the rigid nature of most current dialogue systems keeps them far from human-like performance, but the importance and potential benefits of reciprocal learning in language coordination between humans and interactive agents is receiving more and more attention [4].

The chunking mechanism presented here provides a cognitively plausible basis for the computational modelling of routinisation effects. But interactive alignment does not just lead to more natural discourse, it can also aid in optimising and guiding computational processing through a unified theory of dialogue.

Tracking of discourse referents and anaphora resolution are often treated as modular problems which are not handled by core parsing components but using extra-linguistic systems. Since routines are derived from more specific cases of use than their individual constituents, humans use them naturally to express association to specific discourse referents, a fact easily exploited by systems making use of dynamically-derived redundant representations.

5 Conclusion

In this article we argued for the relevance of redundant representations in the linguistic inventory and presented an algorithm for dynamically deriving holistic constructions from sets of dependent constructions which are used to build compositional structure. The model crucially relies on some of the properties of Construction Grammar in general and some features of Fluid Construction Grammar in particular. Construction Grammar makes use of only a single representation for all kinds of linguistic structure which is also capable of handling the additional complexity that characterises chunked constructions. Lexical and grammatical constructions can be combined just as easily, and parts of a chunked phrase can also be left unexpressed. Constructions derived by chunking can themselves become part of even larger chunks using exactly the same algorithm. The fact that FCG is unification-based enables the combination and composition of chunked constructions to be carried out relatively straightforward.

Another important feature is the bidirectional applicability of constructions in both parsing and production. Routinisation has been shown to cover both language understanding as well as generation, and a homogeneous linguistic representation for both tasks allows to support this aspect and enable positive feedback loops for alignment processes between interlocutors. Most natural language processing frameworks on the other hand are optimised for one task (most prominently parsing), and this one-sidedness is often reflected in the representations and data structures they employ. Consequently, these approaches can not easily capture and take advantage of cognitive mechanisms such as routinisation.

Although we pointed out some potential applications in language modelling and processing, the mechanism is by far not limited to these cases. Chunking is a theory-neutral operation and can also be used for other purposes. Since chunked constructions form autonomous units, their content is immediately amenable to modifications, be it capturing semantic idiosyncracies or simplifying syntactic structure. The algorithm presented is thus not only useful for questions of optimising linguistic processing, but also extensible to any area of linguistics research in which entrenchment processes play a role.

Acknowledgements. This research was carried out at the Artificial Intelligence Laboratory at Vrije Universiteit Brussel with funding from the Vrije Universiteit Brussel. I would like to thank Luc Steels, Pieter Wellens and Joachim De Beule for their help with the work and Remi van Trijp for useful comments on an earlier draft.

References

[1] Bybee, J.: From usage to grammar: The mind's response to repetition. Language 82(4) (2006)

[2] De Beule, J.: A Formal Deconstruction of Fluid Construction Grammar. In: Steels, L. (ed.) Computational Issues in FCG. LNCS (LNAI), vol. 7249, pp. 215–238. Springer, Heidelberg (2012)

[3] De Beule, J., Steels, L.: Hierarchy in Fluid Construction Grammars. In: Furbach, U. (ed.) KI 2005. LNCS (LNAI), vol. 3698, pp. 1–15. Springer, Heidelberg (2005)

[4] Fernández, R., Larsson, S., Cooper, R., Ginzburg, J., Schlangen, D.: Reciprocal learning via dialogue interaction: Challenges and prospects. In: Proceedings of the IJCAI 2011 Workshop on Agents Learning Interactively from Human Teachers (ALIHT), Barcelona, Catalonia, Spain (2011)

[5] Goldberg, A.E.: Constructions. A Construction Grammar Approach to Argument Structure. The University of Chicago Press (1995)

[6] Hay, J.: Causes and Consequences of Word Structure. Routledge (2003)

[7] Langacker, R.W.: Foundations of Cognitive Grammar, vol. I: Theoretical Prerequisites. Stanford University Press (1987)

[8] Langacker, R.W.: A usage-based model. In: Rudzka-Ostyn, B. (ed.) Topics in Cognitive Linguistics, Current Issues in Linguistic Theory, vol. 50, pp. 127–161. John Benjamins Publishing Company (1988)

[9] McQueen, J.M., Cutler, A.: Morphology in word recognition. In: Spencer, A., Zwicky, A.M. (eds.) The Handbook of Morphology, pp. 406–427. Blackwell Handbooks in Linguistics, Blackwell (1998)

[10] Mos, M.B.J.: Complex Lexical Items. Netherlands Graduate School of Linguistics (2010)

[11] O'Donnell, T.J., Snedeker, J., Tenenbaum, J.B., Goodman, N.D.: Productivity and reuse in language. In: Proceedings of the Thirty-Third Annual Conference of the Cognitive Science Society (2011)

[12] Pickering, M.J., Garrod, S.C.: Toward a mechanistic psychology of dialogue. Behavioral and Brain Sciences 27(2), 169–190 (2004)

[13] Steels, L., De Beule, J., Neubauer, N.: Linking in Fluid Construction Grammars. In: Proceedings of BNAIC, pp. 11–18. Transactions of the Belgian Royal Society of Arts and Sciences, Brussels (2005)

[14] Steels, L.: Emergent adaptive lexicons. In: Proceedings of the Simulation of Adaptive Behavior Conference. The MIT Press, Cambridge (1996)

[15] Steels, L.: The origins of ontologies and communication conventions in multi-agent systems. Journal of Agents and Multi-Agent Systems 1(2), 169–194 (1998)

[16] Steels, L.: Language as a Complex Adaptive System. In: Schoenauer, M., Deb, K., Rudolph, G., Lutton, E., Merelo, J.J., Schwefel, H.-P. (eds.) PPSN 2000. LNCS, vol. 1917, pp. 17–26. Springer, Heidelberg (2000)

[17] Steels, L. (ed.): Design Patterns in Fluid Construction Grammar. John Benjamins, Amsterdam (2011)

[18] Steels, L., De Beule, J.: Unify and Merge in Fluid Construction Grammar. In: Vogt, P., Sugita, Y., Tuci, E., Nehaniv, C.L. (eds.) EELC 2006. LNCS (LNAI), vol. 4211, pp. 197–223. Springer, Heidelberg (2006)

[19] Steels, L., De Beule, J., Neubauer, N.: Linking in Fluid Construction Grammar. In: Proceedings of BNAIC. Transactions of the Belgian Royal Society of Arts and Sciences (2005)

[20] Steels, L., van Trijp, R., Wellens, P.: Multi-level Selection in the Emergence of Language Systematicity. In: Almeida e Costa, F., Rocha, L.M., Costa, E., Harvey, I., Coutinho, A. (eds.) ECAL 2007. LNCS (LNAI), vol. 4648, pp. 425–434. Springer, Heidelberg (2007)
[21] van Trijp, R.: Analogy and Multi-level Selection in the Formation of a Case Grammar. A Case Study in Fluid Construction Grammar. Ph.D. thesis, University of Antwerp, Antwerp (2008)
[22] Wellens, P.: Organizing constructions in networks. In: Steels, L. (ed.) Design Patterns in Fluid Construction Grammar. John Benjamins, Amsterdam (2011)
[23] Zuidema, W.: What are the Productive Units of Natural Language Grammar? A DOP Approach to the Automatic Identification of Constructions.. In: Proceedings of the Tenth Conference on Computational Natural Language Learning, pp. 29–36. Association for Computational Linguistics, New York City (2006)

Part III
Case Studies

Expressing Grammatical Meaning with Morphology: A Case Study for Russian Aspect

Kateryna Gerasymova

Sony Computer Science Laboratory Paris, France

Abstract. Phrasal structures form the backbone of any sentence, and they provide key information about, respectively, the constituent structure of a sentence and how its meanings are to be used in achieving a communicative purpose. In addition, languages typically feature several other systems that express meaning through grammatical rather than lexical means. Examples are a tense-aspect system, which expresses information about the timing and temporal structure of events, a mood-modality system, which concerns the epistemic status and opinion of the facts reported in a sentence and a determination system, which provides information about the access status of the referent of nominal phrases. This chapter shows how such grammatical meanings are approached within the framework of Fluid Construction Grammar through a concrete example of the Russian aspect system.

1 Introduction

Certainly a large part of the meaning of a sentence is expressed through lexical items, but languages also package a lot more information into the sentence by expressing additional meanings through grammatical devices like morphology and syntax, resulting in the need for a discussion of *grammatical meaning* instead of simply *lexical meaning*. Languages of the world differ widely in terms of which meanings they express grammatically. One language may grammatically express a very specific nuance in meaning that may be completely ignored in the grammar of another language. Here are some examples:

1. To describe events in time, some languages employ tenses to locate situations in the past, present or future from a particular moment in time. In French, a speaker can say "il pleut" (it rains), "il pleuvait" (it rained) and "il pleuvera" (it will rain) so as to relate the event of rain to the moment of speech. In Bamileke-Dschang (spoken in Cameroon), a finer-grained distinction holds that includes past and future tenses of five different degrees of remoteness, such as immediate past and the past within one day from today, whereas in English only the distinction of past/non-past is expressed morphologically [4].
2. Other languages focus more upon how events unfold in time using the grammatical category of aspect. Aspect does not annotate the passage of time in a situation according to an external clock, but reveals the internal timing of an

L. Steels (Ed.): Computational Issues in FCG, LNAI 7249, pp. 91–122, 2012.

event by describing its temporal structure, such as, "it rained" versus "it was raining" [3].

3. By means of modality, the status of the proposition that describes the situation can be indicated, as in the German utterance "Ich glaubte, er wäre krank" where the subjunctive mood of "wäre" marks the belief of the speaker.
4. In Japanese, a sophisticated system of honorifics may be used to convey information about the social distance or disparity in rank between speaker and hearer, or to emphasize social intimacy or similarity in rank.
5. In Romance languages such as French, the ubiquitous articles serve as an expression of definiteness, as in "Les fruits que j'ai achetés" (The fruit that I bought), which, in contrast, are completely absent from Japanese or Slavic languages.

This chapter presents a case study that demonstrates how grammatical meanings can be expressed through grammar and how this expression can be represented in constructions for Fluid Construction Grammar [15, 17]. Examples are drawn from Russian aspect. Although the Russian aspectual system is notorious for its complexity, it is possible to crystallize a regular subsystem out of it and to address the issues of grammatical expression of this subsystem, serving the didactic purposes of this chapter. Thus, no attempt is made here to give a comprehensive description of the total verbal system of Russian with its numerous exceptions and grammaticalization processes. Rather, we only address the principle or idea of Russian aspect as a grammatical category.

The ultimate goal of this study is to be able to process dialogues in FCG that appeared in the comprehension experiment of [19], who investigated how Russian children develop their understanding of aspectual forms. Preschool children were interviewed after watching pairs of short movies, each illustrating what would be described by a different aspectual form of the same verb stem. The comprehension of those dialogues was the test condition for the ability to manage aspect. For example, the question Кто нарисовал лицо? (*Kto narisoval lico?*, 'Who has drawn the face?') tested whether a child understood the concept of completion of the event of drawing expressed by the perfective aspect. The grammar presented in this chapter constitutes part of a larger study on aspect acquisition [8], which consequently motivated the choice of the test examples.

This chapter assumes that the reader has had a first encounter with FCG, for example by reading [16, 18] and is also acquainted with the templates for implementing phrasal constructions [5, 14]. Section 2 begins with a sketch of the linguistic background in order to build a foundation for the grammar developed later. Section 3 introduces some general design principles on how to organize complex grammars and how to divide labor between constructions. In the next stage, the full grammar is implemented with the help of templates (Section 4), raising new questions in the process, such as how to deal with an unmarked case of imperfective (Section 5). Section 6 briefly outlines the language processing, and, finally, the Appendix provides an insight into what actually happens behind the scenes by offering a tutorial on how to write fully-fledged constructions and how to develop templates for them.

2 Linguistic Insights into Russian Aspect

When modeling a nontrivial linguistic phenomenon, it is crucial to find a linguistic theory capable of providing the necessary grip for its in-depth computational treatment. The analysis in this chapter is based on the view that aspect is a *grammatical* category, manifested in Russian through the contrast between perfective and imperfective.[1] As formulated by [6], perfective aspect expresses the action as a *total event* summed up with reference to a single *juncture*, and imperfective is characterized by the absence of that notion. In Russian, in contrast to many other languages such as Turkish, English or the broader family of Romance languages, it is the perfective rather than the imperfective that is morphologically marked in verbs.

2.1 Dimensions of Aspect

However, the story does not simply end with this basic opposition of perfective versus imperfective. In order to comprehensively describe the Russian aspectual system, another distinction needs to be introduced – the *semantic* category of Aktionsart. Aktionsart expresses additional, often temporal, properties of the event introduced by a verb. For instance, *telic* Aktionsart conveys that the event has an inherent goal or result; *ingressive* Aktionsart profiles the beginning of the event; *delimitative* Aktionsart conveys that the event has a limited time span and so on. The categories of aspect and Aktionsart are linked by the fact that perfective aspect is defined as a means to highlight the boundaries of the event. It is not important which boundaries are profiled (initial, final or both), as long as at least one of them is actually profiled. While the notion of perfectivity does not discriminate between the different possible positions of the boundary, the boundary's position is fundamental for the Aktionsart of the verb [2, 19]. For example, in the verb нарисовать (*narisovat'*, 'draw.PFV') perfective highlights the inherent notion of completeness of the event by focusing on the final boundary, and in the verb заплакать (*zaplakat'*, 'start-crying.PFV'), perfective signals the notion of beginning (the initial boundary), viewing the beginning of *crying* as a single indivisible whole. Imperfective is often connected with the durative Aktionsart, but due to its unmarked nature it is also compatible with a wide range of contexts, even those where most languages would use perfective [20].

Overall, aspect is omnipresent in Russian grammar, and every verb in all forms and tenses is either perfective or imperfective. For instance:

(1) Нечего было^{i} делать^{i}, мы приютились^{p} у
nothing be.PT.IPFV do.INF.IPFV we harbor.PT.PFV.REFL near
огня, закурили^{p} трубки, и скоро чайник
fire smoke.PT.PFV pipe and soon tea kettle
зашипел^{p} приветливо. *Nečego bylo*^{i} *delat'*^{i}, *my prijutilis'*^{p} *u*
hiss.PT.PFV friendly

[1] Perfective is hereafter indicated as PFV and imperfective as IPFV.

ognja, zakurili^p *trubki, i skoro čajnik zašipel*^{p} *privetlivo.*

'There was nothing to do but to make ourselves comfortable by the fire, we lighted up our pipes, and soon the teakettle began to hiss happily.'
[M. Y. Lermontov. Герой нашего времени ('A hero of our time')]

The above sentence exhibits examples of verbs in different aspects and Aktionsarten. The two verbs at the beginning of the sentence are imperfective (indicated by the superscript ^{i}). All the rest are perfectives (indicated by the superscript ^{p}) of various Aktionsarten. For instance, both perfectives закурили^p (*zakurili*, 'began to smoke.PFV.PT.1PS.PL')[2] and зашипел^p (*zašipel*, 'began to hiss.PFV.PT.3PS.SG') portray the beginning of events of smoking and hissing, respectively, and are of the ingressive Aktionsart.

2.2 Morphology

The morphology of the Russian aspect mirrors the complexity of its semantics. Again, in contrast to other languages like English, there is no single morphological marker that marks either of the two aspects. In English, the progressive aspect is marked with the conjugated 'to be' + infinitive of the verb + '-ing', as in "it is raining" in contrast to "it rains", and thus the progressive is marked unambiguously. In contract to this, Russian verbs can be roughly divided into 'simple' verbs, consisting of a stem and a conjugated ending, such as читать (*čitat'*, 'read.IPFV'), щипать (*ščipat'*, 'pinch.IPFV'), and 'complex' verbs, which are derived from the 'simple' verbs by the addition of aspectual markers, such as by prefixation перечитать (*perečitat'*, 're-read.PFV') and выщипать (*vyščipat'*, 'pinch-out.PFV'). Simple verbs typically describe activities and are imperfective, such as резать (*rezat'*, 'cut.IPFV'). The addition of a prefix changes the aspect of simple verbs into perfective, such asнарезать (*narezat'*, 'cut.PFV'),порезать (*porezat'*, 'cut-for-a-while.PFV'), дорезать (*dorezat'*, 'cut-to-the-end.PFV') and so on, indicated schematically in Figure 1. Russian has nineteen verbal prefixes that productively form perfective [12]. There is also a perfectivizing suffix -ну- leading to such forms as резануть (*rezanut'*, 'cut-once.PFV').

Moreover, Russian verbs can undergo more than one aspectual derivation. After the prefix is added to the simple verb (e.g., думать, *dumat'*, 'think.IPFV') making it perfective (придумать, *pridumat'*, 'invent.PFV'), the so-called imperfectivizing suffixes can flip the verb's aspect to imperfective again, as in придумывать (*pridumyvat'*, 'invent.IPFV'). However, another prefix can be attached to this form, changing the aspect to perfective again – попридумывать (*popridumyvat'*, 'invent-for-a-while.PFV'). This chapter focuses on the first aspectual derivation: the addition of prefixes to simple verbs, which changes them from imperfective to perfective. These forms account for roughly 80 percent of

[2] The following abbreviations are used throughout the chapter: PFV – perfective, IPFV – imperfective, PR – present tense, PT – past tense, FT –future tense, REF – reflexive, PS – person, PL – plural, SG – singular.

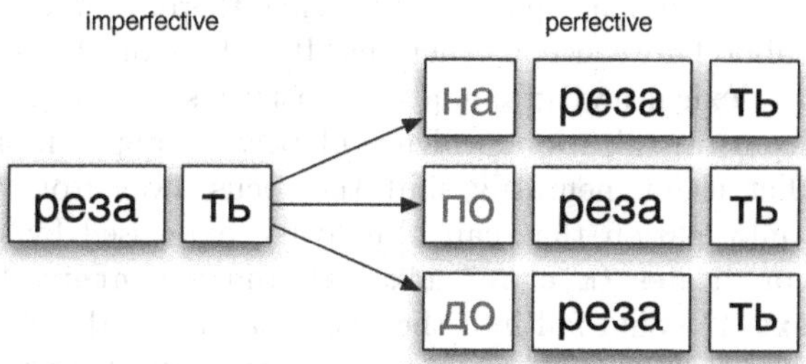

Fig. 1. Schema of the simple verb резать (*rezat'*, 'cut.IPFV') and its perfective derivatives нарезать (*narezat'*, 'cut.PFV'), порезать (*porezat'*, 'cut-for-a-while.PFV') and дорезать (*dorezat'*, 'cut-to-the-end.PFV'), which are formed by prefixation

the total verb occurrences in written corpora, and, as stated by [7], awareness of the aspectual opposition is therefore likely to be focused precisely on the contrast between simple imperfective and prefixed perfective forms (and not on that of perfective and secondary imperfective).

3 Designing a Grammar

3.1 What Is a Suitable Grammar Architecture?

Rather than immediately start writing FCG constructions, it is important first to develop a general strategy as to how the grammar should be organized. The production procedure starts with a meaning that has to be communicated and tries to construct an utterance that would convey this meaning in a given context. In the following example, the speaker wishes to communicate the event of Michael completing the drawing of a face, which in English might be expressed as "Michael has drawn a face" and in Russian "Миша нарисовал лицо" (*Miša narisoval lico*). The meaning underlying the target utterance can be represented in the following way in the notation of the first-order predicate calculus:

```
(2) (michael michael-indiv context-1)
    (draw draw-ev context-1)
    (drawer draw-ev michael-indiv)
    (drawee draw-ev face-obj)
    (event-type draw-ev complete)
    (face face-obj context-1)
    (context context-1)
```

The above notation essentially indicates four main components in the context: 1) there is an individual Michael and 2) a draw event (`draw-ev`) which has a drawer and a drawee, 3) that event is complete, and 4) the object of that event, the drawing, is a face.

When dealing with a nontrivial language subsystem and trying to write constructions to handle it, it is easier to split up the whole constructicon in sets of constructions with similar functions, arriving thereby at a clearer design and division of labor between constructions. It is first of all useful to distinguish between the lexical and grammatical pathways. There are a lot of advantages to such an organization, which will become apparent in the course of the chapter. Let us momentarily shift the focus away from the grammar and toward the information that can already be expressed by purely lexical items. The two predicates `(michael michael-indiv context-1)` and `(face face-obj context-1)` could fall into the responsibility of the lexical constructions that have the corresponding meaning of `michael` and `face` on their semantic poles. (See the introductory chapter in this volume [18].) Similarly, the three predicates

```
(draw draw-ev context-1)
(drawer draw-ev michael-indiv)
(drawee draw-ev face-obj)
```

can be expressed by the lexical entry for the verb "to draw." The meaning left unprocessed is `(event-type draw-ev complete)`, which, in Russian, is grammaticalized and morphologically expressed in the verb. Thus, this predicate should be captured by grammatical constructions different from the lexical ones for the case of Russian, although, in some languages, this meaning can very well be expressed lexically. Now we turn to the question as to which grammatical constructions are needed in order to capture this meaning in a way consistent with the Russian grammar.

As shown in the previous section, the notion of completeness is an integral part of the semantics of some Russian verbs, which are said to belong to the telic Aktionsart. There are other Aktionsarten characterized by the notions of ingressivity, durativity, deliminativity, and so forth. In other words, Aktionsart describes the lexical temporal semantics of a verb and is therefore a semantic category. This principle can be formalized with the help of a special construction, which puts the semantic feature of *completeness* – the predicate `(event-type draw-ev complete)` – in relation to the semantic category of Aktionsart of the corresponding verb. Additionally, the semantic dimension of Aktionsart has to be translated into its grammatical counterpart of aspect by another grammatical construction. For example, for the telic Aktionsart this mapping construction should state that the notion of telicity is grammatically expressed by the perfective aspect. It is then the duty of another kind of construction – the morphological construction – to express the perfective aspect by the attachment of a prefix to a verb stem, with the particular string of a prefix depending on the semantic category of Aktionsart.

The notion of totality characteristic of all perfective verbs does not constitute a part of meaning (which is supposed to come from the world model), it is rather a semantic constraint captured in the semantic category of the corresponding verb. This design decision is motivated by the theory of genesis of aspect proposed by [7], underlining that the "perfectivity" (i.e. the notion of totality) of a prefixed verb is basically nothing more than a by-product of the word-building process out of which the forms with new semantic nuances are derived.

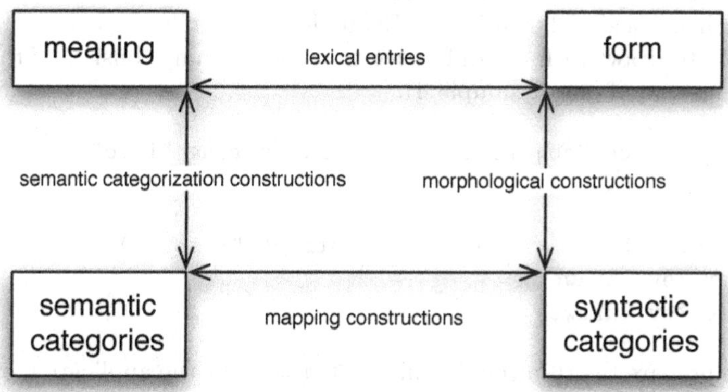

Fig. 2. The grammar square for aspect shows the different relations that grammars need to establish. They are done here by different construction types: lexical, semantic categorization, mapping and morphological. Lexical constructions map lexical stems to their meanings (top, horizontal arrow), semantic categorization constructions recategorize meaning in terms of semantic categorizations (left arrow), mapping constructions map abstract semantic structures to abstract syntactic structures (bottom arrow), and morphological constructions express syntactic categories using morphology (right arrow).

3.2 Division of Labor between Constructions

Writing effective operational constructions is complicated. One has to consider many aspects, such as unification and merging procedures, hierarchical organization, bidirectional applicability and so on. Tackling all of the issues simultaneously is possible only in simple cases. In more complicated ones, it is useful to first look at a construction as a "black box" and attempt to determine its exact behavior resulting from a specific body of input, especially in light of its interaction with other constructions.

Grammatical meaning works through the intermediary of semantic and syntactic categorizations as illustrated in the grammar square (see Figure 2), and for clarity of design, constructions are used that correspond to each of these steps, even though all of them can involve criteria from any level of the grammar. For example, morphological constructions (further called *morph-constructions*) focus on mapping syntactic categorizations to surface forms, but they may take semantic as well as phonological criteria into account.

Lexical entries provide the base material for further grammatical processing; therefore, they are applied first both in production and parsing. Given a particular stretch of meaning to be expressed, these lexical entries should grab that meaning in production, encapsulate it in a new unit, and associate a word string with that unit. In so doing, the lexical entry for the noun 'face' should trigger in the presence of the meaning (face ?obj ?ctx) and associate it with the string “lico", as schematically shown in the Example 3. A similar association applies for the verb ‘to draw’ with the difference that the meaning consists of the three predicates instead of one (Example 4).

(3) `meaning: (face ?obj ?ctx)` ⟷ `form: (string "lico")`

```
(4) meaning:                          form:
    (draw ?ev ?ctx)          ⟷        (string "risova")
    (drawer ?ev ?drawer)
    (drawee ?ev ?drawee)
```

In order to prepare the resulting linguistic structure for the application of grammatical constructions, lexical entries should also introduce additional semantic and/or syntactic categorizations of the unit, thereby providing constraints for the latter to trigger on. For example, if a morphological marker should only be used with verbs, the lexical entry of the verb should supply the information that it is a verb.

We now look at the constructions that establish the relations in the grammar square, focusing first on production to make the construction types easier to understand.

1. After applying lexical constructions, the additional meaning of the event-type should be re-categorized in terms of the language-internal semantic category of Aktionsart and encapsulated in the unit of the verb introduced by the lexicon. This task is undertaken by semantic categorization constructions (called *sem-cat constructions*). A sem-cat construction is needed here, stating that if the event type of the event expressed in a unit is *complete*, then the semantic category ‘telic Aktionsart’ is added to this unit. We need these sem-cat constructions because this categorization is not always so straightforward and different meanings could map into the same Aktionsart depending on the context. The relation that the sem-cat construction has to put in effect is schematically captured in the following way:
   (5) `meaning: (event-type ?ev complete)` ⟷
   `sem-cat: (aktionsart telic)`
   Sem-cat constructions could in principle take into account many other aspects of the linguistic context, such as syntactic criteria, but the examples treated here are sufficiently simple so that this is not necessary.
2. The next step in production is the translation of Aktionsarten into their grammatical counterparts of aspect. This is necessary because the same Aktionsart can be mapped to both perfective or imperfective aspect depending on the context. For instance, a distinction between перерисовать (*pererisovat’*, ‘redraw.PFV’) and перерисовывать (*pererisovyvat’*, ‘redraw.IPFV’), which are both of the totalizing Aktionsart, is in aspect (the perfective in the former and imperfective in the latter). Moreover, the notion of *totality*

characteristic of all perfective verbs is not yet captured in the transient structure. We achieve this effect through *mapping constructions*, which implement the bottom bi-directional relation of the grammar square. Our example must then have a construction triggering on the semantic category of telic Aktionsart. It should not only link this category to perfective aspect, but also add the feature *totality* characteristic of all perfective verbs. Here is the mapping:

(6) `sem-cat: (aktionsart telic)`
`sem-cat: (view ?ev totality)`
$\longleftrightarrow$ `syn-cat: (aspect perfective)`

Such mapping constructions implement the core of aspectual grammar by establishing the subtle interplay between Aktionsarten and aspect, thereby achieving a distinguished role for each category: Aktionsart is responsible for the semantics of telicity, whereas perfective aspect is responsible for the notion of totality.

3. As the last step in production, a construction is needed that implements the expression of perfective aspect by means of prefixation. Which one of nineteen prefixes is attached to the verb depends on the semantics of the perfective form, that is, on the Aktionsart. These kinds of constructions are called *morphological constructions* because they settle morphology, even if it may involve taking additional pragmatic, semantic or other linguistic contexts into account. Morph-constructions establish the following relation:

(7) `sem-cat: (aktionsart telic)`
$\longleftrightarrow$
`syn-cat: (aspect perfective)`
`prefix: (string "na-")`

Morph-constructions thus provide the missing strings of grammatical markers (similar to the lexical constructions that supply strings for lexical entries) and thereby finalize the production process.

This organization, already proposed in [9], is schematically illustrated in Figure 2. Let us see how these different construction types now operate in parsing:

1. The lexical entries again provide the base material for further grammatical processing, so they apply first. Given a particular word in the utterance, the lexical entry encapsulates it in a new unit and associates the relevant meaning with that unit. Lexical entries also add semantic and syntactic categories to the unit that will be relevant in further grammatical processing.
2. Next, the morph-constructions are applied, because they detect additional form elements in the utterance and translate them into syntactic categories. For example, they detect that a verb is prefixed and add the relevant syntactic categorizations to the unit that covers the base verb.
3. All syntactic and semantic categorizations are now available to apply the mapping constructions, which map some of the syntactic categories (e.g., perfective aspect) into a semantic categorization (telic Aktionsart), constrained by the syntactic and semantic context.

4. Finally, sem-cat constructions are applied that map the language-internal semantic categories into meaning, in our case Aktionsart, to the event type of the verb.

Hence, parsing uses the same construction sets, but they are ordered in the opposite direction from that in production: clockwise when looking at the grammar square for parsing and counter-clockwise for production (Figure 2).

4 Implementing a Grammar

This section uses templates to introduce an implementation of the grammar design outlined in the previous section. Templates allow the grammar engineers to abstract away from the technical details of the FCG formalism and instead concentrate on linguistic aspects. The Appendix at the end of the paper offers an explanation of how to develop such templates.

Our starting point in production is on the meaning that has to be expressed (as presented in Example 2):

(8)
```
(michael michael-indiv context-1)
(draw draw-ev context-1)
(drawer draw-ev michael-indiv)
(drawee draw-ev face-obj)
(event-type draw-ev complete)
(face face-obj context-1)
(context context-1)
```

4.1 Lexical Constructions

Face-Construction. As discussed previously, the lexical construction for the noun 'face' produces the following bidirectional mapping:

(9) `meaning: (face ?obj ?ctx)` ⟷ `form: (string "lico")`

However, a lexical construction usually has to do more in order to prepare the resulting linguistic structure for the application of grammatical constructions. It should also introduce some additional semantic and/or syntactic categories of the unit, thereby providing constraints for the grammatical constructions to trigger on. Instead of using only one template `def-lex-cxn` specifying everything that is needed to build a construction, the entire task can be split into different templates for handling different issues, as discussed by [14]. Thus, the template for defining a lexical entry for the noun "face" is shown below, where, in addition to the simple meaning-to-form mapping with `def-lex-skeleton`, there is also a specification of semantic and syntactic categories of the construction with the help of the `def-lex-cat` template.[3]

[3] All templates (`def-lex-cxn, def-lex-skeleton and def-lex-cat`) are discussed in detail in [14].

(10)
```
(def-lex-cxn face-cxn
     (def-lex-skeleton face-cxn
          :meaning (== (face ?obj ?ctx))
          :args (?obj ?ctx)
          :string "lico")

     (def-lex-cat face-cxn
          :sem-cat (==1 (class indiv))
          :syn-cat (==1 (lex-cat noun)
                        (gender neuter)
                        (case ?case))))
```

Draw-Construction. The lexical entry construction for the verb рисовать (*risovat'*, 'draw') (more precisely, for the stem рисова- because endings of verbs in Russian are subject to conjugation) has to establish the following mapping:

(11)
```
meaning:                          form:
  (draw ?ev ?ctx)        ⟷        (string "risova")
  (drawer ?ev ?drawer)
  (drawee ?ev ?drawee)
```

The corresponding template for defining a draw-construction with additional semantic and syntactic categories appears as the following:

(12)
```
(def-lex-cxn draw-cxn
     (def-lex-skeleton draw-cxn
          :meaning (== (draw ?ev ?ctx)
                       (drawer ?ev ?drawer)
                       (drawee ?ev ?drawee))
          :args (? ev ?ctx)
          :string "risova")
     (def-lex-cat draw-cxn
          :sem-cat
           (==1 (class event)
                (sem-val
           (==1 (agent ?ev ?drawer)
                (patient ?ev ?drawee))))
          :syn-cat (==1 (lex-cat verb)
                        (gender ? gender))))
```

Of particular interest is the verb-specific semantic category of semantic valency (`sem-val`), which contains information regarding who the agent and patient of the event described by the verb are. This valency is used later to establish a grammatical agreement between the subject and the verb in a sentence.[4]

Scaling Up the Lexicon. Once the language-specific slots for a `def-lex-cxn` template have been worked out, it is very simple to scale up the lexicon. New nouns can be defined as in Examples 13 and 14 and other verbs as in Example 15.

[4] More about the verb agreement can be found in [21].

(13)
```
(def-lex-cxn masha-cxn
     (def-lex-skeleton masha-cxn
          :meaning (== (masha ?obj ?ctx))
          :args (?obj ?ctx)
          :string "Masha")
     (def-lex-cat masha-cxn
          :sem-cat (==1 (class indiv))
          :syn-cat (==1 (lex-cat noun)
                        (gender feminine)
                        (case ?case))))
```

(14)
```
(def-lex-cxn letter-cxn
     (def-lex-skeleton letter-cxn
          :meaning (== (letter ?obj ?ctx))
          :args (?obj ?ctx)
          :string "pis'mo")
     (def-lex-cat letter-cxn
          :sem-cat (==1 (class indiv))
          :syn-cat (==1 (lex-cat noun)
                        (gender neuter)
                        (case ?case))))
```

(15)
```
(def-lex-cxn read-cxn
     (def-lex-skeleton read-cxn
          :meaning (== (read ?ev ?ctx)
                       (reader ?ev ?reader)
                       (readee ?ev ?readee))
          :args (?ev ?ctx)
          :string "cita")
     (def-lex-cat read-cxn
          :sem-cat
           (==1 (class event)
                (sem-val
                 (==1 (agent ?ev ?reader)
                      (patient ?ev ?readee))))
          :syn-cat (==1 (lex-cat verb)
                        (gender ?gender))))
```

4.2 Sem-cat Constructions

The next step in production is the application of the sem-cat constructions, which translate those parts of the meaning not directly expressed by lexical items into semantic categories that are later mapped onto syntactic features of the utterance, such as morphological markers and word order.

Telic-construction. In the case at hand, the sem-cat construction has to trigger on the meaning `(event-type ?ev complete)` and re-categorize it into the

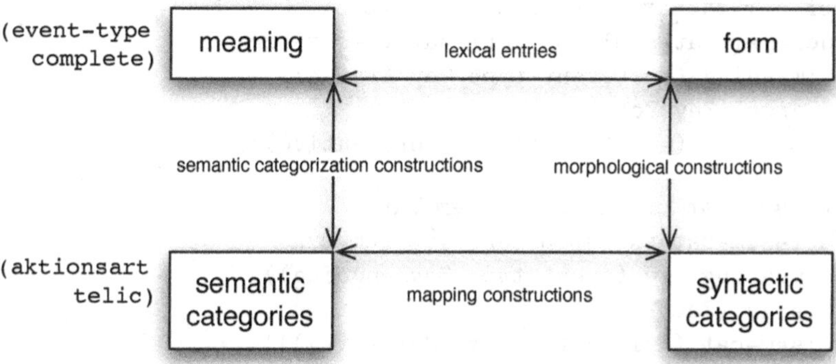

Fig. 3. The semantic construction translates the meaning of the complete event type into the telic Aktionsart and back

semantic category of telic Aktionsart, as depicted on the grammar square in Figure 3. (If we look at the meaning in Example 8, this predicate is precisely what remained unprocessed after the lexical constructions applied.)

(16) `meaning: (event-type ?ev complete)` ⟷
`sem-cat: (aktionsart telic)`

It is very important to note that the meaning of the event type is allocated to the already existing unit of the verb. The sem-cat construction does not create any new units to host this meaning; it rather enhances the verb with the event type and Aktionsart information that is expressed later by means of morphology.

The template `def-sem-cat-cxn` is used to define such constructions. It has a subtemplate called `def-sem-cat-skeleton` which defines the basic relation between meaning and semantic categorization. It also needs the `args` feature to provide a link between the event variable `?ev` of the construction and the one used with the unit in the transient structure by the lexicon based on the meaning of the verb. Thus, the completed form of a template looks as follows:

(17)
```
(def-sem-cat-cxn telicity-sem-cxn
  (def-sem-cat-skeleton telicity-sem-cxn
    :meaning (== (event-type ?ev complete))
    :args (?ev ?ctx)
    :sem-cat (==1 (aktionsart telic))))
```

Scaling Up. The sem-cat constructions for other Aktionsarten can be defined in a way similar to the `telicity-sem-cxn`. The corresponding event-types are represented with analogous predicates, such as `(event-type ?ev begin)` standing for ingressive, `(event-type ?ev finish)` for terminative, `(event-type ?ev for-a-while)` represents delimitative, `(event-type ?ev ongoing)` durative Aktionsarten and so on.

(18)
```
(def-sem-cat-cxn terminative-sem-cxn
  (def-sem-cat-skeleton terminative-sem-cxn
    :meaning (== (event-type ?ev finish))
    :args (?ev ?ctx)
    :sem-cat (==1 (aktionsart terminative))))
```

(19)
```
(def-sem-cat-cxn durative-sem-cxn
  (def-sem-cat-skeleton durative-sem-cxn
    :meaning (== (event-type ?ev ongoing))
    :args (?ev ?ctx)
    :sem-cat (==1 (aktionsart durative))))
```

4.3 Mapping Constructions

The next step in production is the transformation of the abstract semantic categories, which re-conceptualize meaning, into the abstract syntactic categories that are expressed through morphology. For Russian aspect, this transformation is the place where the interplay between semantic and grammatical categories of aspect is captured.

Telic-perfective-Construction. For the case of telic Aktionsart, the semantic dimension of telicity has to be translated into its grammatical counterpart of perfective aspect with all the consequences involved. Here is the mapping discussed earlier:

(20)
```
sem-cat: (aktionsart telic)
sem-cat: (view ?ev totality)
⟷ syn-cat: (aspect perfective)
```

As it was the case with the previous construction types, a template called `def-map-cxn` is used to create a mapping construction, which realizes this schematic translation. Instead of defining everything within the body of a single template, the different facets of the mapping construction are captured in several other templates grouped together with `def-map-cxn`. The `def-map-skeleton` is used to realize the basic transformations of categories; the addition of any supplementary categories is delegated to another template. In this case, the basic mapping is the translation of telic Aktionsart into perfective aspect (as long as the unit is a verb) and vice versa. Basic here means that one of the categories is triggered during the unification phase and is translated into the other during merging.

In production, the construction is triggered by the presence of the telic verb in the transient structure (assigned by the semantic categorization construction). Whereas in parsing, the construction is triggered by the syntactic category of the perfective aspect (assigned by a morphological construction due to the presence of a prefix). In contrast, the supplementary category of the *event view* is never present in the transient structure and is added by the construction both in

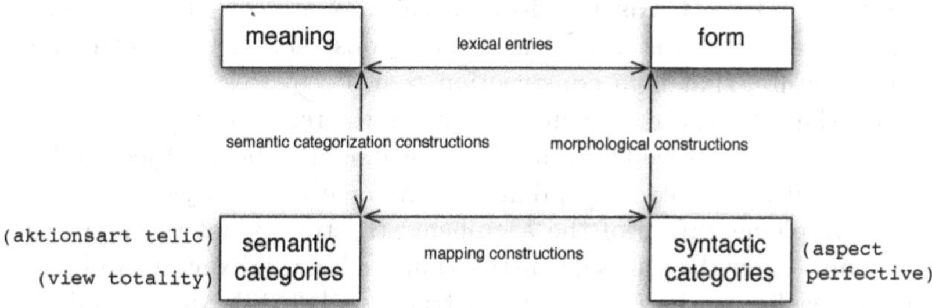

Fig. 4. The mapping telic-perfective-construction couples the semantic category of telic Aktionsart to its syntactic counterpart of perfective aspect, thereby capturing the semantic flavor of totality that is characteristic of all perfective verbs in an additional semantic category – totality view of event

parsing and production. The special template **def-map-cxn** is used for this purpose. Summing up thus far, the schematic mapping from Example 20 is equivalent to the following template:

(21)
```
(def-map-cxn telicity-map-cxn
     (def-map-skeleton telicity-map-cxn
       :sem-cat (==1 (aktionsart telic))
       :syn-cat (==1 (lex-cat verb)
                     (aspect perfective)))
     (def-map-impose telicity-map-cxn
       :cxn-sem-cat (==1 (view totality))))
```

Figure 4 summarizes the semantic and syntactic dimensions of aspect, upon which the construction operates, with the help of the grammar square.

Scaling Up. Other Aktionsarten correspond to analogous constructions, for example, the delimitative, ingressive and terminative Aktionsarten are also signaled through the perfective aspect. Thus, their mapping constructions differ only in the name of **aktionsart**, as in Example 22. However, the construction for the durative links durative Aktionsart to the imperfective aspect, which lacks any notion of totality and is an unmarked case, so the structure of the construction will differ as well. Section 5 is dedicated to the discussion of dealing with the unmarked case of imperfective.

(22)
```
(def-map-cxn terminative-map-cxn
     (def-map-skeleton terminative-map-cxn
        :sem-cat (==1 (aktionsart terminative))
        :syn-cat (==1 (lex-cat verb)
                      (aspect perfective)))
     (def-map-impose terminative-map-cxn
        :cxn-sem-cat (==1 (view totality))))
```

Argument Structure Construction. Because we are considering a complete transitive sentence, there is also a need for a construction that actualizes the argument structure, that is, a construction that 1) equates the referent of the subject with that of the verb's agent, 2) equates the referent of the direct object with the verb's object, as well as 3) settles case assignments of subject and direct object, and, finally, 4) makes the predicate agree with the subject.

Since the implementation of the argument structure is not the focus of this chapter, we only show the phrasal construction used in this example and refer the reader to the earlier work on phrasal constructions [13, 14]. More sophisticated argument structures are discussed in [1, 21].

```
(def-phrasal-cxn transitive-phrase-cxn
   (def-phrasal-skeleton transitive-phrase-cxn
        :phrase
        (?phrase-unit)
        :constituents
        ((?subject-unit)
         (?predicate-unit)
         (?object-unit)))
   (def-phrasal-agreement transitive-phrase-cxn
        (?subject-unit
         :sem-cat (==1 (class indiv))
         :syn-cat (==1 (lex-cat noun)
                       (gender ?agent-gender)
                       (case nominative)))
        (?predicate-unit
         :sem-cat
          (==1 (class event)
               (sem-val ((agent ?ev ?agent)
                         (patient ?ev ?patient))))
         :syn-cat (==1 (lex-cat verb)
                       (gender ?agent-gender)))
        (?object-unit
         :sem-cat (==1 (class indiv))
         :syn-cat (==1 (lex-cat noun)
                       (case accusative))))
   (def-phrasal-linking transitive-phrase-cxn
        (?subject-unit
         :args (?agent ?ctx))
        (?predicate-unit
         :args (?ev ?ctx))
        (?object-unit
         :args (?patient ?ctx))))
```

4.4 Morphological Constructions

The last processing step in production is the application of morphological constructions. Such constructions operate mostly only on the syntactic pole of linguistic structures and specify the surface form of abstract syntactic categories.

Prefix-Construction. The morphological constructions expressing the perfective aspect have to determine which prefix out of the possible nineteen prefixes should apply. This decision has also to take semantics into account, illustrating the non-modular nature of grammar. Here is the proposed schematic mapping:

(23)`sem-cat: (aktionsart telic)`
$\longleftrightarrow$
`syn-cat: (aspect perfective)`
`prefix: (string "na-")`

The template for defining syntactic constructions is called `def-morph-cxn` and is able to take constituents such as prefix, stem and suffix, some of which are optional. It starts by defining a basic skeleton using the template `def-morph-skeleton`. The mapping (23) corresponds to the following template, which specifies the prefix на- (*na-*) and a stem as constituents of a `telic-prefix-cxn` construction, with some constraints put on the latter:

(24)
```
(def-morph-cxn telic-prefix-cxn
  (def-morph-skeleton telic-prefix-cxn
     :prefix "na-"
     :stem
     (?stem-unit
      :sem-cat (==1 (aktionsart telic))
      :syn-cat (==1 (aspect perfective)))))
```

The prefix-construction states that the prefix на- (*na-*) can serve as an expression of the telic Aktionsart, such as in написать (*napisat'*, 'write'), нарвать (*narvat'*, 'cut/pluck/pick'), налгать (*nalgat'*, 'lie') and so on. Other prefixes have similar morphological constructions. What the prefix-construction does in terms of aspectual dimensions is summarized in the grammar square in Figure 5.

Scaling Up. Other prefixes can be defined in a similar way, as shown:

(25)
```
(def-morph-cxn terminative-prefix-cxn
  (def-morph-skeleton terminative-prefix-cxn
     :prefix "do-"
     :stem
     (?stem-unit
      :sem-cat (==1 (aktionsart terminative))
      :syn-cat (==1 (aspect perfective)))))
```

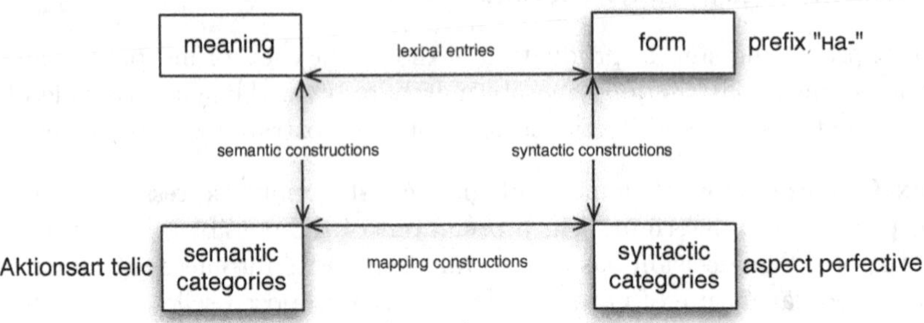

Fig. 5. The prefix-construction specifies the surface expression of telic Aktionsart and perfective aspect through the prefix на- (*na-*)

Ending-Construction. Additionally, all Russian verbs require a conjugated ending to complete their form. The ending is implemented here with the help of a similar template, specifying the ending -л (*-l*), which has to be attached to all masculine verbs in the past tense:[5]

```
(def-morph-cxn masculine-ending-morph-cxn
  (def-morph-skeleton masculine-ending-morph-cxn
     :suffix "-l"
     :stem
     (?stem-unit
      :syn-cat (==1 (lex-cat verb)
                    (gender masculine)))))
```

The feminine ending -ла (*-la*) is defined analogously.

5 Dealing with the Unmarked Case

Imperfective aspect is the unmarked case in Russian grammar. This raises the question of how to treat the unmarked forms in FCG, as pointed out in the previous section. The difficulty, namely, lies in parsing: if in the course of the application of the morphological constructions there is no marker indicating perfectivity, the syntactic category of aspect remains unassigned in the transient structure. The question arises, then, as to how to fill something in based on the *absence* of information.

One can imagine several possible ways of dealing with unmarked cases. A rather unfortunate solution is to have an explicit representation of an absent marker, such as the empty prefix (NIL-prefix), and then to have a morphological construction that triggers on it, assigning the imperfectivity to a verb.

[5] Expression of tense falls out of the scope of the present chapter.

Although it is widely used, this solution creates unnecessary search because such null-forms would have to be assumed all the time. The second possible way is to assume the default (unmarked) feature value from the very beginning, so, in the case at hand, the default imperfective aspect would already appear in the definition of the verb stem. To be realizable, this solution requires that linguistic processing is able to override these defaults when a specific grammatical marking is encountered. At this point, FCG does not allow overriding values of features and with good reason, one of which is that although overriding significantly extends the representational power, it also increases the risk in grammar design. More importantly, all the decisions that were made based on the default (such as all constructions applying under the assumption of imperfective) have to be reverted, which creates the need for complex backtracking mechanisms. Such mechanisms are not currently part of the FCG-interpretation process due to the great costs connected to them. What is the alternative solution for handling unmarked cases?

It is important to postpone the decision on a feature value until it is definitely sure that no counter evidence of marking can be expected anymore; and only then is the default case assumed. One way to actualize this approach is by organizing constructions into sets and ordering their application (as discussed in [22], and used in a case study on Hungarian by [1]). Specifically, after the application of the morphological constructions, the system runs special constructions for unmarked cases. The drawback of this solution is that this special construction set is only needed in parsing. Thus, one ends up with the application of different constructions in different processing directions, which is counter to the general design philosophy of FCG. Another solution explored here requires the constructions that need to know about the possibly unmarked feature values to add this information, which is explained in detail below.

Durative-Imperfective Construction. The mapping construction needed here has to relate the durative Aktionsart to the imperfective aspect. This construction is the first one to notice the lack of grammatical marking in parsing. After all morphological constructions have been tried out and none of them have detected an expression of perfective, the aspect feature on the syntactic pole of the transient structure remains empty due to the unmarked nature of imperfective. At this point the decision concerning the unmarked case can be made with certainty, and the language processing requires the mapping of the *newly assumed* imperfective into the durative Aktionsart. Being the first one to apply at this point, our construction, besides the mapping realization, has to also fill in the default case of the imperfective aspect. Since imperfective is never present in unification, it cannot be specified in the skeleton of the construction and has to be added afterwards by using the `def-map-impose` template which adds the information about the imperfective aspect as illustrated in Example 26:

(26)
```
(def-map-cxn durativity-map-cxn
     (def-map-skeleton durativity-map-cxn
          :sem-cat (==1 (aktionsart durative))
          :syn-cat (==1 (lex-cat verb)))
     (def-map-impose durativity-map-cxn
          :cxn-syn-cat
             (==1 (aspect imperfective))))
```

In case there are many constructions that require the information supplied by such an unmarked case, this solution implies that all of them make the decision separately upon application. This redundancy is not problematic here, since in the case at hand, only the durative has to be translated to imperfective. In other cases, however, this way of solving the default case may become less elegant.

6 Language Processing

The goal of this section is to examine, in more detail, how all the constructions introduced in earlier sections apply in production and in parsing.

6.1 Production

At the beginning of production, the FCG engine creates an initial linguistic structure, which is a meaning-form mapping similar to constructions, as shown in Figure 6: the semantic pole contains the meaning that has to be expressed, and the syntactic pole is empty so far. In the process of production this linguistic structure gradually becomes enhanced with other linguistic information, especially on the syntactic side, finally creating an utterance as an outcome of production.

The first construction set to apply in production is the lexical entries set. Upon its application, each lexical construction creates a new unit in both poles

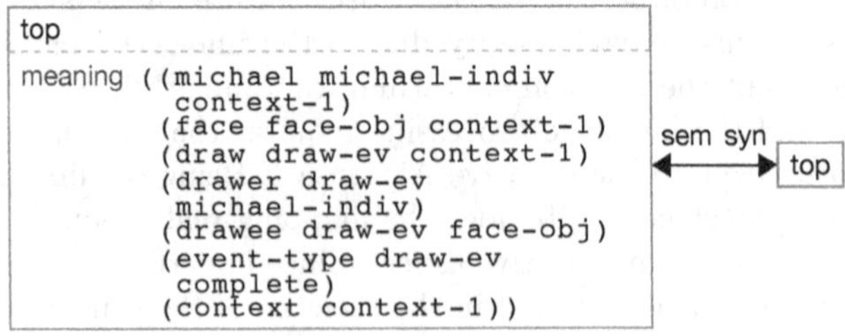

Fig. 6. Initial transient structure in production. Its semantic pole contains the meaning that has to be expressed; the syntactic pole is empty.

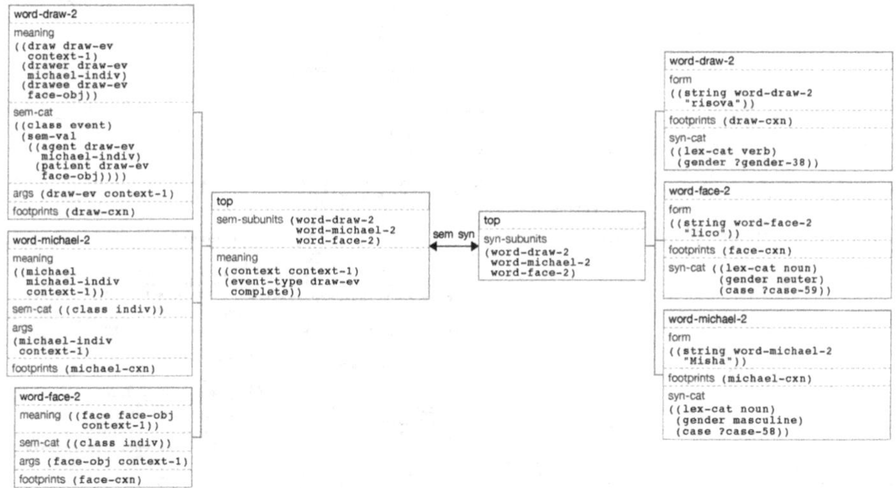

Fig. 7. Current transient structure after the application of all lexical entries. Each lexical entry creates a new unit in both poles of the linguistic structure and relocates all the relevant information to it.

of the transient structure and relocates there all the relevant information of the found word.[6] After all the lexical entries that could be applied – in our example, these are the face-, michael- and draw-constructions – have been applied, the current transient structure contains three units hanging from the top-unit, each corresponding to one lexical stem, as shown in Figure 7.

This way, starting from the initial structure in Figure 6 with an empty syntactic pole, the FCG engine gradually enhances the transient structure by trying out different lexical, semantic, mapping and finally morphological constructions until no more constructions can be applied. Figure 8 shows the syntactic pole of the resulting structure. The head of the hierarchy builds the `top-unit`, followed by the `phrase-unit` that was created by the argument structure construction to capture all the constituents of the transitive sentence under one parent. The units for each of the constituents were established by the lexical constructions; in the course of production other grammatical constructions have gradually filled them with linguistic information. In later stages, the morphological constructions have attached two units to the verb with information about the prefix and ending. The final linguistic structure is rendered into the utterance *Misha na- risova -l lico* ('Misha has drawn a face'), which was the target of the production process.

6.2 Parsing

The great advantage of FCG is that in parsing the exact same events occur as in production except for the direction of the construction application. The parsing

[6] The detailed application of lexical constructions is covered in [14, 16].

Fig. 8. The syntactic pole of the transient structure at the end of production. It is rendered into the utterance *Misha na- risova -l lico* ('Misha has drawn a face').

```
                 top
                 form ((string lico-6 "lico")
                       (string -l-1 "-l")
         sem syn       (string risova-6 "risova")
[top] <---------->     (string na--4 "na-")
                       (string misha-6 "Misha")
                       (meets misha-6 na--4)
                       (meets na--4 risova-6)
                       (meets risova-6 -l-1)
                       (meets -l-1 lico-6))
```

Fig. 9. Initial feature structure by parsing of *Misha na- risova -l lico*

process is initiated by an agent's perceiving an utterance: *Misha na- risova -l lico*. This information is captured by the FCG system in the initial coupled feature structure (Figure 9): on the syntactic side the top unit consists of parsed strings and ordering constraints explicating which string meets which, while the semantic pole remains empty. Note the mirroring of poles when compared to initial structure in production in Figure 6. From this stage, the system constructs the meaning of the observed utterance by simply reversing the order of the construction application: the unification takes place on the syntactic pole followed by the merging of the semantic pole (and the syntactic pole). This difference leads also to the reversed order of application of the various types of constructions: lexical constructions still come first but are immediately followed by the morphological constructions. This order is necessary because these two construction types provide the syntactic information that is required by mapping constructions for determining a verb's Aktionsart and aspect. Finally, once the mapping constructions have been applied, the

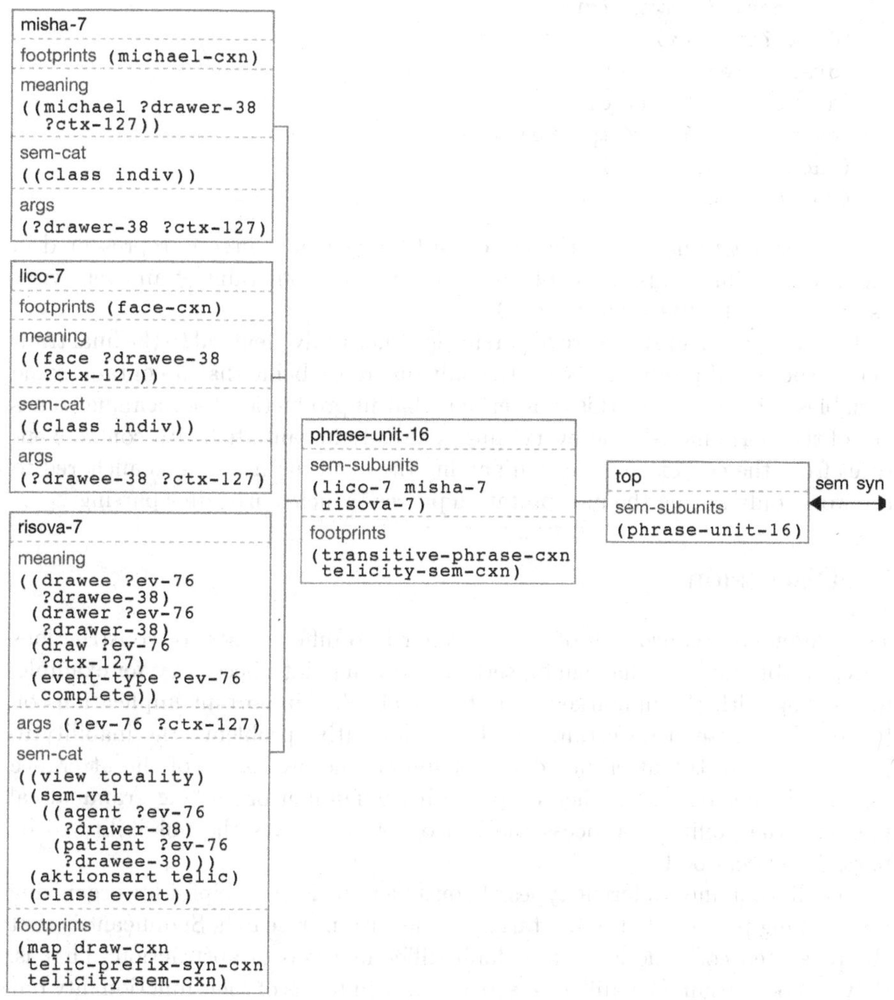

Fig. 10. The semantic pole of the final structure built in parsing of *Misha na- risova -l lico*. The underlying meaning is in Example (27).

semantic constructions are able to reveal the meaning encoded in the semantic categories. Thus, in production, the movement along the grammar square (Figure 2) is clockwise.

Analogous to production, the application of available constructions enhances the initial transient structure with an empty semantic pole to the final transient structure in Figure 10, which contains elaborate semantics. This transient structure codes for the underlying meaning of the perceived utterance *Misha na-risova -l lico* (Миша нарисовал лицо), which is the combination of all meaning features of its units:

```
(27) (michael ?drawer ?ctx)
     (draw ?ev ?ctx)
     (drawer ?ev ?drawer)
     (drawee ?ev ?drawee)
     (event-type ?ev complete)
     (face ?drawee ?ctx)
     (context ?ctx)
```

It is important to note that the notion of totality is not directly represented in the meaning, but is instead captured as a semantic constraint of an event view `(sem-cat (==1 (view totality)))`.

The final transient structure of parsing is structurally identical to the final transient structure of production with the only difference being that it contains some variables. The reason for this difference is that in production the meaning comes out of the world model, and everything is already instantiated with concrete entities from the context, whereas in parsing the resulting meaning is anchored to the world only during the interpretation process which starts after parsing.

7 Discussion

The presented organization of the grammar into different sets of constructions provides not only a mechanism for setting decision points, necessary, for example, for dealing with the unmarked case, but it also has important implications on flexibility. In case of uncertainty and communicative problems, the inability to process parts of the utterance does not inhibit the processing of the utterance as a whole. For instance, when encountering unfamiliar or missing grammatical markers, the ability to process the lexicon already gives the possibility to be partially understood.

The division into different types of constructions is also helpful for organizing the learning process that is the target of the current research. Significant is that the presented construction sets exhibit different levels of abstraction. That is, they can be subsumed in different sets not only in terms of their functionality but also in terms of abstractness, with the lexical entries being much less abstract than the most abstract mapping constructions. During the acquisition process, lexical constructions can be learned independently of the complex aspect system; aspect markers can be learned first in an ad hoc way, and then the more abstract and more difficult to learn categories can be acquired [8].

Another approach for grammar organization is discussed in [22]. It shows how families of related constructions can be organized in a network-based relationship, how this organization is useful during linguistic processing and how it can be learned by the FCG-engine during the linguistic processing. The latter point, that the constructicon organization can stem from the linguistic processing itself, demonstrates that the division of labor between constructions as shown in this chapter is not a pure artifact imposed by the grammar architect.

Overall, the presented chapter is relevant to some current questions in linguistics. One interesting issue of speculation for linguists is what in a language is learned in an individual instance and what is represented in a rule-based fashion. The grammar presented in this chapter comprised prefixes that are likely to be learned as a rule, or in our terminology as semantic item-based constructions. However, there are many inconsistent cases in Russian, which is also the reason for the difficulties that aspect causes to language learners. There is essentially no one-to-one mapping between prefixes and Aktionsarten: one can say that each verb basically *decides* itself how to interpret a particular prefix, which in conjunction with 19 existing prefixes generates a terrifying number of cases that have to be memorized. To account for this complexity, the presented didactic example could be extended with respect to the intertwinement between prefixes and verbs. One possible way to enact this conjoining is to enhance constructions for verbs with the information about the prefixes they employ in order to build different Aktionsarten. Another alternative would be to create separate holophrastic constructions for each of the idiosyncratic perfective forms.

A further issue concerning Russian aspect that intrigues linguists is that not all verbs behave the same way with respect to aspectual derivation. Recent studies in cognitive linguistics suggested that it is the lexical meaning of a verb that constrains its possibilities for deriving different Aktionsarten [10, 11]. For instance, the verb пахнуть^{i} (*pachnut'*, 'smell') is inherently atelic and cannot derive the telic Aktionsart. To account for these constraints, the presented grammar could be extended to incorporate a new category – *potential* to derive a particular aspectual form – into the knowledge about a verb.

8 Conclusion

This chapter presented a case study of the Russian aspect as a didactic example demonstrating how to deal with grammatical meaning in FCG. The reader was introduced to a general methodology for designing complex grammars and dividing labor between constructions. The success of the approach was highlighted by demonstrating the grammar in operation using example dialogues that were produced and parsed. During the development of aspect grammar, the case of imperfective raised the issue of unmarked forms, which was plausibly solved on the basis of the current grammar organization. The key to the solution was the division of the constructicon into different construction sets providing potential decision points for influencing the language processing. When developing grammars for other grammatical categories, the design described in this study can aid grammarians in their decision process, especially for those domains that are expressed morphologically or feature unmarked forms.

Acknowledgements. Research reported in this chapter was partly funded by the EU project ALEAR and carried out at the Sony Computer Science Laboratory in Paris. I thank the whole team working on FCG at the University of Brussels (VUB AI lab) and at Sony CSL for their contributions in making FCG such a superb environment for doing sophisticated experiments in construction grammar.

References

[1] Beuls, K.: Construction sets and unmarked forms: A case study for Hungarian verbal agreement. In: Steels, L. (ed.) Design Patterns in Fluid Construction Grammar. John Benjamins, Amsterdam (2011)
[2] Bickel, B.: Aspectual scope and the difference between logical and semantic representation. Lingua 102, 115–131 (1997)
[3] Comrie, B.: Aspect: An Introduction to the Study of Verbal Aspect and Related Problems. Cambridge University Press, Cambridge (1976)
[4] Comrie, B.: Tense. Cambridge University Press, Cambridge (1985)
[5] De Beule, J., Steels, L.: Hierarchy in Fluid Construction Grammars. In: Furbach, U. (ed.) KI 2005. LNCS (LNAI), vol. 3698, pp. 1–15. Springer, Heidelberg (2005)
[6] Forsyth, J.: A Grammar of Aspect: Usage and Meaning in the Russian Verb. Cambridge University Press, Cambridge (1970)
[7] Forsyth, J.: The nature and development of the aspectual opposition in the Russian verb. The Slavonic and East European Review 50(121), 493–506 (1972)
[8] Gerasymova, K., Spranger, M.: Acquisition of Grammar in Autonomous Artificial Systems. In: Proceedings of the 19th European Conference on Artificial Intelligence, ECAI 2010 (2010)
[9] Gerasymova, K., Steels, L., van Trijp, R.: Aspectual morphology of Russian verbs in Fluid Construction Grammar. In: Proceedings of the 31th Annual Conference of the Cognitive Science Society (2009)
[10] Janda, L.A.: Aspectual clusters of Russian verbs. Studies in Language 31(3), 607–648 (2007)
[11] Janda, L.A.: Semantic motivations for aspectual clusters of Russian verbs. In: American Contributions to the XIV International Congress of Slavists, p. 22 (2008)
[12] Krongauz, M.A.: Pristavki i glagoly v russkom jazyke: semantičeskaja grammatika. Jazyki russkoj kul'tury, Moscow (1998)
[13] Steels, L., De Beule, J., Neubauer, N.: Linking in Fluid Construction Grammars. In: Proceedings of BNAIC, pp. 11–18. Transactions of the Belgian Royal Society of Arts and Sciences, Brussels (2005)
[14] Steels, L.: A design pattern for phrasal constructions. In: Steels, L. (ed.) Design Patterns in Fluid Construction Grammar. John Benjamins, Amsterdam (2011)
[15] Steels, L. (ed.): Design Patterns in Fluid Construction Grammar. John Benjamins, Amsterdam (2011)
[16] Steels, L.: A first encounter with Fluid Construction Grammar. In: Steels, L. (ed.) Design Patterns in Fluid Construction Grammar. John Benjamins, Amsterdam (2011)
[17] Steels, L. (ed.): Computational Issues in Fluid Construction Grammar. Springer, Berlin (2012)
[18] Steels, L.: Design Methods for Fluid Construction Grammar. In: Steels, L. (ed.) Computational Issues in FCG. LNCS (LNAI), vol. 7249, pp. 3–36. Springer, Heidelberg (2012)
[19] Stoll, S.: The role of aktionsart in the acquisition of Russian aspect. First Language 18(54), 351–376 (1998)
[20] Stoll, S.: Beginning and end in the acquisition of the perfective aspect in Russian. Journal of Child Language 32(4), 805–825 (2005)

[21] van Trijp, R.: A design pattern for argument structure constructions. In: Steels, L. (ed.) Design Patterns in Fluid Construction Grammar. John Benjamins, Amsterdam (2011)
[22] Wellens, P.: Organizing constructions in networks. In: Steels, L. (ed.) Design Patterns in Fluid Construction Grammar. John Benjamins, Amsterdam (2011)

Appendix: Defining a Grammar or How to Write Templates

Templates are useful abstractions; however, they hide what happens behind the scenes. This section is targeted to those readers who are interested in the technical details of the implementation. For an example of a semantic categorization construction, a general methodology of how to develop templates is illustrated in detail. The reader can get acquainted with how to write real FCG-constructions that serve a particular function and, thereafter, how to turn them into self-defined templates.

Methodology for Writing Templates. Templates can be very large or quite small, complicated or basic, highly specialized or multi-purpose, but the development of almost all of them goes through the following four steps:

1. The linguistic dimensions that play a key role are identified.
2. An example of a complete construction is developed into which a future template expands.
3. When scaling up, the changeable elements of a construction are identified.
4. A template emerges as a parametrized version of a construction.

Taking an example of a semantic categorization construction for a case of the telic Aktionsart, let us develop the template `def-sem-cat-cxn` used in the previous section to define all semantic categorization constructions.

1. Key Linguistic Dimensions. Semantic categorization constructions have to re-categorize parts of the meaning into the language-internal semantic categories. Hence, they operate on the dimensions of meaning and sem-cats. For the case of the telic Aktionsart, the schematic mapping was already identified in Section 3.2 as the following:

(28) `meaning: (event-type ?ev complete)` $\longleftrightarrow$
`sem-cat: (aktionsart telic)`

2. Writing a Complete Construction. By this time the reader is familiar with several FCG-constructions. Our telic-construction differs from all the previous ones in that it operates only on one pole of the linguistic structure to which it applies, namely, only on the semantic pole. This is the case because the transformation it realizes – translation of meaning into semantic categories and back – affects only semantics.

It is important to note that our telic-construction still contains two coupled poles; yet, both its left and its right poles refer to the semantic pole of a linguistic structure.

In building a construction, let us start by creating a skeleton and pinning down the meaning it should trigger on. After the application of the lexical constructions, the information about the event type is still located in the top of the linguistic structure (Figure 7), so the construction has to search for it there. Additionally, we tag this meaning to make it movable in order to allocate it later to an appropriate unit.

```
((?top-unit
  (tag ?meaning (meaning (== (event-type ?ev complete)))))
<-->
((?top-unit))
```

There are some things to take into account before we relate this meaning to the telic Aktionsart. First, the preliminary construction shown above has to be constrained in a way so that it unifies with only specific kinds of structures. Namely, we want it to apply only in the presence of a verb because this is where the aspectual information about the internal structure of events is expressed in Russian. Thus, we extend the construction by the desired hierarchical structure, i.e., the top unit should contain a subunit (`?ev-unit`), which is responsible for an event. To assure that it is an event, we constrain the sem-category of this unit to the `(class event)`, under the assumption that the lexical entry for this verb has already applied creating this separate unit. The extended version looks as follows:

```
((?top-unit
  (tag ?meaning
       (meaning (== (event-type ?ev complete))))
  (sem-subunits (== ?ev-unit)))
 (?ev-unit
  (sem-cat (==1 (class event)))))
<-->
((?top-unit
  (sem-subunits (== ?ev-unit))))
```

Now the time has come to translate the *completeness* of the event into the category of the telic Aktionsart of the corresponding verb. For this we have to add the sem-cat of Aktionsart to the event unit and move the corresponding meaning of event-type from the top-unit into it.

Important to note is that this construction actualizes merging of the new information into an existing structure. It accesses the substructure and alters it, augmenting the existing unit with some parts of meaning and a semantic category. To specify the semantic category of Aktionsart, we simply add it to the event unit on the *right* pole of the construction, because this is where the merging phase takes place in production:

```
((?top-unit
  (tag ?meaning
       (meaning (== (event-type ?ev complete))))
  (sem-subunits (== ?ev-unit)))
 (?ev-unit
  (sem-cat (==1 (class event)))))
<-->
((?top-unit
  (sem-subunits (== ?ev-unit)))
 (?ev-unit
  (sem-cat (==1 (aktionsart telic)))))
```

On the other hand, the addition of the tagged meaning on the *left* pole has to be done with the help of the J-operator. This addition cannot be done here by merging as well due to the nature of parsing. When writing FCG-constructions, one has to consider the flow of information in both application directions in order to ensure bi-directionality. With regard to production in the previous case, the information about the telic Aktionsart would already be present in the event unit after the application of the morphological construction: the construction for the prefix will already have translated the prefix into the telic Aktionsart of the prefixed verb. Thus, when the right pole of our semantic construction unifies with the linguistic structure, the presence of the sem-cat of the telic Aktionsart has to serve as a constraint in order to ensure that the translation only occurs by those verbs that are telic. Therefore, this condition is specified in the sem-cat of the event unit on the right pole. However, with respect to the current case of parsing, at this point in parsing there is no information about the meaning – it is specifically the job of the semantic construction to add meaning to the transient structure. The meaning cannot simply be put on the right pole of the event unit as a condition; it has to be added with the J-operator:

```
((?top-unit
  (tag ?meaning
       (meaning (== (event-type ?ev complete))))
  (sem-subunits (== ?ev-unit)))
 (?ev-unit
  (sem-cat (==1 (class event))))
 ((J ?ev-unit)
  ?meaning))
<-->
((?top-unit
  (sem-subunits (== ?ev-unit)))
 (?ev-unit
  (sem-cat (==1 (aktionsart telic)))))
```

The next step in building our telic-construction is the addition of footprints. Normally, the footprints are put in the same unit once with an excludes (==0) and once with an includes operator (==1) on each pole of the construction, respectively. The excludes first ensures that the construction applies for the very first time, and the includes leaves a mark (usually, the name) after the construction's application. In our case, however, the footprints have to be attached to separate units on the left and right poles because both refer to the semantic pole, and hence the added mark on one pole would cause conflicts by the merging of the other pole with an excludes operator and vice versa. The footprints are attached on the left pole to the event-unit and on the right pole to the top-unit:

```
((?top-unit
  (tag ?meaning
       (meaning (== (event-type ?ev complete))))
  (sem-subunits (== ?ev-unit)))
 (?ev-unit
  (sem-cat (==1 (class event)))
   (footprints (==0  telicity-sem-cxn)))
 ((J ?ev-unit)
  ?meaning
   (footprints (==1  telicity-sem-cxn))))
<-->
((?top-unit
  (sem-subunits (== ?ev-unit))
   (footprints (==0  telicity-sem-cxn)))
 (?ev-unit
  (sem-cat (==1 (aktionsart telic))))
  ((J ?top-unit)
   (footprints (==1 telicity-sem-cxn))))
```

Our construction is already fully operational and behaves in the desired manner during production. However, in parsing a small detail is still missing. What the present construction lacks is that the variable `?ev` in the event-type predicate refers to the same event as the one in the event-unit `?ev-unit`. Up until now there was nothing linking the two, which means that nothing stated that *this particular event* is of the type complete, although the event-type predicate was moved into the event-unit, and the variable names happened to be the same locally in both feature structures. The gap can be closed with the help of the `args` feature. Recall that the lexical entry for event has specified its arguments in the list `(?ev ?ctx)`, the purpose of which has hitherto remained mysterious. It can now be made use of, in order to specify the variables' equality by means of referring to both the event argument of the event unit and the event of the event-type predicate with the same name *within the same construction.* In this way, we arrive at the following telic-construction:

```
((?top-unit
  (tag ?meaning
       (meaning (== (event-type ?ev complete))))
  (sem-subunits (== ?ev-unit)))
 (?ev-unit
  (sem-cat (==1 (class event)))
  (args (?ev ?ctx))
  (footprints (==0  telicity-sem-cxn)))
 ((J ?ev-unit)
  ?meaning
  (footprints (==1  telicity-sem-cxn))))
<-->
((?top-unit
  (sem-subunits (== ?ev-unit))
  (footprints (==0  telicity-sem-cxn)))
 (?ev-unit
  (sem-cat (==1 (aktionsart telic))))
  ((J ?top-unit)
  (footprints (==1 telicity-sem-cxn))))
```

Now the construction is complete. Note that it is concerned neither with perfective aspect nor the notion of totality characteristic to all perfective verbs. This design decision underlines that Aktionsarten alone are not responsible for the emergence of the grammatical aspect. Another point to note is that this telic-construction is item-based; item being a specific kind of temporal semantics fixed for a construction, whereas the event that this temporal semantics refers to is unspecified and represented as a slot to fill in by a verb.

3. Identifying the Pattern. To discover a pattern, one has to consider what the semantic categorization constructions for other Aktionsarten look like. As already mentioned, other semantic nuances are also represented with the predicate of event type, such as `(event-type begin)`. Respectively, they get mapped onto different Aktionsarten, such as the notion of beginning onto the `(aktionsart ingressive)`. Thus, these elements of a construction differ for other Aktionsarten. The rest of the construction's structure remains the same except for its name and the event variable present in the `:args` feature.

4. Template def-sem-cxn. As soon as the changeable elements of a construction definition are known, a construction can be easily converted into a template, where concrete values are substituted by parameters that are supplied later by a template. In the case at hand, the feature value components for `meaning`, `sem-cat`, `args` as well as the name of the construction will be different for different constructions, thus they are turned into parameters in a template definition (i.e., the underlined list).[7] When the template is called, these parameters

[7] &key means that parameters are named.

are substituted inside the construction by the actual values supplied in the call. Shown below is the template definition with substituted parameters indicated in bold:

```
(defmacro def-sem-cat-cxn (name &key meaning args sem-cat)
  `(((?top-unit
      (tag ?meaning (meaning ,meaning))
      (sem-subunits (== ?unit-name)))
     (?unit-name
      (sem-cat (==1 (class event)))
      (args ,args)
      (footprints (==0 ,name)))
     ((J ?unit-name)
      ?meaning
      (footprints (==1 ,name))))
    <-->
    ((?top-unit
      (sem-subunits (== ?unit-name))
      (footprints (==0 ,name)))
     (?unit-name
      (sem-cat ,sem-cat))
     ((J ?top-unit)
      (footprints (==1 ,name))))))
```

With the def-sem-cat-cxn template, the definition of the entire telic-construction can be folded into the following call:

```
(29) (def-sem-cat-cxn telicity-sem-cxn
       :meaning (== (event-type ?ev complete))
       :args (?ev ?ctx)
       :sem-cat (==1 (aktionsart telic)))
```

Handling Scope in Fluid Construction Grammar: A Case Study for Spanish Modals

Katrien Beuls

Artificial Intelligence Laboratory, Vrije Universiteit Brussel, Belgium

Abstract. This paper demonstrates one way how the Spanish epistemic modal system can be implemented in Fluid Construction Grammar. Spanish is a Romance language with a rich morpho-phonological system that is characterized by paradigmatic stem changes, a considerable degree of syncretism in verbal suffixes and a sophisticated usage of modal markers. Because the choice of mood does not only depend on the linguistic expression that is used (e.g. "probablemente", "creo que ..."), but also on the position of such expression in the utterance and its scope, the processing engine needs to be flexible enough to capture these conditions. The formal implementation of the Spanish conjugational paradigm with special focus on syncretic markers forms a prerequisite for the processing of verbal mood and modal expressions.

1 Introduction

Language is a product of its users. Conversation partners usually do not hesitate to package their utterances in such a way that the interlocutor understands their attitude toward the proposition that is expressed. This strategy is operational in many language systems around the world and is mostly realized by means of mood and modal expressions that create different shades of meaning. Since these forms are inextricably tied to the field of (inter)subjective communication, the main question of this paper is concerned with the way in which such expressions can be captured by a formal representation of grammar. This paper shows one way in which a modal language system for (peninsular) Spanish[1] can be modeled in Fluid Construction Grammar (hereafter: FCG) [3, 8, 12]. Linguists traditionally make the distinction between *propositional modality* and *event modality* [7]. Since this paper reports on a first case study of the implementation of a modal system in FCG, only propositional modality has been considered, with special focus on epistemic modality.

The following requirements are specific to this FCG grammar and make this case study an interesting workbench for grammar formalizations:

1. Since the Spanish language is characterized by frequent *stem changes* in the verbal conjugational paradigm and *syncretic suffixes* (single form for

[1] Modal expressions are often dependent on the geographical and social situation of the language community.

L. Steels (Ed.): Computational Issues in FCG, LNAI 7249, pp. 123–142, 2012.

multiple functions), the formalization needs to be robust enough to handle such morpho-phonological incongruencies.
2. Multiple modal constructions are needed to actualize differences in meaning and form (e.g. mood suffixes). The *organization* of such a series of constructions poses an interesting challenge: The moment in the processing pipeline when the modal constructions apply is crucial for their success.
3. A modal grammar requires the use of subclauses and therefore launches the handling of *scoping* and the start of possible long distance dependencies between clauses.
4. Flexible processing allows the grammar to come up with multiple solutions for one meaning, influenced by the *discourse context.* The constructions themselves are thus not the only decision makers in the production process.

After the introduction of some basic linguistic facts about the language system that forms the subject of this case study in Section 2, the paper addresses the four requirements listed above in their order of appearance. Section 3 demonstrates the processing of syncretic forms in FCG and introduces a template that handles verbal stem changes. Modal constructions form the subject of Section 4: their functionality as well as their role in the processing pipeline are discussed. Section 5 launches the use of modal subclauses and the presence of a scoping relation between the main clause and the subordinated clause. Section 6 discusses deviant uses of modal expressions and their implications for the processing engine. Finally, Section 7 concludes the paper and gives directions for further research on the topic.

2 Linguistic Facts

Since this paper is concerned with a case study on the implementation of epistemic modality in Spanish, some basic linguistic background information is required in order to fully grasp its computational complexity and relevance for theories of grammar formalization. Section 2.1 addresses the meaning of the term epistemic modality; Section 2.2 concentrates on the building blocks of the verbal conjugational paradigm in Spanish. Section 2.3 briefly discusses the use of the subjunctive mood in Spanish.

2.1 Epistemic Modality

Modality typically encodes the speaker's attitude towards the proposition that is expressed. In the case of epistemic modality, the speaker forms his or her modal "judgement" based on the kind of knowledge (< Gr. *epistèmè*) he or she has acquired about the proposition (truth, probability, certainty, belief, evidence). The use of the term epistemic is relatively straightforward, with *possibility* and *probability* as two major epistemic meaning predicates. Another epistemic category is *certainty*, which is used when the speaker has good reason to believe that the statement is true (e.g. 'There must be some way to get from New York to

San Francisco for less than $600.'). Consider the clear contrast in the notional features involved in the following pairs of examples (adopted from [7]):

(1) Kate may be at home now.
Kate must be at home now.

(2) Kate may come in now.
Kate must come in now.

The distinction between (1) and (2) is usually made in terms of propositional modality and event modality. This is illustrated by the use of paraphrases using 'possible' and 'necessary':

(3) It is possibly the case that Kate is at home now.
It is necessarily the case that Kate is at home now.

(4) It is possible for Kate to come in now.
It is necessary for Kate to come in now.

In Example (4), the speaker expresses his personal attitude toward a potential future event, that of Kate coming in. Example (3) is concerned with the speaker's judgement of the proposition that Kate is at home.

2.2 Spanish Verbal Paradigm

Spanish is a member of the Indo-European language family and belongs to the branch of Romance languages. This branch comprises all languages that descend from vulgar Latin, the language of Ancient Rome. Today, Spanish is the third most spoken language in the world with about 500 million native speakers.

A defining feature of Spanish phonology is its diphthongization of the Latin short vowels *e* and *o* into *ie* and *ue*, respectively, in stressed contexts (e.g. Lat. *petram* > Sp. *piedra*). This difference in stress pattern has been preserved in the current stem morphology, which has lead to four main cases that a language user has to account for when conjugating a verb in Spanish:

1. Regular stem, regular endings: 'cortar', 'deber', 'vivir', etc. (see Table 1)
2. Irregular stem, regular endings: e.g. 'empezar' > 'empiezo' (*begin.inf* > *begin.1sg.present*), 'volver' > 'vuelvo' (*return.inf* > *return.1sg.present*)
3. Regular stem, irregular endings: e.g. 'andar' > 'and-uve' (*walk.inf* > *walk.1sg.past.pf*)
4. Irregular stem, irregular endings: 'hacer' > 'hic-e' (*do.inf* > *do.1sg.past.pf*)

Irregular uses do not always show a deviant conjugation over the full paradigm[2]. Depending on the class a verb belongs to and the verb tense and mood that is required, verbs may or may not be conjugated in an irregular manner. There

[2] The term paradigm is used here to refer to one column in the conjugational table; e.g. 1st verb class indicative present.

are three verb classes in Spanish: verbs ending on *-ar*, *-er* and *-ir*. Without taking into account the compound tenses (auxiliary *haber* + past participle), there are five different tenses in the indicative mood: present, past imperfect, past perfect, future and conditional. The subjunctive mood only occurs with three tenses: present, past imperfect and future. Table 1 presents parts of the (regular) Spanish conjugational paradigm that have been implemented for the current case study: indicative present, indicative past perfect and subjunctive present. All forms for the three regular verb classes have been included.

Table 1. Indicative present, past perfect and subjunctive present conjugation paradigms for regular verbs of the three main verb classes: 'cortar' ('to cut'), 'deber' ('have to'), 'vivir' ('to live')

-ar			-er			-ir		
ind.		subj.	ind.		subj.	ind.		subj.
pres.	past pf.	pres.	pres.	past pf.	pres.	pres.	past pf.	pres.
cort-**o**	cort-é	cort-e	deb-o	deb-í	deb-a	viv-o	viv-í	viv-a
cort-as	cort-aste	cort-**es**	deb-**es**	deb-iste	deb-as	viv-**es**	viv-iste	viv-as
cort-a	cort-**ó**	cort-e	deb-e	deb-ió	deb-a	viv-e	vivió	viv-a
cort-**amos**	cort-**amos**	cort-emos	deb-emos	deb-imos	deb-amos	viv-imos	viv-imos	viv-amos
cort-áis	cort-asteis	cort-éis	deb-éis	deb-isteis	deb-áis	viv-ís	viv-isteis	viv-áis
cort-an	cort-aron	cort-en	deb-en	deb-ieron	deb-an	viv-en	viv-ieron	viv-an

There is a considerable number of syncretic forms present in Table 1. Syncretism occurs where two or more distinct morphosyntactic values are collapsed in a single inflected word form [1]. Table 1 contains three main instances of syncretic forms:

1. indicative present and past suffixes for 1st person plural are equal in form, e.g. 'cort-amos' (present/past);
2. 1st person indicative present and past forms are the same in writing but receive a different emphasis (*o* vs. *ó*), e.g. 'cort-o' (1sg) vs. 'cort-ó' (3sg);
3. subjunctive present suffixes of the first verb class and indicative present suffixes of the second and third verb classes are shared across all persons except 1st person singular: e.g. 'cort-es' (subjunctive) vs. 'viv-es'/'deb-es' (indicative).

2.3 Subjunctive

The difference between the indicative and the subjunctive mood is linked to the degree of affirmation of an utterance. When the speaker is confirming that what he or she is saying is valid at the moment of speaking, the indicative is used. In the contrary case, the subjunctive shows up to mark the non-affirmative stance of the speaker towards his or her proposition. The following sentences illustrate the use of the two moods in a conditional subordinated clause:

(5) *Aunque llueve, vamos a la playa.*
although rain-(3sg.ind.pres), go-(1sg.ind.pres) to the beach.
Although it is raining, we are going to the beach.

(6) *Aunque llueva, vamos a la playa.*
although rain-(3sg.subj.pres), go-(1sg.ind.pres) to the beach.
Even if it rains, we are going to the beach.

The indicative ending in (5) expresses the fact that it is raining right now, imposing an 'although' meaning onto the conditional adverb *aunque*. The subjunctive verb form in (6) signals a rather hypothetical statement: 'even if' it is raining now, we will go to the beach. The speaker indicates that the condition of the weather cannot be confirmed at the moment of the utterance.

3 Capturing Syncretism

The previous section has already pointed at the presence of syncretic forms in the conjugational paradigm of verbs in Spanish. There are two main elements of processing complexity when multiple values are conflated into one morpho-phonological form: First, all values of the single form need to be learned to lead to successful parsing. When the suffix '-amos' is encountered, three alternative values will usually be activated: 1st person plural indicative present, indicative past perfect or subjunctive present. According to the morphological verb form and the semantics of the verbal clause, one of these gets selected. Second, in production, a language user needs to know which forms go together with which meaning. This second element is thus an additional (syntactic) operation one needs to perform in order to find the right form. In order to express the indicative present first person plural form of the verb 'cantar' ('to sing'), a speaker of Spanish needs to have access to the fact that there are three suffixes that can fill this slot ('-amos', '-emos' and '-imos') so he can select the appropriate form matching the verb class of the verb ('-amos').

Section 3.1 illustrates how such syncretic forms can be implemented in FCG to assure optimal processing in parsing as well as production. Section 3.2 discusses one way for dealing with morpho-phonological elements that share the same function but are used with different forms. Stem changes form the main focus of the discussion.

3.1 Morpho-phonological Constructions

The standard way of dealing with morphological variation in FCG is through morphological constructions. There have been many case studies on this issue ranging from Russian aspectual affixes [4], over German case markers [11], to Hungarian verbal agreement markers [2]. The general FCG template that instantiates a morphological construction has two main slots (apart form the obligatory construction name): `suffix` and `stem`. The suffix slot contains the marker string; its grammatical function is specified in the stem slot. The function of a marker is usually implemented as a list of syntactic categories that a verb stem must have in order to license the presence of the marker string.

By definition, syncretic markers share the same marker string. The following lines of code show how such markers can be instantiated by means of the morphological template `def-morph-cxn`. The suffix "-e" is syncretic since it is used for the 3rd person singular present indicative (2nd and 3rd conjugation) and the 3rd person singular present subjunctive (1st conjugation). The only difference in functional use is the verbal mood.

```
(def-morph-cxn present-ind-3sg-2/3-morph-cxn
    :suffix "e"
    :stem (?stem-unit
           :syn-cat (==1! (verb-class (==1 (1 -) (2 ?vc2) (3 ?vc3)))
                          (agreement (==1 (singular + - - +)
                                          (plural - - - -)))
                          (tam (==1 (indicative + - + -)
                                    (subjunctive - - - -))))))
```

```
(def-morph-cxn present-subj-1sg/3sg-1-morph-cxn
    :suffix "e"
    :stem (?stem-unit
           :syn-cat (==1! (verb-class (==1 (1 +) (2 -) (3 -)))
                          (agreement (==1 (singular ?sg ?1sg - ?3sg)
                                          (plural - - - -)))
                          (tam (==1 (indicative - - - -)
                                    (subjunctive + - + -))))))
```

The syntactic categories[3] that constitute the grammatical function of these markers contain three elements: the verb class (`verb-class`), subject-verb agreement information (`agreement`) and values for tense, aspect and mood categories (`tam`). Each of these is implemented as a so-called feature matrix, which contains the actual and potential functional values (see also [13]). The actual values are indicated by a '+' or a '−' sign, the potential values by variables: e.g. the verb class value of the first construction (`(==1 (1 −) (2 ?vc2) (3 ?vc3))`) is 2 or 3 but never 1. Agreement values are read as follows: `(singular ?sg ?1sg ?2sg ?3sg)` and `(plural ?pl ?1pl ?2pl ?3pl)`. Third person singular is thus formalized as `(==1 (singular + - - +) (plural - - - -))`. Tense and mood are specified as

[3] The special operator `==1!` needs to be interpreted as follows: The elements that follow it should occur only once in the list in any order (regular `==1`) and they should always be matched to the transient structure, even in merging (`!`). This operator avoids merging the wrong feature values into a unit in parsing.

`(indicative ?ind ?ind-past ?ind-present ?ind-future)` and `(subjunctive ?subj ?subj-past ?subj-present ?subj-future)`, resulting in `(==1 (indicative + - + -) (subjunctive - - - -)` for present indicative. A more detailed example that discusses the functioning of feature matrices can be found elsewhere in this Volume [5].

Syncretism can also occur across lexical class boundaries. Remember the Spanish "-o" and "-a" suffixes to mark agreement in gender (masculine, feminine) between nouns and adjectives: 'una torta delicios-a', 'a delicious cake'. These cases are captured through the grammatical function that is expressed by these markers. A verbal marker "-a" will never conflate with an adjectival marker "-a" since they differ on substantial syntactic categories such as agreement (person, number vs. gender, number) and lexical category (verb vs. adjective).

Even though underspecification costs something in terms of ambiguity, it also facilitates processing. Having a construction inventory with less markers can reduce the storage cost considerably. Within the same verb class, the "-e" marker can be used for 1st and 3rd person singular subjunctive present. The final decision on whether the person value is 1 or 3 does not have to be stored in the inventory but can be delayed toward the moment of processing. It is then the grammar that fills in the person slot as soon as it is needed. However, such a reduction only works within one verb class.

3.2 Stem Changes

The previous section has shown that, in production, the decision of which form goes with which meaning can be guided by morpho-syntactic categories such as the verb class of the stem. There is one more aspect that plays a role in choosing the right form: phonology. Examples (7) and (8) illustrate a difference in stem vowel between the 1st person singular and plural of the indicative present paradigm.

(7) ***Vuelv***-*o* *mañana.*
return-(1sg.ind.pres) tomorrow.
I will return tomorrow.

(8) ***Volv***-*emos* *mañana.*
return-(1pl.ind.pres) tomorrow.
We will return tomorrow.

How does one represent such stem changes in a formal grammar? Generally, there are two possible approaches:

- A series of lexical entries can be created for to cover all different forms that might be encountered (e.g. 'vuelv-', 'volv-', etc.). However, this approach would lead to a processing overload in the lexical construction set (subset in the construction inventory containing all lexical constructions), since not only lexical but also morpho-phonological decisions would have to be made within this single processing step.

- By separating multiple concerns, the alternative option divides the work over three types of constructions: lexical, stem and morpho-phonetic. The lexical constructions contain the verb infinitive (e.g. 'volver'), the stem constructions instantiate the infinitive so it becomes a morphological stem (e.g 'vuelv-', 'volv-') and the morpho-phonetic constructions match a stem with a suffix.

This case study follows the second approach. Separation of concerns implies that processing is separated into distinct modules that overlap in functionality as little as possible. Organizing constructions into construction sets fulfills this requirement (see also [2]). Figure 1 shows how two different verb forms of the verb 'volver' ('return'), see (7) and (8) can be rendered in a production process. The constructional application order is set to: lexical, (functional, grammatical,) stem, morpho-syntactic. The role of the functional and grammatical construction sets can currently be ignored. Section 4 addresses their functional use.

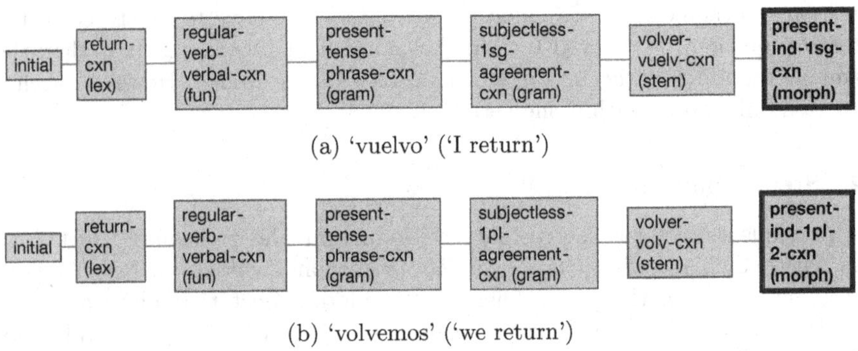

Fig. 1. Resulting application processes in production for 'vuelvo' (a) and 'volvemos' (b). The lexical construction for the verb (**return-cxn**) is shared, the stem and morpho-syntactic constructions differ

The only difference that is visible in the processing pipelines of both verb forms is the application of the stem and morpho-syntactic constructions: `volver-vuelv-cxn` vs. `volver-volv-cxn` and `present-ind-1sg-cxn` vs. `present-ind-1pl-2-cxn`. In order to better understand how the production of a single verb form proceeds, we run step by step through the application of 'vuelvo', ignoring functional and grammatical constructions (responsible for subject-verb agreement and time).

- The initial transient structure contains the following semantic representation:

```
((1sg-agent indiv-1 context) (return event-1 context)
 (return-returner event-1 indiv-1) (event-overlaps event-1 now)
 (current-time-point now))
```

- First, the lexical construction `return-cxn` triggers on the presence of `(return event-1 context) (return-returner event-1 indiv-1)` in the initial structure. The lexical template that creates this construction consists of a skeleton covering its meaning and form (infinitive) and a lexical categorization which specifies its semantic class, lexical category and syntactic verb class.

```
(def-lex-cxn return-cxn
  (def-verb-skeleton return-cxn
      :meaning (== (return ?event ?base-set)
                   (return-returner ?event ?agent))
      :args (?event ?base-set)
      :string "volver")
  (def-lex-cat return-cxn
      :syn-cat (==1 (lex-cat (regular verb))
                    (verb-class (==1 (1 -) (2 +) (3 -))))
      :sem-cat (==1 (class event))))
```

- Second, after grammatical constructions have done their work and added the necessary syntactic information for agreement (covering meaning predicate `(1sg-agent indiv-1 context)`) and tense and mood (covering meaning predicates `(event-overlaps event-1 now) (current-time-point now)`), the stem construction `volver-vuelv-cxn` translates the infinitive "volver" into "vuelv-". This happens only when the verb form is specified as indicated by the syntactic slots `agreement` and `tam`, that is in the present tense indicative or subjunctive with all a singular person or the third person plural.

```
(def-stem-cxn volver-vuelv-cxn
    :infinitive "volver"
    :string "vuelv-"
    :syn-cat (==1 (agreement
                   (==1 (singular ?sg ?1sg ?2sg ?3sg)
                        (plural ?3pl - - ?3pl)))
                  (tam
                   (==1 (indicative ?ind-pres - ?ind-pres -)
                        (subjunctive ?subj-pres - ?subj-pres -)))))
```

- Finally, the morpho-syntactic construction that adds the matching suffix to the stem form "vuelv-" can apply. According to the morpho-syntactic template included below, the "o" suffix triggers when the subject is first person singular and the tense is present indicative. All three verb classes take this suffix.

```
(def-morph-cxn present-ind-1sg-cxn
    :suffix "o"
    :stem
    (?stem-unit
     :syn-cat (==1 (agreement
                    (==1 (singular + + - -)
                         (plural - - - -)))
                   (tam
                    (==1 (indicative + - + -)
                         (subjunctive - - - -)))
                   (verb-class (==1 (1 ?vc1) (2 ?vc2) (3 ?vc3))))))
```

In parsing, the processing pipeline is traversed in almost the opposite direction: morpho-syntactic constructions trigger before grammatical constructions and stem constructions before lexical ones.

4 Formalizing Modal Constructions

Now that all morpho-phonological machinery for dealing with the Spanish conjugational paradigm has been introduced, it is time to move on to the real topic of this paper: modals in FCG. Modal expressions typically belong to one of the following three classes of modal assessment:

1. **Mental expressions** including cognition verbs such as *believe* and *doubt* and complex expressions such as *have the impression*, etc.
2. **Modal adjuncts** such as adverbs like *perhaps*, prepositional phrases like *in all likelihood* and clauses such as *there is a good chance that*, etc.
3. **Modal auxiliaries** such as *may, can* and *must.*

Each of these classes is related to a different subjective position a speaker can take according to a proposition. Take the proposition "Anna is pregnant". There are many possible sentences a speaker could utter when he or she forms a modal assessment of this proposition: e.g. '*I believe that* Anna is pregnant', 'Anna is *probably* pregnant', 'Anna *may* be pregnant', etc. Each of these utterances is characterized by a certain degree of belief the speaker has about the proposition that Anna is pregnant.

This section only concentrates on the FCG processing of modal adjuncts (adverbs) and modal auxiliaries. Apart from introducing a new range of constructions needed to operationalize main clauses that contain these modal expressions (Section 4.1), the remainder of the current section zooms in on the organization of the application process of these modal clauses (Section 4.2). Section 5 deals with cognition verbs, and consequently with subclauses and modal scoping.

4.1 Expanding the Construction Inventory

Lexical Constructions. Lexical constructions map meaning to form and reversely. While the form part of modal adjuncts and auxiliaries is straightforward to implement, more questions arise when the meaning is considered. Is it possible to attribute a particular semantic representation to them? And moreover, how does one capture the semantic difference between modal adjuncts and auxiliaries in predicate logic terms? According to Nuyts [6], modal auxiliaries show the same functional position as the modal adverbs. Both adverbs and auxiliaries are neutral with respect to all functional factors in his model. He argues that an illustration of this is that they only very rarely occur in a focus position (as opposed to modal adjectives ('it is possible that') and mental state predicates ('I think that')).

The current case study follows this finding and does not distinguish between modal auxiliaries and adverbs in terms of their semantic representation. Spanish has three main modal auxiliaries that differ in the epistemic strength they express: 'puede', 'debe' and 'tiene que'. Three "corresponding" modal adverbs are, respectively: 'posiblemente', 'probablemente' and 'seguramente'. The meaning predicates that have been implemented for these modals look as follows:

```
(speaker ?speaker ?base-set)
(judgement ?evaluation ?speaker ?proposition)
(proposition ?proposition ?event)
(qual-strength ?evaluation [possibility|probability|certainty])
```

By using a modal expression, a *speaker* makes a *judgement* about a *proposition* concerning a particular event. Such an evaluation is characterized by a certain *qualitative strength*, which ranges from possibility over probability to certainty, depending on the modal expression that is used. Note that only the speaker predicate is linked to the physical context (`?base-set`). This implementation illustrates the fact that modal meaning is not directly observable from the context but that it needs to be constructed by a speaker.

Modal Constructions. Apart from its presence in the lexicon of a construction inventory, the modal meaning also needs to be propagated to the rest of the utterance that a modal expression occurs in. This is the task of the modal constructions. For the modal auxiliaries, this means that a verbal complex (auxiliary + main verb) is created, and it is marked as a modal verb. Embedded modal adverbs are processed similarly.

The template for creating a modal auxiliary-verb construction is included here for the purpose of illustration. It comprises three main modules: a template skeleton, percolation of agreement features and percolation of variables for semantic linking. The template used here is the standard FCG template for creating phrasal constructions [9].

- The skeleton contains three main slots: `:cxn-set`, `:phrase` and `:constituents`. The phrasal unit that this template creates is a modal verb phrase that has a modal auxiliary and a verb as its constituents. The modal features of the auxiliary unit (provided by the lexicon) are percolated upwards so that the complete verbal complex gets marked for modality. The `:cxn-form` slot within the `?modal-verb-complex` sets the word order of the constituents.

```
(def-phrasal-skeleton modal-auxiliary-verb-cxn
    :cxn-set modal
    :phrase
    (?modal-verb-complex
     :sem-function predicator
     :cxn-form (== (meets ?modal-aux ?verb))
     :phrase-type (modal verbal-phrase))
    :constituents
    ((?verb
      :sem-function predicator
      :syn-cat (==1 (lex-cat (?type verb))))
     (?modal-aux
      :sem-cat (==1 (class (epistemic evaluation)))
      :phrase-type (modal verbal-phrase))))
```

- The phrasal agreement template percolates some values from the constituents to the newly created phrasal unit. Valency information is provided by the verb unit, while the auxiliary unit contributes the agreement information. The mood value is here merged into the syntactic category of the modal auxiliary. The indicative is the default mood but can be overridden by additional constructions that have scope over the `modal-auxiliary-verb-cxn`. An example of this is included in Section 5.

```
(def-phrasal-agreement modal-auxiliary-verb-cxn
    (?modal-verb-complex
     :sem-cat (==1 (sem-val ?sem-val))
     :syn-cat (==1 (syn-val ?syn-val)
                   (agreement ?agreement)))
    (?verb
     :sem-cat (==1 (sem-val ?sem-val))
     :syn-cat (==1 (syn-val ?syn-val)))
    (?modal-aux
     :syn-cat
     (==1 (agreement ?agreement)
          (tam
           (==1 (indicative ?ind ?ind-past ?ind-present ?ind-future)
                (subjunctive - - - -))))))
```

- Finally, the phrasal linking template percolates the values from the verb unit to the new modal verb unit so they can be accessed in later grammatical processing (agreement constructions, argument structure constructions). Note also that it is secured that the `?event` variable is shared across all units.

```
(def-phrasal-linking modal-auxiliary-verb-cxn
  (?modal-verb-complex
   :args (?event ?context))
  (?verb
   :args (?event ?context))
  (?modal-aux
   :args (?speaker ?event ?context)))
```

The template for the adverbial modal construction functions analogously. The slot of the modal auxiliary is filled in by a modal adverb and the agreement and mood information is provided by the main verb unit this time. Also here, the default mood is the indicative. Examples of a change in mood that is guided by the adverbial's position in the clause are included in Section 5.

4.2 Processing Modals

This section demonstrates the bi-directional processing of the previously introduced modal constructions. The following example sentences accompany this demonstration.

(9) *Ana* ***puede*** *estar* *embarazada.*
Anna could-(3sg.ind.pres) be.temp(inf) pregnant.
Anna could be pregnant.

(10) *Ana* *está* ***posiblemente*** *embarazada.*
Anna be.temp(3sg.ind.pres) possibly pregnant.
Anna is possibly pregnant.

Let us first concentrate on Sentence (9). The sentence contains one modal auxiliary ('puede'), which expresses a weak epistemic assessment of the proposition 'Ann is pregnant'. Figure 2 contains its production process (a) and the resulting linguistic structure (b). The application order is guided by construction sets that group constructions that share a certain functionality. Figure 2a illustrates this processing chain of construction sets, which starts off with the lexical construction set and reaches its goal (cf. the bold search node) when the last morpho-syntactic construction could apply. In order for the modal meaning to propagate, it is important that the modal construction set precedes other grammatical constructions (argument structure, agreement, word order) in both processing directions. Since the modal construction first groups modal auxiliary and main verb, argument structure and agreement constructions can then use use the values of the modal verb phrase as its input and propagate them further in the clause.

Note that the order of application of the argument structure and agreement constructions is reversed in parsing. This is a consequence of the fact that in

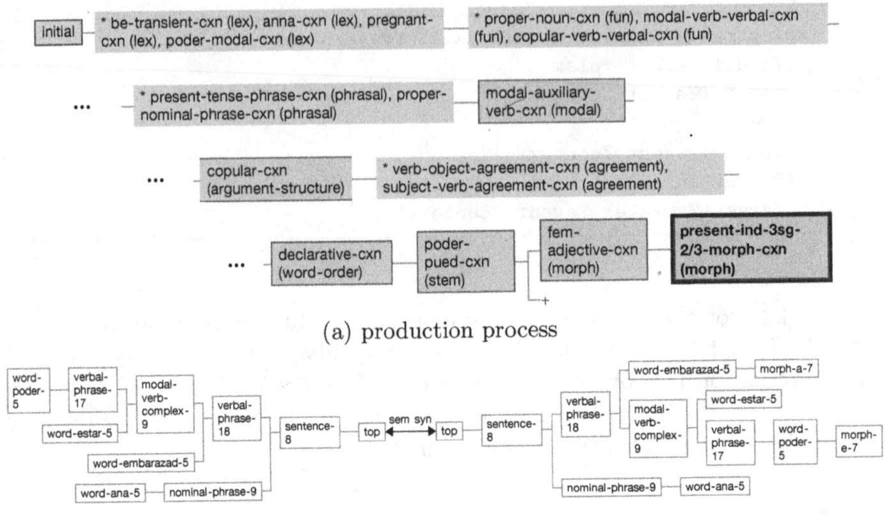

Fig. 2. Search process and resulting linguistic structure for the production of Sentence (9). 18 different constructions applied to build the resulting linguistic structure that contains the utterance: "Ana puede estar embarazada".

production, the argument structure relations are provided by the semantic representation and need to be translated into agreement feature matrices in order to express the appropriate form. In parsing, the process starts from the form side, so that the available agreement information needs to be converted into argument structure relations.

Figure 2b shows the final linguistic structure that has been built during the production process. The semantic and syntactic pole are symmetric with each a sentence unit directly under the top unit, which has a nominal phrase (subject: 'Ana') and a verbal phrase as its constituents (predicate: 'puede estar embarazada'). The verbal phrase unit then comprises the main verbal complex ('puede estar') and its complement ('embarazada'). It is through feature percolation that the agreement values (number and gender) of the adjectival complement are synchronized with the subject's. The same goes for the agreement information needed for conjugation of the verb (person and number).

The processing of Sentence (10) proceeds in a similar fashion. Since the modal is an adverb and not an auxiliary anymore, it is the main verb 'estar' that receives the conjugational ending this time. The following slight difference in the meaning representations of Sentences (9) and (10) is responsible for this processing effect: `(event-overlaps speaker-1 time-1)` vs. `(event-overlaps event-1 time-1)`. In the sentence with the modal auxiliary, it is the speaker constant that is linked to the present time span. Since the modal auxiliary construction `poder-modal-cxn` also guarantees such a speaker link (see above) while the `be-transient-cxn` does not, it is assured that the present tense construction inserts conjugational information to the appropriate unit. Since the semantic difference between the use of a modal auxiliary and a modal adverb only becomes visible in the phrasal constructions, that is, after the lexical constructions have been processed, there are always two main branches in the search tree. One branch will finally fail in re-entrance, because the `event-overlaps` variables do not correspond.

5 Modal Scope

Section 4 has shown that the indicative is the default mood that modal constructions assign to the finite verb form of a clause. The current section shows how this default can be overridden through the application of an additional modal construction that has *scope* over the indicative verb form. The sentence that illustrates this scoping process builds further on Example Sentence (9):

(11) *Dudo* *que* *Ana* ***pueda*** *estar*
doubt-(1sg.ind.pres) that anna could-(3sg.subj.pres) be.temp(inf)
embarazada.
pregnant.

I doubt that Anna could be pregnant.

This sentence demonstrates the use of the third most common linguistic expression of modality (see Section 4): *mental state predicates.* A mental state predicate ('dudo' in (11)) is a cognition verb in the first person singular present that expresses the speaker's degree of certainty toward the realization of the proposition (following or preceding this predicate). In the first position of a sentence, mental state predicates are always followed by a complementizer such as "that" in English or "que" in Spanish.

First, we update the construction inventory with two new constructions: a lexical construction for the cognition verb 'dudar' and a grammatical construction that takes care of the scoping relation. The lexical construction takes the verbal infinitive (without 'que') as its form. Its meaning representation includes two additional predicates compared to the previous modal meanings:

```
(speaker ?speaker ?base-set)
(judgement ?evaluation ?speaker ?proposition)
(proposition ?proposition ?event))
(qual-strength ?evaluation unlikelihood)
(evidence ?proposition personal-knowledge)
(responsibility ?speaker ?evaluation)
```

The `evidence` predicate indicates the evidential source the speaker used to make his evaluation of the proposition 'Ann is pregnant'. In the case of 'dudar' ('to doubt'), this evidence stems from personal knowledge of the speaker. The last predicate relates the responsibility of the evaluation and its impact to the realm of the speaker.

The grammatical construction that regulates the use of a subjunctive mood in the subordinated clause that depends on a mental state predicate is characterized by three main tasks:

- guaranteeing a scoping relation between the evaluation of the mental state predicate 'dudo' and the modal subordinated clause 'ana pueda estar embarazada'
- adding agreement and valency features for a 1st person singular agent (speaker)
- providing the complementizer 'que'.

Scoping has an effect on both structural poles of the transient structure. On the semantic side, this construction is responsible for the variable linking of speaker, event, proposition, context and time variables in the subordinated clause and the mental state predicate. The evaluation variables are kept different, since we are dealing with a second evaluation ('dudo que') of an earlier evaluation ('puede estar'). On the syntactic side, the clausal mood feature (`tam`) is set to subjunctive mood. Since the mood feature already had a specified value, this value needs to be "overridden". This is done with help of the -> operator:

```
(tam (==1 (-> (subjunctive - - - -)
              (subjunctive + ?subj-past ?subj-present ?subj-fut))
          (-> (indicative + ?ind-past ?ind-present ?ind-fut)
              (indicative - - - -)))
```

The semantics of the overrides operator are specified as follows: `(-> original-value new-value)`. The subjunctive value was already set to – by the modal construction that operated in the subordinated clause, but it is now replaced by the subjunctive mood (any tense). The indicative feature receives the previous value of the subjunctive feature.

The syntactic pole of the resulting linguistic structure of parsing sentence (11) is visualized by Figure 3. Processing the mental state predicate has lead to a considerable increase in structural complexity. A sentence unit now unites the subordinated clause (`clause-489`) and the mental state predicate (`verbal-phrase-2927`). The complementizer 'que' is present in the structure as a subunit of the `verbal-phrase-2927` unit. The scoping construction only changes the mood feature values in the `clause-489`, since they are automatically percolated among all children that carry such a feature. Eventually, this results in the presence of the subjunctive '-a' marker that the stem 'pued' receives, as opposed to a default indicative '-e' marker.

Another frequent example of overriding the default mood feature is the fronting of a modal auxiliary such as in:

(12)	***Posiblemente***	*Ana*	*esté*	*embarazada.*
	possibly	anna	be.temp(3sg.subj.pres)	pregnant.

Possibly Anna is pregnant.

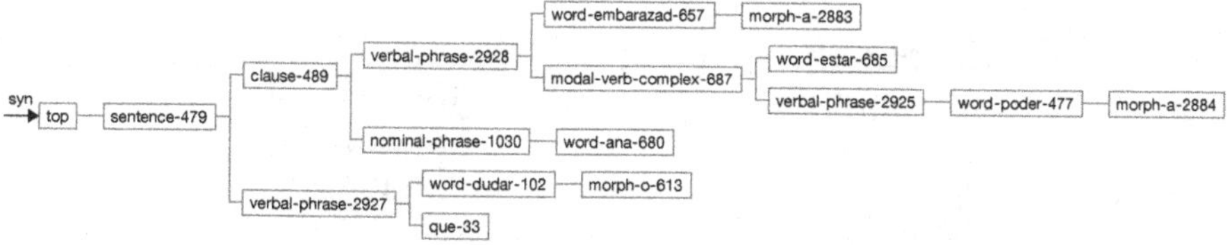

Fig. 3. The syntactic pole of the final transient structure after parsing "Dudo que Ana está embarazada"

Also here, the modal is not part of the clause that expresses the proposition but precedes it and can thereby influence the use of the subjunctive mood. Note that in this case, the modal has a direct influence on the presentation of the proposition itself, whereas the example of the mental state predicate 'dudo que' showed that there can also be an influence on another modal expression.

6 Robustness

Modality is generally a domain that has not been explored very much in implementations of grammar formalizations. This is probably due to the fact that it is an extreme example of an open-ended system, which has a negative effect on the robustness of the formalization. There are two main issues to consider when making a modal grammar more solid toward internal and external incongruencies:

1. The exact semantic representation of a modal expression can vary across speakers and between linguistic communities, since modality concerns personal judgements of individual language users. Moreover, depending on the situation, the choice of verbal mood for a particular proposition might differ.
2. Due to deviating meanings, the modal forms that are parsed by a hearer dot not always conform to his or her constructional knowledge. This happens when the speaker is being innovative, when he belongs to a different linguistic community or when he speaks carelessly.

In terms of semantic robustness, a single user grammar does not really encounter the issue of variable semantic representations across speakers. There is only one speaker, which is the system itself. It is only in multi-agent experiments that make use of FCG, where semantic representations are built by every agent individually. Nevertheless, once semantic representations are constructed from grounded scenes, discrete modal categories such as qualitative strength, have to be replaced by continuous values.

Syntactic robustness is a different issue. Previous FCG research on robust parsing has focused on unknown words and coercion (for an overview see [10]).

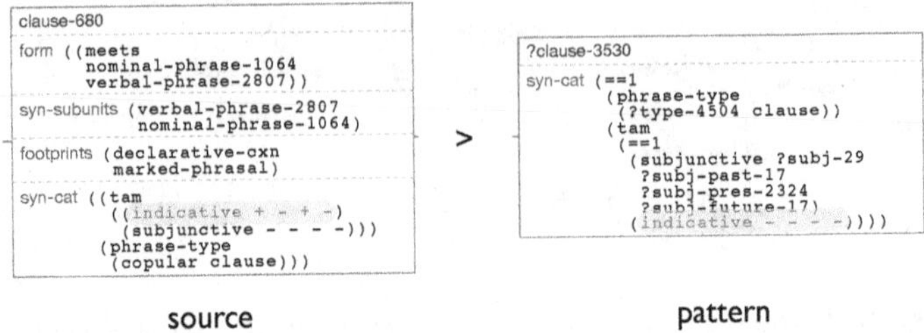

Fig. 4. In parsing the marked sentence "Dudo que Ana está embarazada", the source unit of the transient structure (left) is matched with the pattern unit of the `mental-state-predicate-cxn` (right). The match fails since the values of the indicative feature do not correspond: the source unit contains a present indicative mood, while the pattern expects a subjunctive mood.

The most straightforward deviating use of a modal expression, is an unexpected mood marker: the subjunctive instead of the indicative or reversed. Take the following mood alternation:

(13) *Dudo* *que* *Ana* *esté* *embarazada.*
doubt-(1sg.ind.pres) that anna be.temp-(3sg.subj.pres) pregnant.
I doubt that Anna is pregnant. (default reading)

(14) *Dudo* *que* *Ana* *está* *embarazada.*
doubt-(1sg.ind.pres) that anna be.temp-(3sg.ind.pres) pregnant.
I doubt that Anna is pregnant. (marked reading)

Sentence (13) illustrates the default use of the mood marker that follows a mental state predicate which expresses a high degree of uncertainty: the subjunctive ("-e" in "esté"). Parsing this sentence with the construction inventory that supports this case study, leads to a successful parsing process with 20 search nodes and a single search branch, the goal node being the scope construction `mental-state-predicate-cxn`. Now, parsing the marked mood marker in the subordinate clause, that is the indicative "-a", results in an explosion of the search space: 18 search branches with each 19 nodes and no correct solution found. The reason for this is the lacking of the twentieth node, namely that of the scope construction.

The FCG inspector tells us that there was no match between the transient structure after the 19th construction has applied and the scope construction. Figure 4 shows that the match failed exactly because of the presence of the indicative mood feature in the transient structure (source), whereas the scope construction (pattern) requires a subjunctive feature (of any tense).

The traditional FCG solution to such a problem in processing, is to create a diagnostic that notifies the mismatch in mood and then instantiate a repair process that adjusts the mood in the clausal unit. The diagnostics and repairs form part of the so-called 'meta-layer' in processing. On top of the routine processing layer, diagnostics check whether there has been some unexpected processing result, and if so, they call on a series of repair methods to solve the problem and continue regular processing.

7 Conclusion and Outlook

This paper has presented basic insights into the operationalization of modal constructions and their organization in terms of processing efficiency. Modal constructions are best processed before other grammatical constructions can apply so that the latter take over the modal values left in the verb unit by the former. Scope constructions (mental state predicates) are processed at the end of the grammatical construction batch. In production, this is right before morpho-syntactic constructions start to fill in the appropriate marker forms. A scope construction can thus modify a mood value left by the modal constructions and processed by the grammatical ones at the very last moment.

Since all the modal constructions that have been introduced in this paper work on verbal units, also the Spanish conjugational paradigm had to be captured in FCG constructions. A considerable degree of syncretism (same form shared across multiple functions) and variation in verbal stem morphology has been reported and covered by the current implementation. The use of the `==1` operator in the morpho-syntactic templates and the introduction of stem templates that translate infinitives into stems and reversely have been essential in this process.

The importance of building robust grammars has been pointed at through the incorporation of the parsing process of a sentence with an indicative subordinate clause where a subjunctive was expected. The FCG meta-layer has proved to be a valuable processing extension to capture unusual language use. By means of a repair strategy that modified the matching pattern of the modal construction, processing can be continued from the point where an earlier problem had been reported.

The goal of this paper has been to present a feasibility study on the implementation of modal expressions in FCG. The potential of such an implementation has become clear throughout the different sections. Nevertheless, an expansion of the current test grammar within the domain of epistemic modality (more modals, more sentences) as well as toward a wider application of modality (evidentials, event modality) is in order. The implementation of more modal systems that cover a number of different languages can offer a better understanding of the current Spanish test grammar.

Acknowledgements. This research was conducted at the Vrije Universiteit Brussel, financed by a strategic basic research grant (IWT-489) from the agency for Innovation by Science and Technology (IWT). Additional funding came from the European research project ALEAR (FP7, ICT-214856). Apart from the members of our team in Brussels and at the Sony CSL lab in Paris, I especially want to thank Johan van der Auwera (University of Antwerp) for his help in my quest for the right modal terminology.

References

[1] Baerman, M.: Syncretism. Language and Linguistics Compass 1(5), 539–551 (2007)
[2] Beuls, K.: Construction sets and unmarked forms: A case study for Hungarian verbal agreement. In: Steels, L. (ed.) Design Patterns in Fluid Construction Grammar. John Benjamins, Amsterdam (2011)
[3] De Beule, J., Steels, L.: Hierarchy in Fluid Construction Grammars. In: Furbach, U. (ed.) KI 2005. LNCS (LNAI), vol. 3698, pp. 1–15. Springer, Heidelberg (2005)
[4] Gerasymova, K., Steels, L., van Trijp, R.: Aspectual morphology of Russian verbs in Fluid Construction Grammar. In: Taatgen, N., van Rijn, H. (eds.) Proceedings of the 31th Annual Conference of the Cognitive Science Society, pp. 1370–1375. Cognitive Science Society (2009)
[5] Höfer, S.: Complex Declension Systems and Morphology in Fluid Construction Grammar: A Case Study of Polish. In: Steels, L. (ed.) Computational Issues in FCG. LNCS (LNAI), vol. 7249, pp. 143–177. Springer, Heidelberg (2012)
[6] Nuyts, J.: Epistemic Modality, Language and Conceptualization. John Benjamins, Amsterdam (2001)
[7] Palmer, F.: Mood and Modality. Cambridge University Press, Cambridge (2001)
[8] Steels, L., De Beule, J., Neubauer, N.: Linking in Fluid Construction Grammars. In: Proceedings of BNAIC, pp. 11–18. Transactions of the Belgian Royal Society of Arts and Sciences, Brussels (2005)
[9] Steels, L.: A design pattern for phrasal constructions. In: Steels, L. (ed.) Design Patterns in Fluid Construction Grammar. John Benjamins, Amsterdam (2011)
[10] Steels, L., van Trijp, R.: How to make construction grammars fluid and robust. In: Steels, L. (ed.) Design Patterns in Fluid Construction Grammar. John Benjamins, Amsterdam (2011)
[11] van Trijp, R.: Argumentsstruktur in der Fluid Construction Grammar. In: Fischer, K., Stefanowitsch, A. (eds.) Konstruktionsgrammatik II: Von der Konstruktion zur Grammatik, Stauffenburg Linguistik, vol. 47. Stauffenburg Verlag, Tübingen (2008)
[12] van Trijp, R., Steels, L., Beuls, K., Wellens, P.: Fluid construction grammar: The new kid on the block. In: Proceedings of the 13th Conference of the European Chapter of the Association for Computational Linguistics. ACL, Avignon (2012)
[13] van Trijp, R.: Feature matrices and agreement: A case study for German case. In: Steels, L. (ed.) Design Patterns in Fluid Construction Grammar. John Benjamins, Amsterdam (2011)

Complex Declension Systems and Morphology in Fluid Construction Grammar: A Case Study of Polish

Sebastian Höfer

Robotics and Biology Laboratory, Technische Universität Berlin, Germany

Abstract. Different languages employ different strategies for grammatical agreement. Slavic languages such as Polish realize agreement with rich declension systems. The Polish declension system features seven cases, two number categories and is subdivided further with respect to gender and animacy. In order to differentiate among these different grammatical categories Polish exhibits a complex, syncretistic and highly irregular morphology. But not only the morphology is complex, the grammatical rules that govern agreement are, too. For example, the appropriate case of a noun in a verbal phrase does not only depend on the verb itself but also on whether the verb is in the scope of a negation or not.

In this paper we give an implementation of the Polish declension system in Fluid Construction Grammar. In order to account for the complexity of the Polish declension system we develop a unification-based formalism, called *nested feature matrices*. To demonstrate the power of the proposed formalism we investigate its appropriateness for solving the following linguistic problems: a) selecting appropriate morphological markers with respect to the noun's gender and stem for expressing case and number, b) establishing phrasal agreement between nouns and other parts of speech such as verbs, and finally c) dealing with long-distance dependencies in phrasal agreement. We show that our formalism succeeds in solving these problems and that the presented implementation is fully operational for correctly parsing and producing simple Polish transitive sentences.

1 Introduction

Developing computational models for Slavic languages is very beneficial for understanding language in general, as Slavic languages exhibit many complex grammatical and morphological structures that English and other Western European languages lack. A particularly intriguing part of Slavic languages is their declension system. The Polish declension system, for instance, features seven cases, two number categories and is subdivided further with respect to gender and animacy. In order to differentiate among these different grammatical categories Polish exhibits a complex, syncretistic and highly irregular morphology.

L. Steels (Ed.): Computational Issues in FCG, LNAI 7249, pp. 143–177, 2012.

But not only the morphology is complex, the grammatical rules that govern agreement are, too. For example, the appropriate case of a noun in a verbal phrase does not only depend on the verb itself but also on whether the verb is in the scope of a negation or not.

Due to their inherent linguistic complexity, there has been growing interest in formalizing Slavic languages in computational grammar theories in recent years [3, 19]. One of the currently most prominent grammar formalisms is Head-Driven Phrase Structure grammar (HPSG) [17] and therefore most of the Slavic community focussed on the implementation of Slavic languages theories in this formalism.

In this paper, the implementation of different aspects of the Polish noun declension system in Fluid Construction Grammar (FCG) is presented. The main purpose is to show that the FCG formalism provides a uniform way of dealing with the Polish declension system at the morphological, syntactical and semantical level. In order to account for the complexity of the Polish declension system we develop a unification-based formalism, called *nested feature matrices*. To demonstrate the power of the proposed formalism we investigate its appropriateness for solving the following linguistic problems: a) selecting appropriate morphological markers with respect to the noun's gender and stem for expressing case and number, b) establishing phrasal agreement between nouns and other parts of speech such as verbs, and finally c) dealing with long-distance dependencies in phrasal agreement in terms of a weak form of the so-called long distance genitive of negation. We show that our formalism succeeds in solving these problems and that the presented implementation is fully operational for correctly parsing and producing simple Polish transitive sentences.

The work presented in this paper builds upon many studies concerning the operationalization of lexical, phrasal and morphological constructions in FCG. It follows the FCG design pattern approach presented in this volume [25], and shares the implementation of morphological constructions with operationalizations of Hungarian verbs [1], Spanish modals [2] and Russian verbal aspect [12]. Furthermore, we develop an extension of the feature matrix formalism which has been originally introduced in [27] for dealing with syncretisms in the German declension system.

As the Slavic community has conducted a lot of work on the implementation of Slavic linguistic phenomena in HPSG, the reader might also refer to another chapter in this volume presenting FCGLight [7]. This formalism makes a link between HPSG and FCG by implementing a core subset of the latter in LIGHT, a system previously used for the implementation of large-scale HPSG grammars [5]. Another related study on a Slavic language example in FCG which deals with verbal aspect in Romanian can be found in [6].

The remainder of this paper is structured as follows: first, the linguistic problems addressed in this paper are explained. Next, feature matrices and nested feature matrices are introduced, which constitute the core formalism used to model the declension system and establish agreement on the morphological and syntactic level. Finally, the operationalization of the Polish case study in FCG is presented, and the results are summarized and evaluated.

2 Linguistic Insights

This case study presents a formalization of the Polish noun declension system, the so-called genitive of negation and the long distance genitive of negation. The main part of the implementation deals with morphological aspects of the Polish noun declension system, and, in particular, how this complex system can be represented in FCG in a uniform manner. The long distance genitive of negation phenomenon is considered in order to illustrate that FCG is also suitable for the operationalization of long distance dependencies. In order to grasp the implementational details of the formalism presented later, some linguistic background on these phenomena is required which is provided in the following section.

2.1 Polish Noun Declension System

Nominal inflections in Polish conflate two grammatical categories: case and number. There are seven cases (nominate, genitive, dative, accusative, instrumental, locative and vocative) and two numbers (singular and plural). Additionally, Polish nouns are traditionally divided into three inflectional paradigms or *declension schemes* in terms of the three genders (masculine, feminine, neuter). However, the paradigms are not entirely consistent; for almost every case and number there exist several endings, and the appropriate ending depends mainly on the morphological and syntactic properties of the noun. Therefore the number of distinct paradigms is very large [16]. Things get even more complicated, since some nouns can have two different endings in the genitive case, depending on the meaning that a speaker wants to express.

Let us look at an example in order to illustrate the complexity of the Polish declension system. Consider the following examples, which deal with the two masculine nouns *przypadek* (case) and *człowiek* (man):

(1)

W	*żadnym*	***przypadku***	*nie*	*znajdziemy*	*całej*	*prawdy*
In	no.LOC	case.LOC	not	(we) find	whole.GEN	truth.GEN
o	***człowieku.***					
about	man.LOC					

'In no case do we find out the whole truth about mankind.'

This example shows that *-u* is a marker for the locative case for masculine nouns, and indeed it is so quite consistently. The next examples consider the *-a* ending:

(2) *Nie ma ani jednego* ***człowieka.***
Not is even one.GEN man.GEN
'There is not even one man.'

(3) *Widzę jednego* ***człowieka.***
(I) see one.ACC man.ACC.
'I see one man.'

(4) *Przyimek 'zamiast' wymaga użycia drugiego* ***przypadka.***
Preposition.NOM 'zamiast' requires usage.GEN second.GEN case.GEN
'The preposition 'zamiast' requires usage of the second case.'

(5) *Pierwszy raz widzę taki* ***przypadek.***
first time (I) see such.ACC case.ACC
'It is the first time that I see such a case.'

The first thing to be noticed is that the ending -*a* occurs with both nouns, but not always in the same cases. The examples 2 and 4 suggest that -*a* serves as a marker for genitive. However, things are more complicated: as seen in example 3, the accusative of *człowiek* corresponds to its genitive, that is, it takes the -*a* too. On the other hand, the accusative of *przypadek* corresponds to its nominative and is therefore unmarked. Why is this so? As a rule of thumb, nouns that denote virile (masculine-human) individuals agree in the genitive and the accusative case, while nouns denoting non-animate objects agree in nominative and accusative. Therefore, in many Polish textbooks the masculine gender is subdivided into three: virile (animate and personal), animate (and not personal) and impersonal. In current Polish language the amount of nouns following the virile scheme is steadily expanding [16]; particularly neologisms like *email* follow the virile declension scheme and therefore exhibit the -*a* marker in accusative, although they denote inanimate objects.

Yet, the whole issue of the declension scheme becomes even more puzzling, as the following example shows:

(6) *Nie było takiego* ***przypadku*** *choroby.*
Not was such.GEN case.GEN illness.GEN.
'There was no such case of illness.'

The noun *przypadek* is an example from a small group of nouns which can take either -*a* or -*u* in the genitive case. Whether one or the other ending is preferred sometimes depends on idiomatic use. In this case it depends on the intended meaning of the word: if the grammatical case is meant, as in example 4, the noun takes the -*a* marking. If a certain circumstance or fact is to be expressed, the -*u* marking is used. See, for example, [10] for an extensive discussion of the distribution of the two endings in genitive masculine.

Table 1 exemplifies in which cases the ending *-a* can actually occur. It shows that the marker is completely independent from the grammatical categories case, number and gender.

Table 1. The ending *-a* occurs across different cases, genders and numbers. An example of a noun form is given for each of the possible entries occurrences of the ending. The nominative singular forms of the inflected nouns are *książe* (duke), *pole* (field), *człowiek* (man) and *cud* (miracle).

-a	SG			PL		
Case	**SG-M**	**SG-F**	**SG-N**	**PL-M**	**PL-F**	**PL-N**
NOM	*sędzia* (judge)	*dziewczyna* (girl)	–	*książa* (dukes)	–	*pola* (fields)
GEN	*człowieka* (man)	–	*pola* (field)	–	–	–
DAT	–	–	–	–	–	–
ACC	*człowieka*	–	–	*cuda* (miracles)	–	*pola*
INS	–	–	–	–	–	–
LOC	–	–	–	–	–	–
VOC	–	–	–	–	–	*pola*

Stem Palatalization. As in many other Slavic languages, during the evolution of Polish several sound changes subsumed under the term *palatalization* occurred. In this process mid, close front vowels (e.g. /i/, /e/) and the semi-vowel /j/ shift nearby phonemes, usually preceding consonants, towards the palatal articulatory position. There exist several types of palatalization, such as the so-called *iotation*, as in the occurrence of the *i* in *nie* (no / not) results in changing the sound of /n/ to /ɲ/. In Polish, the /ɲ/ phoneme is represented by *ni* in the beginning and by *ń* in the end of a syllable. Consider, for example, *dzień* (day) and *nie*, which both contain this very same phoneme.

The Polish declension system includes two palatalizing endings denoted by *-'e* and *-'i*. The way the stem of a noun is changed depends on the stem or the stem consonant of a noun, respectively. Hence, consider for example the changes that occur in feminine nouns that exhibit the *-'e* in the dative singular case: *ryba* becomes *rybie* (fish), *łąka* becomes *łące* (meadow), *skóra* becomes *skórze*, etc. There do exist reliable rules as to how palatalization affects nearby phonemes. For a more complete analysis see, for example, [13].

Note that the non-palatalizing counterparts *-e* and *-i* also appear in the declension scheme, for example, the dative singular of the noun *szansa* (chance) takes the palatalized ending and becomes *szansie*, but the noun's nominative plural is *szanse*.

In any case, this brief analysis shows that beside the support for parsing and production of nouns and their endings, an operationalization of the Polish declension scheme must also account for changes which affect the stem of a noun.

2.2 Genitive of Negation

Another interesting grammatical phenomenon in Slavic languages, including Polish, is the so-called *genitive of negation (GoN)*. The phenomenon can be explained as follows: in the presence of verbal negation, the genitive case is assigned to the argument of the verb if the verb requires the argument to take the accusative in the absence of negation. The following example demonstrates that the case of the accusative object needs to be changed due to the appearance of the negative marker *nie*:

(7) *Michał* *widzi* ***Marię.***
Michael.NOM sees Maria.ACC
'Michael sees Maria.'

(8) *Michał* *nie* *widzi* ***Marii.***
Michael.NOM not sees Maria.GEN
'Michael does not see Maria.'

Note that the GoN only applies to accusative objects:

(9) *Michał* *macha* ***patykiem.***
Michael.NOM waves stick.INS.
'Michael waves the stick.'

(10) *Michał* *nie* *macha* ***patykiem.***
Michael.NOM not sees stick.INS
'Michael does not wave the stick.'

Moreover, the GoN does not only affect finite verb forms but also non-finite verb forms such as infinitivals and participles.

Whereas in languages such as Russian, the application of GoN is not obligatory but often depends on pragmatic, semantic or idiosyncratic factors, GoN in Polish is fully grammaticalized, that is, it is triggered by the morphosyntactic structure of the negative marker *nie*.[1]

2.3 Long Distance GoN

An interesting property of the GoN in Polish is that it appears even in cases where the *nie* does not negate the verb directly, but only a verb higher in the hierarchical structure of the sentence [18]. This is illustrated in the following example, where the negation applies to the auxiliary verb but still causes the object of the infinitival to take genitive case:

---

[1] However, as already noted in [4], there exist some exceptional cases in Polish where the GoN is indeed optional, for example [18]:

Marię / Marii *nie boli* *głowa.*
(11) Maria.ACC / Maria.GEN not aches head.NOM
'Maria does not have a headache.'

(12) *Michał* *nie* *chce* *widzieć* ***Marii.***
Michael.NOM not want see Maria.GEN
'Michael does not want to see Maria.'

This phenomenon is discussed in more detail in [18] and additional cases are presented where the long distance GoN is not obligatory or is singled out by Polish native speakers. In the following analysis, a simple example consisting of an auxiliary and an infinitival as shown above is considered. In spite of its simplicity, it reflects well how long distance relationships can be handled in FCG.

3 Feature Matrices

The previous section demonstrated the need for an efficient formalism that is able to account for the complexity of the presented declension system. The approach in this paper is based on *feature matrices* which constitute a solely unification based method for handling syncretisms in terms of case, gender and number distinctions [27]. Common accounts for the issue of case syncretism involve *disjunctive feature representations* which represent the multifunctionality by disjunctions, i.e. alternatives. Let us contrast the two approaches with an example and consider the representations for the proper name *Maria* and the *-a* ending. To be more precise, not the feature matrix of *Maria*, but only of its stem *Mari-* is considered, since the former already is a combination of a noun stem with an ending. The noun stem can be represented by the following concise disjunctive feature representation:

Mari-:

$$\begin{bmatrix} \text{GENDER} & f \\ \text{NUM} & sg \\ \text{CASE} & nom \vee gen \vee dat \vee acc \vee ins \vee loc \vee voc \end{bmatrix}$$

Since *Mari-* is considered a noun stem, all cases are allowed and have to be specified either by being left unmarked or by acquiring a suffix. Because *Maria* is a female proper name, this example assumes that it only occurs in the singular case. The representation for the ending *-a* looks as follows:

-a:

$$\begin{bmatrix} \text{GENDER} & m \\ \text{NUM} & sg \\ \text{CASE} & nom \vee gen \vee acc \end{bmatrix} \vee \begin{bmatrix} \text{GENDER} & m \\ \text{NUM} & pl \\ \text{CASE} & nom \vee acc \end{bmatrix} \vee$$
$$\begin{bmatrix} \text{GENDER} & f \\ \text{NUM} & pl \\ \text{CASE} & nom \end{bmatrix} \vee \begin{bmatrix} \text{GENDER} & n \\ \text{NUM} & sg \\ \text{CASE} & gen \end{bmatrix} \vee \begin{bmatrix} \text{GENDER} & n \\ \text{NUM} & pl \\ \text{CASE} & nom \vee acc \end{bmatrix}$$

The respective feature matrix representation for *Mari-* is shown in Table 2.

Table 2.

Mari-		SG			PL		
Case	**C**	**SG-M**	**SG-F**	**SG-N**	**PL-M**	**PL-F**	**PL-N**
NOM	*?n*	*?n-sg-m*	*?n-sg-f*	–	*?n-pl-m*	–	*?n-pl-n*
GEN	*?g*	*?g-sg-m*	–	*?g-s-n*	–	–	–
DAT	–	–	–	–	–	–	–
ACC	*?a*	*?a-sg-m*	–	–	*?a-pl-m*	–	*?a-pl-n*
INS	–	–	–	–	–	–	–
LOC	–	–	–	–	–	–	–
VOC	*?v*	*?v-sg-m*	–	–	–	–	*?v-pl-n*

Table 3 shows the feature matrix for the ending *-a* which can directly be read from Table 1 on page 147.

Table 3.

-a		SG			PL		
Case	**C**	**SG-M**	**SG-F**	**SG-N**	**PL-M**	**PL-F**	**PL-N**
NOM	*?n*	*?n-sg-m*	*?n-sg-f*	–	*?n-pl-m*	–	*?n-pl-n*
GEN	*?g*	*?g-sg-m*	–	*?g-s-n*	–	–	–
DAT	–	–	–	–	–	–	–
ACC	*?a*	*?a-sg-m*	–	–	*?a-pl-m*	–	*?a-pl-n*
INS	–	–	–	–	–	–	–
LOC	–	–	–	–	–	–	–
VOC	*?v*	*?v-sg-m*	–	–	–	–	*?v-pl-n*

In the given feature matrix representations, strings preceded by a quotation mark denote *variables* which can be bound during the unification process to either '–', '+', or other variables. As opposed to variables, strings without quotation marks are called *symbols*, such as 'NOM', '–' and '+'. Additionally, the matrix cells contained in the columns beginning with the *SG-M* column are called *feature cells*. The symbol '–' occurring in a feature cell means that the particular case-gender-number combination is not possible for the linguistic item. A variable displays the possibility of this combination, and the '+' symbol makes a final commitment, determining the grammatical categories of the item. The upcoming example shows how a well-formed feature matrix should look and how feature matrix unification works.

Whereas disjunctive features prove elegant in easily separable cases without intermingling categories like for the form *Mari-*, they obviously do not form a very compact representation for irregular systems as the Polish case system, as can be seen for the *-a* ending. Feature matrices, on the other hand, may be fairly sparse for very specific linguistic items. However, disjunctions were proven to be computationally expensive [11]. Moreover, unification of disjunctive features is, in general, NP-complete [20]. In contrast, feature matrix unification is a rather simple task in terms of computational effort. Unification based processing of disjunctive features cannot be covered in detail at this point, since this paper concentrates solely on feature matrices. For a more detailed comparison, see [27].

Let us take a look at the unification result of the feature matrices for *Mari-* and *-a*. What exactly happens during unification? The formal details of unification and merging in FCG are given in [9], however, an intuitive notion of unification of feature matrices is given in the following.

Table 4.

Mari-a		SG			PL		
Case	**C**	**SG-M**	**SG-F**	**SG-N**	**PL-M**	**PL-F**	**PL-N**
NOM	*?n-sg-f*	–	*?n-sg-f*	–	–	–	–
GEN	–	–	–	–	–	–	–
DAT	–	–	–	–	–	–	–
ACC	–	–	–	–	–	–	–
INS	–	–	–	–	–	–	–
LOC	–	–	–	–	–	–	–
VOC	–	–	–	–	–	–	–

All cells of both matrices are compared pairwise, that is, the cell in row i, column j from the first matrix is compared to the cell in row i, column j from the second matrix. If both cells contain symbols (in this case a string like 'NOM', '–' or '+'), they must be identical; if one cell contains a variable and the other a symbol, the variable is bound to this symbol – if the variable is not bound to another symbol yet. Similarly, if both cells contain variables, the first variable is bound to the second one. Thus, for example, the variable *?n-sg-m* from the *-a*-matrix is bound to '–', since this is the value of the corresponding cell in the *Mari-* matrix. Obviously, as shown in Table 4 the right solution is obtained, because all possibilities except nominative singular feminine get sorted out this way.

At this point, the role of the matrix's second column, *C*, has not yet been explained. The *C* actually stands for *case* and will be called the *case column*. In order to understand what that case column does, let us take a look at the resulting *Mari-a* matrix in Table 4 again. The feature cell corresponding to nominative singular feminine contains the same variable *?n-sg-f* as the cell in the *C* column in the nominative row. That means that if *?n-sg-f* is bound to '+' or '–', both cells are affected. It was mentioned before that a '+' would signal full commitment; obviously, the result is unique, but why does no '+' occur in the resulting matrix then? The reason is that neither of the two linguistic items, neither the noun stem nor the suffix, can make a definite commitment for a case on its own. Assuming that the *-a* ending would only occur in nominative, there would be a '+' in the nominative case column of the *-a* feature matrix, and this '+' would also make its way into the result matrix through unification.

Whether to put a '+' in a feature cell, too, depends on the number of alternatives in this row: if the item can mark singular and plural or different genders, there would be variables like before. Otherwise, if a specific case-gender commitment could be made, there would be a '+' in the corresponding column as well.

Although in the *Mari-a* example no final commitment in terms of '+'s could be made, it is not harmful in practice when constructions that commit to case are involved. This is illustrated by the following sentence:

(13) *Maria* *śpi.*
Maria.NOM sleeps.
'Maria sleeps / is sleeping.'

In parsing or producing this sentence the construction for the verb *śpi* would contain a feature matrix for phrasal agreement, which would specify the case of the subject (also usually including feature matrices for the cases of potential objects, shown later). The verb's feature matrix related to the subject or agent in this phrase is shown in Table 5.

Table 5.

śpi $_{Subject}$		**SG**			**PL**		
Case	**C**	**SG-M**	**SG-F**	**SG-N**	**PL-M**	**PL-F**	**PL-N**
NOM	+	*?n-sg-m*	*?n-sg-f*	*?n-sg-n*	*?n-pl-m*	*?n-pl-f*	*?n-pl-n*
GEN	–	–	–	–	–	–	–
DAT	–	–	–	–	–	–	–
ACC	–	–	–	–	–	–	–
INS	–	–	–	–	–	–	–
LOC	–	–	–	–	–	–	–
VOC	–	–	–	–	–	–	–

Clearly evident, when the *śpi* $_{Subject}$ feature matrix and the *Mari-a* feature matrix are unified, the resulting matrix contains a '+' in the nominative case column and another '+' in the feature cell corresponding to nominative singular feminine. This example illustrates the purpose of the case column: the hypothesis is that information about the case comes from the wider context, such as a verb requiring its arguments to taking specific cases, while information about number and gender can be inferred from the noun or at least from a nominal phrase. The latter is the case for languages which mainly mark case by articles like German.

3.1 Limitations of Feature Matrices

The last section explained the basic idea and application mechanism of feature matrices. This section will show that the previously introduced feature matrix formalism is not flawless. However, the issues can be remedied by a canonical extension called *nested feature matrices* in the forthcoming section.

Revisiting the previous example, the *-a* is combined with a masculine noun, choosing *człowiek* (man), which is also a noun stem since the nominative case is unmarked here. For the sake of completeness, provided are both the feature matrix (Table 6) and the disjunctive feature representation for this noun:

człowiek:

$$\begin{bmatrix} \text{GENDER} & m \\ \text{NUM} & sg \vee pl \\ \text{CASE} & nom \vee gen \vee dat \vee acc \vee ins \vee loc \end{bmatrix}$$

Table 6.

człowiek		SG			PL		
Case	**C**	**SG-M**	**SG-F**	**SG-N**	**PL-M**	**PL-F**	**PL-N**
NOM	*?n*	*?n-sg-m*	–	–	*?n-pl-m*	–	–
GEN	*?g*	*?g-sg-m*	–	–	*?g-pl-m*	–	–
DAT	*?d*	*?d-sg-m*	–	–	*?d-pl-m*	–	–
ACC	*?a*	*?a-sg-m*	–	–	*?a-pl-m*	–	–
INS	*?i*	*?i-sg-m*	–	–	*?i-pl-m*	–	–
LOC	*?l*	*?l-sg-m*	–	–	*?l-pl-m*	–	–
VOC	*?v*	*?v-sg-m*	–	–	*?v-pl-m*	–	–

As before, the feature matrices for the noun stem and the ending *-a* whose feature matrix was shown in Table 3 are unified. The result is shown in Table 7.

Table 7.

człowiek-a		SG			PL		
Case	**C**	**SG-M**	**SG-F**	**SG-N**	**PL-M**	**PL-F**	**PL-N**
NOM	*?n*	*?n-sg-m*	–	–	*?n-pl-m*	–	–
GEN	*?g*	*?g-sg-m*	–	–	–	–	–
DAT	–	–	–	–	–	–	–
ACC	*?a*	*?a-sg-m*	–	–	–	*?a-pl-m*	–
INS	–	–	–	–	–	–	–
LOC	–	–	–	–	–	–	–
VOC	*?v*	*?v-sg-m*	–	–	*?v-pl-m*	–	–

Notice that there are many variables, thus many possibilities are still open. Next, *człowiek-a* is embedded into a full sentence:

(14) *Nie* *widzę* *człowieka.*
Not (I) see man.GEN
'I do not see the man.'

As known from Section 2.2, a negated verb calls for the genitive of negation, therefore *człowiek-a* definitely takes the genitive case. Suppose that *nie widzę* has a feature matrix for its direct object as in Table 5 (the subject matrix for *śpi*), but it contains a '+' and variables in the genitive row instead of the nominative row. If now the matrix for *człowiek-a* from Table 7 and the object feature matrix of *nie widzę* are unified, the resulting feature matrix looks as shown in Table 8.

Table 8.

(nie widzę) człowiek-a		**SG**			**PL**		
Case	**C**	**SG-M**	**SG-F**	**SG-N**	**PL-M**	**PL-F**	**PL-N**
NOM	–	–	–	–	–	–	–
GEN	+	*?g-sg-m*	–	–	–	–	–
DAT	–	–	–	–	–	–	–
ACC	–	–	–	–	–	–	–
INS	–	–	–	–	–	–	–
LOC	–	–	–	–	–	–	–
VOC	–	–	–	–	–	–	–

Something strange has occurred, namely that the case column and the feature cell for the genitive singular masculine do not match. Why did this happen? By checking all the feature matrices involved so far, it can be seen that none of these matrices contain the same variable in the genitive case column and the regarded feature cell. Therefore, these two cells cannot be related to each other in the final result. In fact, it is not possible for any matrices to make the genitive case column cell equal to a genitive feature cell since each matrix allows more than one possibility in the genitive case – although after the application of *all* the constructions, only one possibility remains.

The reader may wonder if this behavior poses an actual problem, which, unfortunately, indeed it does for production. In production processing goes the other way around, that is, first the phrase structure with its agreement and dependencies is processed, and the selection of the appropriate ending is made in the very end. Thus, before any ending is added to *człowiek*, the feature matrix looks like in Table 8. Now imagine that there are not one possible ending for the genitive but many different ones. To take a concrete example, let us look only at the genitive row of the feature matrix of the ending *-ów* which marks genitive and accusative plural masculine and neuter:

Now comes the problem: Although the ending *-ów* is not allowed for the masculine singular, its feature matrix unifies with the one from Table 8. More precisely, the variable *?g* will be bound to '+' and all others will be bound to '–'. The meaning of the resulting feature matrix can be read as "the linguistic

Case	**C**	**SG-M**	**SG-F**	**SG-N**	**PL-M**	**PL-F**	**PL-N**
GEN	*?g*	–	–	–	*?g-pl-m*	–	*?g-pl-n*

Table 9. A nested feature matrix for Polish

	SG				PL			
Case	**S**	**S-M**	**S-F**	**S-N**	**PL**	**PL-M**	**PL-F**	**PL-N**
?n	*?n-s*	*?n-s-m*	*?n-s-f*	*?n-s-n*	*?n-pl*	*?n-pl-m*	*?n-pl-f*	*?n-pl-n*
?g	*?g-s*	*?g-s-m*	*?g-s-f*	*?g-s-n*	*?g-pl*	*?g-pl-m*	*?g-pl-f*	*?g-pl-n*
?d	*?a-s*	*?a-s-m*	*?a-s-f*	*?a-s-n*	*?a-pl*	*?a-pl-m*	*?a-pl-f*	*?a-pl-n*
?a	*?d-s*	*?d-s-m*	*?d-s-f*	*?d-s-n*	*?d-pl*	*?d-pl-m*	*?d-pl-f*	*?d-pl-n*
?i	*?i-s*	*?i-s-m*	*?i-s-f*	*?i-s-n*	*?i-pl*	*?i-pl-m*	*?i-pl-f*	*?i-pl-n*
?l	*?l-s*	*?l-s-m*	*?l-s-f*	*?l-s-n*	*?l-pl*	*?l-pl-m*	*?l-pl-f*	*?l-pl-n*
?v	*?v-s*	*?v-s-m*	*?v-s-f*	*?v-s-n*	*?v-pl*	*?v-pl-m*	*?v-pl-f*	*?v-pl-n*

item takes the genitive case but has no gender and number" – which obviously does not make any sense for nouns in Polish[2].

3.2 Nested Feature Matrices

Before a way to solve the issue raised in the previous paragraphs is presented, the reason for the problem should be formulated in a more abstract way. As mentioned before, Polish knows three grammatical categories for nouns, case, gender and number. Thus, it can be stated that the grammatical category of a Polish noun is threefold or three-dimensional. A feature matrix, on the other hand, is in this sense only *two*-dimensional: the rows encode different cases, but the columns have to encode gender *and* number. Let us look at the feature matrix for *człowiek* in Table 6 again: the noun *człowiek* fully determines the gender, but this fact cannot be explicitly expressed in this formalism. The intuition is that a *gender column* or a *number column* are needed, which can be related to the feature cells.

In fact, this is the basic idea of *nested feature matrices.* Table 9 introduces two extra columns for number – of course gender could also be used, but then one more column would have to be added, since there are three genders but only two numbers. Now the trick is the following: if a construction containing a feature matrix can make a commitment to gender, it makes the gender column and the feature cell equal. Therefore, the nested version for *człowiek* appears as shown in Table 10. Of course, all of the other feature matrices have to be transformed to their nested versions as well.

Notice that also commitment to number can easily be modeled without the need for nesting number separately. The only requirement is to make the case and number columns equal.

In summary, in order for the resulting nested feature matrix to be well-formed and to uniquely determine case, feature and number of a syntactic form, for each of the syntactic categories, there must be at least one nested feature matrix that determines its value.

[2] In Polish, even indefinite pronouns like *nic* (nothing) have to be declined.

Table 10.

człowiek	SG				PL			
C	S	S-M	S-F	S-N	PL	PL-M	PL-F	PL-N
?n	*?n-s-m*	*?n-s-m*	–	–	*?n-pl-m*	*?n-pl-m*	–	–
?g	*?g-s-m*	*?g-s-m*	–	–	*?g-pl-m*	*?g-pl-m*	–	–
?d	*?a-s-m*	*?a-s-m*	–	–	*?a-pl-m*	*?a-pl-m*	–	–
?a	*?d-s-m*	*?d-s-m*	–	–	*?d-pl-m*	*?d-pl-m*	–	–
?i	*?i-s-m*	*?i-s-m*	–	–	*?i-pl-m*	*?i-pl-m*	–	–
?l	*?l-s-m*	*?l-s-m*	–	–	*?l-pl-m*	*?l-pl-m*	–	–
?v	*?v-s-m*	*?v-s-m*	–	–	*?v-pl-m*	*?v-pl-m*	–	–

To illustrate the whole application chain, let us look at the genitive row of the nested version of the *-a* ending (Table 11).

Table 11.

	SG				PL			
C	S	S-M	S-F	S-N	PL	PL-M	PL-F	PL-N
?g-sg	*?g-sg*	*?g-sg-m*	–	*?g-sg-n*	–	–	–	–

The commitment to number is expressed by using the same variable *?g-sg* in the case and the singular column. Finally, the genitive row of the result looks as follows (all the cells in the other rows are '-'):

Table 12.

	SG				PL			
C	S	S-M	S-F	S-N	PL	PL-M	PL-F	PL-N
+	+	+	–	–	–	–	–	–

The first '+' means that the case is genitive and is introduced by the *nie widzę* object feature matrix. The '+' in the second column appears due to the fact that the case column is made equal to the singular number column by the *-a* ending matrix (Table 11). Eventually, the last '+' is in place because the *człowiek* matrix (Table 10) links the number columns to the masculine feature cells.

3.3 Modeling the Case System

The previous demonstrated how nested feature matrices can be used for dealing with commitment and making it explicit. Before the presentation of the actual FCG implementation for Polish, there is one last issue to solve which is related to ambiguity. Consider the following case which is the positive version of example 14:

(15) *Widzę człowieka.*
(I) see man.ACC
'I see the man.'

It was previously mentioned that virile nouns take the same form in the genitive and accusative. Let us take a look at the accusative row of the feature matrix for the ending *-a*, shown in Table 13, this time in nested form. Notice that no number commitment can be made, since both the singular and plural are allowed. However, the noun *człowiek* cannot take the *-a* ending in plural: In fact, the accusative plural entry refers to another class of masculine nouns such as *cud* (miracle). So the question is, how can this suffix be prevented from applying to the wrong noun?

Table 13.

-a	SG				PL			
C	**S**	**S-M**	**S-F**	**S-N**	**PL**	**PL-M**	**PL-F**	**PL-N**
?a	*?a-sg-m*	*?a-sg-m*	–	–	*?a-pl-m*	*?a-pl-m*	–	–

There are several possible solutions. The first thing to do in any case is to subdivide the declension schemes further. Following [16], there are more than 26 basic declension schemes. One possibility would be to put them into a huge feature matrix, which would yield more than 26 columns. Obviously, this is not a very elegant solution, for most of the matrices will be extremely sparse. Additionally, the fact that the specific declension schemes can be grouped together and share most of the endings is not taken into account by this solution either.

The possibility chosen here is to add supplementary features which denote the declension scheme to the lexical constructions and to the suffix constructions. It is important to note that no *disjunctive* features are needed here; rather the feature matrix is used together with a *conjunction* of new features. Additionally, the masculine declension scheme is subdivided into three schemes for *virile*, *animate* and *inanimate* and this distinction is introduced into the feature matrix paradigm. However, as mentioned before, this categorization is not always valid, since there are inanimate objects following the animate scheme; therefore, the three schemes are denoted by *M1*, *M2* and *M3*. In total, this results in nested feature matrices consisting of ten feature columns, one case column and two number columns (overall 13 columns).

Another special case is the ending pair *-i* and *-y*, for they mostly mark the same cases. Which one is to be applied depends on the stem: In some declension schemes *-y* is the default ending, and it is substituted by *-i* after *k* and *g*. In other schemes, *-i* is the default ending and has to be exchanged by *i*.

In the remainder of this paper the focus is not to implement all the different schemes, but rather to show how the pursued approach can be used to represent the whole complexity of this intricate declension system. The next section deals with the actual implementation of the system in FCG and explains it step by step.

4 Operationalization in FCG

The forthcoming section aims to show how a subset of the Polish grammar can be implemented in FCG and how nested features matrices (further called feature matrices) can be used to facilitate morphological and phrasal agreement. As mentioned in an earlier chapter of this Volume [25], the key idea of construction grammars is to treat every linguistic item as a *form-meaning pair*, a construction. However, not all constructions in FCG have to be form-meaning pairs. Morphological processing can be modeled by exploiting the fact that FCG also allows *form-form pairs*, that is, pure syntactic constructions. The need for syntactic constructions will become obvious when the implementation of morphological processing in the Polish example is explained.

Moreover, the generation of constructions is facilitated by templates which also have been introduced in earlier chapters [2, 12, 25]. In particular the morphological templates from [12] and [2] were adapted to deal with inflection and stem affixes. Additional templates for feature matrix creation were already developed for [27] and were extended for this study to cover nested feature matrices.

The actual application order of the constructions is guided by two factors. On one hand, only appropriate constructions are considered during the application process, since they have to match the current transient structure. In this sense, constructions are looking for and triggered by certain unit features of the current transient structure. One the other hand, the grammar designer can also group constructions into *construction sets* and induce an explicit ordering on the families. In the presented grammar constructions are grouped into the following sets:

Lexical constructions provide the basic lexical items.
Functional constructions map lexical items to their syntactic function in a phrase or sentence.
Negative and positive verb constructions determine if the phrase has a negative sense, expressed by the word *nie*.
Marked inflection constructions handle the proper case, number and gender related endings for nouns.
Unmarked inflection constructions treat noun forms which do not exhibit an ending.
Stem constructions provide the appropriate changes to stems of nouns, according to their stem class and the attached ending.
Number constructions determine the right number of a noun.
Phrasal constructions take care of phrasal agreement.
Sentential constructions add context on the meaning side and punctuation on the form side.

In the following the most important constructions are explained in detail. In order to give the reader an overview of the machinery necessary for the implementation of the formalized linguistic problems, the constructions will be presented both from the design as well as the operational level; that is, template definitions as well as graphical representations of constructions (using the tools presented earlier in [14]) are given.

4.1 Feature Matrices

So far, feature matrices were only considered in an abstract way, now their implementation in FCG is presented. In fact, the implementation is rather straightforward, since a matrix can be modeled as a list of lists. Thus, the following code shows the nested feature matrix for the noun *człowiek* (man) (see Table 10) in FCG notation:

```
((nom ?nom (nom-sg ?nom-sg-m1 ?nom-sg-m1 - - - -)
           (nom-pl ?nom-pl-m1 ?nom-pl-m1 - - - -))
 (gen ?gen (gen-sg ?gen-sg-m1 ?gen-sg-m1 - - - -)
           (gen-pl ?gen-pl-m1 ?gen-pl-m1 - - - -))
 (dat ?dat (dat-sg ?dat-sg-m1 ?dat-sg-m1 - - - -)
           (dat-pl ?dat-pl-m1 ?dat-pl-m1 - - - -))
 (acc ?acc (acc-sg ?acc-sg-m1 ?acc-sg-m1 - - - -)
           (acc-pl ?acc-pl-m1 ?acc-pl-m1 - - - -))
 (ins ?ins (ins-sg ?ins-sg-m1 ?ins-sg-m1 - - - -)
           (ins-pl ?ins-pl-m1 ?ins-pl-m1 - - - -))
 (loc ?loc (loc-sg ?loc-sg-m1 ?loc-sg-m1 - - - -)
           (loc-pl ?loc-pl-m1 ?loc-pl-m1 - - - -)))
 (voc ?voc (voc-sg ?voc-sg-m1 ?voc-sg-m1 - - - -)
           (voc-pl ?voc-pl-m1 ?voc-pl-m1 - - - -)))
```

The overall structure is a list which contains one sublist per case. Each case list consists of a symbol denoting the case name (e.g. `nom`), the case (column) variable (`?nom`) and two sublists, one for each number. Again, the number lists contain a symbol for the case-number combination (`nom-sg`), a number (column) variable (in this example the first `?nom-sg-m1`) and finally the actual feature cells. In the example, all entries except the one at the *M1* positions are marked by a '-', since *człowiek* follows the masculine virile declension scheme.

4.2 Lexical and Morphological Constructions

One one hand, there are lexical constructions which are simple form-meaning mappings that translate a semantic entity denoting an individual, an object or an event into an appropriate lexical representation. On the other hand morphological constructions deal with the attachment of the right stem and endings to these representations. The focus of this study is on the morphology of nouns. Therefore, first the lexical construction for the noun *dziewczyna* (girl) is given, and it is explained how production and parsing on the lexical level works in FCG. The following example parses the utterance `("dziewczy" "-n" "-a")` and yields its semantic representation `(girl girl-set context)`. It is important to note that the very same constructions can also be used to produce the utterance from the latter semantic representation.

Semantics. In FCG, semantic representations roughly correspond to second order predicates. However, FCG does not use a formal inference system, so the way of using the predicates is not as strict as in formal predicate calculus. On the semantic side, a girl is presented by the predicate `(girl ?girl-set ?context)`. The first position of the predicate denotes the predicate name, followed by an arbitrary number of arguments. In this case, a helpful interpretation is to consider predicates as functions which calculate output sets or entities from input sets. Hence, the girl predicate calculates the set of girl individuals from a given context set (consisting of different objects and individuals). In a more common predicate calculus representation, the girl predicate might be written as Girl(X, Y), where the predicate calculus set variables X and Y correspond to the FCG variables `?girl-set` and `?context`, respectively. In the full FCG grammar solution presented in this paper, each noun is accompanied by another predicate denoting whether only one individual or a set of individuals is referenced, namely `(single-entity ?entity-set)` or `(set ?entity-set)`. A good way to interpret the `single-entity` and `set` predicates is to regard them as additional constraints rather than functions. For example, the following predicate set denotes one specific girl individual in the base set, at least if such an individual exists in the context:

```
(girl ?girl-set ?context) (single-entity ?girl-set)
```

Note how the variable `?girl-set` appears in both predicates ensuring the correct variable binding. The `single-entity` and `set` predicates are introduced by the constructions from the *number* construction set.

Lexicon. The following code uses lexical templates as presented in [25] to create the *girl* construction, at first without feature matrices:

```
(def-lex-cxn girl-cxn
    (def-lex-skeleton girl-cxn
        :meaning (== (girl ?girl-set ?context))
        :args (?girl-set ?context)
        :string "dziewczy")
    (def-lex-cat girl-cxn
        :sem-cat (==1 (class indiv))
        :syn-cat (==1 (lex-cat noun)
                      (gender feminine))
        :phon-cat (==1 (stem "-n")
                       (stem-class hard)
                       (palatal-plural-endings -)))
```

The resulting construction is depicted in Figure 1. The construction is actualized by a coupled feature structure, consisting of a semantic (left) and a syntactic (right) pole. The upper boxes above the dashed line basically state how the transient feature structure should look in order to be manipulated by this construction. The lower part contains information that should be added to the transient feature structure by this construction in terms of J-Units.

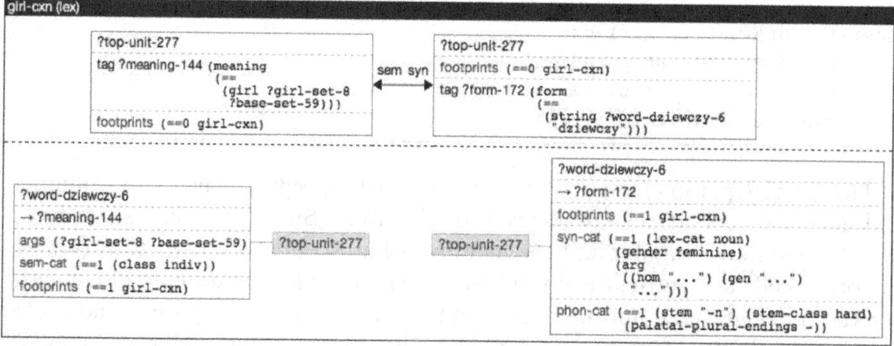

Fig. 1. Lexical construction for the (stem of the) noun *dziewczyna* (girl). Due to space constraints, the full feature matrix is omitted.

As visible in the `string` argument of the `def-lex-skeleton`, the lexical item for girl only contains the form `dziewczy`, lacking the stem and a concrete case marking. These must be added by other constructions, considering the intended case and number of the expression. Therefore, the `def-lex-cat` template is used to add more information, particularly about the syntactic and phonetic properties of the word. It assigns the lexical category to be a noun with feminine gender (lines 8 and 9), additionally, it adds phonetic categories (lines 10 to 12): by specifying the default stem and the stem class, only the right endings (in terms of the right constructions) for this noun are considered during further processing. Finally, the feature `palatal-plural-endings` specifies whether this noun can take palatal plural endings which affect the noun stem. This noun obviously does not, for its nominative plural is *dziewczyn-y* and not **dziewczyn-i*.

After defining the syntactic, semantic and phonetic features, a feature matrix is added to the girl construction. In the first instance, the declension paradigm has to be created which specifies which genders, cases and numbers are available:

```
(defparameter *polish-paradigm*
  (make-matrix-paradigm
   :dimensions ((nom gen dat acc ins loc)
                (sg pl)
                (m1 m2 m3 f n))))
```

Note that the vocative case is left out as it is not be used in this example. The paradigm is an object which is bound to the variable `*polish-paradigm*` and is used throughout the following construction definitions.

Next, the feature matrix is created and added to the girl construction by using the following command:

```
(def-feature-matrix girl-cxn
    :paradigm *polish-paradigm*
    :dimensions (sg-f pl-f)
    :feature (:syn-cat :agr))
```

The crucial parameter is `:dimensions` which specifies which case, number and gender combinations are allowed for this item. Since the noun is feminine, only the feminine singular and the feminine plural columns are set to variables, the other cells are automatically set to '-'. The template takes care of converting the necessary case and number columns into variables or pluses, and looks for the possibility of unifying variables. The `feature` parameter specifies at which exact location in the coupled feature structure the matrix is inserted. In this example, a new feature *agr* (for agreement) containing the feature matrix is created, which is appended to the *syn-cat* feature of the syntactic pole.

Noun Inflection. At this point, only the constructions for the core of the noun *girl* is available, now the constructions which deal with the endings are shown. The following template creates a construction for the *-a* ending:

```
(def-inflection-affix-cxn inflection-suffix-a
    (def-inflection-affix-skeleton inflection-suffix-a
        :suffix "-a"
        :syn-cat (==1 (lex-cat noun)
                      (gender ?gender))
        :phon-cat (==1 (stem-class ?stem-class))
        :impose-phon-cat (==1 (stem-palatalized -)))
    (def-inflection-affix-feature-matrix
        inflection-suffix-a
          :paradigm *polish-paradigm*
          :feature (:syn-cat :agr)
          :dimensions
           (nom-sg-f
            gen-sg-m1 gen-sg-m2 gen-sg-m3 gen-sg-n
            acc-sg-m1 acc-sg-m2)
          :feature (:syn-cat :agr)))
```

Several new templates arise here, which are adapted to the creation of inflection affixes. Again, there is an overarching template as well as a skeleton and feature matrix template. An important difference is that the resulting construction will not consist of a semantic and a syntactic, but of two syntactic poles. The reason for this is that the ending suffix does not add any new information on the semantic side, but only actualizes the case and number marking. Role assignment and all other semantically relevant tasks are taken care of by phrasal constructions which will be shown later.

The application mechanism for pure syntactic constructions is the same as for normal constructions, that is, it is divided into a matching and a merging phase.

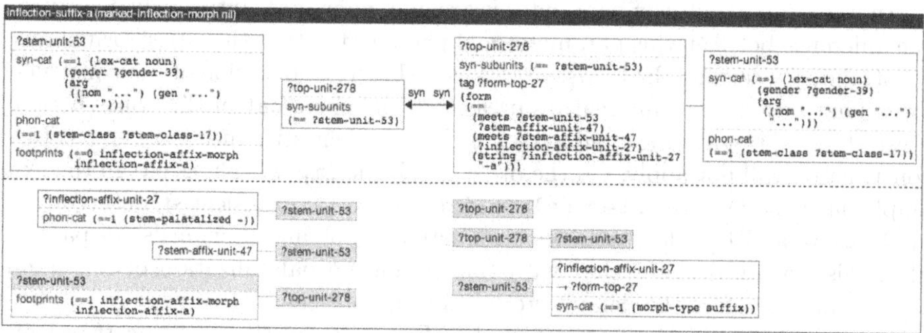

Fig. 2. Morphological construction for the *-a* ending. Due to space constraints, the full feature matrices are omitted.

However, both matching and merging apply to the syntactic pole of the current transient feature structure.

The most important difference is the `suffix` parameter by which a string denoting the actual ending is passed. Alternatively, the parameter `infix` may be used which also takes a string as its value. This is necessary since there exist cases which are in principle unmarked, but which introduce a gap vowel before the stem. For example, the genitive plural of the feminine noun *deska* (board) is *desek*, that is, an *e* is introduced before the stem consonant *k*. This phenomenon can be handled if the *e* is treated like a normal inflection ending, but which occurs in the infix instead of suffix position.

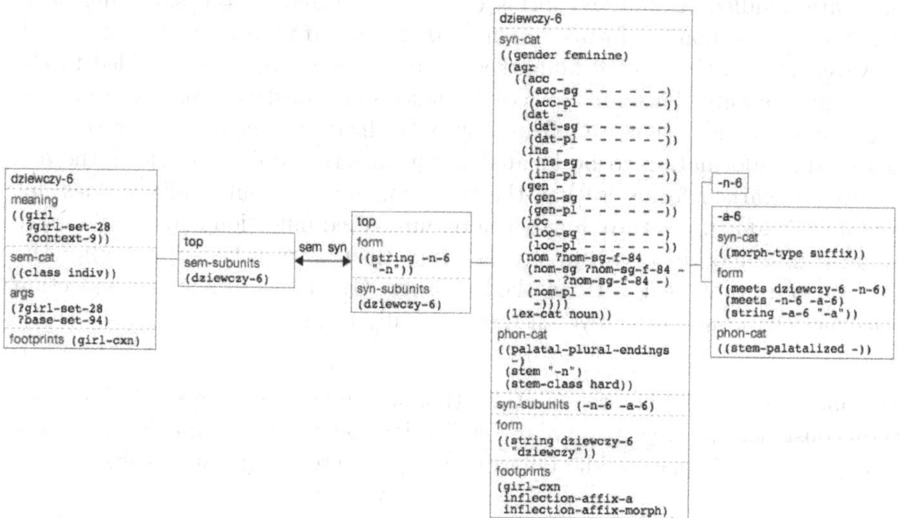

Fig. 3. Transient structure resulting after the application of *girl-cxn* and *inflection-suffix-a-cxn*

Another important new parameter is `impose-phon-cat`. Intuitively speaking, the difference between this parameter and `phon-cat` is that the latter formulates constraints concerning the transient structure before application of the construction. That means that any feature present in the `phon-cat` of the construction must also be present in the `phon-cat` of the transient structure – otherwise the construction will not apply. On the other hand, the `impose-phon-cat` in the example *adds* the feature `(stem-palatalized -)` to the transient structure after application, and therefore affects constructions applying afterwards. In particular, this feature declares that with this ending no palatalization of the stem occurs, and therefore the default stem has to be attached.

The *-a* ending construction depicted in Figure 2 and the resulting transient structure after the application of *girl-cxn* and *inflection-suffix-a-cxn* shown in Figure 3 illustrate the parsing and production process. For a syntactic ending construction only the right pole of the transient structure has to be considered. The *inflection-suffix-a-cxn* attaches a new subunit to the noun unit. In the construction, the noun unit is called `?stem-unit-73`, that is, its name is a variable. Therefore, it can be bound to the `dziewczy-6` unit in the transient structure. Similarly, `?inflection-unit-33` transforms to `-a-6`. The `-a-6` unit contains the feature `(morph-type suffix)` in its `syn-cat` which determines that the stem added in the next step must be an infix. Note that the feature matrix in the `syn-cat` of `dziewczy-6` has already determined the nominative singular case to be the right solution after application of the *inflection-suffix-a-cxn*. Furthermore, the *inflection-suffix-a-cxn* adds another empty unit named `-n-6`, which functions as a placeholder for the stem added by the construction presented in the next section.

Before turning to stem constructions, it should be mentioned how unmarked cases are handled. Unmarked forms can by actualized by the same inflection templates as for marked forms, but no `suffix` or `infix` arguments are passed. However, also in the case of unmarked forms an inflection-unit is added to the transient structure. This unit is necessary since stem constructions need information whether or not they are affected by palatalization. The stem constructions expect this information to be located in an inflection unit. Therefore, the difference to marked forms is that the inflection unit for null endings does not contain any `string` feature. Furthermore, unmarked inflection constructions are grouped into another construction set, since they have to be applied after the constructions that deal with marked endings. Otherwise, unmarked inflection constructions would apply even if there actually is an ending.

Stems. As explained before, palatalization has an effect on the stem of a noun. Stem constructions are very similar to inflection constructions and also use structurally related templates. The following template creates the stem infix *-n*:

```
(def-stem-affix-cxn stem-infix-n
    (def-stem-affix-skeleton stem-infix-n
        :infix "-n"
        :syn-cat (==1 (lex-cat noun)
                      (gender ?gender))
        :phon-cat (==1 (stem "-n") (stem-class hard))
        :inflection-phon-cat  (==1 (stem-palatalized -))))
```

Most of the parameters contain the same function as the ones in the inflection template. An important new parameter is `inflection-phon-cat` which is the counterpart of the `impose-phon-cat` from the inflection construction. In this example, it states that the inflection attached to the noun must not palatalize the stem; otherwise this construction would not be applied and a different one would have to be chosen. If needed, a feature matrix can be added to the stem as well, which is not necessary in this case because the *-n* stem occurs in all cases. Figure 4 shows the resulting construction.

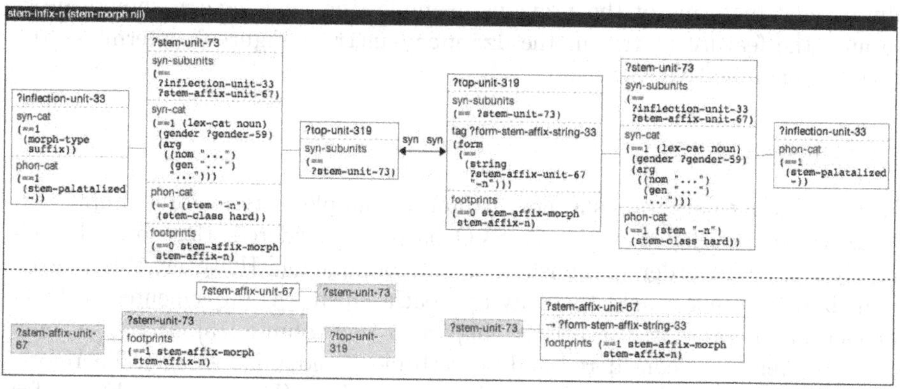

Fig. 4. Morphological construction for the *-n* stem

After parsing `("dziewczy" "-n" "-a")` or producing `(girl girl-set context)` the `-n-6` unit on the syntactic pole now contains the actual string representation for the stem. The syntactic pole of the obtained coupled feature structure are depicted in Figure 5.

Number. Now that all work on the syntactic side is done, a predicate denoting the right number of individuals must be introduced on the semantic side. There are two specific constructions, *singular-cxn* and *plural-cxn*. For the sake of brevity, the constructions are not depicted here, also because they do a fairly simple job: in the semantic pole, they introduce the `single-entity` or `set` predicate, respectively. In order to do so, each of them includes a feature matrix in the syntactic pole which either contains variables in all the singular or in the

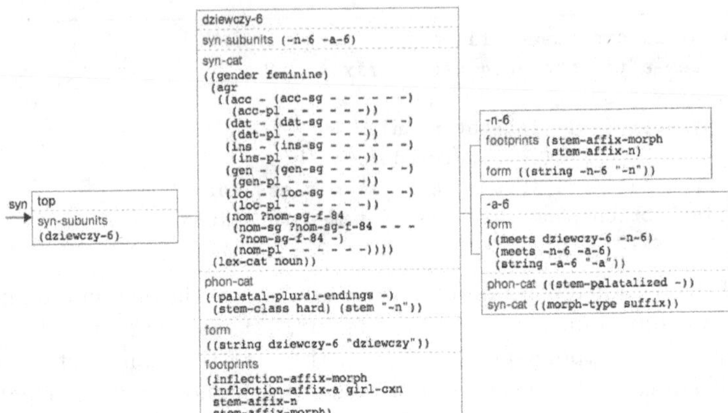

Fig. 5. Syntactic pole of the coupled feature structure after the application of lexical and morphological constructions

plural cells. In terms of the previous example, the *singular-cxn* should apply because the feature matrix in the `dziewczy-unit` in Figure 5 determines the case to be nominative singular.

4.3 Phrases

In the following paragraphs a more complex example in terms of a simple sentence will be developed. Only the SVO pattern considered, therefore, the relatively free word order of Polish is not accounted for. However, this can be actualized by using a field topology approach which was implemented in FCG for German as presented in a later chapter of this volume [15]. Moreover, only transitive verbs are considered and no verb morphology is modeled. Therefore, all verbs are in the third person singular or infinitives. However, morphology for verbs can be added in a similar way as the noun morphology presented in the preceding sections. The grammar can be also easily extended with more complex phrases by adding constructions for more complex patterns similar to the ones presented in the forthcoming explanation.

Verbs. First, constructions for verb forms are added. The following lexical construction defines the verb form *widzi* (he/she/it sees):

```
(def-lex-cxn see-cxn
    (def-lex-skeleton see-cxn
        :meaning (== (see ?see-set ?base-set)
                     (seer ?see-set ?seer)
                     (seee ?see-set ?seee))
        :args (?see-set ?seer ?seee ?base-set)
        :string "widzi")
    (def-lex-cat see-cxn
        :sem-cat (==1 (class event)
                      (sem-val
                       (==1 (agent ?see-set ?seer)
                            (patient ?see-set ?seee))))
        :syn-cat (==1 (lex-cat verb)
                      (verb-form inflected)))
    (def-feature-matrix see-cxn
        :paradigm *polish-paradigm*
        :dimensions (nom)
        :feature (:syn-cat :subject-agr))
    (def-feature-matrix see-cxn
        :paradigm *polish-paradigm*
        :dimensions (acc gen)
        :feature (:syn-cat :direct-object-agr)))
```

This construction is very similar to the lexical noun constructions presented before, only the semantic features are different because the verbs considered here describe events rather than individuals. Notice that the construction contains two feature matrices, one for agreement with the subject, another for agreement with its direct object. The subject is forced to take the nominative case, while the direct object can take either the accusative or genitive case – owed to the genitive of negation. In order to distinguish the two feature matrices, the feature matrix corresponding to the subject is located in the `subject-agr` feature, while the other one is located in the `direct-object-agr` feature.

The constructions for verbs which do not take the accusative look almost the same, such as *macha* (he/she/it waves), which takes the instrumental case. The main difference is that they only allow the instrumental case in the direct object agreement feature matrix, since they are not affected by the genitive of negation.

Since verb morphology is not covered in this paper a new construction for every verb form has to be defined. However, this is not too much work since only infinitives and verbs in the third person singular are considered. The `see -infinitive-cxn` looks almost the same as the `see-cxn` construction, except for having the `verb-form` feature, which is set to `infinitive`. Note that this means that there is no difference on the meaning side between an inflected and an uninflected verb construction. As shown later, this can become a problem in production which is overcome by the introduction of sentential constructions.

Beside the full verbs also inflected forms of auxiliaries like *chce* (he/she/it wants) are defined. In order to distinguish these verbs, the auxiliaries take the additional `(verb-type auxiliary)` feature in their `syn-cat`.

Negation. In order to handle the genitive of negation, in the first instance, another lexical construction for the negation marker *nie* (not) is needed. It is fairly trivial, for it translates this *nie* string into the predicate `(not ?event)`. The argument of the `not` predicate is an event which is introduced in the meaning of the verbal construction above.

```
(def-lex-cxn not-cxn
    (def-lex-skeleton not-cxn
        :meaning (== (not ?event))
        :args (?event)
        :string "nie")
    (def-lex-cat not-cxn
        :syn-cat (==1 (lex-cat particle))
        :sem-cat (==1 (class modifier))))
```

In terms of FCG hierarchy [8], it also adds a new unit to the transient structure which represents this negation marker or predicate, respectively. Note that only sentential negation is considered in this example, that is, no constituent negation. This type of negation also exists in Polish and is marked by the same word *nie*.

In the next step, a construction is needed which propagates the appearance of the negation marker to the verbal unit. It must bind the `?event` variable in the *not-cxn* to the verbal unit, and must also affect the direct object agreement feature matrix of a verbal unit. More precisely, it sets the accusative row of this feature matrix to '-'. The nominative row is also set to '-', since direct objects of transitive verbs do not take this case either. The *sentential-negation-cxn* is depicted in Figure 6.

However, a construction which discovers negation is not sufficient, but also a construction for the positive case is necessary. The reason for this is that there must be a way to sort out the possibility that the direct object of a verb like *widzieć* (see) can take the genitive case, if the phrase is not negated. This *positive-verb-cxn* is much simpler than its negative counterpart, for it does not introduce any new units, but just sets the genitive row of the direct object feature matrix of the affected verb unit to '-'.

Note that these constructions are also able to deal with verbs which always require their direct object to be in the genitive case, that is, also if no negation is present. An example of such a verb is *szukać* (search). In this case neither the *sentential-negation-cxn* nor the *positive-verb-cxn* apply, for the feature matrix for the direct object of *szukać* contains a '+' in the genitive row. The *sentential-negation-cxn* does not apply because no negation marker is present, the *positive-verb-cxn* cannot apply, for its feature matrix contains a '-' in the genitive row. Hence, their feature matrices cannot be unified and no change is made to the verbal unit.

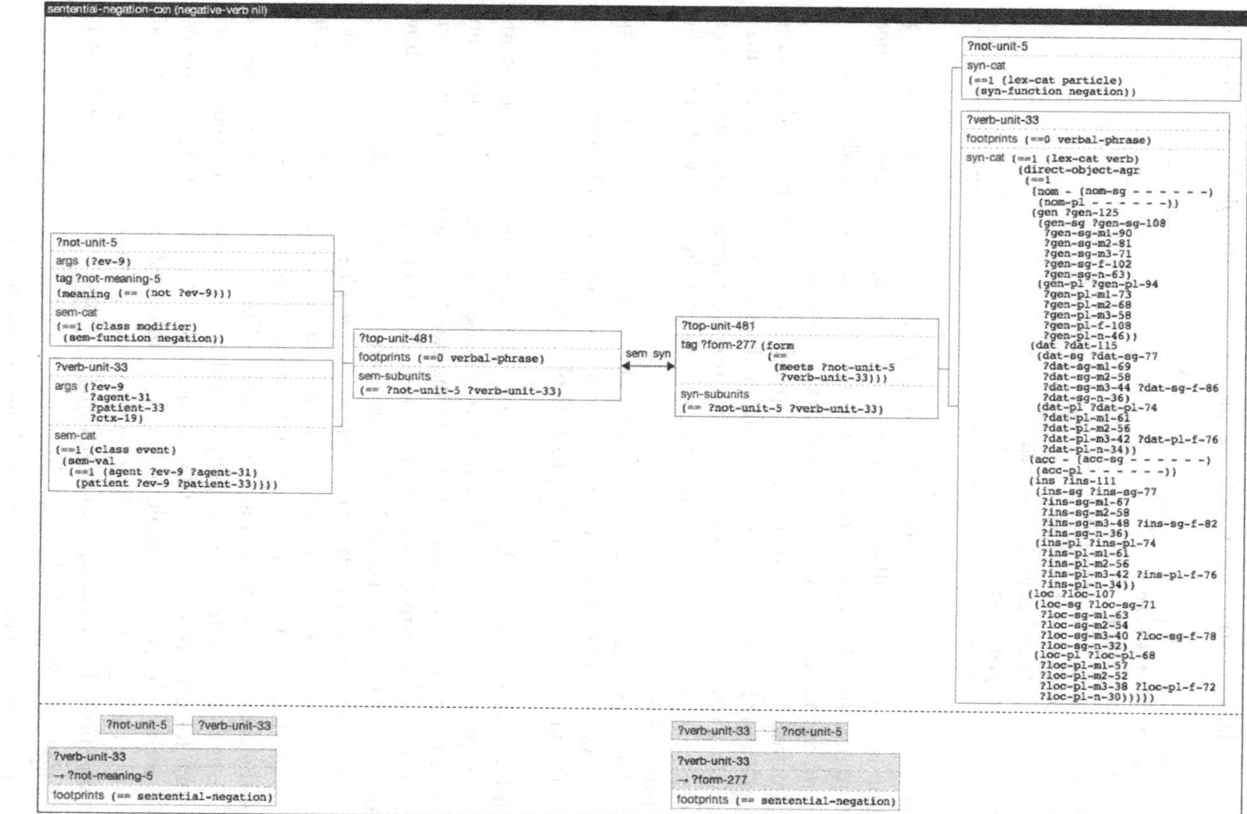

Fig. 6. The *sentential-negation-cxn* prevents the direct object of the verb construction from taking the accusative case if the negation marker *not* is present

Functional Constructions. Before the units created by the lexical constructions can be processed by phrasal constructions, the functional role of the parts of speech has to be determined. This is the task of the functional constructions which are created by the `def-fun-cxn` template. They are fairly simple, therefore only one exemplary construction which assigns the predicate role to an inflected verb is given here:

```
(def-fun-cxn predicate-cxn
    :sem-function action
    :sem-cat (==1 (class event))
    :syn-cat (==1 (lex-cat verb)
                  (verb-form inflected))
    :syn-function predicate)
```

Verbal Phrases. In order to model the long distance genitive of negation a construction is created that allows auxiliary verbs and infinitives to be grouped into a verbal phrase. The construction is depicted in Figure 7. In order to apply, it requires an `auxiliary-unit` and an `infinitive-unit`.

It is important to see how long distance dependencies get propagated. During the application of the construction the feature matrices of the `infinitive-unit` are moved into a new `auxiliary-infinitive-verbal-phrase-unit` which then heads the verbal units. This new unit behaves as if it were a verb, and the *sentential-negation-cxn* can apply to it.

In a similar way also the processing of a chain of infinitives could be implemented: Pairs of infinitives are headed by a new phrasal unit, and the last infinitive's feature matrices are moved to this phrasal unit.

Sentential Phrases. In the last step, phrasal constructions are used to arrange all the parts of speech with transitive phrase constructions. Since they are quite complex constructions, only the templates for creating feature matrices and feature matrix agreement are presented. For more information on how phrasal agreement is realized in FCG by this templates, see also [22].

Figure 8 shows the general structure of a *transitive-phrase-cxn*. The construction requires three units, namely a *subject-unit*, an *object-unit* and a *verb-unit*. During application, it introduces a new unit called *transitive-phrase-unit*, which subsumes the aforementioned units. The construction's main task is to assign the right cases to its constituents. In fact, several constructions are needed, more precisely, one for each possible case that a direct object can take. This is necessary because the construction should assign a '+' in one of the case rows and set all other rows to '-'. This is especially needed in production, where the phrasal constructions precede the morphological constructions, which must be able to select the right ending without ambiguity[3].

[3] Another possibility would be to use a phrasal construction containing a feature matrix, forcing one row to be '+' and all others to be '-' but changing the case name (e.g. `nom`) of all the rows to variables. This solution is not pursued here, since it is computationally very expensive.

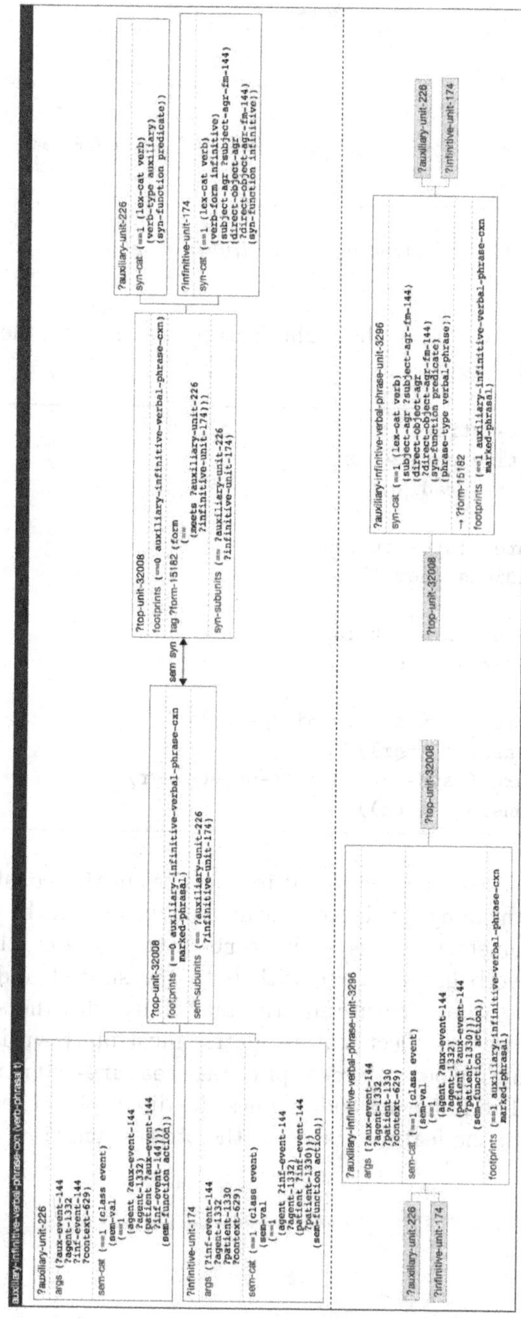

Fig. 7. The *auxiliary-infinitive-verbal-phrase-cxn* groups an inflected auxiliary verb and an infinitive

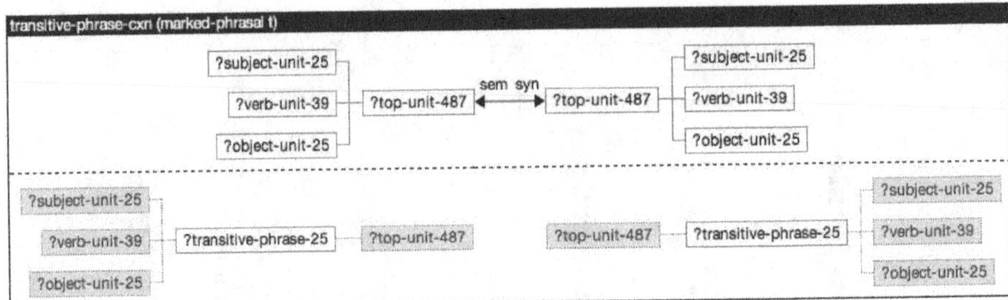

Fig. 8. General structure of the *transitive-phrase-cxn*

The following template adds the right feature matrices to the *accusative-transitive-phrase-cxn*:

```
(def-phrasal-feature-matrix
  accusative-transitive-phrase-cxn
    :paradigm *polish-paradigm*
    (?subject-unit
            (:feature (:syn-cat :agr)
             :dimensions (nom)))
    (?object-unit
            (:feature (:syn-cat :agr)
             :dimensions (acc)))
    (?verb-unit
            (:feature (:syn-cat :subject-agr)
              :dimensions (nom))
            (:feature (:syn-cat :direct-object-agr)
              :dimensions (acc))
```

In total, this template creates four feature matrices in this construction: one that will match with the `subject-unit`'s feature matrix, one for the `object-unit` and two for the agreement matrices of the `verb-unit`. However, this is still insufficient, since the verb has to agree with both the subject and the object. Therefore, the verb's subject feature matrix must unify with the subject's feature matrix and the verb's object feature matrix must unify with the object's feature matrix. For this purpose, the `def-phrasal-feature-matrix-agreement` template is needed. The following code unifies the direct object feature matrix of the `verb-unit` with the feature matrix of the `object-unit`:

```
(def-phrasal-feature-matrix-agreement
  accusative-transitive-phrase-cxn
    :paradigm *polish-paradigm*
    :agreement
        ((?verb-unit
            :feature (:syn-cat :direct-object-agr))
         (?object-unit
            :feature (:syn-cat :agr))))
```

Similarly, the subject-verb agreement can also be established.

When the construction applies, the units feature matrices unify with the matrices of the phrasal construction. Because of the pairing of the subject-verb and object-verb feature matrices, the right cases are propagated to the units.

4.4 Sentence Parsing and Production

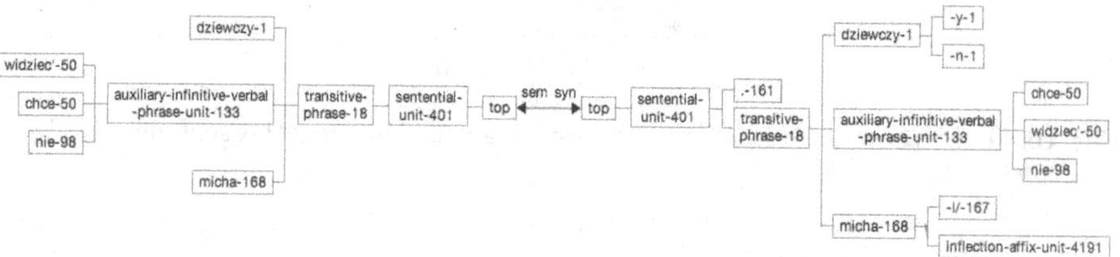

Fig. 9. Transient structure resulting after parsing the sentence *Michael does not want to see the girl*

Figure 9 shows the transient structure after parsing the following sentence:

"Micha" "-ł" "nie" "chce" "widzieć" "dziewczy" "-n" "-y" ".".
(*Michael does not want to see the girl.*)

The following semantical representation is parsed from this sentence:

```
(michal michal-indiv-1 context-1)
(single-entity michal-indiv-1)
(girl girl-indiv-1 context-1)
(single-entity michal-indiv-1)
(not want-ev-1)
(want want-ev-1 context-1)
(wanter want-ev-1 michal-indiv-1)
(wantee want-ev-1 see-ev-1)
(see see-ev-1 context-1)
(seer see-ev-1 michal-indiv-1)
(seee see-ev-1 girl-indiv-1)
(context context-1))
```

In order to see the result of the feature matrix agreement, the syntactic `dziewczy-unit` is shown in more detail in Figure 10. As can be clearly seen, the feature matrix determines that the noun takes the genitive singular case.

```
dziewczy-1
form ((string dziewczy-1 "dziewczy"))
phon-cat ((palatal-plural-endings -)
          (stem-class hard) (stem "-n"))
syn-cat ((syn-function nominal)
         (gender feminine)
         (agr
          ((acc - (acc-sg - - - - - -)
            (acc-pl - - - - - -))
           (dat - (dat-sg - - - - - -)
            (dat-pl - - - - - -))
           (ins - (ins-sg - - - - - -)
            (ins-pl - - - - - -))
           (gen + (gen-sg + - - - + -)
            (gen-pl - - - - - -))
           (loc - (loc-sg - - - - - -)
            (loc-pl - - - - - -))
           (nom - (nom-sg - - - - - -)
            (nom-pl - - - - - -))))
         (lex-cat noun))
syn-subunits (-n-1 -y-1)
footprints (stem-affix-morph
            stem-affix-n
            noun-nominal-cxn cat
            girl-cxn lex
            inflection-affix-y
            inflection-affix-morph
            singular-cxn number-cxn)
```

Fig. 10. The syntactic `dziewczy-unit` resulting after parsing the sentence *Michael does not want to see the girl*

The *sentence-cxn*, not yet explicitly mentioned so far, adds the `(context context-1)` predicate on the semantic and the full stop on the syntactic side. It applies if all units have been subsumed under a phrasal unit and ensures that no units are uncovered. This might happen in production since the semantic poles of the inflected and the infinitive constructions look exactly the same – their meanings are identical, but their form realizations are different. Therefore, FCG considers the possibility of using the inflected verb form construction for both *want* and *see*. Of course, two inflected verbs forms cannot be grouped together by the *auxiliary-infinitival-verbal-phrase-cxn*, and therefore the following defective sentence is produced:

`*"Michał" "nie" "widzi" "dziewczyny" "chce".`
(**Michael does not see the girl, wants.*)

However, the sentence construction will not apply in this case and leave the *(context context-1)* predicate uncovered. This will signal FCG that it should look for a better solution that processes all the meaning predicates.

Note that multiple subclauses do not pose a problem in principle. In order to actualize them, several slightly differing sentence constructions that require a finite amount of subphrases could be used in order to group the subphrases in an appropriate way.

5 Conclusion

This paper has explained how a complex declension system can be operationalized in FCG. Polish was chosen as a representative from the group of Slavic languages in order to verify if FCG can cope with highly irregular natural language examples. Feature matrices have proven to be an elegant representation for this system. They can be used to model agreement from the morphological to the phrasal level. The key idea is to include the feature matrices in constructions for nouns, morphological suffixes and phrases. Each of the constructions contains a feature matrix encoding in which the possible cases, numbers and genders of the item are encoded. Indeed, different constructions for the same ending might be necessary, if they are required for the disambiguation of declension variations within the same gender. Which variation a noun must exhibit in order to be combined with an ending is stored in supplementary features which are added to the constructions of the noun and the ending. Moreover, the endings contain more features which encode their effect on the stem. This allows palatalization to be modeled. The presented approach can also deal with unmarked cases. In some of these unmarked cases, a gap vowel has to be introduced before the stem consonant. This special case can be solved by treating the gap vowel as an infix marking. In the same way as palatalizing endings, a gap vowel is indicated by adding supplementary features to the construction that represents the gap vowel. This way, the right constructions are triggered in order to parse and produce a noun form in a grammatically and syntactically correct manner.

Furthermore, a simple example of the long distance genitive of negation has been implemented. A special focus has been on the case where the genitive of negation has an effect on the direct object of a nested infinitive when the predicate is negated. Phrasal constructions subsume the predicate and the infinitive in a new unit and propagate information about verbal agreement up to this unit. This allows for the right constructions to apply and to change the feature matrices representing the verbal agreement correctly.

The presented grammar can be extended in several ways. For instance, the grammar can be scaled up by adding adjectives and pronouns. Morphologically, these grammatical items can be treated in an analogue way to the nouns, that is, every item will exhibit its own feature matrix and specific endings. From a syntactic point of view, more flexible phrasal constructions will be necessary. However, it has already been extensively shown how these different grammatical items can be handled in FCG (see this volume and also [23]).

More work on how to handle long distance dependencies in FCG in general could be done. Polish exhibits a strong negative concord, that is, a negative particle such as *nikt* (nobody), which always requires the negation marker *nie*, despite not expressing double negation [21]. This phenomenon calls for a general way to represent long distances, and future work should concentrate on how these dependencies can be modeled in FCG.

Acknowledgements. This research was conducted at the Sony Computer Science Laboratory in Paris and at the University of Brussels (VUB AI Lab).

Funding has come from the Sony Computer Science Laboratory as well as from the European research project ALEAR (FP7, ICT-214856). I would like to thank all members of the language groups at Sony CSL and at the VUB AI Lab for insightful discussions and helpful comments, and Liviu Ciortuz for pointing out relationships of my work to other work in the Slavic linguist community.

References

[1] Beuls, K.: Construction sets and unmarked forms: A case study for Hungarian verbal agreement. In: Steels, L. (ed.) Design Patterns in Fluid Construction Grammar. John Benjamins, Amsterdam (2011)

[2] Beuls, K.: Handling Scope in Fluid Construction Grammar: A Case Study for Spanish Modals. In: Steels, L. (ed.) Computational Issues in FCG. LNCS (LNAI), vol. 7249, pp. 123–142. Springer, Heidelberg (2012)

[3] Borsley, R.D., Przepiórkowski, A.: Slavic in Head-Driven Phrase Structure Grammar. CSLI Publications, Stanford (1999)

[4] Buttler, D., Kurkowska, H., Satkiewicz, H.: Kultura języka polskiego. Zagadnienia poprawności gramatycznej [Culture of Polish language: Issues on grammatical correctness]. Państwowe Wydawnictwo Naukowe, Warszawa (1973)

[5] Ciortuz, L.: *LIGHT* - A Constraint Language and Compiler System for Typed-Unification Grammars. In: Jarke, M., Koehler, J., Lakemeyer, G. (eds.) KI 2002. LNCS (LNAI), vol. 2479, pp. 3–17. Springer, Heidelberg (2002)

[6] Ciortuz, L., Saveluc, V.: Learning to unlearn in lattices of concepts: A case study in Fluid Construction Grammars. In: Proceedings of SYNASC 2011, pp. 160–167. IEEE Computer Society, Timişoara (2011)

[7] Ciortuz, L., Saveluc, V.: Fluid Construction Grammar and Feature Constraint Logics. In: Steels, L. (ed.) Computational Issues in FCG. LNCS (LNAI), vol. 7249, pp. 289–311. Springer, Heidelberg (2012)

[8] De Beule, J., Steels, L.: Hierarchy in Fluid Construction Grammars. In: Furbach, U. (ed.) KI 2005. LNCS (LNAI), vol. 3698, pp. 1–15. Springer, Heidelberg (2005)

[9] De Beule, J.: A Formal Deconstruction of Fluid Construction Grammar. In: Steels, L. (ed.) Computational Issues in FCG. LNCS (LNAI), vol. 7249, pp. 215–238. Springer, Heidelberg (2012)

[10] Dąbrowska, E.: Learning a morphological system without a default: the Polish genitive. Journal of Child Language (28), 545–574 (2001)

[11] Flickinger, D.P.: On building a more efficient grammar by exploiting types. Natural Language Engineering 6(1), 15–28 (2000)

[12] Gerasymova, K.: Expressing Grammatical Meaning with Morphology: A Case Study for Russian Aspect. In: Steels, L. (ed.) Computational Issues in FCG. LNCS (LNAI), vol. 7249, pp. 91–122. Springer, Heidelberg (2012)

[13] Kowalik, K.: Morfonologia. In: Grzegorczykowa, R., Laskowski, R., Wróbel, H. (eds.) Gramatyka współczesnego języka polskiego: Morfologia [A Grammar of Contemporary Polish: Morphology], vol. 1. Państwowe Wydawnictwo Naukowe, Warszawa (1998)

[14] Loetzsch, M.: Tools for Grammar Engineering. In: Steels, L. (ed.) Computational Issues in FCG. LNCS (LNAI), vol. 7249, pp. 37–47. Springer, Heidelberg (2012)

[15] Micelli, V.: Field Topology and Information Structure: A Case Study for German Constituent Order. In: Steels, L. (ed.) Computational Issues in FCG. LNCS (LNAI), vol. 7249, pp. 178–211. Springer, Heidelberg (2012)

[16] Orzechowska, A.: Rzeczownik. In: Grzegorczykowa, R., Laskowski, R., Wróbel, H. (eds.) Gramatyka współczesnego języka polskiego: Morfologia [A Grammar of Contemporary Polish: Morphology], vol. 1. Państwowe Wydawnictwo Naukowe, Warszawa (1998)

[17] Pollard, C., Sag, I.A.: Information-based syntax and semantics: vol. 1: fundamentals. Center for the Study of Language and Information, Stanford, CA, USA (1988)

[18] Przepiórkowski, A.: Long distance genitive of negation in Polish (2000)

[19] Przepiórkowski, A., Kupść, A.: Why formal grammar? (1999)

[20] Ramsay, A.: Disjunction without tears. Computational Linguistics 16(3), 171–174 (1990)

[21] Richter, F., Sailer, M.: Negative Concord in Polish. CSLI Publications, Stanford (1999)

[22] Steels, L.: A design pattern for phrasal constructions. In: Steels, L. (ed.) Design Patterns in Fluid Construction Grammar. John Benjamins, Amsterdam (2011)

[23] Steels, L. (ed.): Design Patterns in Fluid Construction Grammar. John Benjamins, Amsterdam (2011)

[24] Steels, L. (ed.): Computational Issues in Fluid Construction Grammar. Springer, Berlin (2012)

[25] Steels, L.: Design Methods for Fluid Construction Grammar. In: Steels, L. (ed.) Computational Issues in FCG. LNCS (LNAI), vol. 7249, pp. 3–36. Springer, Heidelberg (2012)

[26] Steels, L. (ed.): Experiments in Cultural Language Evolution. John Benjamins, Amsterdam (2012)

[27] van Trijp, R.: Feature matrices and agreement: A case study for German case. In: Steels, L. (ed.) Design Patterns in Fluid Construction Grammar. John Benjamins, Amsterdam (2011)

Field Topology and Information Structure: A Case Study for German Constituent Order

Vanessa Micelli

Sony Computer Science Laboratory Paris, France

Abstract. A widely used approach for handling German constituent ordering is based on the so called field topology surface model. This model proposes five fields of varying complexity in linear order whereby each field imposes more or less flexible constraints on the number and the types of sentence constituents it can capture. Both the placement of constituents into fields and the order of the constituents within a field can vary widely subject to an intricate interplay of diverse constraints including information structure. This chapter works out a complete operational solution illustrating this field topology approach within the context of Fluid Construction Grammar. It focuses in particular on the double object construction in ditransitive sentences.

1 Introduction

> An average sentence, in a German newspaper, is a sublime and impressive curiosity; it occupies a quarter of a column; it contains all the ten parts of speech – not in regular order, but mixed;" ([40], Appendix D).

German language learners in particular will agree with Mark Twain that German constituent order presents a difficult but also intriguing subject of study. Despite several strict rules, it is often the case that German constituent order is quite free. For instance, the finite verb must appear in the second position in declarative sentences but subject or objects can shift around without restriction.[1]

One way of formally describing the seemingly free constituent order in German sentences is through a topological surface model. This model traditionally proposes a maximum of five fields of varying complexity in linear order as discussed for example in [29].[2] Each field then imposes constraints on which and also on how many parts of the sentence it can capture. There are ongoing debates on the acceptability of constituent orders in German utterances. Examples of potential factors determining constituent order are focus, definiteness,

[1] This claim only holds as long as the noun phrases are either case marked or identifiable by the context they appear in or by selectional restrictions. Else reordering is not freely permitted (see [46, 45]).

[2] [19] gives a review of the topological fields. He proposes one additional field preceding the Vorfeld to accommodate left-dislocated-elements. This approach is, however, not accounted for in this case study.

L. Steels (Ed.) Computational Issues in FCG, LNAI 7249, pp. 178–211, 2012.

case and animacy. (See for instance [16, 21, 24, 41].) In the present study, we focus on the constraints identified by [24]. He found that German constituent order, especially within the proposed fields, is subject to an intricate interplay of a number of diverse semantic, pragmatic or syntactic constraints. Significantly, these constraints must interact with aspects of *information structure* that are often ignored or treated as peripheral to grammar rather than as integral to it.

The information structure of a sentence refers to how that sentence is structured regarding its focus, ground, topic, comment and so forth. Identification of those issues within a sentence is still discussed in the literature, and so far no common consensus has been reached. Although it is often described in terms of general discourse principles or pragmatic parameters, empirical studies show that almost every language has developed concrete strategies for marking information structure. Within those languages, those strategies are conventionalized and are more systematic than often assumed.

This chapter tries to answer the question as to how a speaker's knowledge of the information structure of his or her language can be operationalized so that it can influence constituent order, focusing as a first step on the double object construction in declarative sentences in German. The chapter describes a Fluid Construction Grammar (FCG) implementation that follows a field topological approach and that tightly incorporates information structure into the grammar, making it an integral part of it. We refer to other papers in this volume [38] as well as [36] for introductions to FCG. The grammar is fully operational and can be used for both parsing and production of German interrogative and declarative sentences with intransitive, transitive or ditransitive verbs. This achievement is noteworthy as many other approaches to grammar are often purely descriptive.

The main points of the grammar implementation described in detail in this chapter are the following:

1. As previously suggested by [11], information structure has to be tightly integrated into the grammar, as it interacts both with phonology and syntax. FCG's openness with respect to features and constraints offers an elegant way for achieving this. To capture German's complex constituent order it is important to deal with various constraints on various levels of the language, which necessarily interact with aspects of information structure. Therefore, the syntactic, semantic and pragmatic constraints identified by [24] will be explicitly represented, evaluated and determined during language processing. Their states are accessible to other constructions from any other part of the grammar at all times. Pragmatic information is incorporated into the grammar without assuming a separate discourse layer so that all 'levels' of language are tightly coupled in a non-modular way.
2. The grammar engineer can either put all constructions in one big 'constructicon', (one construction set), or group them into several construction sets, whose order of application can then be controlled. The second option is

> chosen in this study, although it may seem to conflict at first glance with a non-modular approach to grammar. However, one must keep in mind that constructions can reach across layers and they only apply when all their constraints are met. So most of the time it is not at all relevant at which point in processing they operate. On the other hand, sometimes constraints in constructions are left as variables (i.e. they are underspecified). Therefore constructions might apply too early, thereby imposing an incorrect value on an underspecified constraint. One way of preventing this strongly undesirable behavior is to put the constructions that determine those values correctly into one construction set. It then has to be specified that this set is applied before other constructions which rely on these constraints.

In order to determine the focus of a proposition, it is common practice to assume that the proposition provides the answer to a lead-in information question. This question sets the context and ensures that the answer incorporates the most appropriate information structure, i.e. focus-marks the sentence constituent corresponding to the WH-constituent of the question [7, 23]. The presented grammar serves as the language representation in such a question-answering dialogue and can be used both for producing and interpreting questions and respective answers.

The remainder of this chapter is structured as follows: Section 2 presents the linguistic background of the present case study, introducing the notions of field topology and information structure. Section 3 takes a step back from the actual implementation and describes the different steps necessary for engineering a grammar, including the previously discussed linguistic findings. Section 4 highlights the main design patterns of the implementation, with Section 5 diving into several implementation details and presenting the constructions needed to produce an utterance. Section 6 briefly summarizes the handling of information structure in several other grammar formalisms and concludes the chapter.

2 Constituent Order of German Declaratives

The ordering of constituents in German declarative sentences is an intriguing subject, because, although several strict rules non-ambiguously determine some sentence constituents' position, it is often the case that German exhibits quite a free constituent order. The approach in this chapter assumes that German constituent order can be accounted for by following rules forming a topological model. This model divides sentences into topological domains or fields. All sentence constituents are captured by a field and then those fields are linearly ordered. Information structure plays a role in partially determining the constituent order within sentences and determining the ordering inside those topological fields that capture more than one constituent. This section introduces the notions of *field topology* and *information structure*.

2.1 Field Topology

The topological surface model traditionally proposes a maximum of five fields of varying complexity in linear order as discussed for example in [18] and displayed in Figure 1.[3] The two sentence brackets (called *linke Klammer* (LK; 'left bracket') and *rechte Klammer* (RK; 'right bracket')) form the sentence frame, embracing the *Mittelfeld* (MF; 'middle field'), preceded by the *Vorfeld* (VF; 'fore field'), followed by a *Nachfeld* (NF; 'end field'). All of those fields are optional, however, some of them more than others. For example, the linke Klammer is typically occupied by a finite verb, however, never in relative clauses.[4]

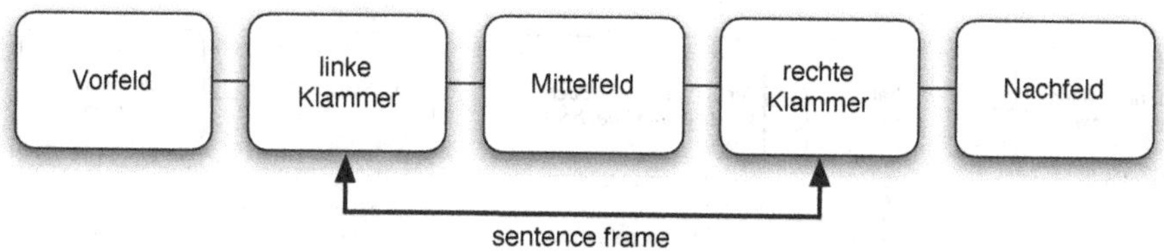

Fig. 1. Model of the five topological fields

Each of these fields imposes constraints about the type and number of sentence constituents it can capture. The finite verb, for instance, is always positioned in the LK, whereas non-finite verb forms as for example the past participle, in case the verb is in perfect tense are considered to be always included in the RK. This study does not account for cases where the participle occurs in another position as this goes beyond the scope of this study. Here we only consider possible declarative sentences which can answer a WH-question about one of the event participants. The Vorfeld is generally composed of exactly one sentence constituent (every constituent is permitted except the finite verb).[5] Figure 2 shows an example of how a sentence can be divided into five fields.

Despite the previously mentioned constraints determining which constituent can go into which field, this sentence has more than a dozen possible constituent orders. The ordering of constituents in the Mittelfeld seems to be relatively free, but there are factors of varying nature that interact with one another and affect the sentence constituents' order in that field, particularly factors related to information structure.

[3] There is, however, controversial literature highlighting possible problems when assuming this approach. (See for instance [28].)

[4] For more detailed information on topological fields or a historical overview see for instance [18], [19] or [10] who first used the field-based terminology. For a discussion of sentences with an empty left bracket see [28].

[5] In this chapter, the investigations are constrained to declarative sentences and WH-questions. There are, of course, exceptions to the mentioned rules, but these are beyond the scope of this case study. See [26, 27] for an HPSG approach to account for multiple frontings in German.

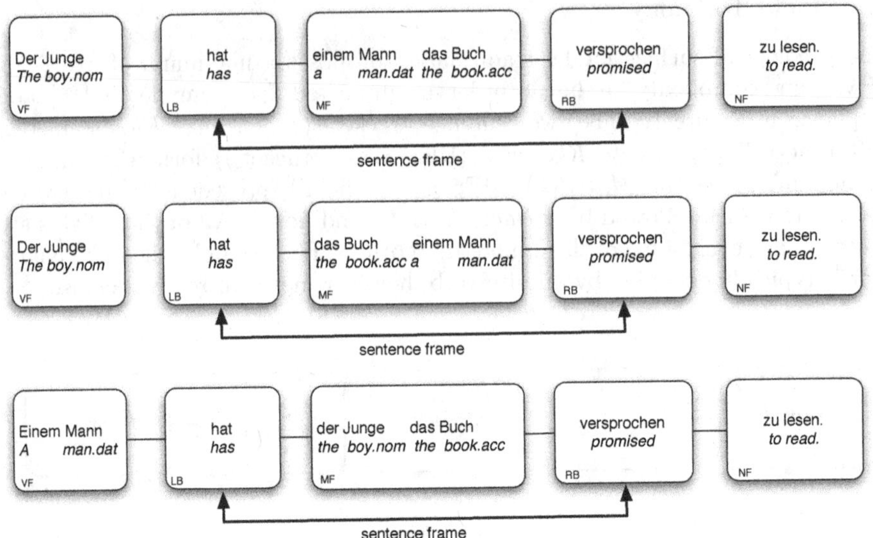

Fig. 2. Example sentences demonstrating three possibilities of placing sentence constituents into the fields. English translation: "The boy has promised a man to read the book". The glosses show the literal English translation.

2.2 Information Structure

The term *information structure* has been first introduced by Halliday [14]. It refers to information that is provided to the listener about what aspect is assumed to be in focus, what is given and new, what perspective is emphasized. Within a shared communicative context, a speaker aims at avoiding misunderstandings in communication. Therefore, he follows certain conventions with regard to information structure so that the listener can understand it with minimal processing effort [45].

Strategies of Information Structure. Different languages use different strategies to express information structure in their utterances depending on different communicative circumstances. It can be expressed prosodically, by grammatical markers or by a specific order of syntactic constituents in the form of complex grammatical constructions. English, for instance, uses constituent order as in (1) and (2), with possibly additional intonational stress or lexical means as in (3), to emphasize particular parts of sentences (underlined in the example sentences):

(1) *He likes flowers.*

vs.

(2) *Flowers he likes.*

(3) *As for flowers, he likes them.*

A language can have competing language strategies for expressing similar phenomena. German, like English, is an intonation language. Therefore, one of the strategies used for expressing information structure is the use of pitch accents on new or prominent parts of the sentence [32]. Those parts are here called the *focus* of the sentence. A different, frequently used strategy is for instance fronting of the most salient sentence constituents as exemplified in (3) for English.

Focus-Marking in Question-Answering. One of the main assumptions of traditional analyses of information structure is that the utterance answers a previously asked question which presents the relevant context [17, 42]. Different questions (see (4) and (6)) force different prosodic focus-marking (by using a pitch accent) on the truth-conditionally similar answers as exemplified in the following example sentences (The focus-marked constituent is put in square brackets; the index FOC stands for focus.):

(4) *Wer gibt dem Mann das Buch?*
Who gives the man the book?
transl.: 'Who gives the book to the man?'

(5) $[DerJunge_{FOC}]$ *gibt dem Mann das Buch.*
The boy gives the man the book.
transl.: 'The boy gives the book to the man'

(6) *Was gibt der Junge dem Mann?*
What gives the boy the man?
transl.: 'What does the boy give the man?'

(7) *Der Junge gibt dem Mann* $[einBuch_{FOC}]$.
The boy gives the man a book.
transl.: 'The boy gives the book to the man'

In these cases, the use of pitch accent focus-marks that part of the utterance asked for by the indicated question.

In this chapter, we focus exclusively on focus-marking for the following reasons:

1. Information about focus-marking is helping to account for an acceptable order of two objects in the Mittelfeld. (See the end of this section.)
2. Through the use of pitch accent the cognitive effort for the hearer is reduced, because the part of the response that answers directly the question is made more salient.
3. In some cases, intonation is necessary for disambiguation.

Example sentences (8) – (11) present a case where intonation helps disambiguate which sentence constituent plays which role in the situation. Sentence (9) presents an ambiguous answer to the question in (8): It is not clear who is seeing whom in that answer.

(8) *Wen sieht sie?*
transl.: 'Whom does she see?'

(9) *Die Professorin sieht die Studentin.*
transl.: 'The professor sees the student.' or
'The student sees the professor.'[6]

Sentences (10) and (11) are, however, unambiguous: in (10) the student sees the professor, in (11) the professor sees the student. However, the constituent order of both sentences is identical, and only intonation disambiguates the two different readings.

(10) $[DieProfessorin_{FOC}]$ *sieht die Studentin.*
transl.: 'The student sees the professor'.

(11) *Die Professorin sieht* $[dieStudentin_{FOC}]$.
transl.: 'The professor sees the student'.

The assumption that focused noun phrases are emphasized through prosodic means (through pitch accent) is based on Selkirk's findings [31]. She argues that questions allow control over which syntactic constituent in the answer has to be emphasized.

The present case study will not make a fine-grained difference of nuclear or prenuclear accents of declarative sentences. It additionally does not distinguish between rising or falling accents (adapted for German e.g. in [13]) as we are only interested in general focus-marking of newly introduced noun phrases to help determine constituent order. In this chapter we follow [30, 32] and use the term *focus* in the sense of particularly prominent or new. We concentrate on how information structure, and to be more precise, how focus-marking helps determine the ordering of noun phrases (NPs) in the Mittelfeld. To determine unmistakably which element should be focus-marked in an utterance, a preceding question is assumed.

Different Criteria Influencing Constituent Order. Certainly there are several properties of very different kinds that have an impact on constituent order. Some studies concentrate on definiteness [22], animacy [16, 21] or length of the argument NP in question. (see [1, 139], [2, 86], or [15]). In his seminal work on constituent order in German, Lenerz identified three different constraints on definiteness, case and focus-marking that co-determine the ordering of noun phrases in the double object construction in the Mittelfeld [24]:

[6] The first reading is preferred slightly more, as 'the professor' is in front position of the sentence.

1. definite NP *precedes* indefinite NP (*Definiteness constraint*)
2. non-focused NP *precedes* focused NP (*Focus constraint*)
3. dative NP *precedes* accusative NP (*Case constraint*);[7] *unmarked* constituent order

These three constraints are taken into account in this study.[8] Speakers of German have to establish knowledge of these constraints to successfully produce and understand utterances. There are five valid ordering scenarios regarding the interplay of the identified constraints. Most interesting about those constraints is their complex interaction with each other. Table 1 displays the valid scenarios with the respective truth values of the constraints.

Table 1. Constraints and their interaction between each other (+ means that a constraint is met, – means that it is not)

Scenarios	Definiteness	Focus	Case
1	+	+	+
2	+	+	–
3	–	–	+
4	–	+	+
5	+	–	+

Assuming the question in (6), the example sentence in (7) displays Scenario 1. The sentence in (12), however, presents an example of an invalid ordering of NPs in the Mittelfeld, assuming the same preceding question.

(12) Der Junge gibt ein Buch FOC dem Mann.
The boy gives a book FOC *the man.*
transl.: 'The boy gives the man a book'.

The answers in (14) and (15) to the question in (13) present the Scenarios 2 and 3 respectively.

[7] Especially the case constraint is currently under debate: As described for instance in [25] or [8], the order of sentence constituents in the MF is dependent on the kinds of verbs and the type of its arguments. Cook suggests, for example, to not assume a case constraint as suggested by Lenerz but to divide dative objects into low and high datives regarding their grammatical function. Noun phrases are then ordered in the MF depending on their grammatical function and not on their case. This approach has the advantage that the grammar then captures all kinds of ditransitive verbs not only those that are captured by following Lenerz' approach. However, in this chapter we follow solely Lenerz seminal study and consider the further division of dative objects as future work.

[8] To ensure that two objects occur both in the MF, it is assumed in this case study that the subject of the sentence is fixed in first position. This decision, however, is not linguistically motivated but chosen to ensure the occurrence of the double object construction in the MF.

(13) Wem gibt der Mann das Buch?
Whom gives the man the book?
transl.: 'To whom does the man give the book?'

(14) Der Mann gibt das Buch einem Jungen FOC.
The man gives the book a boy FOC.
transl.: 'The man gives the book to a boy.'

(15) Der Mann gibt einem Jungen FOC das Buch.
The man gives a boy FOC *the book.*
transl.: 'The man gives the book to a boy.'

Lenerz' findings can be summed up as follows: As soon as the case constraint holds, i.e. as soon as the dative NP precedes the accusative NP, it is irrelevant which of the remaining two constraints is positive. For this reason, this constituent order is called *unmarked* [24].[9] However, in case it does not hold, both of the other two constraints have to be met (*marked* constituent order). All these special constraints and their interaction between each other are explicitly integrated into the present FCG case study.

3 Progressive Plan Refinement

Before diving into the actual grammar implementation, it is important to consider which different steps have to be taken when composing an utterance using a grammar that integrates the previously discussed linguistic findings. This planning process collects different constraints, tests their validity, makes refinements and in the end, composes the utterance, satisfying all constraints, hopefully leading to communicative success. After the first and foremost goal has been reached in the process of producing an utterance, i.e. **what** will be said has been decided, the planning of the actual **how** to say it starts: what are the utterance's smallest constituents?

3.1 Which Words to Use?

Let us focus on the sentence "The man gives the book to a boy". A question can be asked about each event participant. Here it is assumed that the question in (13) (repeated here for convenience in (16)) precedes the production of the utterance and sets the context necessary to determine which event participant has to be focus-marked.

(16) Wem gibt der Mann das Buch?
Whom gives the man the book?
transl.: 'Whom does the man give the book to?'

[9] See additional remarks on unmarked constituent order in Section 6.

Producing an utterance is a sequential process in which the planning is constantly refined. It generally starts with selecting the required lexical items depending on the speaker's lexicon. There are several possible answers to the question in (16), two of which take into account the constraints mentioned in the last section.

(17) Der Mann gibt das Buch einem Jungen FOC.
The man gives the book a boy FOC.
transl.: 'The man gives the book to a boy.'

Another appropriate answer, investigated more closely here, is the following:

(18) Der Mann gibt einem Jungen FOC das Buch.
The man gives a boy FOC *the book.*
transl.: 'The man gives the book to a boy.'

When composing the utterance that answers the context question, the previously mentioned constraints are considered: the event participant being asked for is made more salient by being marked with a pitch accent and the noun phrase newly introduced to the context is preceded by an indefinite article, according to convention.[10]

Figure 3 shows which lexical constructions are used to compose the utterance. Each lexical item is a bi-directional mapping of a form which traditionally is constituted by the actual string and a meaning. A first order predicate logic-based representation of the meaning is used, which, for the lexical item Buch (engl.: 'book'), looks like this: `(book ?x)`. The predicate `book` stands for the ontological class describing books, and the variable `?x` can be bound to the actual book in the real world, which is referenced in this specific context. Determiners do not yet have a form, depending on the semantic and syntactic role that the item they are combined with plays. The appropriate string is added in a later step. For simplification, Figure 3 does not list all predicate-logic meanings but only the placeholder `meaning`. (See Figure 11 for a meaning representation of the complete sentence.)

The foundational material for building the utterance has been collected. The next step is to decide which low-level constituents can be determined thus far.

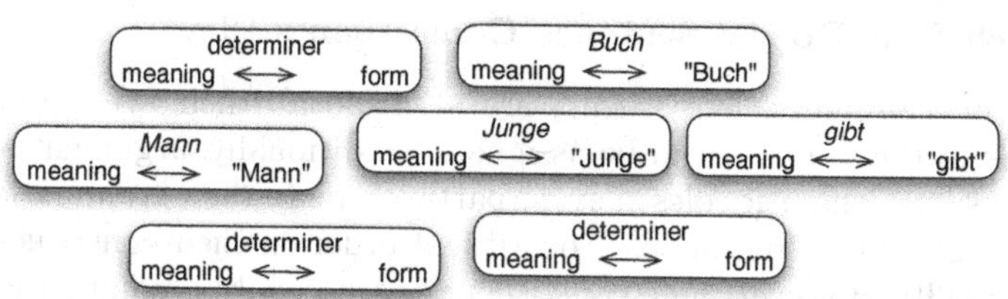

Fig. 3. All lexical items needed to produce the utterance

[10] This means that we assume that the NP has not been aforementioned to ensure the possibility to determine constituent order in the MF by accounting for Lenerz' findings (here the determination constraint respectively).

3.2 What Are Possible Sentence Constituents?

Each noun is preceded by a determiner, therefore, in this step nouns and determiners are combined into determined noun phrases. Syntactic and semantic information from each of the two components of a determined noun phrase are percolated up to the newly created noun phrase. In addition, the construction creating the noun phrases adds additional information both to its form part (i.e. constituent order constraints that the determiner has to precede the noun) and to its meaning part. The speaker wishes to emphasize the noun phrase asked for ('einem Jungen'), in order to minimize the cognitive effort of the hearer. Focus-marked sentence constituents are more salient than others, which is why the hearer immediately draws his or her attention to that constituent. Formally, this is represented by adding the marker "FOC" following the noun phrase in question. Figure 4 shows the constituents identified so far.

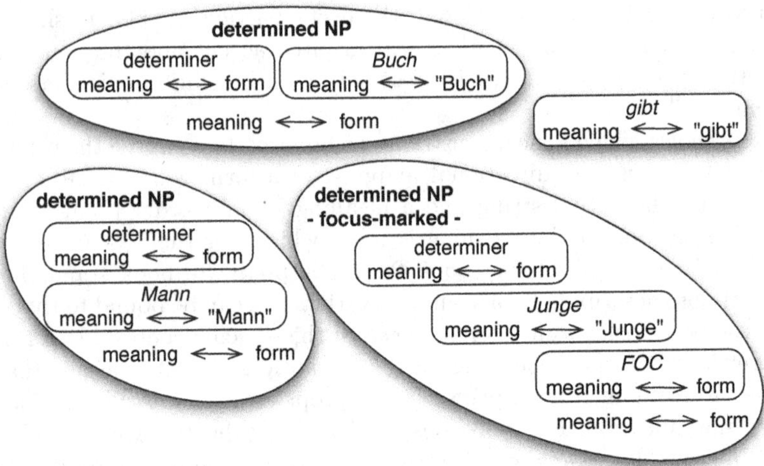

Fig. 4. The sentence constituents which so far have been identified

3.3 Which Role Do the Sentence Constituents Play?

Knowing which sentence constituents are at disposal, their syntactic and semantic roles in the sentence can be assigned. Traditionally, argument structure constructions link semantic roles of event participants to their grammatical roles, and additionally they often impose constituent order on their constituents. (See for instance [43]). However, here constituent order is only accounted for in the very last step of building the utterance, when the topological fields have been determined and can be sorted. One of the reasons for this approach is that the same argument structure constructions can apply for both declaratives and questions.

After each sentence constituent's semantic and syntactic role in the sentence has been identified, the determiners can be assigned their final forms. Figure 5

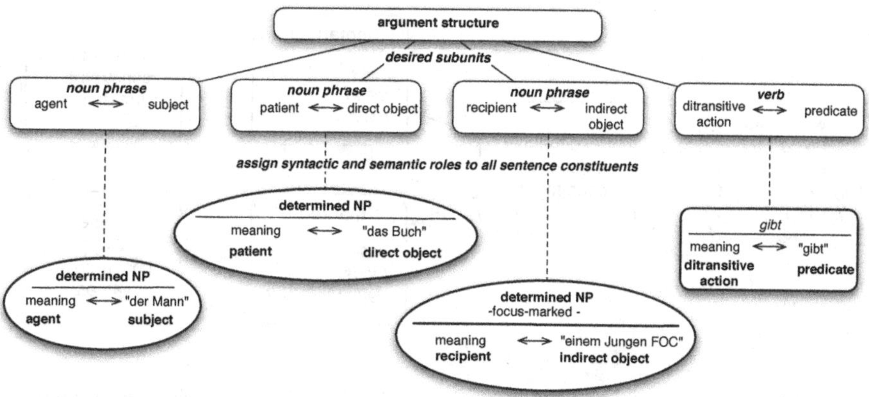

Fig. 5. Event participants are assigned their semantic and syntactic roles

shows the constituents identified so far, their semantic and syntactic roles and the forms of the appropriate determiners. It shows that an argument structure construction asks for four subunits which are assigned semantic and syntactic roles, assuming that they meet the constraints the construction imposes on them beforehand.

3.4 What Will Be the Order of the Two Objects in the Mittelfeld?

Before putting sentence constituents that have been determined so far into the appropriate topological fields, another decision has to be verified: Will the order of the two objects in the Mittelfeld be *marked* or *unmarked*? (See Figure 6.) This study accounts for three different constraints determining the constituent order of the two objects in the double object construction. Those constraints are all initially underspecified as presented in Figure 6 by a question mark (?) following the three keywords designating the three mentioned constraints: case, focus and definiteness.

In the case of the chosen constituent order being unmarked (as in sentence (16)), the case constraint is satisfied, i.e. it is positive. This decision is made when exactly **what** to say is decided, i.e. the predicate `(unmarked)` is listed in the meaning of the complete utterance to be produced. (See Figure 11.) Figure 6 shows that the question mark following the term case has been substituted by a +, because the constituent order is going to be unmarked. This step does not happen magically, but there are mechanisms in the grammar whose job it is to check if a constraint is met and determine the explicitly presented values of the constraints. As soon as the case constraint is determined to be positive, however, it is irrelevant if the other two constraints are fulfilled. The next step in the plan can be executed, i.e. which constituent is captured by which field and – in the case of the Mittelfeld – in which order are the constituents put into the field? (See Section 3.5.)

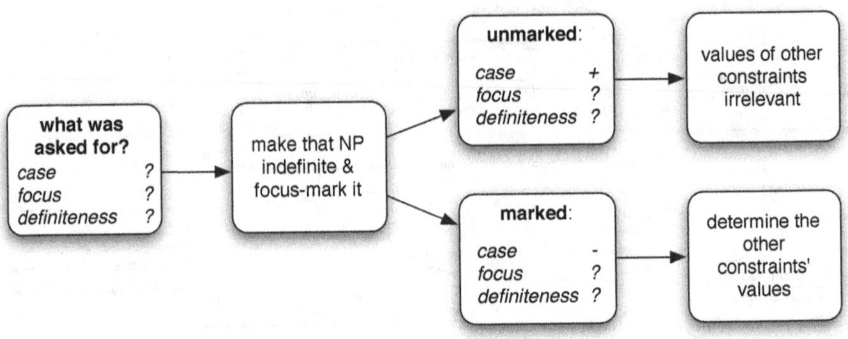

Fig. 6. Which order in the Mittelfeld is preferred (marked or unmarked) and what are the subsequent steps after the decision has been made?

Before that step is executed, the case should also be considered in which marked constituent order has been chosen (i.e. the accusative object NP precedes the dative object NP) (see (17)). In that case, the two other constraints regarding focus-marking and definiteness have to be determined (and in fact have to be

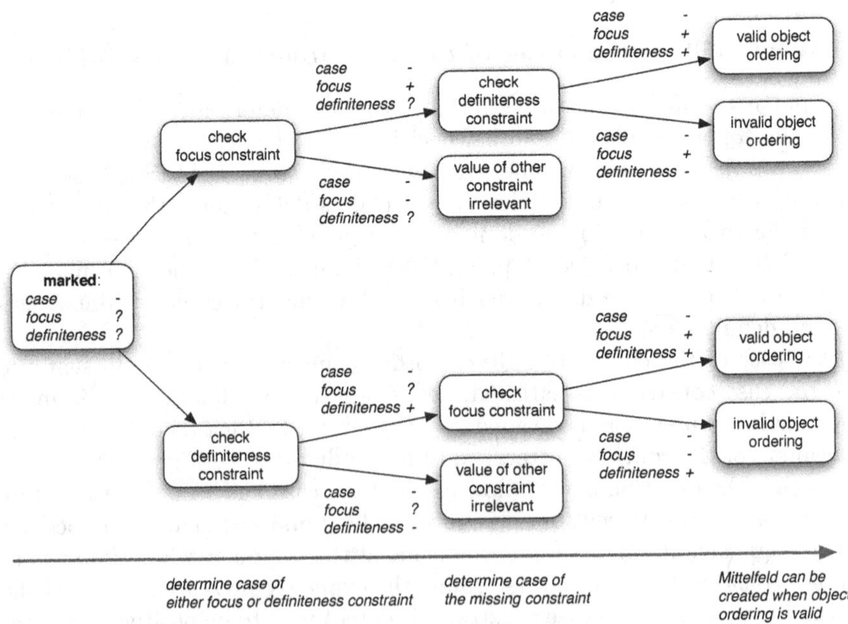

Fig. 7. When marked constituent order is preferred, all other constraints have to be checked successively. Both the definiteness and the focus constraint have to be positive to yield appropriate object ordering.

met) in order to yield an appropriate utterance. Figure 7 shows the decision tree which is traversed in that case. Having decided on producing marked constituent order in the Mittelfeld, the case constraint can be assigned a negative value, which means that there is a split in the tree: either the focus constraint or the definiteness constraint has to be checked as a subsequent step. If the first one picked tests negative, the value of the remaining last constraint is irrelevant, since no appropriate ordering of the noun phrases is possible. Remember, that if the case constraint does not hold, both other constraints must be positive. Therefore, ideally at the end of this planning phase all three constraints will have been determined, and will describe Scenario 2 of Table 1.

3.5 Which Sentence Constituent Goes into which Field?

As already mentioned, each field poses specific constraints on the constituent it can capture. If the constraints are met, the sentence constituent in question is put into the respective field. In this example study, the subject is always preferred to be in the Vorfeld, to make sure that the two objects are definitely in the Mittelfeld. Their order has already been determined in the last step where the three constraints and their validity were checked. The linke Klammer is in declarative sentences typically occupied by a finite verb. In the example sentence three topological fields result, which capture all of the present sentence constituents but which still have to be ordered linearly. Figure 8 illustrates the state in processing identified so far.

3.6 How Are the Topological Fields Ordered?

The last step of the plan still has to be executed: The topological fields have to be put into linear order. The Vorfeld is always in first position, followed by the linke Klammer, which is in turn followed by the Mittelfeld in which the order of constituents has previously been determined (see Figure 9). The construction that creates the linear order of the fields is a declarative construction, which is not affected by the type of constituents in the fields but simply puts those fields that are at its disposal into the appropriate order. In this example this means that after the declarative construction has applied, the Vorfeld precedes the linke Klammer, which in turn precedes the Mittelfeld.

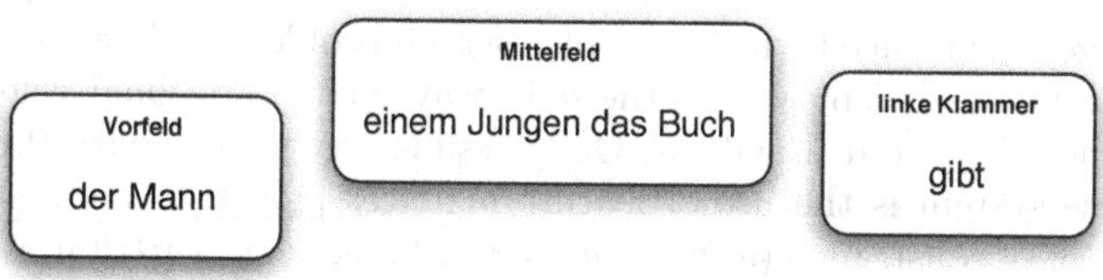

Fig. 8. Identified topological fields capturing their respective constituent(s) in arbitrary order. The order of the two objects in the Mittelfeld has already been determined.

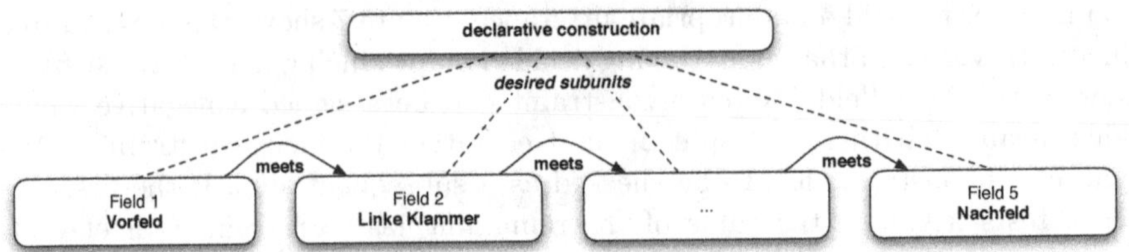

Fig. 9. A declarative construction puts the fields into linear order. The field containing the dots stands for any field that is put within the Linke Klammer and the Nachfeld.

3.7 Analyzing an Utterance

To parse the previously discussed utterance, exactly the same mechanisms are used. All steps are taken similar to the production process described above but starting from the surface form. The goal in this process is to pick the utterance apart and collect the sentence's expressed meaning. The order of the application of the mechanisms has, however, been slightly altered. First all lexical items (including the determiners) are picked out, and their meanings are collected. Determined noun phrases are then detected, semantic and syntactic roles of all event participants are assigned, the validity of the constraints are checked, fields and their constituents are assigned and the application of the declarative construction shows that the utterance is in fact a declarative.

After having discussed on a more general level how an utterance is built by assuming the approach of creating topological fields, sorting them and incorporating information structure to determine the fields' constituents' order, the next section presents some actual design patterns used in the applied FCG grammar to operationalize all of what has been mentioned before.

4 Design Patterns

This section highlights the main design patterns that have been used to implement the linguistic decision-making process discussed in the previous section.

4.1 Feature Matrices

The language user is faced with a complex search problem and needs to manage this problem in an efficient way. In the same way, a computational system has to find an efficient way to deal with it. One possible way to deal with the complex German case system is the use of feature matrices [44]. It is more efficient to represent a set of constraints (as case, gender and number) as attributes that take an array of values. Postponing the decision of a noun's case, gender and number to a point in the analysis where there is no longer ambiguity avoids unnecessary search or backtracking, in case a wrong hypothesis has been followed. As a result processing cost is highly reduced.

However, not only are feature matrices used to determine the case, gender and number of noun phrases or definiteness in determiners, attribute-value pairs are also put into the top-unit by the argument structure construction. Those attributes and their values are used to help determine the final constituent order of the double object construction in the Mittelfeld. That means that the final surface form of the utterance depends on a complex interaction of constraints. Only when the validity of the constraints has been identified, can the final constituent order be determined.

4.2 Construction Sets

Despite the fact that the linguistic inventory is a continuum from lexicon to grammar, various sets of constructions can be identified based on their function in the grammar. Particularly complex sentences, such as the one examined in this chapter, involve a considerable number of constructions of a different nature. Although FCG can also autonomously organize the search [47], the process of identifying the various **types** of constructions involved in the sentences' analysis is a first and necessary step into understanding and operationalizing a grammar. Hence, constructions are grouped into several construction sets regarding their function in interpretation and production.[11] (See Figure 10.) All constructions are bi-directional form–meaning pairings, however, they differ in their complexity.

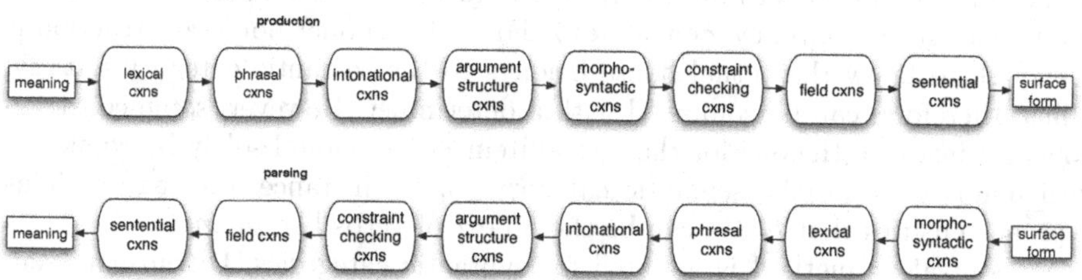

Fig. 10. The order in which FCG constructions are applied in production (upper part) and in interpretation (lower part)

Another major reason for arranging constructions in different sets is that the order of processing can thereby be controlled. Normally, the order of application does not matter, as constructions only apply when their conditions are fulfilled. However, aside from the fact that they can be grouped in functionally similar sets, making the application process more readable and easier to follow, it is important that some constructions only apply after other sets have already applied. Argument structure constructions add attribute value pairs to the top-unit, where the value is initially a logic variable. (See paragraph on explicit

[11] For more details on construction sets see [3].

constraint representation below.) Later in processing, there are constructions that check the value of those constraints, whose application requires for instance either an explicit negative value (i.e. a –) or a positive one (+). However, construction application can also successfully happen if the value of the constraint is still a variable for which the technical reason is that `(unify '(a b c) '(a b c))` clearly unifies, however, `(unify '(a ?x c) '(a b c))` unifies as well and binds the variable `?x` to `b`. Certainly, this binding is not desired in this case where all variables should first clearly be determined.

4.3 Ontological Categories

Constructions usually have a `syn-cat` and a `sem-cat` unit-feature that list the syntactic or semantic categories, respectively. Examples are for instance the part of speech of a word, its `function` like `nominal` or a plain semantic category like `entity`. These categories are further used by higher-level constructions: For instance a determiner-noun-construction asks for two subunits: one whose `function` is `nominal` and whose semantic category is an `entity` and one whose part of speech is `determiner` and whose semantic category contains a definiteness value. When having found units that conform to those constraints, these units are combined into a determined noun phrase. In this grammar, whenever necessary, instead of single category values, a list of semantic or syntactic categories is given, describing the same item, but with differing granularity or specificity.

Let's have a closer look at one example construction: The `sem-cat` feature of the construction describing the lexical item *house*, for instance, lists the semantic categories `(entity container)`. For a determiner-noun-construction it is enough to know the actual house belongs to the semantic category `entity`, which, therefore, can be combined with a determiner. However, some constructions, for instance the one for the lexical item *enter*, should solely be combined with nouns of a specific semantic category as, for instance, `container`. This approach ensures that *house* can be the object of verbs like *to enter*.

An equivalent method is adopted for syntactic categories: Ditransitive sentences have two objects: a direct and an indirect object. Both belong to the more general category `object`, therefore their `syn-cat` feature includes both `(direct-object object)` and `(indirect-object object)` respectively. A higher level construction like the one building the Mittelfeld for questions considers only that the constituents it captures are objects and not them being direct or indirect. Other constructions, however, need to make that distinction and therefore need more fine-grained information.

This method is chosen to account for simple ontological 'hierarchies', which theoretically can be as fine-grained as desired. *Hierarchy* here does not imply the integration of a real ontological hierarchy but refers to a list of ontological categories which are not linked in the construction at all. However, those categories can be mapped to ontological classes in a separate ontological model where properties and links have been established. The downside of this method is that so far many categories have to be copied and manually integrated into constructions again and again.

4.4 Explicit Representation of Constraints' Status

Constituent order in German is influenced by various kinds of constraints. Three of them and their interaction among each other have been discussed in 2.2. Those are all treated in the same way in the grammar implementation: The argument structure construction adds one attribute-value pair for each constraint to the `top-unit` of the transient structure representing the status of each of those constraints. This also shows that information structure as it is represented here is strongly interwoven with the rest of the grammar. The following pairs are explicitly added to the `top-unit` in a newly created unit-feature called `constraint-status`:

```
(constraint-status (==1 (focus-constraint ?fc)
                                       (definiteness-constraint ?dc)
                                      (case-constraint ?cc))
```

Each attribute is followed by its value, which initially is a variable, indicated by the ? preceding it. Only when it can be decided unambiguously which constraint is met, will the respective variable be changed either into a + (indicating that this constraint is met) or a – (indicating that it is not met). Similar category value pairs, where the value can either be a +, a – or a variable, will be used throughout the grammar on both the semantic and syntactic poles.

All mentioned high-level design patterns of the grammar will recur in the following section, where parts of the actual implementation are described.

5 Operationalization

Now that the linguistic background and more abstract ideas behind the presented grammar have been examined, technical issues that arise during operationalization can be addressed. Basic knowledge about FCG is assumed [37]. In the course of this section, several constructions are highlighted that contribute to the production of the answer to the respective question in (18). The answer is repeated in (19) for the reader's convenience.

(19) Der Mann gibt einem Jungen FOC das Buch.
The man gives a boy FOC *the book.*
transl.: 'The man gives the book to a boy.'

Extensive detail of the application of all of these constructions is not provided, rather mostly how they are created and what they look like is highlighted.[12] The interested reader is referred to `www.fcg-net.org` to inspect a complete dialogue where a question as well as a respective answer is produced and also parsed using the presented constructions. In the web demonstration, single constructions, as well as transient structures and their modifications after construction application, can be inspected. In the following sections, the constructions are described in their order of application in production as depicted in Figure 10.

[12] See [5] for a detailed explanation how constructions are applied.

5.1 Initial Linguistic Structure

Each production process starts with the creation of an initial transient structure that couples a syntactic and a semantic structure or pole. The semantic structure specifies the meaning of a sentence, while the syntactic structure specifies its form. Linguistic processing essentially involves the mapping of a semantic structure to a syntactic structure (i.e. meaning to form) during production, and the inverse during parsing. In terms of FCG, this is accomplished through the application of constructions to a transient structure. The consecutive application of constructions adds additional units and constituent structure to both poles of the structure as well as additional parts of meaning and form. All meaning to be rendered into an utterance is stored in the so-called *top-unit* (cf. Figure 11). The meaning is represented in first order predicate logic expressions.

Constructional meanings are stored in a frame-based ontology. A construction's meaning is represented by one of the frames present in the ontology, i.e. the value of its meaning feature is equivalent to a frame in the ontology. For example, the frame representing the meaning of the verb *to give* looks as follows:

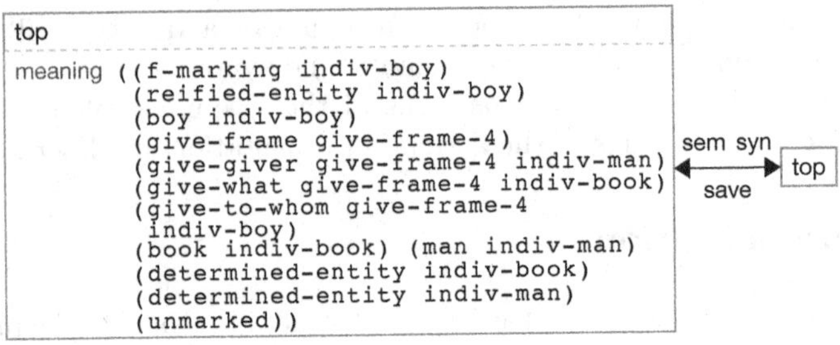

```
top
meaning ((f-marking indiv-boy)
         (reified-entity indiv-boy)
         (boy indiv-boy)
         (give-frame give-frame-4)                          sem syn
         (give-giver give-frame-4 indiv-man)   <----------> top
         (give-what give-frame-4 indiv-book)        save
         (give-to-whom give-frame-4
          indiv-boy)
         (book indiv-book) (man indiv-man)
         (determined-entity indiv-book)
         (determined-entity indiv-man)
         (unmarked))
```

Fig. 11. Initial transient structure. The semantic pole (to the left of the arrow) contains the meaning which will be rendered into an utterance, the syntactic pole (to the arrow's right) is still empty.

```
((give-frame ?give-frame)
 (give-giver ?give-frame ?a-giver)
 (give-what ?give-frame ?the-given-thing)
 (give-to-whom ?give-frame ?the-recipient))
```

Again, names starting with a question mark are variables. The use of the same variable name ensures that every instance of its use refers to the same referent. You can see in Figure 11 that those variables which designate the actual objects and events the speaker wishes to talk about have been replaced by unique symbol names. For instance, instead of the variable `?give-frame`, an indexed `give-frame-4` is used, referring to the give-action in the context.

5.2 Lexical Constructions

To define a lexical construction, the same templates as described in [37] are used. The following template creates a lexical construction called Mann-cxn by first creating a skeleton, then incrementally adding syntactic and semantic categorizations and finally a feature matrix to account for case:

```
(def-lex-cxn Mann-cxn
 (def-lex-skeleton Mann-cxn
         :meaning (== (man ?man))
         :args (?man)
         :string "Mann")
 (def-lex-cat Mann-cxn
         :sem-cat (==1 mann person entity
                       (sem-function identifier)))
         :syn-cat (==1 (pos noun)
                       (syn-function nominal))
 (def-feature-matrix Mann-cxn
         :feature (:syn-cat :case-number-gender)
         :paradigm *german-case*
         :dimensions (nom-s-m acc-s-m dat-s-m)))
```

In this state of processing it is not yet possible to unambiguously determine the lexical item's case. It can potentially be nominative, dative or accusative masculine singular. Feature matrices are used to express that there is still ambiguity. (See [44].) To include the respective feature matrix into the Mann-cxn the template def-feature-matrix is called within def-lex-cxn. Within that template, the feature to which the matrix is added to is specified (here: case-number-gender). Also the unit-feature to which case-number-gender is added to is listed (here: syn-cat). Then the kind of paradigm to be used – here *german-case* – is indicated. The possible values (nom-s-m acc-s-m dat-s-m) are listed as the Mann-cxn can be of all three cases, however always being masculine and singular.[13] The German case paradigm has to be created before with a template called define-paradigm:

```
(define-paradigm :dimensions ((nom acc dat gen)
                              (s-m s-f s-n)))
```

The resulting paradigm defined by that template is the following:

```
(syn-cat (==1 (case-number-gender
                ((nom ?nom ?nom-s-m ?nom-s-f ?nom-s-n)
                 (acc ?acc ?acc-s-m ?acc-s-f ?acc-s-n)
                 (dat ?dat ?dat-s-m ?dat-s-f ?dat-s-n)
                 (gen ?gen ?gen-s-m ?gen-s-f ?gen-s-n)))))
```

[13] Please see [44] for more information on the feature matrices, including a detailed description of the design choices and the respective templates.

For illustration purposes, plural is ignored in this example. Please refer to [44] for a complete treatment of German determiners. The paradigm that is included in the Mann-cxn, then, looks as follows. Some possibilities are already ruled out (i.e. marked with a –), as the gender and number of the lexical item is already known:

```
(syn-cat (==1 (case-number-gender ((nom ?nom-s-m ?nom-s-m - -)
                                    (acc ?acc-s-m ?acc-s-m - -)
                                    (dat ?dat-s-m ?dat-s-m - -)
                                    (gen - - - -)))))
```

In production, the application of the construction is triggered by the meaning (man indiv-man) in the ?top-unit. A new unit is then created, which contains both a semantic and a syntactic pole. On the semantic side, an args feature, whose value is the same referent as the one in the meaning predicate, and a sem-cat feature, whose value is a simple hierarchy listing the unit's semantic categories (mann person entity), are added. (See Section 4.3.) The syntactic pole contains the part of speech and the syntactic function of the unit (nominal). Each construction has a specific syntactic function. The function of more complex noun phrases is also nominal. Those functions enable the usage of the output unit in higher level constructions. For instance, the determiner-noun-phrase construction does not care if the determiner is combined with a common noun or an adjective-noun phrase. It only imposes one constraint on the unit the determiner is combined with: The function of that unit has to be nominal. All lexical constructions are created in the same way as described for the Mann-cxn.

5.3 Grammatical Constructions

Grammatical constructions are needed to determine semantic or syntactic roles of the sentence, its phrase structure and the topological sentence structure. The following sections describe the types of constructions needed to produce the utterance.

Phrasal and Intonational Constructions. The only phrasal construction to apply three times is the determiner-nominal-phrase-cxn. To create this construction the def-phrasal-cxn template is used, which heavily resembles the one described in detail in [35] and utilizing the J-operator [9]. That chapter goes step by step through the creation of a phrasal construction by exploring different mechanisms handling each single issue in the construction. The following shows the template as it is used here:

```
(def-phrasal-cxn determiner-nominal-phrase-cxn
   (def-phrasal-skeleton determiner-nominal-phrase-cxn
     :phrase
      (?nominal-phrase
       :cxn-form (== (meets ?determiner-unit ?nominal-unit))
       :sem-function referring
       :phrase-type nominal-phrase)
      :constituents
      ((?determiner-unit
        :sem-function reference
        :syn-function determiner)
       (?nominal-unit
        :sem-function identifier
        :syn-function nominal)))
    (def-phrasal-agreement determiner-nominal-phrase-cxn
     (?nominal-phrase
      :sem-cat (==1 (determined +)
                    (definite ?definiteness)
                    referent)
      :syn-cat (==1 (definite ?definiteness)
                    (determined +)
                    (pos (== ref-expression))
                    (case-number-gender ?case) referent))
     (?determiner-unit
      :sem-cat (==1 (definite ?definiteness))
      :syn-cat (==1 (definite ?definiteness)
                    (pos determiner)
                    (case-number-gender ?case)))
     (?nominal-unit
      :sem-cat (==1 entity)
      :syn-cat (==1 (case-number-gender ?case))))
    (def-phrasal-linking determiner-nominal-phrase-cxn
     (?nominal-phrase
      :args (?referent))
     (?determiner-unit
      :args ?referent)
     (?nominal-unit
      :args (?referent))))
```

The construction created by the template does not add a constructional meaning but only specifies a constructional form (constituent order). However, the choice in semantic or syntactic categories presents the main differences to the construction creation described in [35]. To ensure agreement in case, number and gender, the `case-number-gender` categories of both the determiner and the nominal units carry the same value `?case`.

The rule's application is triggered by the presence of a `?determiner-unit` and a `?nominal-unit` complying with the semantic and syntactic constraints imposed on those units. Each nominal and its associate determiner are made subunits of a newly created noun phrase unit. Depending on which kind of determiner has triggered the application of the `determiner-nominal-phrase-cxn`, the respective definiteness value, `(definite +)` or `(definite -)`, is percolated both to the semantic and syntactic poles of the newly created noun phrase. Similarly, the value of the variable `?case`, which is a complete feature matrix including case, number and gender information, is percolated to the new unit `?nominal-phrase` where the same variable name is used. The part of speech of each newly created unit is `ref-expression`. This attribute is needed for the unit's later use in the ditransitive construction.

One of the created noun phrases is going to be the one that carries the pitch accent, i.e. that is focus-marked. On the form side, this is expressed by adding the marker "FOC" to the noun phrase that was asked for in the previously asked question ("einem Jungen"). Also a syntactic category will be added: `(f-marked +)`. On the meaning side, this is represented by the meaning `(f-marking indiv -boy)`. The semantic category `(focused +)` is additionally added. The construction which takes care of focus-marking that noun phrase is created with the same `def-phrasal-cxn` template. The only differences are in the choice of semantic and syntactic categories. Most important are those in the `def-phrasal -agreement` template:

```
(def-phrasal-agreement focus-unit-construction
       (?emphasized-phrase
        :sem-cat (==1 (focused +) referent)
        :syn-cat (==1 (f-marked +)
                      (pos (== ref-expression))
                      (case-number-gender ?case))))
```

After successful construction application, the newly created unit `?emphasized -phrase` contains the listed semantic and syntactic categories. They will later be needed to determine the value of the focus constraint in the `?top-unit` to determine the order of the two objects in the Mittelfeld. (See Section 5.3.) Additionally, case, number and gender information of the unit to be emphasized is percolated from the noun phrase to `?emphasized-phrase`.

Argument Structure. The main task of argument structure constructions is to link semantic roles of event participants to their grammatical roles [34]. This section briefly examines the ditransitive construction needed to produce the utterance. For a complete chapter on how to deal with argument structure of utterances and how they can be created see [43]. There are several differences between the argument structure construction used here and argument structure constructions presented in that chapter:

1. It does not explicitly add any meaning in form of a meaning predicate, but it assigns semantic and syntactic roles to the event participants.

2. It does not impose constituent order on its subunits. The main reason for that design choice is that it can be used both in questions and declarative sentences, differing in their surface structure. Constituent order is only accounted for by ordering the topological fields. (See Section 5.3.)
3. It creates a new unit-feature `constraint-status` in the top-unit and adds three attribute-value pairs to this unit-feature which are needed to determine the order of the nominal objects in the Mittelfeld:

```
(constraint-status (==1 (focus-constraint ?fc)
                        (definiteness-constraint ?dc)
                       (case-constraint ?cc))
```

   After the application of the ditransitive construction, the values of those three attributes are still underspecified (marked by the preceding question mark (?) of the symbol name). They become atomic (either + or −) after their truth-value has been checked by the respective constructions (cf. Section 5.3). This is a requirement to decide whether or not a scenario as listed in Table 1 is valid.

The decision which sentence constituent plays which semantic or syntactic role in a sentence has been delayed to a point where it can unambiguously be decided. After application of that construction all event roles are specified, i.e. the mapping of semantic roles like `agent` and syntactic roles like `subject` has been taken care of, which means that the respective cases of the event participants can ultimately be assigned. For instance the feature matrix for the determiner noun phrase "*der Mann*" looks now as follows:

```
(syn-cat (==1 (case-number-gender ((nom + + - -)
                                   (acc - - - -)
                                   (dat - - - -)))))
```

Morphological Constructions. Morphological constructions operating solely on the syntactic part of the structure determine the eventual form of the articles. Since the case, number and gender of determined noun phrases has been determined by the argument structure construction, the determiners' case, number and gender is known, as well. Therefore, their form can be assigned at this point in processing. The template to create a morphological construction for the determiner *der* looks like the following:

```
(def-morph-cxn der-morph
    :syn-cat (==1 (pos determiner)
                  (case-number-gender ?case)
                  (definite +)
                  (syn-function determiner))
    :string "der")
```

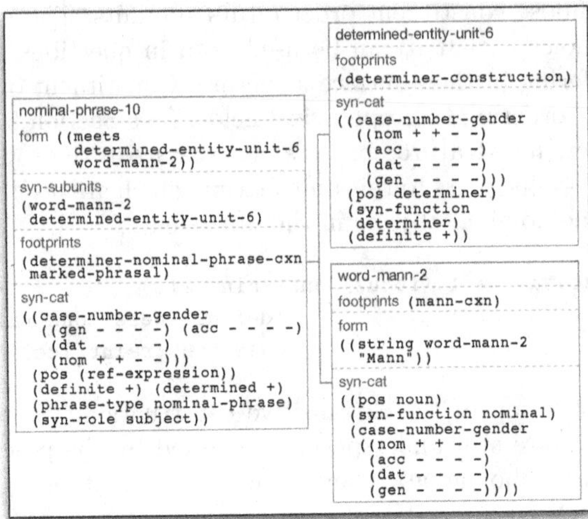

Fig. 12. The syntactic part of the noun phrase unit with its two subunits

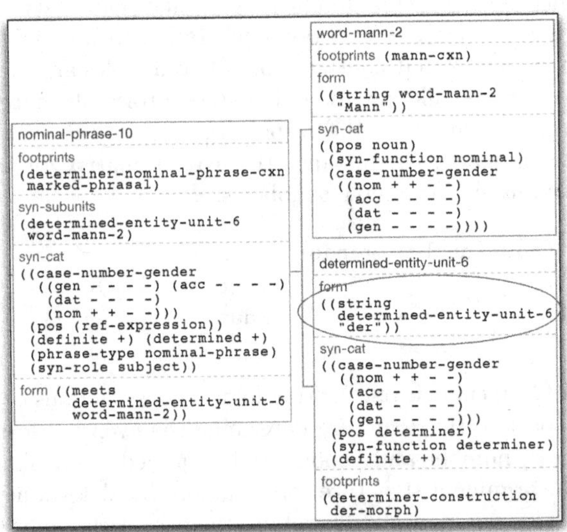

Fig. 13. The same unit as above after the application of a morphological construction having added the form feature to the determination unit

Figure 12 shows the syntactic part of the noun phrase unit combining the `Mann-unit` and the `determination-unit` before the application of the morphological construction. After its application the form feature with the string "der" has been added to the `determination-unit`, depicted in Figure 13.

Constraint-Checking Constructions. Constraint-checking constructions determine which of the three constraints, whose status is monitored in the `top-unit`, are met, regarding a certain order of noun phrases in the Mittelfeld. Depending on the result of the test, the value of each attribute will be either + or −. When the case constraint is met (dative NP *precedes* accusative NP), none of the other constraints no longer have to be checked (see Scenarios 1, 3, 4 and 5 of Table 1), which means their attribute value can stay underspecified. Only in the second scenario, i.e. when marked constituent order is chosen, the values of the definiteness and the focus constraint have to be validated. (See description of the decision process in Section 3.)

To account for the utterance in (19), only the construction checking the case constraint applies. All constructions checking any kind of constraint look very similar and are created with the `def-constraint-check` template. The following creates the `case-check-construction-positive` construction.

```
(def-constraint-check case-check-construction-positive
     :constituent-order (?first-object ?second-object)
     :meaning (unmarked)
     :constraint-status (case-constraint +)
     :constituents ((?first-object
                       :args (?recipient)
                       :sem-cat (==1 (sem-role recipient))
                       :syn-cat (==1 (syn-role (== indirect-object))))
                      (?second-object
                       :args (?patient)
                       :sem-cat (==1 (sem-role patient))
                       :syn-cat (==1 (syn-role (== direct-object))))))
```

On its syntactic side, the construction imposes a constituent order on its two constituents `?first-object` and `?second-object`. This constituent order is specified in the slot `:constituent-order`, then the construction's meaning is given. The following slot allows for the manipulation of the values of the constraints that are in the `top-unit`. Here, it is specified, that the case-constraint is going to be met (it is positive). When applied, the construction assigns a + to the previous variable `?cc` of the case constraint `(constraint-status (==1 (case-constraint +)))`. In the slot `:constituents`, both semantic and syntactic categories of all constituents (here `?first-object` and `?second-object`) are specified. The constituent `?first-object` must have the `(sem-role recipient)` and the `(syn-role (== indirect-object))`. Similarly, it is constrained that the constituent `?second-object` must have the `(sem-role patient)` and the `(syn-role (== direct-object))`. Those constraints and the imposed constituent order on the constituents equal the case constraint: dative NP *precedes* accusative NP.

The following shows what the created construction looks like. The information which has been provided by the template is printed in bold:

```
(def-cxn case-check-construction-positive ()
       ((?top (sem-subunits (== ?first-object ?second-object))
              (sem-cat (==0 question-to-be-answered))
              (meaning (== (unmarked)))
              (footprint (==0 case-check-construction)))
        (?first-object
         (sem-cat (==1 (sem-role recipient)))
         (args ?recipient))
        (?second-object
         (sem-cat (==1 (sem-role patient)))
         (args ?patient))
        ((J ?top)
          (constraint-status (==1 (case-constraint +)))
          (footprint (== case-check-construction))))
       <-->
       ((?top (syn-subunits (== ?first-object ?second-object))
              (form (== (meets ?first-object ?second-object)))
              (syn-cat (==0 question-to-be-answered))
              (footprint (==0 case-check-construction)))
        (?first-object
         (syn-cat (==1 (syn-role (== indirect-object)))))
        (?second-object
         (syn-cat (==1 (syn-role (== direct-object)))))
        ((J ?top)
         (constraint-status (==1 (case-constraint +)))
         (footprint (== case-check-construction)))))
```

After it has been determined that the case constraint is positive, the stage is set for the topological constructions to apply.

Topological Constructions. To account for sentence structure in German, a field topology approach is followed as briefly described in Section 2. Each field is considered as a box in which constituents are put when they meet several conditions. They all look very similar and apply in exactly the same way as all previously discussed constructions. The following shows the template `def-field-cxn` used to create constructions that build fields:

```
(def-field-cxn field name
               :constituent-order  list constituents that should follow each other
               :constituents ( ?unit-name
                               :args  arguments
                               :sem-cat  features
                               :syn-cat  features))
```

In the first slot `:constituent-order` the constituents that are supposed to follow each other are listed. The slot `:constituents` can capture a varying number of constituents. Those constituents will be put into the respective field.

This is operationalized by creating a new field-unit and making the constituents subunits of that field-unit. A new unit-feature is introduced in the newly created field unit called `field-role`. This unit-feature is needed later by the sentential construction which puts the fields into linear order. The value of this feature is the actual name of the respective field the unit designates. The following subsections show how that template is used to create the linke Klammer, Vorfeld and Mittelfeld.

Linke Klammer. The first field to be inspected is the linke Klammer. The following shows the template creating it:

```
(def-field-cxn linke-klammer-full-verb-constituent
     :constituents ((?clause-constituent
                     :args (?referent)
                     :sem-cat (==1 event)
                     :syn-cat (==1 (verb-form finite)
                                   (pos (== full-verb))
                                   (syn-role predicate)))))
```

This field is the simplest one here, as there is only one option which sentence constituent it can capture: the finite verb. Therefore, the semantic category of this clause constituent have to be of type event `(sem-cat (== event))` and the syntactic categories have to include `(syn-cat (==1 (verb-form finite) (pos (== verb)) (syn-role predicate)))`.

After the application of this construction, a new unit is created which captures the constituent and takes it as its subunit. To both its syntactic and semantic pole a new unit-feature is added:

```
(field-role (== linke_klammer))
```

Vorfeld. Generally, each sentence constituent except the finite verb are allowed in the Vorfeld. There are, however, exceptions which are discussed in detail in [25]. With an interest in the double object construction in the Mittelfeld, only the subject is permitted in the Vorfeld in this grammar implementation. It is, however, also possible to implement the Vorfeld construction in a way so that it accepts other sentence constituents, but this construction will not be described here. To make sure that the subject will be put into the Vorfeld, the syntactic category of the constituent the construction applies on is required to be of `(syn-role subject)` and the semantic category of `(sem-role agent)`. Again – behind the scenes – a `field-role` unit-feature and a footprint are added to the newly created unit.

The following shows the `def-field-cxn` template used to create a construction that builds the Vorfeld:

```
(def-field-cxn Vorfeld-construction
    :constituent-order (?clause-constituent ?left-bracket)
    :constituents ((?clause-constituent
                     :args (?agent)
                     :sem-cat (==1 (sem-role agent))
                     :syn-cat (==1 (syn-role subject)))
                    (?left-bracket
                     :field-role (==1 linke_klammer))))
```

Mittelfeld. In our implementation, there are two different constructions that can create a Mittelfeld, however, only one of them can apply here based on the positive value of the case-constraint: `(constraint-status (==1 (case -constraint +)))`.

Below, the `def-field-cxn` template is used to create that Mittelfeld:

```
(def-field-cxn Mittelfeld-construction
    :constraint-status (case-constraint +)
    :word-order (?first-object ?second-object)
    :constituents ((?first-object
                     :sem-cat (==1 (sem-role recipient))
                     :syn-cat (==1 (syn-role (==1 indirect-object))))
                    (?second-object
                     :sem-cat (==1 (sem-role patient))
                     :syn-cat (==1 (syn-role (==1 direct-object)))))
```

In parsing, the `Mittelfeld-construction` applies when two subunits are present fulfilling the syntactic constraints that both of their `syn-roles` have to be objects, one being `(syn-role (== indirect-object))` and the other one `(syn -role (== direct-object))` respectively.

In production, the construction imposes semantic constraints on its constituents, i.e. their `sem-role` has to be either patient or recipient: `(sem-cat (==1 (sem-role (== patient))))` or `(sem-cat (==1 (sem-role (== recipient))))` respectively.
As soon as those constraints are met, a Mittelfeld-unit is created, taking the direct object and the indirect object as subunits and imposing constituent order on them `(form (== (meets ?first-object ?second-object)))`. By now, all necessary sentence constituents are captured in a topological field. The created fields are still in no specific order. Sentential constructions put the fields into linear order, how exactly is explained in the following.

Sentential Constructions. Sentential constructions, as for instance an interrogative or a declarative construction, put the created fields into linear order. The declarative construction is triggered as soon as there are three fields, here called `?vorfeld`, `?linke-klammer` and `?mittelfeld`, which fulfill the following constraints on both semantic and syntactic poles of the source structure:

```
(?vorfeld (field-role (== vorfeld)))
(?linke-klammer (field-role (== linke_klammer)))
(?mittelfeld (field-role (== mittelfeld)))
```

The declarative construction does not add additional conceptual meaning, however it contributes to the meaning by adding a semantic and a syntactic category to the top-unit: `(sem-cat (==1 assertion))` and `(syn-cat (== declarative -clause))`. It additionally does not care about the number and type of constituents captured in the fields. It solely sorts the fields by imposing `meets`-constraints on them in its form feature:

```
(form (== (meets ?vorfeld ?linke-klammer)
          (meets ?linke-klammer ?mittelfeld)))
```

Finally, all constructions which are needed to create the utterance in (19) have applied and the utterance, therefore, can be rendered.

6 Discussion and Conclusion

There are various efforts operationalizing German constituent order which have inspired this work. In [12], for instance, the implementation of a grammar is described, dealing with German constituent order based on a topological model starting from a syntactic dependency tree. The main emphasis of that work is, however, to cover all acceptable linear orders of German declarative sentences. There is no semantic or contextual information integrated in their formalism yet. Furthermore, they do not account for syntactic structure of the sentence at all, playing a fundamental role in constituent order, but only care about the topological phrase structure, i.e. about the order or the fields per se and not the order of elements within those fields or other phrases' structure. The HPSG description of German constituent order in [20] also describes linearization rules exclusively based on the topological structure of sentences.

Information structure is usually ignored in present-day computational systems, however, there are some efforts where its inclusion is regarded beneficial. [39] reports on the incorporation of information structure into UCCG – Unification-based Combinatory Categorial Grammar. The main goal of the involvement of information structure in that grammar implementation is to improve the performance of speech generation systems. Similar to the account taken here, pitch accents are implemented as autonomous units which can be combined with the constituent that has to be emphasized. This ensures that the lexicon is not unnecessarily expanded as it is, for instance, in Combinatory Categorial Grammar [33] where each lexical word is represented multiple times in the lexicon: one separate entry is created for the non-emphasized word and several entries for each possible accent that word can carry. However, that grammar implementation includes a much more fine-grained analysis of intonation as its main purpose is completely different to the grammar presented here, which is to be further used in a speech generating system.

In [11], the integration of information structure into the HPSG framework is described. This study is conform with this approach in several points, such as that information structure should be an integral part of the grammar instead of representing it independently. However, their analysis has never been expressed as a working computational implementation, but only describes a potential computational system. From the point of view taken here, it is considered to be essential to implement the analyses proposed to validate their assumptions.

There are other efforts in HPSG dealing with the implementation of grammars including aspects of information structure. For instance [4] describes an HPSG grammar implementation which takes into account the thematic role of clitic left dislocated arguments in Spanish, assuming that part of the focus of an utterance depends on that thematic role.

Most inspiring to our work is the approach taken in [6] who presents a detailed analysis – only descriptive and not computationally implemented – based on Optimality Theory grammar, accounting for the same linguistic constraints mentioned in Section 2.2. His main focus, the same proposed here, is to present a case study of the interaction of constituent order, prosody and focus. As we did in our study, he is limiting his discussion mainly to the double object construction.

This paper has presented an operational solution illustrating a field topology approach and including one aspect of information structure. The grammar can be used to produce and parse WH-questions and corresponding answers which not only include the most efficient and also context-sensitive focus-marking, but also account for a complete phrase structure of both questions and answers.

Various design choices have been made to achieve the desired grammar. One main aspect includes the tight integrating of focus-marking into the grammar which highlights the non-modular approach to language that FCG is attributed to. This way, the grammar can use information structure to determine constituent order (and vice versa). Besides several other design choices, a novel design pattern of representing the status of constraints in the top-unit of the transient structure has been explored. It has been shown that FCG is open enough to offer an appropriate framework to deal with the mentioned issues. Future work includes the further exploration of the monitoring of constraint status and the integration of further aspects of information structure into the grammar, such as for instance focus/background marking.

Acknowledgements. Research reported in this paper was funded by the Sony Computer Science Laboratory Paris and the EU FP7 ALEAR project. I thank Luc Steels and the whole team working on FCG at the University of Brussels (VUB AI lab) and at Sony CSL for their contributions in making FCG such a superb environment for doing sophisticated experiments in construction grammar. Also I would like to thank Remi van Trijp for his help in bug-fixing the grammar and Stefan Müller and Philippa Cook for helpful comments on an earlier version of this chapter. All remaining errors are mine.

References

[1] Behaghel, O.: Beziehung zwischen Umfang und Reihenfolge von Satzgliedern. Indogermanische Forschungen 25, 110–142 (1909)
[2] Behaghel, O.: Von deutscher Wortstellung. Zeitschrift für Deutschkunde 44, 81–89 (1930)
[3] Beuls, K.: Construction sets and unmarked forms: A case study for Hungarian verbal agreement. In: Steels, L. (ed.) Design Patterns in Fluid Construction Grammar. John Benjamins, Amsterdam (2011)
[4] Bildhauer, F.: Clitic left dislocation and focus projection in Spanish. In: Proceedings of the 15th International Conference on Head-Driven Phrase Structure Grammar, pp. 346–357. CSLI Publications (2008)
[5] Bleys, J., Stadler, K., De Beule, J.: Search in linguistic processing. In: Steels, L. (ed.) Design Patterns in Fluid Construction Grammar. John Benjamins, Amsterdam (2011)
[6] Büring, D.: Let's phrase it!—Focus, word order, and prosodic phrasing in German double object constructions. In: Müller, G., Sternefeld, W. (eds.) Competition in Syntax. Studies in Generative Grammar, vol. 49, pp. 101–137. de Gruyter, Berlin (2001)
[7] Comrie, B.: Language universals and linguistic typology: Syntax and morphology. University of Chicago Press, Chicago (1981)
[8] Cook, P.: The datives that aren't born equal. Beneficiaries and the dative passive. In: Hole, D. (ed.) Datives and Other Cases. Between Argument Structure and Event Structure, pp. 141–184. John Benjamins, Amsterdam (2006)
[9] De Beule, J., Steels, L.: Hierarchy in Fluid Construction Grammars. In: Furbach, U. (ed.) KI 2005. LNCS (LNAI), vol. 3698, pp. 1–15. Springer, Heidelberg (2005)
[10] Drach, E.: Grundgedanken der deutschen Satzlehre. Diesterweg, FRANKFURT (1937)
[11] Engdahl, E., Vallduví, E.: Information packaging in HPSG. In: Edinburgh Working Papers in Cognitive Science, pp. 1–32 (1996)
[12] Gerdes, K., Kahane, S.: Word order in German: a formal dependency grammar using a topological hierarchy. In: ACL 2001: Proceedings of the 39th Annual Meeting on Association for Computational Linguistics, pp. 220–227. Association for Computational Linguistics, Morristown (2001)
[13] Grice, M., Baumann, S., Benzmüller, R.: German intonation in autosegmental phonology. In: Prosodic Typology (2003)
[14] Halliday, M., Hasan, R.: Notes on transitivity and theme in English. Journal of Linguistics 3, 199–244 (1967)
[15] Hawkins, J.: A performance theory of order and constituency. Cambridge University Press, Cambridge (1994)
[16] Hoberg, U.: Die Wortstellung in der geschriebenen deutschen Gegenwartssprache. Heutiges Deutsch. Linguistische Grundlagen. Forschungen des Instituts für deutsche Sprache, vol. 10. Max Hueber Verlag, München (1981)
[17] Höhle, T.N.: Explikation für "Normale Wortstellung". In: Abraham, W. (ed.) Satzglieder im Deutschen - Vorschläge zur Syntaktischen, Semantischen und Pragmatischen Fundierung. Studien zur deutschen Grammatik, pp. 75–153. Gunter Narr Verlag, Tübingen (1982)
[18] Höhle, T.N.: Topologische Felder. ms, Köln (1982)

[19] Höhle, T.N.: Der Begriff Mittelfeld, Anmerkungen über die Theorie der topologischen Felder. In: Weiss, W., Wiegand, H.E., Reis, M. (eds.) Textlinguistik Contra Stilistik? Wortschatz und Wörterbuch - Grammatische Oder Pragmatische Organisation von Rede? Kontroversen, alte und neue, pp. 329–340. Max Niemeyer Verlag, Tübingen (1986)
[20] Kathol, A.: Linearization-based German Syntax. Ph.D. thesis, Ohio State University, Berkeley (1995)
[21] Kempen, G., Harbusch, K.: A corpus study into word order variation in German subordinate clauses: Animacy affects linearization independently of grammatical function assignment. In: Pechman, T., Habel, C. (eds.) Multidisciplinary Approaches to Language Production, pp. 173–181. Mouton de Gruyter, Berlin (2004)
[22] Kurz, D.: A statistical account on word order variation in german. In: Proceedings of the COLING Workshop on Linguistically Interpreted Corpora (2000)
[23] Lambrecht, K.: Information Structure and Sentence Form: Topic, Focus, and the Mental Representations of Discourse Referents (Cambridge Studies in Linguistics). Cambridge University Press (1996)
[24] Lenerz, J.: Zur Abfolge nominaler Satzglieder im Deutschen. Narr, Tübingen (1977)
[25] Müller, S.: Deutsche Syntax deklarativ. Head-Driven Phrase Structure Grammar für das Deutsche. Linguistische Arbeiten, vol. 394. Max Niemeyer Verlag, Tübingen (1999)
[26] Müller, S.: Multiple frontings in German. In: Jäger, G., Monachesi, P., Penn, G., Winter, S. (eds.) Proceedings of Formal Grammar 2002, Trento, pp. 113–124 (2002), `http://hpsg.fu-berlin.de/~stefan/Pub/mehr-vf.html`
[27] Müller, S.: Zur Analyse der scheinbar mehrfachen Vorfeldbesetzung. Linguistische Berichte 203, 297–330 (2005), `http://hpsg.fu-berlin.de/~stefan/Pub/mehr-vf-lb.html`
[28] Müller, S.: Elliptical constructions, multiple frontings, and surface-based syntax. In: Jäger, G., Monachesi, P., Penn, G., Winter, S. (eds.) Proceedings of Formal Grammar 2004, Nancy. CSLI Publications, Stanford (to appear)
[29] Reis, M.: On justifying topological frames: Positional field and the order of nonverbal constituents in German. Documentation et Recherche en Linguistique Allemande Contemporaine 22/23, 59–85 (1980)
[30] Rooth, M.: A theory of focus interpretation. Ph.D. thesis, University of Massachusetts, Amherst (1985)
[31] Selkirk, E.: Sentence prosody: Intonation, stress, and phrasing. In: Goldsmith, J. (ed.) Handbook of Phonological Theory, pp. 550–569. Blackwell (1995)
[32] Stechow, A.V., Uhmann, S.: Some remarks on focus projection. In: Topic, Focus, and Configurationality, pp. 295–320 (1986)
[33] Steedman, M.: The Syntactic Process. MIT Press, Cambridge (2000)
[34] Steels, L., De Beule, J., Neubauer, N.: Linking in Fluid Construction Grammars. In: Proceedings of BNAIC, pp. 11–18. Transactions of the Belgian Royal Society of Arts and Sciences, Brussels (2005)
[35] Steels, L.: A design pattern for phrasal constructions. In: Steels, L. (ed.) Design Patterns in Fluid Construction Grammar. John Benjamins, Amsterdam (2011)
[36] Steels, L. (ed.): Design Patterns in Fluid Construction Grammar. John Benjamins, Amsterdam (2011)
[37] Steels, L.: A first encounter with Fluid Construction Grammar. In: Steels, L. (ed.) Design Patterns in Fluid Construction Grammar. John Benjamins, Amsterdam (2011)

[38] Steels, L. (ed.): Computational Issues in Fluid Construction Grammar. Springer, Berlin (2012)
[39] Traat, M.: Information Structure in a Formal Framework. In: Gelbukh, A. (ed.) CICLing 2009. LNCS, vol. 5449, pp. 28–40. Springer, Heidelberg (2009)
[40] Twain, M.: A Tramp Abroad. Oxford University Press Inc. (1880)
[41] Uszkoreit, H.: Word Order and Constituent Structure in German. CSLI Publications, Stanford (1987)
[42] Vallduví, E.: The dynamics of information packaging. In: Engdahl, E. (ed.) Information Structure into Constraint-Based Categorial Approaches. HCRC Publications, University of Edinburgh, Edinburgh (1994)
[43] van Trijp, R.: A design pattern for argument structure constructions. In: Steels, L. (ed.) Design Patterns in Fluid Construction Grammar. John Benjamins, Amsterdam (2011)
[44] van Trijp, R.: Feature matrices and agreement: A case study for German case. In: Steels, L. (ed.) Design Patterns in Fluid Construction Grammar. John Benjamins, Amsterdam (2011)
[45] Van Valin, R.D., LaPolla, R.J.: Syntax: Structure, Meaning, and Function. Cambridge University Press, Cambridge (1998)
[46] Wegener, H.: Der Dativ im heutigen Deutsch. Studien zur deutschen Grammatik, vol. 28. Originally Gunter Narr Verlag now Stauffenburg Verlag, Tübingen (1985)
[47] Wellens, P.: Organizing constructions in networks. In: Steels, L. (ed.) Design Patterns in Fluid Construction Grammar. John Benjamins, Amsterdam (2011)

Part IV
Formal Analysis

A Formal Deconstruction of Fluid Construction Grammar

Joachim De Beule

Artificial Intelligence Laboratory, Vrije Universiteit Brussel, Belgium

Abstract. Fluid construction grammar was primarily developed for supporting the on-line processing and learning of grammatical language in robotic language game setups, and with a focus on semantics and constructrion grammar. In contrast, many related formalisms were developed to support the formulation of static, primarily syntactic theories of natural language. As a result, many of FCG's features are absent in other formalisms, or take a somewhat different form. This can be confusing and give FCG a 'peculiar' status from the perspective of those more familiar with other formalisms. This chapter aims to clarify some of these peculiarities by providing a formal deconstruction of FCG based on a reconstruction of it's history.

1 Introduction

FCG was primarily developed for supporting the on-line processing and learning of grammatical language in robotic language game setups.[1] In contrast, many related formalisms were developed to support the formulation of static theories of natural language. As a result, many of FCG's features are absent in other formalisms, or take a somewhat different form. This can be confusing and give FCG a 'peculiar' status from the perspective of those more familiar with other formalisms. This chapter aims to clarify some of these peculiarities.

In the hope that this will help to accomplish this goal, our strategy will be to reconstruct (most of) FCG in a bottom up fashion. We start from the fact that the history and development of FCG are part of a longer tradition to make use of robotic and computational setups for investigating the emergence and evolution of language. As the complexity of these setups grew, the need arose to handle ever more complex aspects of language. Many of FCG's peculiarities today represent concrete solutions to specific problems encountered in this process. The strategy taken in this paper is therefore to give a deconstruction of FCG based on a reconstruction of its history.

It would also be possible to achieve clarification in another way, by providing a detailed account of the formal differences that exist between FCG and related formalisms. Although this is not the main approach taken here, some high level

[1] In a language game setup, robotic agents interact in order to establish a communication system or *artificial language* [17].

L. Steels (Ed.): Computational Issues in FCG, LNAI 7249, pp. 215–238, 2012.

differences are touched upon in the next section. This will at least provide some dimensions along which such a comparison could take place, and helps to set the stage for the rest of the paper.

2 General Considerations

One of the most distinguishing and, perhaps, confusing aspects of FCG is that it lacks any notion of *well formedness*, at least not in the sense as is customary in other approaches. For instance, in most unification or constraint based formalizations of language, one is typically interested in the minimal consistent set of constraints that specifies, say, all of English (see e.g. [15].) In contrast, in FCG, the validity of a constraint or construction is not measured by its consistency or by how it restricts the set of well formed sentences. Rather, it is measured by how it enables communication. This calls for a *functional* approach to language rather than a *declarative* one.

The notion of "unification" in FCG is also somewhat peculiar. In general, unification is about finding conditions under which certain things can be done, that is, are "valid" or "well formed". Particularly, in other approaches, the set of well formed structured equals the the set of structures entailed by a given grammar through the process of unification. A particular sentence, in this view, specifies a number of specific constraints – the particular word forms in the sentence and their order. These carve out a subset of the set of all well formed sentences. As mentioned, determining this subset is what processing in most unification based approaches is about. In FCG, unification is used for somewhat different purposes, and therefore in different ways.

According to Construction Grammar (CxG), linguistic knowledge is organized in *constructions*. These are entrenched routines that are generally used in a speech community and that involve a pairing of meaning components to form elements [6]. In FCG, constructions are more specifically *routines for expressing a meaning and for understanding a form*. Like functions, FCG constructions transform meaning specifications to form specifications during production, and vice versa during parsing. In this view, a particular sentence specifies a number of '*seeds*' rather than constraints. Each 'seed' (e.g. a word or specific syntactic category) triggers constructions which in turn add more 'seeds' (e.g. the meaning or semantic category of the word). This is the reason why, in FCG, there are *two* sorts of "unification": one for determining the set of "valid" constructions (those that are triggered), and one that governs the actual application of activated constructions ("merge").

Another important distinction in FCG is the notion of *processing direction*. In the tradition of generative grammar, the two processing modes normally distinguished are *parsing* and *generation*. Parsing refers to bottom-up process by which a particular sentence is analyzed in terms of production rules. Generation refers to the top-down process of determining all possible sentences that can be generated with the production rules. The two processing modes in FCG, normally called parsing and *production*, have nothing to do with all this. In FCG, parsing refers to the process of determining the meaning of a given sentence, and production refers to the process of determining a form by which a meaning can be expressed. The duality between FCG's processing modes is thus of a different nature than the one typically conceived of in the generative tradition. Some of FCG's peculiarities, like the fact that feature structures have two poles (a *semantic* and a *syntactic* pole), directly derive from this difference.

Finally, since FCG was developed for supporting *artificial* language processing, it makes the least possible amount of claims about the structure or nature of language.[2] Almost everything in FCG was introduced because it was required for solving a problem of language processing. For instance, certain generalizations require that it is possible to distinguish between specific word forms and the word classes they can belong to (e.g. their part of speech). FCG provides ways to make such kinds of distinctions, but it does not specify what particular distinctions *should* be made. There are no type hierarchies –at least none that can not be easilly circumvented or changed or extended; no intrinsic restrictions on the number or sort of features in feature structures; no restrictions on the values of features, etc.

In the following, we trace back the origins of these and other features of FCG by incrementally building up the machinery required to process an increasingly complex set of language phenomena. Throughout the paper, it will be useful to keep in mind a robotic agent that faces the task of parsing or producing an utterance. Producing an utterance amounts to transforming a given *meaning specification* into a *form specification.* Parsing amounts to transforming a given form specification into a meaning specification. This bi-directional problem structure is formalized throughout the chapter with the help of *production* and *parsing* functions, denoted as $g_{\rightarrow}$ and $g_{\leftarrow}$ respectively. The precise form of these functions, as well as of the meaning and form specifications upon which they operate, will gradually be changed and their complexity increased, mimicking the evolution of FCG itself. In the next section, we start by specifying the most basic elements of meaning and form specifications, called components, in more detail.

3 Meaning and Form Specifications

In general, with language processing we mean the transforming of meaning specifications into form specifications and vice versa. By definition, such specifications are built from primitive *meaning* and *form components* respectively. As is customary in FCG, such components will be represented as expressions in prefix-list notation. Furthermore, names of frames and frame relations will be used in components as specified in the on-line FrameNet database [2, 8]. For example, the following meaning component specifies the '`[line]`' frame:

```
(frame x [line]).
```

[2] Although recent advances, e.g. so calles "design patterns", can be seen as such.

The symbol 'x' is a skolem constant: it represents a specific instance of the [line] frame. I will sometimes further refer to skolem constants in meaning components as *meaning constants.*

By definition, meaning specifications are collections of meaning components. For example, the meaning of the phrase "natural line" is

```
{(frame x [line]), (frame y [natural]),
              (fe-relation y [entity] x)}.
```

The second component in this set introduces 'y' as an instance of the '[natural]' frame. The third component specifies that the '[entity]' frame element of this frame is the frame 'x'.

Similarly, form specifications are collections of form components. The form of the phrase "natural line" for example is represented as below.

```
{(lexeme a "line"), (lexeme b "natural"), (meets a b)}.
```

The skolem constants 'a' and 'b' are *form constants.*

In the next section, we start investigating the processing of language in the case of the simplest meaning and form specifications possible: those consisting of a single meaning and form component only.

4 Holistic Language Processing

We first restrict the discussion to "holistic languages". In a holistic language, phrases are always 'atomic': they are not structured or made out of smaller components in any meaningful way. Formally, this corresponds to the case that meaning and form specifications specify exactly a single component each. In other words, we only consider *singleton* specifications in this section.

4.1 Constructions

The bi-directional processing of singleton meaning and form specifications calls for a bi-directional lookup table. Each entry in the table associates a meaning component with a form component, and in this sense is a construction. The following is an example construction that associates the meaning specification '{(frame x [line])}' with the form specification '{(lexeme a "line")}'.

$$c\_1(x,a) = \boxed{\texttt{\{(frame x [line])\}} \leftrightarrow \texttt{\{(lexeme a "line")\}})}. \tag{1}$$

This construction is not in full concordance with contemporary practices in FCG however, and we will change its form again later. Nevertheless, the convention of displaying constructions in a box will be maintained throughout the chapter. The meaning side is separated from the form side by a double arrow. The meaning and form sides of a construction 'c' will also be referred to as 'c^m' and 'c^f', respectively. For example, with c_1 as above:

$$c_1^m(x) = \texttt{\{(frame x [line])\}} \quad ; \quad c_1^f(a) = \texttt{\{(lexeme a "line")\}}.$$

The semantic part of a construction will generally be referred to as the construction's *semantic pole.* Likewise, the syntactic part is referred to as the construction's *syntactic pole.*

4.2 Variables and Bindings

When faced with the problem of expressing the meaning specification '`{(frame x [line])}`', an agent can retrieve the construction $c_1(x)$ from its lookup table and notice that it specifies the exact same meaning specification in its semantic pole. It can therefore conclude that this meaning is expressed by the construction's syntactic pole.

But when given instead, say, the specification '`{(frame y [line])}`', a problem arises. The problem is that the construction specifies the skolem constant '`x`', whereas the new specification specifies the constant '`y`'. In consequence, there will be no match during lookup. A proper construction, therefore, should specify a *variable* instead of a constant, so that it matches *all* instances of the '[line]' frame.

By convention, variables will be marked by a leading question mark, as in '`?x`'. Variables are implicitly and universally quantified over, so the introduction of variables is like the inverse of skolemization. A variable can take any (but only one) value. A specific assignment $[?x/x]$ of a variable $?x$ to a value x is called a *binding* or a *basic substitution.* A set of bindings B of variables $?x_1, ?x_2, ...$ to values $x_1, x_2, ...$ is represented as $B = [?x_1/x_1, ?x_2/x_2/, ...]$. Every set of bindings B induces a *substitution function* $\sigma_B(e)$, which replaces all variables that occur in an expression e by their value according to the bindings in B.

Replacing the skolem constants '`x`' and '`a`' in construction c_1 by variables and using the abbreviations

$$m_1(?x) = \texttt{(frame ?x [line])} \quad \text{and} \quad f_1(?a) = \texttt{(lexeme ?a "line")},$$

thus gives the following more general definition of construction c_1:

$$c_1(?x, ?a) = \boxed{\{m_1(?x)\} \leftrightarrow \{f_1(?a)\}} \tag{2}$$

This construction associates *any* [line] frame with *any* "line" lexeme.

4.3 Component Matching

We now put everything together. Suppose that C is a constructicon –a collection of constructions, that is, a bi-directional lookup table between singleton meaning specifications and singleton form specifications– and suppose that some specification $\{m(x)\}$ needs to be expressed. For that, the agent goes through the constructions in C and compares their semantic poles to the given specification. The meaning and form components in constructions now contain variables. The operation with which components containing variables can be compared is called component matching. We denote it by U_0. This function takes a pattern component p and a source component s and computes all sets of minimal substitutions

σ_B that make the pattern identical to the source, that is, for which $\sigma_B(p) = s$.[3] An example of component matching is given below.

$$U_0(m_1(?x), m_1(x)) = \{[?x/x]\}.$$

We are now ready to give a first definition for the production and parsing functions. The production function $g_{\rightarrow}$ for now operates on a singleton meaning specification $\{m(x)\}$ and computes the set of form specifications that express it according to the constructicon C:

$$g_{\rightarrow}(m(x), C) = \{c^f : c \in C, U_0(c^m(?x), m(x)) \neq \emptyset\}.$$

Thus, this set contains the syntactic poles of all constructions of which the semantic side matches the given meaning component $m(x)$. For example, with c_1 as defined earlier:

$$g_{\rightarrow}(\{\texttt{(frame y [line])}\}, \{c_1\}) = \{\{\texttt{(lexeme ?a "line")}\}\}.$$

The parsing function $g_{\leftarrow}$ is defined in a similar way. It takes a singleton form specification and computes a set of singleton form specifications:

$$g_{\leftarrow}(\{f(a)\}, C) = \{c^m : c \in C, U_0(c^f(?a), f(b)) \neq \emptyset\}.$$

For example:

$$g_{\leftarrow}(\{\texttt{(lexeme b "line")}\}, \{c_1\}) = \{\{\texttt{(frame ?x [line])}\}\}.$$

It is possible that several constructions are available in a given constructicon that all express the same meaning (synonyms) or cover the same form (homonyms). In this case, the agent will have to select one among them. This could be done for instance on the basis of preference scores. We return to this issue in section 7.

This concludes our discussion of the processing of holistic language. In summary, it requires a bi-directional lookup table of constructions – associations between singleton meaning and form specifications containing variables –, and a component matching function for determining which constructions express a given singleton meaning specification or parse a given singleton form specification.

5 Compositionality

We now relax the assumptions that meaning and form specification may only contain a single component. This opens up the way to *compositional language*, in which phrases are structured and consist of several parts.

---

[3] A minimal substitution is one that does not specify bindings for variables that do not occur in the pattern or source. Component matching corresponds to the notion of standard unification in Artificial Intelligence and logic (See e.g. [13].)

5.1 Set Matching

Suppose again that C is a constructicon (a collection of constructions). As before, it is assumed that meaning and form constants are replaced with variables in constructions. Suppose further that the meaning specification that needs to be expressed is denoted by μ. As before, μ will have to be compared to the semantic poles of constructions in C. This time, however, it is possible that some construction only expresses *part* of μ. This is the case for those constructions of which the meaning pole is a *subset* of μ. The operation that checks whether one set of components is a subset of another is called *set matching*. It is denoted as U_1. This function takes a pattern set p and a source set s and computes the set of minimal substitutions σ_B that make the pattern set a subset of the source, that is, for which $\sigma_B(p) \subset s$. More formally, if μ and μ' are two meaning or form specifications, then:

$$U_1(\mu, \mu') = \{B : \sigma_B(\mu) \subset \mu'\} \tag{3}$$

New versions of the production and parsing functions that use this enhanced matching power can now be defined as follows:

$$g_{\rightarrow}(\mu, C) = \{c^f : c \in C, U_1(c^m, \mu) \neq \emptyset\},$$

$$g_{\leftarrow}(\phi, C) = \{c^m : c \in C, U_1(c^f, \phi) \neq \emptyset\}.$$

These functions now operate on arbitrary meaning and form specifications instead of just singletons. For example, if $\mu_1(x) = \{m_1(x)\}$ and $\phi_1(a) = \{f_1(a)\}$, then:

$$U_1(\{m_1(?x)\}, \mu_1(x)) = \{[?x/x]\} \quad ; \quad U_1(\{f_1(?a)\}, \phi_1(a)) = \{[?a/a]\}$$

and, with $C = \{c_1(?x, ?a)\}$ (see equation 2),

$$g_{\rightarrow}(\mu_1(x), C) = \{\phi(?a)\} \quad ; \quad g_{\leftarrow}(\phi_1(a), C) = \{\mu_1(?x)\}$$

Now consider the following meaning specification:

$\mu(x, y) = \{m_1(x), m_2(y)\} = \{$`(frame x [line]), (frame y [natural])`$\}$.

It must be transformed into the following form specification:

$\phi(?a, ?b) = \{f_1(?a), f_2(?b)\}$=`{(lexeme ?a "line") (lexeme ?b "natural")`.

This is achieved with the following construction h.

$$h = \boxed{\{m_1(?x), m_2(?y)\} \leftrightarrow \{f_1(?a), f_2(?b)\}}$$

Indeed, the semantic side of h matches μ:

$$U_1(h^m(?x, ?y), \mu(x, y)) = \{[?x/x, ?y/y]\}.$$

From this, and from the definition of $g_{\rightarrow}$, it follows that

$$g_{\rightarrow}(\mu, \{h\}) = \{\phi(?a, ?b))\}$$

In a sense this is a "holistic" production because the construction h maps both meaning components to two form components *in one go*. In contrast, a compositional encoding should involve two constructions: one for the 'line' part and one for the 'natural' part. Let us call these constructions c_1 and c_2. Then c_1 is as in equation (2) and c_2 is as below.

$$\begin{aligned} c_2(?y, ?b) &= \boxed{\{m_2(?y)\} \leftrightarrow \{f_2(?b)\}} \\ &= \boxed{\{\texttt{(frame ?y [natural])}\} \leftrightarrow \{\texttt{(lexeme ?b "natural")}\}}. \end{aligned} \quad (4)$$

The semantic sides of both constructions match the given specification $\mu(x, y)$, so that the "lookup" part of processing succeeds for both of them:

$$U_1(c_1^m(?x, ?a), \mu(x, y)) = \{[?x/x]\} \quad ; \quad U_1(c_2^m(?y, ?b), \mu(x, y)) = \{[?y/y]\}.$$

However, the production function $g_{\rightarrow}$ as defined above produces two incomplete productions instead of a single compositional production.

$$g_{\rightarrow}(\mu, C) = \left\{\{c_1^f\}, \{c_2^f\}\right\}.$$

Compositional language processing is thus more demanding than holistic language processing, beyond the fact that it requires a more general mode of unification (set matching). It also requires a *transient linguistic structure* for collecting intermediate results (partial meaning and form specifications).

5.2 The Transient Linguistic Structure and Merge

We introduce the transient linguistic structure for keeping track of intermediate processing results. Since this is needed in the case of compositional encoding regardless of the direction of processing (parsing or production), and since this will turn out to be useful in the following, we define the transient linguistic structure to be an association between a meaning and a form specification. As in the case of constructions, the semantic and syntactic poles of a transient structure s are denoted as s^m and s^f respectively.

The initial meaning and form specifications from which processing starts and that are given as input to the production and parsing functions can also conveniently be specified as transient linguistic structures by simply leaving the appropriate pole empty, that is, the syntactic pole in case of production and the semantic polle in case of parsing. Thus, the meaning specification μ which is given before production starts, corresponds to the transient structure s_μ below.

$$s_\mu = \boxed{\mu \leftrightarrow \emptyset}.$$

Now the semantic poles of the constructions c_1 and c_2 match the semantic pole of the transient structure s_μ:

$$U_1(c_1^m, s_\mu^m) = U_1(c_1^m(?x), \mu(x, y)) = \{[?x/x]\}$$

and

$$U_1(c_2^m, s_\mu^m) = U_1(c_2^m(?y), \mu(x, y)) = \{[?y/y]\}.$$

As before, this indicates that both constructions can be considered for further processing by the production function. The idea is that each of the constructions adds its own parts to the transient structure. This is done through *merging.*

In this section, we do not consider any other relationships between meaning or form components besides the fact that they appear together in meaning and form specifications. In this case, all that needs to happen during merging is that the missing constructional form components are added to the transient structure. In other words, for now we can define the merge operation to be the set theoretic union operation. More formally, we introduce the merge function $U_2(\phi, \phi')$ for merging two component sets ϕ and ϕ' into a single component set as:

$$U_2(\phi, \phi') = \phi \cup \phi'.$$

Clearly, the merge function applies both to meaning and form specifications, since these are all sets.

The notion of merge in FCG should not be confused with Chomsky's merge introduced in [4]. Rather, merging corresponds to unification in traditional unification and constraint based formalisms: both result in extra 'constraints' in the transient linguistic structure. As mentioned in the introduction, in FCG such 'constraints' can also be considered 'seed material'. This will become relevant when even more complex meaning and form specifications are considered below.

We are now in a position to redefine the production and parsing functions again such that they operate on transient linguistic structures and make use of the merge function U_2. Since these functions now should embody an iterative process of applying all applicable constructions one after the other, this is most easily done through induction. Thus, in case that the constructicon only specifies a single construction c, and with s a transient linguistic structure, we have that:

$$g_{\rightarrow}(s, \{c\}) = \begin{cases} \{\boxed{s^m \leftrightarrow U_2(s^f, s^f)}\} \text{ if } U_1(c^m, s^m) \neq \emptyset \\ \{s\} \text{ otherwise.} \end{cases} \tag{5}$$

In words, this says that the production function, when given a transient linguistic structure s and a singleton constructicon $\{c\}$ such that the semantic poles s^m and c^m match (according to U_1), produces a transient linguistic structure with a modified syntactic pole that is equal to the union of the syntactic poles of the given transient structure and the construction. This definition is easily extended to larger collections of construction through the following induction step on larger constructicons:

$$g_{\rightarrow}(s, \{c\} \cup C) = \{g_{\rightarrow}(s', C) : s' \in g_{\rightarrow}(s, \{c\})\}.$$

Note that this definition assumes that the order in which constructions are considered does not matter. If it did, then the constructions would not be independent and a search would be required over possible orderings. This possibility is further discussed in section 7.

Note also that, whereas the processing functions are defined by induction, this does not mean that they are also recursive functions. In recent years, there has been quite a debate over whether or not humans are the only species that possess the capacity for recursion, so this issue is a matter of some importance [7, 9, 11, 12]. However, there is an important difference between genuinely recursive functions and merely tail recursive representations of iterative functions [1]. Only genuinely recursive functions also require a recursive implementation for computation. Compositional language processing as defined in this section does not.

In any case, we now have that:

$$g_{\rightarrow}(s_\mu, \{c_1\}) = \left\{\boxed{\mu \leftrightarrow \{f_1(?a)\}}\right\},$$
$$g_{\rightarrow}(s_\mu, \{c_2\}) = \left\{\boxed{\mu \leftrightarrow \{f_2(?b)\}}\right\}.$$

And:

$$g_{\rightarrow}(s_\mu, \{c_1, c_2\}) = \left\{\boxed{\mu \leftrightarrow \phi(?a, ?b)}\right\}.$$

This accomplishes a compositional encoding of μ into ϕ. The parsing function is defined in a similar fashion.

This concludes our discussion of bi-directional processing in the case that meaning and form specifications are sets of 'independent' meaning or form components. The fact that the components are 'independent' means for instance that they are not allowed to share any of their skolem constants. In summary, in this case a *set* unification function U_1 is required for matching sets of components and for testing which constructions apply. This corresponds to the 'lookup' step in processing. Furthermore, actually applying matching constructions in a compositional fashion amounts to adding their constructional components to a transient linguistic structure through a merge operation. The transient linguistic structure functions to keep 'intermediate results' (partial productions or parses) during processing.

6 Constituent Structure and Hierarchy

So far, we have been considering the English example phrase "natural line" without bothering about the fact that the two lexemes in it are ordered. Indeed, consider again the form specification $\phi(?a, ?b)$ from the previous section, which is the result of applying the production function to the meaning $\mu(x, y)$:

$$\phi(?a,?b) = \{f_1(?a), f_2(?b)\} = \{\texttt{(lexeme ?a "line")}, \texttt{(lexeme ?b "natural")}\}$$

Something is missing in this specification. In fact, it fails to specify the order of lexemes, so that both "natural line" and "line natural" are consistent with it. As mentioned already in section 3, a more correct specification should specify this order, like ψ below.

$$\begin{aligned}\psi &= \{f_1(?a), f_2(?b), f_3(?b, ?a)\}\\ &= \{\texttt{(lexeme ?a "line")},\ \texttt{(lexeme ?b "natural)},\ \texttt{(meets ?b ?a)}\}.\end{aligned}$$

Here, the component $f_3(?b, ?a)$ or '`(meets ?b ?a)`' represents a further constraint on the variables $?a$ and $?b$ besides the fact that they stand for the lexemes '`line`' and '`natural`'. This component specifies that these lexemes should be rendered in a particular order. Only the phrase "natural line" is consistent with this specification, whereas the alternative "line natural" is ruled out.

Similarly, nothing in the meaning specification $\mu(x, y) = \{m_1(x), m_2(y)\}$ specifies that it is actually the line (represented by x) that has the property of being natural or, in FrameNet terminology, that fulfills the '`[entity]`' Frame Element relation of the '[natural]' frame. The phrase "natural line" therefore expresses not $\mu(x, y)$, but the more elaborate meaning specification η below.

$$\begin{aligned}\eta &= \{m_1(x), m_2(y), m_3(x, y)\}\\ &= \{\texttt{(frame x [line])},\ \texttt{(frame y [natural])},\\ &\qquad \texttt{(fe-relation y x [entity])}\}.\end{aligned} \tag{6}$$

As on the form side in ψ, components are no longer independent in η: some of the skolem constants are shared between them. In the remainder of this section we investigate what modifications need to be made to the machinery developed so far so that it becomes possible to deal with such dependencies.

We start by recalling that, in English, the order of words in the example phrase "natural line" is licensed by a modifier-head construction for combining adjectives with nouns. On the meaning side, this construction links the corresponding meaning components by specifying an `[entity]` frame element relation. How could such a construction be defined with the representational tools developed so far? The answer, unfortunately, is that it can not.

To see this, consider that it should apply to the transient structure obtained from applying the lexical constructions c_1 and c_2 to the extended meaning specification η. Since

$$U_1(c_1^m(?x, ?a), \eta(x, y)) = \{[?x/x]\} \quad \text{and} \quad U_1(c_2^m(?y, ?b), \eta(x, y)) = \{[?y/y]\},$$

this transient structure looks as follows:

$$g_{\rightarrow}(\eta, \{c_1, c_2\}) = \left\{ \boxed{\begin{array}{c}\{m_1(x), m_2(y), m_3(x, y)\}\\ \leftrightarrow\\ \{f_1(?a), f_2(?b)\}\end{array}} \right\}.$$

The correspondence that exists between the meaning component 'm_1' and the form component 'f_1' (as it is captured in construction c_1) is not reflected in the above transient linguistic structure. Similarly, nothing in the structure shown above indicates that there is a connection between the meaning component m_2 and the form component f_2. However, the modifier head construction needs access to this information.

Once again we will extend our representational toolkit. PArticularly, we will make the poles of constructions and of the transient linguistic structure to be *feature structures* instead of plain sets. In other words, constructions (and the transient structure) now become *coupled feature structures* (or *cfs*'s in short).

6.1 Coupled Feature Structures

In general, a feature structure is a set of named *units*. Each unit represents a lexical or phrasal constituent. In order to find the form components that are associated with the meaning components in a unit, it suffices to look in the corresponding unit (the unit with the same name) on the syntactic side. Units are further organized into features. The MEANING feature holds the unit's meaning specification. The FORM feature holds its form specification. Furthermore, like constituents, one unit may be part of another one. This is encoded in the SUBUNITS feature. Meaning and form constants are kept in the REFERENT feature. This can be summarized as follows using BNF notation:

```
cfs               ::= sem-unit-structure <--> syn-unit-structure
unit-structure    ::= {regular-unit*}
regular-unit      ::= <unit-name,{regular-feature*}>
regular-feature   ::= <feature-name,feature-value>
feature-value     ::= feature-value-element
                    | {feature-value-element*}.
```

The asterisk represents the Kleene star operation, specifying that one or more elements of the type marked with it are possible. So '`regular-unit*`' stands for zero or more regular units. The notation $\langle . \rangle$ denotes an ordered list of elements, i.e. a sequence. Sets, which are unordered lists of elements, are denoted with curly brackets as usual.

Here is an example. The cfs that holds the meaning specification η and nothing else appears as follows:

$$s_\eta = \boxed{\{\langle u_0, \langle \text{MEANING}, \eta \rangle \rangle\} \leftrightarrow \{\}} \tag{7}$$

This cfs has one unit named u_0 (not to be confused with the component unification function U_0). In turn, this unit has the specification η as value for its MEANING feature.

By using feature structures instead of plain sets for representing the poles of constructions and of the transient structure, it becomes possible to capture hierarchical constituent structure relations in them. For instance, as will be explained shortly, the transient linguistic structure after applying the constructions c_1 and c_2 to the coupled feature structure s_η above will look as below:

$$s_{12} = g_{\rightarrow}(s_{\eta}, \{c_1, c_2\})$$

$$= \boxed{\left\{\begin{array}{l} \langle u_0,\ \langle \text{SUBUNITS}, \{u_1, u_2\}\rangle\,, \\ \qquad \langle \text{MEANING}, \{m_3(x, y)\}\rangle\,, \\ \langle u_1,\ \langle \text{MEANING}, \{m_1(x)\}\rangle\,, \\ \qquad \langle \text{REFERENT}, x\rangle\rangle\,, \\ \langle u_2,\ \langle \text{MEANING}, \{m_2(y)\}\rangle\,, \\ \qquad \langle \text{REFERENT}, y\rangle\rangle \end{array}\right\} \leftrightarrow \left\{\begin{array}{l} \langle u_0,\ \langle \text{SUBUNITS}, \{u_1, u_2\}\rangle\,, \\ \qquad \langle \text{FORM}, \{f_3(?b, ?a)\}\rangle\,, \\ \langle u_1,\ \langle \text{FORM}, \{f_1(?a)\}\rangle\,, \\ \qquad \langle \text{REFERENT}, ?a\rangle\rangle\,, \\ \langle u_2,\ \langle \text{FORM}, \{f_2(?b)\}\rangle\,, \\ \qquad \langle \text{REFERENT}, ?b\rangle\rangle \end{array}\right\}} \quad (8)$$

Among other things, this cfs captures precisely the fact that the components m_1 and f_1 'belong together' since they are part of the same unit u_1 (although they are in different poles). Importantly, the constituent structure in this cfs is a *result* of applying the constructions c_1 and c_2 to the initial linguistic structure s_η (which itself only has a flat constituent structure). So it is indeed the construction c_1 that defines the meaning-form pair $m_1(?x) \leftrightarrow f_1(?a)$ as a constituent, but now this is also reflected in the transient linguistic structure.

In FCG, the correspondence between constructions and constituents is not merely one-to-one. In particular, FCG expects that constructions *explicitly specify the way in which they change the constituent structure of the transient linguistic structure* (i.e. add new units and/or move components around etc.) Thus, the modifier head construction we aim to define will have to specify that a new unit can be created that groups an existing adjective unit with an existing noun unit in a specific order. In the next section, it is explained how such manipulations of the transient structure can be specified in constructions through the usage of TAGs and 'J-units'.

6.2 Tags and J-Units

Following the developments in the previous section, we now define constructions as an extension over coupled feature structures as follows:

```
cxn        ::= sem-pole <--> syn-pole
pole       ::= {unit*}
unit       ::= regular-unit | J-unit |
               <unit-name, {[regular-feature | tag]*}>
tag        ::= (TAG [tag-variable regular-feature]*)
J-unit     ::= <(J . ?focus ?parent {?child*}),
                         {[tag-variable | regular-feature]*}>
```

All coupled feature structures are thus constructions, but not the other way around: constructions, in addition, may contain TAGs and *J-units*. J-units are easily recognized by the fact that they do not have a proper name. Instead their name is a list of the form '(J . ?focus-unit ?parent-unit child*)'. The first element in this list is called the 'J-operator'. The dot after the J-operator in the definitions above indicates that the arguments that follow the operator are optional.

J-units are ignored during the matching or 'lookup' process. The workings of the J-operator during merging is most easily explained with an example. Consider therefore again the lexical construction c_1 that couples the meaning component m_1 to the form component f_1. In our new notation it looks as follows:

$$c_1 = \boxed{\begin{array}{c} \left\{ \begin{array}{ll} \langle ?u, & (\textsc{tag}\ \texttt{?m}\ \langle \textsc{meaning}, \{m_1(?x)\}\rangle)\rangle \\ \langle (\texttt{J ?new}\ ?u), & \{\texttt{?m}, \langle \textsc{referent}, ?x\rangle\}\rangle \end{array} \right\} \\ \leftrightarrow \\ \left\{ \begin{array}{ll} \langle ?u, & (\textsc{tag}\ \texttt{?f}\ \langle \textsc{form}, \{f_1(?a)\}\rangle)\rangle \\ \langle (\texttt{J ?new}\ ?u), & \{\texttt{?m}, \langle \textsc{referent}, ?a\rangle\}\rangle \end{array} \right\} \end{array}} \tag{9}$$

This construction specifies one J-unit in both poles. The focus of the J-units is the variable '?new'. Their parent is the variable '?u', which also is the name of a regular unit in the construction. The fact that the focus variable does not refer to a regular unit indicates that a new subunit is introduced by this construction in the transient linguistic structure during merge. This unit will be made a subunit of the parent unit. On the semantic side, the new unit will have a REFERENT feature with value (the binding value of) $?x$. It will also have a MEANING feature with value $\{m_1(?x)\}$, as specified by the TAG variable $?m$. On the syntactic side, it will have a REFERENT feature with value $?a$ and a FORM feature with value $\{f_1(?a)$. The latter is specified by the TAG variable $?f$. By definition, when meaning and form components are tagged and specified in J-units as described, they will be removed from the unit in which they originally occurred. This explains why, in structure (8) above, which is the result of applying constructions c_1 and c_2 to the initial structure (7), the meaning and form components covered by these two constructions only occur in the newly created units u_1 and u_2. The process is explained in more detail in the following.

6.3 Unit Structure Matching and Merging

We now specify the process explained in the previous section in more detail. We first consider the matching or comparing of unit structures for lookup.

Recall the definition of coupled feature structures in BNF notation. In particular, notice that a unit structure is a *set* of units. It follows that unit structures can be matched with the set matching function U_1, provided that the matching of the set elements, which are units now, is properly defined. Two units match when their names match and when their *sets* of features match. The latter is a case of set matching again, and calls for a proper definition of feature matching. It is clear that, continuing in this way and following the BNF definition of coupled feature structure, matching of unit structures can fully be defined in terms of symbol matching (for the names of units and regular features) and the set and component matching functions U_1 and U_0.

It remains to specify how J-units and TAGs affect the matching process. As mentioned, J-units are simply ignored during matching. Their purpose is to specify how a construction modifies constituent structure, *given* that the (appropriate pole of) the construction matches with the (appropriate pole of) the transient linguistic structure.

We now turn to tags. On the one hand, the purpose of tags is to mark parts of the transient structure for later reference. Thus, when the semantic pole of construction c_1 is matched against the initial unit structure s_η, the tag variable $?m$ receives the binding $\langle \text{MEANING}, \{m_1(x)\}\rangle$. On the other hand, their purpose is to allow to move components between units during merge. So we turn to the merging of unit structure. Ignoring the details having to do with the bookkeeping of names of units and features etc., merging regular parts of unit structures boils down to taking their union. J-units additionally change constituent structure and extract tagged components. For simplicity, we continue to use the symbol 'U_2' for the extended merge operation that accomplishes all this. Below is given the result of merging the semantic pole of construction c_1 with the initial structure s_η^m:

$$U_2\left(c_1^m, s_\eta^m\right) = \left\{\begin{matrix} \langle u_0, \langle \text{MEANING}, \{m_2(y), m_3(x,y)\}\rangle\rangle \\ \langle u_1, \langle \text{MEANING}, \{m_1(x)\}\rangle\rangle \end{matrix}\right\} \tag{10}$$

The resulting structure has two units instead of just one (with the new unit arbitrarily named u_1). As explained, this is due to the J-operator in c_1^m. The tagged part of meaning $m_1(x)$ was extracted from the original unit and moved to the new unit.

We can now define new production and parsing functions that work with coupled feature structures. The main difference with the previous versions is that now merging should occur for both poles, regardless of the processing mode. The reason for this is that both constructional poles may contain J-units, implying that both sides of the transient linguistic structure may change. Thus we have:

$$g_\rightarrow(t, \{c\}) = \begin{cases} U_2(t^m, c^m) \leftrightarrow U_2(t^f, c^f) \text{ if } U_1(c^m, t^m) \neq \emptyset \\ t \text{ otherwise.} \end{cases}$$

and

$$g_\rightarrow(t, C \cup \{c\}) = g_\rightarrow(g_\rightarrow(t, \{c\}), C).$$

A new parse function is readily defined in a similar way. Note that, as before, these definitions assume that the order in which constructions are applied is arbitrary. This is not a valid assumption in general, and the consequences of relaxing this assumption are investigated in section 7. Note also that, since it is now possible that constructions specify changes to the transient linguistic structure on the side that was previously only matched, we have entered the domain of context sensitive language processing.

6.4 Grammatical Constructions

We now finish the discussion on constituent structure and hierarchy by working towards a modifier-head construction for processing the phrase "natural line". Consider again construction c_1:

$$c_1 = \boxed{\begin{matrix} \left\{ \begin{matrix} \langle ?u, & (\texttt{TAG ?m } \langle \text{MEANING}, \{m_1(?x)\}\rangle) \rangle \\ \langle (\texttt{J ?new } ?u), & \{\texttt{?m}, \langle \text{REFERENT}, ?x\rangle\}\rangle \end{matrix} \right\} \\ \leftrightarrow \\ \left\{ \begin{matrix} \langle ?u, & (\texttt{TAG ?f } \langle \text{FORM}, \{f_1(?a)\}\rangle) \rangle \\ \langle (\texttt{J ?new } ?u), & \{\texttt{?m}, \langle \text{REFERENT}, ?a\rangle\}\rangle \end{matrix} \right\} \end{matrix}} \tag{11}$$

Its semantic side matches that of the initial cfs s_η repeated below.

$$s_\eta = \boxed{\{\langle u_0, \langle \text{MEANING}, \{m_1(x), m_2(y), m_3(x,y)\}\rangle\rangle\} \leftrightarrow \{\}} \tag{12}$$

Indeed:

$$U_1(c_1^m, s_\eta^m) = [?u/u_0, ?x/x, ?m/\langle \text{MEANING}, \{m_1(x)\}\rangle]. \tag{13}$$

The focus variable '?new' of the J-unit in the construction c_1 does not receive a binding according to the above expression. As explained, merging this construction into the structure s_η therefore results in an additional unit u_1:

$$s_1 = g_{\rightarrow}(s_\eta, \{c_1\}) = \boxed{\begin{matrix} \left\{ \begin{matrix} \langle u_0, & \langle \text{SUBUNITS}, \{u_1\}\rangle, \\ & \langle \text{MEANING}, \{m_2(y), m_3(x,y)\}\rangle, \\ \langle u_1, & \langle \text{MEANING}, \{m_1(x)\}\rangle, \\ & \langle \text{REFERENT}, x\rangle\rangle \end{matrix} \right\} \\ \leftrightarrow \\ \left\{ \begin{matrix} \langle u_0, & \langle \text{SUBUNITS}, \{u_1\}\rangle\rangle, \\ \langle u_1, & \langle \text{FORM}, \{f_1(?a)\}\rangle, \\ & \langle \text{REFERENT}, ?a\rangle\rangle \end{matrix} \right\} \end{matrix}} \tag{14}$$

The additional unit contains the tagged part of meaning that was previously in the top unit u_0. Now consider c_2 below.

$$c_2 = \boxed{\begin{matrix} \left\{ \begin{matrix} \langle ?u, & (\texttt{TAG ?m } \langle \text{MEANING}, \{m_2(?y)\}\rangle) \rangle \\ \langle (\texttt{J ?new } ?u), & \{\texttt{?m}, \langle \text{REFERENT}, ?y\rangle\}\rangle \end{matrix} \right\} \\ \leftrightarrow \\ \left\{ \begin{matrix} \langle ?u, & (\texttt{TAG ?f } \langle \text{FORM}, \{f_2(?b)\}\rangle) \rangle \\ \langle (\texttt{J ?new } ?u), & \{\texttt{?m}, \langle \text{REFERENT}, ?b\rangle\}\rangle \end{matrix} \right\} \end{matrix}} \tag{15}$$

We have that

$$U_1(c_2^m, s_1) = \{[?u/u_0, ?y/y, ?m/\langle \text{MEANING}, \{m_2(y)\}\rangle]\},$$

and

$$U_2(c_2^m, s_1^m) = s_{12}^m \quad , \quad U_2(c_2^f, s_1^f) = s_{12}^f,$$

with s_{12} as before:

$$s_{12} = g_{\rightarrow}(s_\eta, \{c_1, c_2\})$$

$$= \boxed{\left\{\begin{array}{ll}\langle u_0, & \langle \text{SUBUNITS}, \{u_1, u_2\}\rangle, \\ & \langle \text{MEANING}, \{m_3(x,y)\}\rangle, \\ \langle u_1, & \langle \text{MEANING}, \{m_1(x)\}\rangle, \\ & \langle \text{REFERENT}, x\rangle\rangle, \\ \langle u_2, & \langle \text{MEANING}, \{m_2(y)\}\rangle, \\ & \langle \text{REFERENT}, y\rangle\rangle \end{array}\right\} \leftrightarrow \left\{\begin{array}{ll}\langle u_0, & \langle \text{SUBUNITS}, \{u_1, u_2\}\rangle, \\ & \langle \text{FORM}, \{f_3(?b, ?a)\}\rangle, \\ \langle u_1, & \langle \text{FORM}, \{f_1(?a)\}\rangle, \\ & \langle \text{REFERENT}, ?a\rangle\rangle, \\ \langle u_2, & \langle \text{FORM}, \{f_2(?b)\}\rangle, \\ & \langle \text{REFERENT}, ?b\rangle\rangle \end{array}\right\}} \quad (16)$$

This cfs explicitly couples the meanings $m_1(x)$ and $m_2(y)$ to the forms $f_1(?a)$ and $f_2(?b)$ respectively, and this way provides the necessary information required to express the remaining component $m_3(x, y)$. We are finally in a position to specify the modifier head construction c_3 that expresses this component:

$$c_3 = \boxed{\begin{array}{c}\left\{\begin{array}{ll}\langle ?u_0, & \langle \text{SUBUNITS}, \{?u_1, ?u_2\}\rangle, \\ & (\texttt{TAG ?m } \langle \text{MEANING}, \{m_3(?x, ?y)\}\rangle), \\ \langle ?u_1, & \langle \text{REFERENT}, ?x\rangle\rangle, \\ \langle ?u_2, & \langle \text{REFERENT}, ?y\rangle\rangle, \\ \langle (\texttt{J } ?u_2 \ ?u1), & \emptyset\rangle, \\ \langle (\texttt{J } ?u_1), & \{\texttt{?m}\}\rangle \end{array}\right\} \\ \leftrightarrow \\ \left\{\begin{array}{ll}\langle ?u_0, & \langle \text{SUBUNITS}, \{?u_1, ?u_2\}\rangle, \\ & (\texttt{TAG ?f } \langle \text{FORM}, \{f_3(?b, ?a)\}\rangle), \\ \langle ?u_1, & \langle \text{REFERENT}, ?a\rangle\rangle, \\ \langle ?u_2, & \langle \text{REFERENT}, ?b\rangle\rangle, \\ \langle (\texttt{J } ?u_2 \ ?u1), & \emptyset\rangle, \\ \langle (\texttt{J } ?u_1), & \{\texttt{?f}\}\rangle \end{array}\right\}\end{array}}$$

This construction further transforms structure s_{12} to structure s_{123}:

$$s_{123} = g_{\rightarrow}(s_\eta, \{c_1, c_2, c_3\})$$

$$= \boxed{\begin{array}{c}\left\{\begin{array}{ll}\langle u_0, & \langle \text{SUBUNITS}, \{u_1\}\rangle\rangle \\ \langle u_1, & \langle \text{SUBUNITS}, \{u_2\}\rangle \\ & \langle \text{MEANING}, \{m_1(?x), m_3(?x, ?y)\}\rangle \\ & \langle \text{REFERENT}, ?x\rangle\rangle \\ \langle u_2, & \langle \text{MEANING}, \{m_2(?y)\}\rangle \\ & \langle \text{REFERENT}, ?y\rangle\rangle \end{array}\right\} \\ \leftrightarrow \left\{\begin{array}{ll}\langle u_0, & \langle \text{SUBUNITS}, \{u_1\}\rangle\rangle \\ \langle u_1, & \langle \text{SUBUNITS}, \{u_2\}\rangle \\ & \langle \text{FORM}, \{f_1(?a), f_3(?b, ?a)\}\rangle \\ & \langle \text{REFERENT}, ?a\rangle\rangle \\ \langle u_2, & \langle \text{FORM}, \{f_2(?b)\}\rangle \\ & \langle \text{REFERENT}, ?b\rangle\rangle \end{array}\right\}\end{array}} \quad (17)$$

The construction c_3 enforces a head-complement relation between its head and complement units $?u_1$ and $?u_2$ respectively. This is accomplished by the first J-units on both sides, which make unit $?u_2$ a subunit of $?u_1$. The second J-units moves the covered meaning and form components m_3 and f_3 to the head unit. Thus, together, constructions c_1, c_2 and c_3 successfully parse and produce the form specification ψ into the meaning specification η. In other words, we have finally accomplished the parsing and production of the English phrase "natural line".

Note that the usefulness of the REFERENT feature now becomes apparent as well: without it, it would not have been possible to formulate a modifier-head construction c_3, unless through a reference to the particular meaning components that are being combined. In our case these are m_1 and m_2, but a different modifier-head construction would be needed for a different pair of components. This would undermine the whole purpose of the modifier-head construction, which is to separate the expression of a linking relation *between* components from the expression of the components themselves.

This almost concludes our discussion of constituent structure and hierarchy. For completeness, we mention that the processing of natural language in general requires many more refinements to the machinery introduced so far. Consider for instance that our modifier-head construction c_3 for pairing an adjective an a noun actually does not refer to the notions of "adjective" or "noun". In French, and in many other languages, there are even different *types* of adjectives and nouns. For instance, in the phrase "le grand ballon rouge", both "grand" and "rouge" are adjectives ("big" and "red" in English respectively), but they combine differently with the noun "ballon". These distinctions are clearly important for language and language processing, and it should be possible to deal with them in FCG. Luckily, the bulk of the machinery required for this is already in place, and no further extensions need to be introduced besides new types of unit features and new types of operators.

In FCG, semantic and syntactic types and categories are usually specified in the SEM-CAT and SYN-CAT features. Next to the MEANING, FORM and REFERENT features, these are the most commonly used features in FCG, although the set of possible features is open ended. Testing for the semantic or syntactic category of a constituent is easily performed during matching by including the type description in the corresponding regular unit in a construction. Most grammatical languages also involve more refined sorts of restrictions on semantic and syntactic categories. Consider for example the sentence (a) below, which is an instance of the Caused Motion construction.

(a) "Joe broke the vase onto the floor."

Golberg notes that the Caused Motion construction only applies if the cause is *not* an instrument [10], rendering sentence (b) below ungrammatical.

(b) *"The hammer broke the vase onto the floor"

As is discussed at length elsewhere, such and other types of restrictions can be specified with special operators.

7 Constructional Dependencies and Search

So far we have ignored any intricacies that might arise from dependencies between constructions. Such dependencies may interfere with processing. To see this, consider once more the example phrase "natural line". It does not matter in what order the lexical constructions c_1 and c_2 for "natural" and "line" are applied, the resulting structure will be the same. But the modifier-head construction only applies after them. In other words, there is a *dependency* between these constructions. It is also possible that two constructions are *conflicting*, for instance synonyms which both cover the same (set of) form components. In this case there will be several possible parses or productions. Finally if, as in the context of language game experiments, constructions are marked with conventionality or preference scores, then some analysis will be more preferable than others. All of these things imply that processing involves search.

7.1 General Aspects of Processing as Search

In general, search involves the exploration of a *search space* of possible analysis (parses or productions) with the goal to find a suitable one. The search space is not directly accessible however: it needs to be constructed through the actual application of constructions, starting from the initial linguistic structure. All constructions that apply to the initial structure give rise to a new (partial) analysis or state in the search space. At each moment during processing, it therefore needs to be decided which analysis to consider further and, if it triggers several constructions, which construction to actually apply to it. This process of repeatedly selecting a previously obtained transient linguistic structure and selecting and applying a construction to it in order to get a modified transient structure is what search is all about. Different search strategies, like breadth first or depth first, merely correspond to different selection strategies, that is, to different strategies for exploring the search space.

In FCG, we are not primarily interested in *all possible* analysis (i.e. the set of all well formed feature structures compatible with the input initial structure). Rather, processing is goal-driven, and the primary aim is to find a *suitable* analysis as fast as possible. What is a suitable analysis depends on the task at hand. During production, one will typically want that all meaning components are expressed, or that the produced phrase is unambiguous. If there are several alternatives, e.g. synonyms, then the most conventional one is preferred etc. During parsing, all form components should be processed, and the parsed meaning specification should 'make sense', e.g. unambiguously determine a referent in the discourse context.

It is often the case that several analysis (parses or productions) are possible that all meet these primary criteria. For instance, an idiom might express a meaning more concisely than a regular analysis. This situation is somewhat similar to the one that arises when both a holistic and a compositional analysis are possible (see sections 4 and 5). Selecting among such alternative analysis requires additional criteria. In human language, such criteria are often related to frequency and alignment effects: words and constructions that are more common or were used in the nearby past are typically preferred over others. In the following section it is discussed in more detail how the availability of frequency or related constructional scores can be used to guide search such that more desirable analysis are found first before others.

7.2 Optimal Processing

The problem investigated in this section is how to select among a set of available partial analysis for further expansion during processing. To be precise, an analysis consists of an ordered set of constructions that, when applied one after the other to the initial linguistic structure (the input to processing), leads to a modified transient linguistic structure. Obviously, if one of the modified structures meets a given set of primary processing criteria (see section 7.1), then processing stops (a 'solution' is found). If not, however, one of the available analysis and a construction that applies to it are selected. Applying the construction then gives rise to a new, additional analysis, and the process is repeated.

If constructions are marked with a "preference score", for instance reflecting the frequency of usage, then a global score can be calculated for each analysis by combining the scores of the constructions in it. One possibility is to sum all constructional preference scores. However, this introduces a bias towards analysis with many constructions, that is, towards compositional rather than holistic or idiomatic analysis. An alternative is to average over all constructional preference scores. Neither of these approaches take into account that some analysis might be less complete than others (e.g. leave more meaning or form components unanalyzed). As such, an analysis that covers only a small part of all components with highly scored constructions will be preferred over one that covers all components, but with only moderately scored constructions.

The question arises whether there is an objective or otherwise 'optimal' way of combining constructional scores. The answer in general depends on the precise nature of these scores. If they reflect the probability that the construction will "get the message through", that is, is shared between the interlocutors, then one possibility is to optimize the expected communicative success. This makes sense particularly in the context of language evolution experiments, where the aim is precisely to simulate the evolution of an efficient communication system or language between robots, and scores typically reflect a degree of "conventionality" or "sharedness".[4]

So let $\alpha(s_0, c)$ denote the fraction of components in the initial structure s_0 that is covered by a construction c. For example, if $\eta = \{m_1(x), m_2(y), m_3(x, y)\}$ and c_1, c_2 and c_3 are as before, then each of the constructions covers one third of the components in η. The holistic construction h of section 5.1 covers two thirds. Furthermore, let $\beta(c)$ denote the (positive) preference score of the construction c,

[4] Note however that not just any scoring mechanism allows an interpretation in terms of probabilities. For one thing, probabilities must be positive and are subject to normalization constraints etc.

and let A be a (partial) analysis (an ordered set of constructions). An optimistic (or *admissible*) yet informative heuristic score of the analysis A is the *best still achievable score* $\gamma(A)$ defined as follows:

$$\gamma(A) = \sum_{c \in A} \alpha(s_0, c)\beta(c) + (1 - \sum_{c \in A} \alpha(s_0, c))$$

The first term in the above expression is the contribution of the constructions in A, that is, in the set of constructions that already applied, modulated by their proper preference scores. The second part is an optimistic estimate of what can still be achieved for the remaining components not yet covered in the analysis. This term assumes that it will be possible to cover the remaining components with constructions of maximum preference score 1. Considering constructions in order of preference and adjusting the still achievable score accordingly may considerably improve the accuracy of the heuristic, and hence the time and memory required for processing.[5]

In summary, given that a constructional score can be interpreted as the probability that the construction is shared, optimal processing optimizes the expected communicative success. This is particularly relevant within the context of language game experiments, where the goal is to optimize communicative success amongst a population of (simulated) language users, but might also be relevant in relation to frequency effects observed in human language.

7.3 Efficiency Issues and Specialized Techniques

Many other specialized techniques exist for optimizing symbolic language processing. However, many of them rely on assumptions that do not hold in FCG. For instance, a well known optimization technique is chart parsing. In computer science terms, this is a *memoization* technique, which ensures that the same subphrase is never analyzed more than once. Instead, the result is calculated once and 'memoized', so that it can be retrieved again later if needed. Most chart parsing techniques rely on pre-defined and often linear representations of form. FCG adopts a more flexible representation of form that may involve a tree, or even a graph of form components. Nevertheless, some degree of memoization can still be achieved by checking for similarities between different analysis. This can still greatly reduce processing load, particularly during lexical processing where the order in which constructions are applied often does not matter.

Another optimization technique is the usage of *ranks* or *independent construction sets*. For some constructions it is known that they will not apply unless certain other constructions applied (consider again the modifier-head construction for instance), so it makes sense to put them in different constructicons. Considering that increasing the size of the constructicon can quickly lead to

---

[5] This is not a trivial matter however, since in general it cannot be excluded that a highly scored construction is only triggered at a later stage, for instance because it depends on other constructions.

a combinatorial explosion of the search space, such a 'divide and conquer' approach might considerably reduce processing load. More generally, we can keep a detailed record of all dependencies that exist between constructions and compile them into a constructional dependency network. This might eliminate search altogether. However, if the language changes, constructional dependencies change too, so that a 'one time compilation' approach is not possible and more dynamic programming techniques are required. These issues are further discussed elsewhere, e.g. [18] or [5].

8 Discussion and Conclusion

FCG was developed as a computational framework to support artificial language processing in robotic setups. From this perspective, it is actually surprising that it has grown into a formalism in which even complex phenomena of natural language can be captured. This in itself, in my opinion, makes it worthwhile to compare FCG with other formalisms that were developed for capturing natural language from the start.

Thus FCG, like HPSG [14] or ECG [3], is feature structure and unification based. However, despite these similarities, a detailed comparison is not easily made due to fact that these techniques are sometimes employed for different reasons. As such, whereas unification in HPSG is seen as a falsifiability problem that determines the set of well formed structures, in FCG it is sometimes used as a way to perform a "lookup" of constructions during processing (match), and sometimes, in a different form, as an active step in processing itself (merge). This reflects the fact that the development of FCG was driven primarily by the problem of *language processing* rather than that of *language representation.*

Another distinguishing feature of FCG is that linguistic knowledge is organized into constructions. As in construction grammar, these are meaning form pairings. In FCG, constructions are furthermore routines for (partially) transforming meaning specifications into form specifications during production, and vice versa during parsing. There is thus an inherent duality between two processing modes –parsing and production– that is not usually found in other formalisms. This duality should not be confused with the one that exists between parsing and generation in generative approaches.

With this chapter, we aimed to clarify some of these and other 'peculiarities' by tracing them back in the history of FCG. This history more or less follows the development of processing machinery for processing increasingly complex forms of language. For purely holistic language processing, a simple bi-directional lookup table between meaning and form specifications suffices. Matching then amounts to a simple comparison of patterns (component matching) and merging is not even relevant. For compositional language processing of independent components, a slightly more involved form of matching is required, namely set-matching. Merging then amounts to taking the union of sets. It also becomes necessary to introduce the notion of a transient linguistic structure for capturing intermediate processing results. When components are no longer independent but form a network, additionally relations between meaning and form components as captured in constructions need to be represented in the transient linguistic structure as well. This is the reason for introducing feature structures in FCG. Matching now becomes a kind of pattern-matching between feature structures. Merging now formally corresponds to the notion of unification of feature structures in other unification-based language formalisms, augmented with special machinery for specifying manipulations to the constituent structure of the transient linguistic structure. Chapters [16] and [5] can be consulted for a further entanglement of differences and commonalities between FCG and other approaches to unification and constraint based language processing.

Acknowledgements. This work was mainly funded by the FWO through the European Complexity-Net project "EvoSym". The author wishes to thank Luc Steels for making the development of FCG possible and for helping to improve this paper.

References

[1] Abelson, H., Sussman, G.J.: Structure and Interpretation of Computer Programs, 2nd edn. MIT Press (1996)
[2] Baker, C.F., Fillmore, C.J., Lowe, J.B.: The Berkeley FrameNet Project. In: Proceedings of the 17th International Conference on Computational Linguistics. Association for Computational Linguistics, Morristown (1998)
[3] Bergen, B., Chang, N.: Embodied Construction Grammar in simulation-based language understanding. In: Östman, J.O., Fried, M. (eds.) Construction Grammar(s): Cognitive and Cross-Language Dimensions. Johns Benjamins (2005)
[4] Chomsky, N.: The Minimalist Program. MIT Press, Cambridge (1995)
[5] Ciortuz, L., Saveluc, V.: Fluid Construction Grammar and Feature Constraint Logics. In: Steels, L. (ed.) Computational Issues in FCG. LNCS (LNAI), vol. 7249, pp. 289–311. Springer, Heidelberg (2012)
[6] Croft, W.: Logical and typological arguments for radical construction grammar. In: Ostman, J., Fried, M. (eds.) Construction Grammars: Cognitive Grounding and Theoretical Extensions. John Benjamin Publ. Cy., Amsterdam (2005)
[7] De Beule, J.: Compositionality, Hierarchy and Recursion in Language, a Case Study in Fluid Construction Grammar. Ph.D. thesis, VUB Artificial Intelligence Lab. (2007)
[8] Fillmore, C.J.: Frame semantics. In: Linguistics in the Morning Calm, Seoul, pp. 111–137 (1982)
[9] Gentner, T.Q., Fenn, K.M., Margoliash, D., Nusbaum, H.C.: Recursive syntactic pattern learning by songbirds. Nature (2006)
[10] Goldberg, A.: Constructions: A Construction grammar approach to argument structure. University of Chicago Press, Chicago (1995)
[11] Hauser, M.D., Chomsky, N., Fitch, W.T.: The faculty of language: What is it, who has it, and how did it evolve? Science 298, 1569–1579 (2002)
[12] Jackendoff, R., Pinker, S.: The nature of the language faculty and its implications for evolution of language (reply to fitch, hauser, and chomsky). Cognition (September 2005)

[13] Norvig, P.: Paradigms of AI: Case studies in Common Lisp. PWS Publishing Company (1992)

[14] Pollard, C., Sag, I.: Head-driven phrase structure grammar. University of Chicago Press, Center for the Study of Language and Information of Stanford University, Chicago (1994)

[15] Sag, I.A., Wasow, T., Bender, E.M.: Syntactic Theory, A Formal Introduction., 2nd edn. CSLI Publications, Leland Stanford Junior University, United States (2003)

[16] Santibáñez, J.S.: A Logic Programming Approach to Parsing and Production in Fluid Construction Grammar. In: Steels, L. (ed.) Computational Issues in FCG. LNCS (LNAI), vol. 7249, pp. 239–255. Springer, Heidelberg (2012)

[17] Steels, L., Vogt, P.: Grounding adaptive language games in robotic agents. In: Husbands, P., Harvey, I. (eds.) Proceedings of the Fourth European Conference on Artificial Life (ECAL 1997). Complex Adaptive Systems. The MIT Press, Cambridge (1997)

[18] Wellens, P.: Organizing constructions in networks. In: Steels, L. (ed.) Design Patterns in Fluid Construction Grammar., John Benjamins, Amsterdam (2011)

A Logic Programming Approach to Parsing and Production in Fluid Construction Grammar

Josefina Sierra-Santibáñez

Universidad Politécnica de Cataluña,
Campus Nord, 08034 Barcelona, Spain
Maria.Josefina.Sierra@upc.edu

Abstract. This paper presents a Logic Programming approach to parsing and production in Fluid Construction Grammar (FCG) [13]. It builds on previous work on the formalisation of FCG in terms of First Order Logic (FOL) concepts, more specifically on the definition of its core inference operations, *unification* and *merge,* in terms of FOL unification and search in the space of a particular set of FOL terms called *structure arrangements.* An implementation of such inference operations based on Logic Programming and Artificial Intelligence techniques such as unification and heuristic search is outlined.

1 Introduction

Fluid Construction Grammar (FCG) [10] is a grammatical formalism implemented in Lisp [6] which incorporates ideas from Construction Grammar [3] and Cognitive Grammar [5].

It has been used in a number of experiments [11, 15] investigating the *symbol grounding problem* [4] in populations of autonomous agents connected to their environment through sensors and actuators. These experiments focus on the study of the evolution and the acquisition of language [9] in particular on the acquisition of grammar and the role of grammar in language grounding, emphasising the communicative function of grammar as well as the relation between grammar and meaning [14].

FCG also draws inspiration from observations of language usage [18], which suggest that natural languages constantly adapt and evolve to cope with new meanings and variations in the behaviour of language users. The experiments themselves are designed to implement and test a constructivist approach to language development [16], in which grammatical constructions are acquired gradually, beginning with concrete linguistic structures based on particular words, from which they are progressively abstracted.

From a computational point of view, FCG is fully operational [1, 17] and it has been used in a considerable number of experiments. However its basic inference operations, unification and merge, are only defined intuitively in the linguistics literature. A formalisation of the unification and merge algorithms used in FCG has been proposed by its developers in [12]. Formal definitions of FCG concepts

L. Steels (Ed.): Computational Issues in FCG, LNAI 7249, pp. 239–255, 2012.

in terms of First Order Logic and Order-Sorted Feature Constraint Logic have also been presented in [8] and [2]. The present paper outlines an approach to parsing and production in FCG based on Logic Programming and Artificial Intelligence techniques such as unification and heuristic search.

The rest of the paper is organised as follows. Section 2 describes the representation formalism used in FCG. Section 3 summarises the formal definition of *unification and merge* proposed in [8]. Section 4 illustrates the usefulness of such definition with two examples of construction application. Finally, section 5 presents an outline of an FCG-unification algorithm based on logic programming techniques through an extended example.

2 Representation Formalism

2.1 Semantic and Syntactic Structures

Linguistic and semantic information is represented using *syntactic* and *semantic structures* in FCG. A semantic or syntactic structure consists of a *set of units*, which correspond to lexical items or constituents such as noun phrases or relative clauses. A unit has a name and a number of feature-value pairs. In this paper, we will assume that *semantic units* contain the features *sem-subunits, referent, meaning* and *sem-cat,* in that order; and *syntactic units* the features *syn-subunits, utterance, form* and *syn-cat.* Feature values depend on the type of feature: *referent* and *utterance* have a *single value*, whereas the values of *sem-subunits* and *syn-subunits* are *sets of unit names.* The values of the rest of the features are *sets of facts* about different aspects of the components of a structure: *meaning* is a set of facts which can be used to identify the referent (e.g. its shape, colour, type of entity or event); *semantic categories* describe more abstract aspects of the referent (e.g. its role as the agent, object or recipient in an action); *form* and *syntactic categories* specify different aspects of the utterance, such as its number, part of speech, stem or grammatical role (e.g. subject, predicate or object). The set of facts which may be included in the values of these features is not restricted to those just mentioned but open ended.

We will use *lists* to represent those facts. For example, the fact that unit-2 is a *noun* will be represented by the list `(part-of-speech unit-2 noun)`. This notation allows using First Order Logic variables for syntactic and semantic categories [7]. In particular, we will use a *many-sorted language* with two types: list and atom[1]. We shall also assume that the elements of the lists representing facts are always variables or constants of type atom, and that any symbol preceded by a question mark is a variable.

[1] There is a binary function symbol `cons: Atom` × `List` ⟶ `List` and a constant symbol `NIL` of type `list`, which allow constructing terms of type `list`. For example, the term `(part-of-speech unit-2 noun)` is an abbreviation for the first order logic term `(cons part-of-speech (cons unit-2 (cons noun NIL)))`, where `part-of-speech`, `unit-2` and `noun` are constant symbols of type `atom`.

2.2 Constructions

In FCG inference is performed applying *constructions* to *source structures*. A *construction* is a pair *<left-pole>* ⇔ *<right-pole>* of *pattern structures* which usually associates a *syntactic pattern* with a *semantic pattern* (see figures 2 and 1). Constructions play therefore the role of *grammar rules* in *construction grammars* [3]. However they not only relate syntactic patterns to semantic ones but also supply information required for parsing and generation which is not included in lexical items, making it possible to construct sentences whose meaning is more than the sum of the meanings of their parts.

Source structures (i.e. semantic and syntactic structures of the type we have described before) constitute the input to parsing and production processes in FCG, whereas constructions are used to add semantic and syntactic information to source structures, that is, to complete missing aspects in these structures, such as the identity of the agent in an event or the subject of a verb.

Formally, the *application of a construction* is a combination of two operations: *Unification,* which is used to check whether a construction is compatible with a source structure; and *merge,* which extends the structure with information contained in the construction [12].

3 Unification and Merge

3.1 Feature-Value Unification

Unification for feature-values depends on the type of feature. *First Order Logic unification* can be used to compute *the most general unifier (mgu)* of two features whose values are single terms. However, when feature values are sets of terms (unit names or facts represented by lists of atoms), a number of issues must be taken into account before First Order Logic unification can be applied.

Feature-value Arrangement. Let $s = \{t_1, \ldots, t_n\}$ be a feature value of type set of terms (unit names or facts represented by lists of atoms) of a semantic or syntactic source unit. An *m-arrangement* of s is a list $v = (t_{i_1}, \ldots, t_{i_m})$, where $t_{i_j} \in s$ for $j = 1 \ldots m$, and t_{i_j} are all distinct. An m-arrangement is thus a list in which m distinct elements of s are organised in a particular order.

Feature-value Unification. Let $s = \{a_1, \ldots, a_n\}$ be a feature value of type set of terms of a *source* unit and $p = (== b_1, \ldots, b_m)$ a feature value of type set of terms of a *pattern* unit[2]. We say that s and p are *FCG-unifiable* if there is an m-arrangement s' of s such that the First Order Logic terms s' and p of type list of terms are unifiable, and we call the most general unifier σ of s' and p an FCG-unifier of s and p.

The symbol $==$ in the pattern feature value is used in FCG to indicate that the source feature value should include the pattern feature value, but that they

[2] Note that we use *list* notation (round brackets), rather than *set* notation (curly brackets), for specifying *pattern* feature values of type set of terms. The reason is that we need not consider the m-arrangements of pattern values.

need not be exactly the same set. If the symbol == is omitted from the list representing the pattern feature value, then it is understood that both sets, the source and the pattern, must be equal after unification.

Feature values of type set of terms in FCG patterns may take thus one of the following forms:

1. $(== t_1, \ldots, t_m)$, specifying a set of terms which should be included in the value of a particular feature in a source structure; or
2. $(t_1, \ldots, t_m)$, specifying a set of terms which should be equal to the value of a particular feature in a source structure.

Note that there can be several FCG-unifiers for a pair (s, p) of source and pattern feature values. Because two different arrangements s_1 and s_2 of s might be such that p and s_1 are unifiable, and so are p and s_2, but s_1 and s_2 are not.

3.2 Feature-Value Merge

Merge is used to extend a semantic or syntactic source structure with additional information contained in a pattern structure.

If the pattern and source feature values are FCG-unifiable, *merge* is equivalent to unification[3]. However, when the pattern and source are not FCG-unifiable, the source feature value is minimally extended so that its extension and the pattern are unifiable. The source feature value is extended only if this can be done without introducing inconsistencies. Consider the following example:

```
p: ((?unit (sem-cat (== (agent ?e ?a) (entity-type ?a human)))))
s: {(unit (sem-cat {(agent e a) (event-type e motion)}))}
```

The values of the feature `sem-cat` are not unifiable. But if we add the fact `(entity-type ?a human)` to the source value, both feature values can be unified yielding the following extended value, which is the result of merging s with p.

```
s': {(unit (sem-cat {(agent e a) (event-type e motion)
                     (entity-type a human)}))}
```

The steps involved in merging the feature value in source structure s with the feature value in pattern structure p above are:

1. Finding a minimal subset $p_c = \{(\text{entity-type ?a human})\}$ of p such that $s \bigcup p_c$ and p are FCG-unifiable, and an FCG-unifier σ of p and $s \bigcup p_c$.
2. Applying $\sigma = \{?\text{a} = a, ?\text{e} = e\}$ to $s \bigcup p_c$ in order to obtain the extended source feature value $(s \bigcup p_c)\sigma$, which is the result of merging s with p.

In general the result of merging a source feature value s with a pattern feature value p is not unique, because there might be different minimal extensions s' of s such that s' and p are unifiable; and there might be as well different FCG-unifiers for a given extension s' and the pattern p.

[3] In this case, the source feature value is not extended as a result of merging it with the pattern feature value, although some of its variables might be instantiated when an FCG-unifier of both feature values is applied to it.

The Set of Facts Consistency Condition. The first step above requires further clarification. Let us consider another example, where s and p denote the source and pattern structures to be merged respectively.

```
p: ((?unit (form  (== (string ?unit car)))
           (syn-cat (== (number ?unit singular)))))
s: {(unit (form  {(string unit cars)})
          (syn-cat {(number unit plural)}))}
```

In this case, s should not be merged with p, because neither the values of the `form` feature nor those of the `syn-cat` feature are consistent with each other. The value of the source feature `syn-cat` and the value of the same feature in the pattern are not unifiable. But the union of the minimal subset of the pattern feature value p_c = {(number ?unit singular)} and the source feature value s = {(number unit plural)} leads to a contradiction, once the most general unifier σ = {?unit = unit} is applied to it: the number of a unit cannot be singular and plural at the same time.

$$(s \bigcup p_c)\sigma = \text{(syn-cat \{(number unit plural) (number unit singular)\})}$$

In fact, the pattern and source structures above cannot be merged. The minimal subset of the pattern feature value p_c such that $s \bigcup p_c$ and p are FCG-unifiable must satisfy an additional condition which we will call *the set of facts consistency:* the extended source feature value resulting from merging the source with the pattern should not contain any pair of facts $(f\ a_1 \ldots a_n\ u)$ and $(f\ a_1 \ldots a_n\ v)$ such that their elements are all equal but for the last one $(u \neq v)$. The reason for imposing this condition is that a function cannot assign different values to a single tuple of elements, and we are assuming that a fact described by a list such as $(f\ a_1 \ldots a_n\ v)$ represents a statement of the form $f(a_1, \ldots, a_n) = v$, where f denotes a function symbol, $a_1, \ldots, a_n$ its arguments, and v the value that f assigns to $(a_1, \ldots, a_n)$.

In FCG the symbol =1 is used in pattern feature values of type set of terms to indicate that no repetitions are allowed. For example, the pattern of the previous example should be specified as follows in FCG:

```
p: ((?unit (form  (=1 (string ?unit car)))
           (syn-cat (=1 (number ?unit singular)))))
```

We need not use =1, because we assume a *functional interpretation* of lists representing facts and *the set of facts consistency* condition. The reader should be warned that lists representing facts in FCG are interpreted *relationally* and that FCG does not make the set of facts consistency assumption.

Feature-Value Merge. Let s be a source feature value of type set of terms, p a pattern feature value of the same type, p_c a minimal subset of p such that $s \bigcup p_c$ and p are FCG-unifiable[4], and σ an FCG-unifier of $s \bigcup p_c$ and p. If $(s \bigcup p_c)\sigma$

[4] A subset p_c of a pattern feature-value p is *minimal* with respect to a source feature-value s if no subset p_t of p satisfies that: (1) $p_t \subset p_c$; (2) p and $s \bigcup p_t$ are FCG-unifiable; and (3) $(s \bigcup p_t)\sigma$ is fact set consistent.

satisfies *the set of facts consistency condition,* then the extended feature value $(s \bigcup p_c)\sigma$ is a valid result of merging s with p.

3.3 Unification and Merge for Units

Let $p = (p_{name}\ (f_1\ \bar{u}_1)\ (f_2\ u_2)\ (f_3\ \bar{u}_3)\ (f_4\ \bar{u}_4))$ be a pattern unit, where $f_1, \ldots, f_4$ are the feature names *sem-subunits, referent, meaning* and *sem-cat,* if p is a semantic unit; or the feature names *syn-subunits, utterance, form* and *syn-cat,* if p is a syntactic unit.

Unit Arrangement. A *p-arrangement* of a source unit s is a first order logic term of the form $(s_{name}\ (f_1\ \bar{v}_1)\ (f_2\ v_2)\ (f_3\ \bar{v}_3)\ (f_4 \bar{v}_4))$, where s_{name} is the name of s; n_1, n_3 and n_4 are the number of elements in $\bar{u}_1, \bar{u}_3$ and $\bar{u}_4$; $\bar{v}_1, \bar{v}_3, \bar{v}_4$ are n_1, n_3 and n_4-arrangements of the values of features f_1, f_3 and f_4 in s, respectively; and v_2 is the value of feature f_2 in s.

A *p-arrangement.* of a source unit s is thus a unit obtained from s substituting each of its feature values for arrangements of such feature values with respect to the corresponding feature values in the pattern unit p.

Unit Unification. Let p be a pattern unit and s a source unit. We say that s and p are *FCG-unifiable* if there is a p-arrangement s' of s such that the first order logic terms p and s' are unifiable. The most general unifier σ of s' and p is an FCG-unifier of s and p.

Unit Merge. Let s be a source unit $(s_{name}\ (f_1\ sv_1)\ (f_2\ sv_2)\ (f_3\ sv_3)\ (f_4\ sv_4))$; p a pattern unit $(p_{name}\ (f_1\ pv_1)\ (f_2\ pv_2)\ (f_3\ pv_3)\ (f_4\ pv_4))$; pv_1^c, pv_3^c and pv_4^c minimal subsets of pv_1, pv_3 and pv_4 such that the extended unit $s^e = (s_{name}\ (f_1\ \ sv_1 \bigcup pv_1^c)\ (f_2\ \ sv_2)\ (f_3\ \ sv_3 \bigcup pv_3^c)\ (f_4\ \ sv_4 \bigcup pv_4^c))$ and the pattern unit p are FCG-unifiable; and σ an FCG-unifier of s^e and p. If every feature value in $s^e\sigma$ satisfies the *set of facts consistency* condition, then $s^e\sigma$ is a valid result of merging s with p.

3.4 Unification and Merge for Structures

Structure Arrangement. Let $s = \{u_1 \ldots u_n\}$ be a source structure and $p = (== v_1 \ldots v_m)$ a pattern structure. An *m-arrangement* of s is a list of m-units $s' = (u_{i1}^{v_1}, \ldots, u_{im}^{v_m})$, where each $u_{i_j}^{v_j}$ is a v_j-arrangement of some $u_{i_j} \in s$ for $j = 1 \ldots m$, and the u_{i_j} are all distinct.

Structure Unification. Let $s = \{u_1 \ldots u_n\}$ be a source structure and $p = (== v_1 \ldots v_m)$ a pattern structure. We say that s and p are *FCG-unifiable* if there is an m-arrangement s' of s such that the first order logic terms s' and p are unifiable. The most general unifier σ of s' and p is an FCG-unifier of s and p.

Structure Merge. Let s be a source structure; p a pattern structure$(== v_1 \ldots v_m)$; p_c a minimal subset of p such that for each unit $u_i \in s \bigcup p_c\ i = 1 \ldots n$ there is a unit u_i^e which is either equal to u_i or an extension of u_i with respect to a unique unit $v_j \in p$, such that the extended structure $s^e = \{u_1^e, \ldots, u_n^e\}$ and the pattern structure p are FCG-unifiable; and σ an FCG-unifier of s^e and p. If every feature-value in $s^e\sigma$ satisfies the set of facts consistency condition, then $s^e\sigma$ is a valid result of merging s with p.

4 Examples of Construction Application

The semantic and syntactic source structures constructed at an intermediate stage during the parsing process of the sentence *John slides blocks to Mary* are shown in figure 1. These structures result from applying morphological, lexical, semantic categorisation and phrase structure rules (constructions) to an initial structure containing just the words that make up the sentence. *Morphological rules* decompose words into a stem and a set of syntactic categories (e.g. "slides" into a stem "slide" and the categories *verb* and *singular*). *Number* is *grammatical* as opposed to *natural,* because it does not contribute to meaning. *Lexical rules* map the stem of a lexical item into a set of facts specifying its meaning, and natural syntactic categories (e.g. *number* for nouns) into additional meaning. *Semantic categorisation rules* add semantic categories to the semantic structure (e.g. the arguments of "slide" can be mapped into the semantic roles *agent, object* and *recipient* in a *transfer-to-recipient (tr)* event). Finally, *phrase structure rules* relate structural properties of a sentence, such as word order, to syntactic categories, such as *subject, direct object* or *indirect object.*

Note that the variables associated with the referents of semantic units *jo, bl* and *ma,* which represent *John, blocks* and *Mary* respectively, are different from those associated with the roles in the *transfer-to-recipient* event in unit *sl.* Figure 2 shows an example of a construction whose purpose is to ensure that the variables associated with the roles *agent, object* and *recipient* (*ag, obj* and *rec* in unit *?eu*) in a *transfer-to-recipient* (*tr*) event in a semantic structure become equal to the variables associated with the referents of semantic units `?au`, `?ou` and `?ru`, which represent the participants in such an event.

Let us see how the construction shown in figure 2 can be applied to the syntactic and semantic structures associated with the sentence *John slides blocks to Mary,* in order to make the variables representing the roles in the *transfer-to-recipient* event equal to those associated with the referents of the units for John, blocks and Mary.

From a computational point of view, *construction application* is a combination of two operations: unification and merge. *Unification* is used to check whether a construction is compatible with a source structure; and *merge* to extend the structure with information contained in the construction.

In our example unification is first applied to the syntactic pattern of the construction and the syntactic source structure, to determine whether the construction can be used to extend the structure. In this case both structures are unifiable. Then the unifier built during this process {?su=u, ?eu=sl, ?au=jo, ?tu=t, ?ou=bl, ?ru=ma} is applied to the semantic pattern of the construction and the semantic source structure. Next, the semantic source structure is merged with the semantic pattern of the construction.

If the semantic source structure and the pattern are unifiable, merge is equivalent to applying one of their FCG-unifiers to the semantic source structure. In our example they are unifiable. Therefore the result of merging the semantic source structure with the semantic pattern is obtained applying the unifier $\tau =$ {?s=?e, ?j=?a, ?b=?o, ?m=?r} to the semantic structure. As a consequence of this, the variables associated with the roles agent, object and recipient in the transfer to recipient event become equal to those associated with the referents of the units representing John, blocks and Mary in the semantic structure.

```
{(u   (sem-sub {sl jo bl ma}))

 (sl  (referent ?s)
      (meaning {(act ?s slide) (arg1 ?s ?a)
                (arg2 ?s ?o) (arg3 ?s ?r)})
      (sem-cat {(ev-type ?s tr) (ag ?s ?a)
                (obj ?s ?o) (rec ?s ?r)}))

 (jo  (referent ?j)
      (meaning {(entity-type ?j person)
                (count ?j one)}))

 (bl  (referent ?b)
      (meaning {(entity-type ?b block)
                (count ?b several)}))

 (ma  (referent ?m)
      (meaning {(entity-type ?m person)
                (count ?m one)})) }
```

```
{(u   (syn-sub {sl jo bl t ma})
      (form     {(order u (jo sl bl t ma))})
      (syn-cat  {SVOtoO-sentence}))
 (sl  (form     {(string sl slides)})
      (syn-cat  {(stem sl slide)
                 (numb gram sl singular)
                 (speech-part sl verb)
                 (role sl pred)}))
 (t   (form     {(string t to)})
      (syn-cat  {(speech-part t prep)}))
 (jo  (form     {(string jo John)})
      (syn-cat  {(stem jo john),
                 (numb nat jo singular)
                 (speech-part jo noun))
                 (role jo subject)}))
 (bl  (form     {(string bl blocks)})
      (syn-cat  {(stem bl block)
                 (numb nat bl plural)
                 (speech-part bl noun))
                 (role bl dir-obj)}))
 (ma  (form     {(string ma Mary)})
      (syn-cat  {(stem ma mary)
                 (numb nat ma singular)
                 (speech-part ma noun)
                 (role ma ind-obj)})) }
```

Fig. 1. Semantic (left) and syntactic (right) source structures built at an intermediate stage during the parsing process of the sentence *John slides blocks to Mary*

```
(=
(?su (sem-sub (= ?eu ?au ?ou ?ru)))

(?eu (referent ?e)
     (sem-cat (= (ev-type ?e tr) (ag ?e ?a)
                 (obj ?e ?o) (rec ?e ?r))))
(?au (referent ?a))
(?ou (referent ?o))
(?ru (referent ?r)))
```

```
(=
(?su (syn-sub (= ?eu ?au ?tu ?ou ?ru))
     (syn-cat (= SVOtoO-sentence)))
(?eu (syn-cat (= (role ?eu pred))))

(?tu (form    (= (string ?tu to))))
(?au (syn-cat (= (role ?au subject))))
(?ou (syn-cat (= (role ?ou dir-obj))))
(?ru (syn-cat (= (role ?ru ind-obj)))))
```

Fig. 2. Construction which associates a *transfer-to-recipient (tr)* semantic pattern structure (left) with a *Subject + Verb + Dir-Object + to + Indir-Object (SVOtoO)* syntactic pattern structure (right). Features whose values are the empty set or variables which appear only once in the construction are omitted.

However, unifiability is not a necessary requirement for merge. If source and pattern are not unifiable, the source structure might still be merged with the pattern, provided it can be minimally extended so that its extension and the pattern are unifiable, and the result of merge does not violate the set of facts consistency condition.

Let us see an example of construction application where merge cannot be reduced to unification. Figure 3 shows a morphological construction which decomposes the word "slides" into a stem and a number of syntactic categories. We apply this construction to the source structure in figure 4. First, unification is applied to the left pattern of the construction and the source structure (see figure 5), to determine whether the construction can be used to extend the structure. Then the unifier σ constructed during this process is applied to the right pattern of the construction and the source structure.

```
(= (?s (form (= (string ?s slides)))))   |  (= (?s (form    (= (stem ?s slide)))
                                         |        (syn-cat (= (number ?s singular)
                                         |                    (speech-part ?s verb)))))
```

Fig. 3. Construction which decomposes the word "slides" into a stem and a number of syntactic categories

```
{ (sl (syn-sub {})
      (utter    ?u2)
      (form     {(string sl slides)})
      (syn-cat ?sc2)) }
```

Fig. 4. Extended form of a syntactic source structure containing a syntactic unit associated with the word "slides" at an initial stage during the parsing process

```
(= (?s (syn-sub {})                            |  { (sl (syn-sub {})
       (utter    ?u1)                          |        (utter    ?u2)
       (form     (= (string ?s slides)))       |        (form     {(string sl slides)})
       (syn-cat ?sc1)) )                       |        (syn-cat ?sc2)) }
```

Fig. 5. Unification is applied to the left pattern of the construction and the source structure, yielding the unifier σ = {?s = sl, ?u1 = ?u2, ?sc1 = ?sc2}

Next, the source structure is merged with the right pattern of the construction. Given that the pattern and the source structure are not unifiable, the source structure is minimally extended so that its extension and the pattern are unifiable. In particular, the value of feature *form* in the source structure is extended with the subset {(stem sl slide)} of the value of the same feature in the pattern (see figure 6).

Finally, the extended source structure and the right pattern of the construction are unified, and the unifier τ = {?sc2 = {(number sl singular) (speech-part sl verb)}} constructed during this step is applied to the extended source structure in order to obtain the result of merging the source structure with the right pattern of the construction (see figure 7).

```
{ (sl (syn-sub {})                          (= (sl (syn-sub {})
      (utter   ?u2)                                (utter    ?u2)
      (form    {(string sl slides)                 (form     (= (stem sl slide)))
                (stem sl slide)})
      (syn-cat ?sc2)) }                            (syn-cat  (= (number sl singular)
                                                                (speech-part sl verb)))))
```

Fig. 6. Unifier σ is applied to the right pattern of the construction, and the source structure is minimally extended so that it unifies with the pattern in the sense of FCG

```
{ (sl (syn-sub {})
      (utter   ?u2)
      (form    {(string sl slides) (stem sl slide)})
      (syn-cat {(number sl singular) (speech-part sl verb)})) }
```

Fig. 7. Result of merging the source structure with the instantiated right pattern of the construction

5 Outline of an FCG-Unification Algorithm

Let $p = (== v_1 \ldots v_m)$ be a pattern structure and $s = \{u_1 \ldots u_n\}$ a source structure. For each unit v_i in p we define the set $C_i = \{(u_j^k, \sigma_j^k) \mid j = 1 \ldots n,\ k = 1 \ldots n_j\}$, where u_j^k is a v_i-arrangement of unit u_j in s such that u_j^k and v_i are unifiable in the sense of First Order Logic and $\sigma_j^k = mgu(v_i, u_j^k)$.

For example, let $p = (== v_1 \ldots v_6)$ be the syntactic pattern structure in figure 2 and $s = \{u_1 \ldots u_6\}$ the syntactic source structure in figure 1. In order to construct C_2, we first try to unify unit v_2 (i.e. *?eu*) in the pattern and unit u_1 (i.e. *u*) in the source. Units in figures 1 and 2 appear in abbreviated form, where features which do not contain relevant values are omitted. Unification requires using the extended form of these units, which is shown below.

```
(?eu (syn-sub ())                         (u (syn-sub {sl jo bl t ma})
     (utter    ?u1)                          (utter    ?u2)
     (form     ?f )                          (form     {(order u (jo sl bl t ma))})
     (syn-cat (= (role ?eu pred))))          (syn-cat  {SVOtoO-sentence}))
```

In order to unify two units, it is necessary to unify their feature values, and it is clear that the values of feature *syn-cat* are not FCG-unifiable: there is no 1-arrangement of {SVOtoO-sentence} which can be made equal to ((role ?eu pre)). Therefore units v_2 and u_1 are not unifiable.

We consider now the pair of units v_2 (i.e. *?eu* in the pattern) and u_2 (*sl* in the source). The extended form of these units is shown below.

```
(?eu (syn-sub ())                         (sl (syn-sub {})
     (utter    ?u1)                           (utter    ?u2)
     (form     ?f)                            (form     {(string sl slides)})
     (syn-cat (= (role ?eu pred))))           (syn-cat  {(stem sl slide)
                                                         (numb gram sl singular)
                                                         (speech-part sl verb)
                                                         (role sl pred)}))
```

The values of features *syn-sub, utter* and *form* in units *sl* and *?eu* are unifiable. The value of feature *syn-cat* has four 1-arrangements, however only one of them, ((role sl pred)), satisfies the unifiability condition. It is easy to check that unit $?eu$ does not unify with the rest of the units in the source structure. Therefore, set C_2 consists only of the pair (u_2^1, σ_2^1), where σ_2^1 is the unifier {?eu = sl, ?u1 = ?u2, ?f = ((string sl slides))} and u_2^1 the $?eu$-arrangement of unit u_2 (i.e. sl) shown below.

```
(?eu (syn-sub ())                        | (sl (syn-sub ())
     (utter    ?u1)                      |     (utter     ?u2)
     (form     ?f)                       |     (form      ((string sl slides)))
     (syn-cat  (= (role ?eu pred))))     |     (syn-cat   ((role sl pred))))
```

The same reasoning can be applied to units v_3, v_4, v_5 and v_6 (i.e. $?tu, ?au, ?ou$ and $?ru$) in the pattern. Only one arrangement of unit u_3 (i.e. t) and unit v_3 (i.e. $?tu$) are unifiable, and the same happens to the pairs of units $(?au, jo)$, $(?ou, bl)$ and $(?ru, ma)$.

Unit v_1 (i.e. $?su$) is more interesting though, because several v_1-arrangements of source unit u_1 (i.e. u) satisfy the unifiability condition. In fact, the set C_1 contains 120 pairs of the form (v_1-arrangement, unifier), one for each permutation of the set {$sl\ jo\ bl\ t\ ma$}. We just show two of them.

The unifier σ_1^1 = {?su = u, ?eu = sl, ?au = jo, ?tu = t, ?ou = bl, ?ru = ma, ?u1 = ?u2, ?f = ((order u (jo sl bl t ma)))} corresponds to u_1^1, the $?su$-arrangement of unit u_1 (i.e. u) shown below.

```
(?su (syn-sub (= ?eu ?au ?tu ?ou ?ru))   | (u (syn-sub (sl jo t bl ma))
     (utter    ?u1)                      |    (utter     ?u2)
     (form     ?f)                       |    (form      ((order u (jo sl bl t ma))))
     (syn-cat  (= SVOtoO-sentence)))     |    (syn-cat   (SVOtoO-sentence)))
```

The unifier σ_1^2 = {?su = u, ?eu = sl, ?au = jo, ?tu = t, ?ou = ma, ?ru = bl, ?u1 = ?u2, ?f = ((order u (jo sl bl t ma)))} corresponds to u_1^2, the $?su$-arrangement of unit u_1 (i.e. u) shown below.

```
(?su (syn-sub (= ?eu ?au ?tu ?ou ?ru))   | (u (syn-sub (sl jo t ma bl))
     (utter    ?u1)                      |    (utter     ?u2)
     (form     ?f)                       |    (form      ((order u (jo sl bl t ma))))
     (syn-cat  (= SVOtoO-sentence)))     |    (syn-cat   (SVOtoO-sentence)))
```

Given a pattern structure $p = (== v_1 \dots v_m)$, a source structure $s = \{\ u_1 \dots u_n\ \}$ and a tuple of sets $(C_1, \dots, C_m)$ of the sort defined above, the set of FCG-unifiers of p and s can be defined as follows.

$$\{\sigma \mid \exists i_1 \dots \exists i_m (a_1^{i_1} \in C_1 \wedge \dots \wedge a_m^{i_m} \in C_m \wedge \sigma = mgu(p, (a_1^{i_1}, \dots, a_m^{i_m}))\}$$

That is, the set of FCG-unifiers of p and s is the set of most general unifiers of p and s', where s' is any p-arrangement of s of the form $(a_1^{i_1}, \dots, a_m^{i_m})$ such that s' and p are unifiable.

Clearly, constructing all the p-arrangements of a source structure s, and checking whether p and any of them are unifiable is not a practical approach to unification. Consider the unification example discussed above. Sets C_2 to C_6 contain a single pair of the form (arrangement, unifier), but set C_1 has 120 pairs. Therefore, in the worst case we would have to construct 120 structure arrangements and check whether each of them and the pattern are unifiable.

Instead, we use a *heuristic depth first search strategy* to explore the space of structure arrangements. The depth first search part of our approach consists in applying the unifier associated with a unit arrangement in a set C_i to the whole pattern and source structures. This requires undoing substitutions in backtracking steps, but it can be easily implemented in Prolog. The heuristic part is used to determine the order in which the sets C_i will be used to explore the set of structure arrangements. For example, if set C_i has fewer elements than set C_j, then we instantiate the i-esim component of an arrangement earlier than the j-esim one. Similarly, semantic relevance is used as a criterion for determining order of instantiation. For example a unit representing the predicate of a sentence should take precedence over other units representing its subject or its complements. Figure 8 shows part of a preliminary Prolog implementation of the FCG-unification algorithm outlined in this section.

Let us illustrate these ideas describing the application of the algorithm to our previous example of unification of the syntactic pattern of the construction in figure 2 and the syntactic source structure in figure 1. In accordance with the heuristics just mentioned the unit-arrangement and unifier in set C_2 would be used in first place, because unit u_2 describes a predicate and the set C_2 only has one element. Sets C_3 to C_6 also have one element. They might be explored in order of semantic relevance: C_4 subject, C_5 direct object, C_6 indirect object and C_3 preposition. Finally, the last set to be used would be C_1, because it has 120 elements. In fact, as we will see later, set C_1 will not even be constructed explicitly. All its arrangements but one will be pruned out by unification during the depth first search process. It is possible to estimate the number of elements of a set C_i without actually computing it[5]. Therefore, we need not assume that the sets C_i must be computed before starting the depth first search process.

First, unification is applied to units v_2 and u_2, the v_2-arrangement u_2^1 and unifier σ_2^1 in C_2 are used as follows: unit u_2 (i.e. *sl*) in the source is substituted for arrangement u_2^1, and unifier σ_2^1 = { ?eu = sl, ?u3 = ?u4, ?f2 = ((string sl slides)) } is applied to the construction and the source structure (see figure 9).

Next, sets $C_i = \{(u_i^1, \sigma_i^1)\}, i = 4, 5, 6, 3$ are used in that order: unit u_i in the source is substituted for arrangement u_i^1, and unifier σ_i^1 is applied to the pattern and the source structures. The result is shown in figure 10.

As we said before, once variables *?eu*, *?au*, *?ou*, *?tu* and *?ru* have been instantiated during the heuristic depth first search process (see figure 10), the set C_1 of arrangements of units in the source structure which can be made equal to unit v_1 consists of a single element rather than 120. That is, $C_1 = \{(u_1^1, \sigma_1^1)\}$, where unifier σ_1^1 is {?su = u, ?u1 = ?u2, ?f1 = ((order u (jo sl bl to ma)))} and arrangement u_1^1 is as follows.

[5] This is clear in the case of C_1, because the value of feature *syn-sub* in unit *?su* is a set consisting of five variables, therefore all the permutations of such a set unify with the value of the same feature in unit *u*. For the rest of the units one can simply check whether their single element in feature *syn-cat* belongs to the value of the same feature in each of the units in the source structure.

```
% fv_unif(P,S,A)
% P a pattern feature-value and S a source feature-value. If P and S
% are FCG-unifiable this predicate succeeds and A is instantiated to
% Ps, S' is a P-arrangement of S unifiable with P and s = mgu(P,S').

% unit_unif(P,S,A)
% P a pattern unit and S a source unit. If P and S are FCG-unifiable
% this predicate succeeds and A is instantiated to Ps, where S' is a
% P-arrangement of S unifiable with P and s = mgu(P,S').

% str_unif(P,S,A)
% P a pattern structure and S a source structre. If P and S are
% FCG-unifiable this predicate succeeds and A is instantiated to
% Ps, S' is a P-arrangement of S unifiable with P and s=mgu(P,S').

str_unif(P,S,A) :- sort_heur(P,S,SP), str_arr(SP,S,A).

st_arr([],_,[]).
st_arr([H|T],S,[AH|R]) :- member(U,S), unit_unif(H,U,AH),
      delete(S,U,Rest), st_arr(T,Rest,R).

% sort_heur(P,S,SP)
% P is a pattern structure and S a source structure.
% This procedure instantiates SP to a list containing the units in
% P sorted in accordance with the heuristics used by the algortihm.
% Units in P which should be instatiated in first place are charac-
% terised as 'good' with respect to the source structure S, and are
% placed at the front of SP. A predicate better is used to indicate
% that a unit u1 should be instantiated earlier than another u2, i.e.
% that u1 should precede u2 in SP. The following rules describe some
% heuristics used by the FCG-unification algorithm.

good(U,S) :- unique_unifier(U,S).

better(U1,U2,S) :- more_unifiers(U2,U1,S), !.
better(U1,U2,S) :- \+ better(U2,U1,S), predicate_unit(U1),
   \+ predicate_unit(U2), !.
% similar rules for subject, direct object, indirect object...
```

Fig. 8. Partial description of the Prolog code of the FCG-unification algorithm (\+ denotes negation by failure)

```
(= (?su (syn-sub (= sl ?au ?tu ?ou ?ru))
        (utter   ?u1)
        (form    ?f1)
        (syn-cat (= (SVOtoO-sentence)))
   (sl  (syn-sub ())
        (utter   ?u4)
        (form    ((string sl slides)))
        (syn-cat (= (role sl pred))))
   (?tu (syn-sub ())
        (utter   ?u5)
        (form    (= (string ?tu to)))
        (syn-cat ?s1)
   (?au (syn-sub ())
        (utter   ?u7)
        (form    ?f3)
        (syn-cat (= (role ?au subject))))
   (?ou (syn-sub ())
        (utter   ?u9)
        (form    ?f4)
        (syn-cat (= (role ?ou dir-obj))))
   (?ru (syn-sub ())
        (utter   ?u11)
        (form    ?f5)
        (syn-cat (= (role ?ru ind-obj))))
```

```
{(u  (syn-sub {sl jo bl t ma})
     (utter   ?u2)
     (form    {(order u (jo sl bl t ma))})
     (syn-cat {SVOtoO-sentence}))
 (sl (syn-sub {})
     (utter   ?u4)
     (form    ((string sl slides)))
     (syn-cat ((role sl pred))))
 (t  (syn-sub {})
     (utter   ?u6)
     (form    {(string t to)})
     (syn-cat {(speech-part t prep)}))
 (jo (syn-sub {})
     (utter   ?u8)
     (form    {(string jo John)})
     (syn-cat {(stem jo john)
               (numb nat jo singular)
               (speech-part jo noun)
               (role jo subject)}))
 (bl (syn-sub {})
     (utter   ?u10)
     (form    {(string bl blocks)})
     (syn-cat {(stem bl block)
               (numb nat bl plural)
               (speech-part bl noun)
               (role bl dir-obj)}))
 (ma (syn-sub {})
     (utter   ?u12)
     (form    {(string ma Mary)})
     (syn-cat {(stem ma mary)
               (numb nat ma plural)
               (speech-part ma noun)
               (role ma ind-obj)})) }
```

Fig. 9. $C_2 = \{(u_2^1, \sigma_2^1)\}$ is used in first place: unit u_2 in the source is substituted for arrangement u_2^1, and unifier σ_2^1 is applied to pattern and source

```
(= (?su (syn-sub (= sl jo t bl ma))
        (utter   ?u1)
        (form    ?f1)
        (syn-cat (= (SVOtoO-sentence)))
   (sl  (syn-sub ())
        (utter   ?u4)
        (form    ((string sl slides)))
        (syn-cat ((role sl pred))))
   (t   (syn-sub ())
        (utter   ?u6)
        (form    ((string t to)))
        (syn-cat ((speech-part t prep))))
   (jo  (syn-sub ())
        (utter   ?u8)
        (form    ((string jo John)))
        (syn-cat ((role jo subject))))
   (bl  (syn-sub ())
        (utter   ?u10)
        (form    ((string bl blocks)))
        (syn-cat ((role bl dir-obj))))
   (ma  (syn-sub ())
        (utter   ?u12)
        (form    ((string ma Mary)))
        (syn-cat ((role ma ind-obj)))))
```

```
{(u  (syn-sub {sl jo bl t ma})
     (utter   ?u2)
     (form    {(order u (jo sl bl t ma))})
     (syn-cat {SVOtoO-sentence}))
 (sl (syn-sub ())
     (utter   ?u4)
     (form    ((string sl slides)))
     (syn-cat ((role sl pred))))
 (t  (syn-sub ())
     (utter   ?u6)
     (form    ((string t to)))
     (syn-cat ((speech-part t prep))))
 (jo (syn-sub ())
     (utter   ?u8)
     (form    ((string jo John)))
     (syn-cat ((role jo subject))))
 (bl (syn-sub ())
     (utter   ?u10)
     (form    ((string bl blocks)))
     (syn-cat ((role bl dir-obj))))
 (ma (syn-sub ())
     (utter   ?u12)
     (form    ((string ma Mary)))
     (syn-cat ((role ma ind-obj))))}
```

Fig. 10. Result of using the arrangements and unifiers in sets C_4, C_5, C_6 and C_3 in that order to explore the space of structure arrangements

```
(u (syn-sub (sl jo t bl ma))
   (utter    ?u2)
   (form     ((order u (jo sl bl t ma))))
   (syn-cat  (SVOtoO-sentence)))
```

The result of using the arrangement and unifier in C_1, that is of substituting unit u_1 in the source structure for arrangement u_1^1, and applying unifier σ_1^1 to the source structure, is a complete arrangement s' of source structure s which satisfies the unifiability condition.

The heuristic depth first search process described above has allowed us to check that the syntactic pattern of the construction and the syntactic source structure are unifiable. The unifier built during this process can be stored for later use. But in order to implement construction application, we apply the substitutions of previous steps not only to the syntactic source structure and the syntactic pattern of the construction, but also to the semantic source structure and the semantic pattern of the construction (see figure 11).

```
(= (u (sem-sub  (= sl jo bl ma))
      (referent ?r1)
      (meaning  ?m1)
      (sem-cat  ?sc1))
   (sl (sem-sub  ())
       (referent ?e)
       (meaning  ?m3)

       (sem-cat  (= (ev-type ?e tr) (ag ?e ?a)
                    (obj ?e ?o) (rec ?e ?r))))
   (jo (sem-sub  ())
       (referent ?a)
       (meaning  ?m4)

       (sem-cat  ?sc7))
   (bl (sem-sub  ())
       (referent ?o)
       (meaning  ?m5)

       (sem-cat  ?sc9))
   (ma (sem-sub  ())
       (referent ?r)
       (meaning  ?m6)

       (sem-cat  ?sc11)))
```

```
{(u  (sem-sub  {sl jo bl ma})
     (referent ?2)
     (meaning  ?m2)
     (sem-cat  ?sc2))
 (sl (sem-sub  {})
     (referent ?s)
     (meaning  {(act ?s slide) (arg1 ?s ?a)
                (arg2 ?s ?o) (arg3 ?s ?r)})
     (sem-cat  {(ev-type ?s tr) (ag ?s ?a)
                (obj ?s ?o) (rec ?s ?r)}))
 (jo (sem-sub  {})
     (referent ?j)
     (meaning  {(entity-type ?j person)
                (count ?j one)})
     (sem-cat  ?sc8))
 (bl (sem-sub  {})
     (referent ?b)
     (meaning  {(entity-type ?b block)
                (count ?b several)})
     (sem-cat  ?sc10))
 (ma (sem-sub  {})
     (referent ?m)
     (meaning  {(entity-type ?m person)
                (count ?m one)})
     (sem-cat  ?sc12))}
```

Fig. 11. Result of applying the unifiers constructed during the heuristic depth first search process to the semantic pattern of the construction (left) and the semantic source structure (right)

As we explained before, construction application consists of two steps. First, the syntactic pattern of the construction and the syntactic source structure are unified. Then the instantiated semantic source structure is merged with the semantic pattern of the construction. In this example, the semantic source structure and the pattern are unifiable, therefore merge is equivalent to applying one of their unifiers to the semantic source structure.

The result of unifying the instantiated semantic source structure and the instantiated semantic pattern is substitution $\tau = \{$?r1 = ?r2, ?m1 = ?m2, ?sc1 = ?sc2, ?e = ?s, ?m3 = ((act ?s slide) (arg1 ?s ?a) (arg2 ?s ?o) (arg3 ?s ?r)), ?a = ?j, ?m4 = ((entity-type ?j person) (count ?j one)), ?sc7 = ?sc8, ?o = ?b, ?m5 = ((entity-type ?b block) (count ?b several)), ?sc9 = ?sc10, ?r = ?m, ?m6 = ((entity-type ?m person) (count ?m one)), ?sc11 = ?sc12 $\}$, which makes variables $?j$, $?b$ and $?m$, associated with the referents of units jo, bl and ma in the semantic source structure, equal to variables $?a$, $?o$ and $?r$, associated with the roles in the *transfer to recipient* event (tr) in that structure.

6 Conclusions

This paper has presented a logic programming approach to parsing and production in Fluid Construction Grammar (FCG). It builds on previous work on the formalisation of the *unification* and *merge* operations used in FCG in terms of First Order Logic (FOL) unification and search in the space of a particular set of FOL terms called *structure arrangements.*

Its main contribution is to outline a method for implementing unification and merge based on Logic Programming and Artificial Intelligence techniques such as unification and heuristic search. The formulation of the unification and merge problems in FCG as heuristic search problems in the space of structure arrangements not only allows understanding the problems of parsing and production with constructions in FCG as deduction problems, but also opens the door to the application of efficient automated deduction techniques to these problems.

Acknowledgements. Partially supported by BASMATI MICINN project (TIN2011-27479-C04-03) and by SGR2009-1428 (LARCA). I would like to thank Luc Steels and Joachim De Beule for valuable comments on an earlier version of this paper.

References

[1] Bleys, J., Stadler, K., De Beule, J.: Search in linguistic processing. In: Steels, L. (ed.) Design Patterns in Fluid Construction Grammar. John Benjamins, Amsterdam (2011)
[2] Ciortuz, L., Saveluc, V.: Fluid Construction Grammar and Feature Constraints Logics. In: Steels, L. (ed.) Computational Issues in FCG. LNCS (LNAI), vol. 7249, pp. 289–311. Springer, Heidelberg (2012)
[3] Goldberg, A.: A Construction Grammar Approach to Argument Structure. Univ. Chicago Press (1995)
[4] Harnad, S.: The symbol grounding problem. Physica D 42, 335–346 (1990)
[5] Langacker, R.: Foundations of Cognitive Grammar. Stanford Univ. Press (1991)
[6] McCarthy, J.: Recursive functions of symbolic expressions and their computation by machine. Communications of the ACM 3(4), 184–195 (1960)
[7] McCarthy, J.: Formalizing Common Sense. Papers by John McCarthy. Ablex (1990); Lifschitz, V. (ed.)

[8] Sierra-Santibáñez, J.: First order logic concepts in Fluid Construction Grammar. In: Biologically Inspired Cognitive Architectures 2011, pp. 344–350. IOS Press (2011)

[9] Steels, L.: The synthetic modeling of language origins. Evolution of Communication 1(1), 1–35 (1997)

[10] Steels, L.: Constructivist development of grounded construction grammars. In: Proceedings of the Annual Meeting of the Association for Computational Linguistics Conference, pp. 9–19 (2004)

[11] Steels, L.: Modeling the Formation of Language: Embodied Experiments. In: Evolution of Communication and Language in Embodied Agents, pp. 235–262. Springer, Heidelberg (2010)

[12] Steels, L., De Beule, J.: Unify and Merge in Fluid Construction Grammar. In: Vogt, P., Sugita, Y., Tuci, E., Nehaniv, C.L. (eds.) EELC 2006. LNCS (LNAI), vol. 4211, pp. 197–223. Springer, Heidelberg (2006)

[13] Steels, L. (ed.): Design Patterns in Fluid Construction Grammar. John Benjamins, Amsterdam (2011)

[14] Steels, L.: Design Methods for Fluid Construction Grammar. In: Steels, L. (ed.) Computational Issues in FCG. LNCS (LNAI), vol. 7249, pp. 3–36. Springer, Heidelberg (2012)

[15] Steels, L. (ed.): Experiments in Cultural Language Evolution. John Benjamins, Amsterdam (2012)

[16] Tomasello, M., Brooks, P.: Early syntactic development: A Construction Grammar approach. In: The Development of Language, pp. 161–190. Psychology Press (1999)

[17] van Trijp, R.: A Reflective Architecture for Language Processing and Learning. In: Steels, L. (ed.) Computational Issues in FCG. LNCS (LNAI), vol. 7249, pp. 51–74. Springer, Heidelberg (2012)

[18] Wittgenstein, L.: Philosophical Investigations. Macmillan, New York (1953)

Part V
Comparisons

Computational Construction Grammar: Comparing ECG and FCG

Nancy Chang[1], Joachim De Beule[2], and Vanessa Micelli[1]

[1] Sony Computer Science Laboratory Paris, France
[2] Artificial Intelligence Laboratory, Vrije Universiteit Brussel, Belgium

Abstract. This chapter compares two computational frameworks developed over the last decade to support investigations into the emergence and use of language, Fluid Construction Grammar (FCG) and Embodied Construction Grammar (ECG). Both of these representational formalisms are rooted in the construction grammar tradition, sharing basic assumptions about the nature of linguistic units and the crucial role played by contextual factors. Nonetheless, they have arisen from different perspectives and with different goals: FCG was designed to support computational language game experiments that address the evolution of communication in populations of robotic agents, while ECG was designed to support cognitive modeling of human language acquisition and use. We investigate how these differing emphases motivated different design choices in the two formalisms and illustrate the linguistic and computational consequences of these choices through a concrete case study. Results of this comparison sharpen issues relevant to computational construction grammar in general and may hold lessons for broader computational investigations into linguistic phenomena.

1 Introduction

This chapter compares two computational formalisms developed over the last decade: Fluid Construction Grammar (FCG) and Embodied Construction Grammar (ECG). Both formalisms draw broad inspiration from construction grammar and cognitive linguistics, sharing basic assumptions about the nature of linguistic units and the crucial role played by meaning in context. But unlike most other work in this area, both FCG and ECG aspire to provide computational implementations of all proposed linguistic structures and processes. This formalization (or operationalization) requirement reflects an emphasis not just on how linguistic knowledge is *represented* but also on how it is *used*: conceptual and linguistic structures should be seamlessly integrated with processes of language learning and use.

Each formalism is also the centerpiece of a broader scientific framework tackling similar issues, albeit from different perspectives and with different motivations. These may best be captured by examining the core goals and questions driving these respective investigations:

L. Steels (Ed.): Computational Issues in FCG, LNAI 7249, pp. 259–288, 2012.

- FCG supports language game experiments that explore answers to the question: How can communication emerge in populations of embodied agents? Its roots are in artificial intelligence, and historically it has been oriented toward artificial languages evolved and acquired by robotic agents. More recently, however, it has begun to address phenomena inspired by natural languages, as exemplified by the case studies in this and other volumes.
- ECG supports cognitive modeling of human language learning and use, within a framework that asks: What is the neural, embodied basis of thought and language? Its roots are in cognitive science and cognitive linguistics, though it is also motivated by psychological, biological and especially developmental considerations.

While these endeavors are theoretically compatible, they have differing orientations and emphases that have shaped their respective formalizations. Some of the resulting differences may be described as superficial notational variations, but others reflect more substantial divergences.

The two formalisms are thus ideal candidates for comparison. In this chapter, we aim to identify the core differences between FCG and ECG, as well as the open research issues suggested by these differences. We center the discussion around a concrete comparison of how the two formalisms realize the key ideas of construction grammar, using a case study that allows a detailed comparison of several lexical and phrasal constructions (Sections 3-5), as well as the processing models (Section 6) associated with each formalism. Section 7 considers how the results of our comparison sharpen issues relevant to computational construction grammar in general, and what lessons they may hold for broader computational investigations into linguistic phenomena.

Shared Theoretical and Methodological Commitments. Before turning to our case study, we briefly summarize some basic theoretical commitments shared by the two research frameworks under consideration. Broadly speaking, both are identified with constructional, cognitive and usage-based approaches to language. Constructions (mappings between form and meaning), are taken to be the basic units of language [9, 10], and meanings correspond to particular ways of conceptualizing or construing a situation [11, 12]. Language is also assumed to be inherently embodied, grounded and communicative: language users have sensorimotor capacities that shape their conceptual categories, and they are grounded in particular environments with specific communicative goals.

Most relevantly, both formalisms were designed to support working systems that actually instantiate structures and processes that are elsewhere typically described only discursively. This commitment to supporting language *use* means that it is not sufficient merely to represent linguistic knowledge in formal notation; rather, the processes that interact with that knowledge must also be specified, and considerations related to processing (e.g., search space, storage, efficiency) must guide representational choices at the level of both individual constructions and the formal notation itself.

Linguistic representations in both frameworks are also assumed to interact closely with structures in other domains, including in particular embodied, situational and world knowledge. The two frameworks differ in the details of how such interactions are modeled, and even in how terms like *embodiment* are used.[1] For the pursposes of this chapter, however, we focus on the specifically linguistic knowledge expressed by the two grammatical formalisms and their mechanisms of use. Both frameworks take these to be conceptually distinguishable from the details of sensorimotor representations; world (ontological) knowledge; general mechanisms of inference and belief update; and specific mechanisms of contextual grounding and reference resolution. We will also refrain from addressing in detail how language learning is modeled in each framework, though we will highlight some connections to these topics where relevant.

This chapter is not intended as a comprehensive description of either formalism; this volume and [20] provide a detailed introduction to FCG, and overviews of ECG and its associated research framework can be found elsewhere [1, 4, 7]. But to ground our discussion, in the sections to follow we introduce the notational basics of each, sufficient for discussing the noun phrase *the mouse* (also addressed in [21]). Despite the relative simplicity of this example, the side-by-side comparison it affords helps reveal some fundamental design issues and differences.

2 Informal Constructional Analysis of *the Mouse*

A traditional analysis of the phrase *the mouse* might identify a determiner (*the*), a noun (*mouse*), and a noun phrase (NP) combining the determiner and noun in that order. For a construction-based approach, it is crucial to consider the utterance's meaning as well: a speaker uttering "the mouse" is engaging in an act of reference, picking out an individual mouse uniquely identifiable to the hearer in the discourse context. A straightforward constructional analysis might have the structure shown in Figure 1, with three constructions:

- The: The word form *the* constrains the referent to be uniquely identifiable to the hearer in context; other determiners may restrict features like number (*some mice*) or proximity (*these mice*).
- Mouse: The word form *mouse* specifies that the referent's ontological category is a mouse. It might also specify that the referent refers to a single thing (in contrast to the greater quantity specified by *mice*), or that it is animate (or not, in the case of a computer mouse). Other nouns may constrain additional qualities of the referent (e.g., semantic role, gender, countability).
- DeterminedNP: This construction has two constituents, corresponding to the two constructions above. It imposes a word order constraint (*the* must precede *mouse*), and its meaning is a referent in context—in fact the same

[1] Broadly speaking, embodiment in FCG emphasizes the constraints of using physically embodied agents, while embodiment in ECG emphasizes the constraints of the human sensorimotor system.

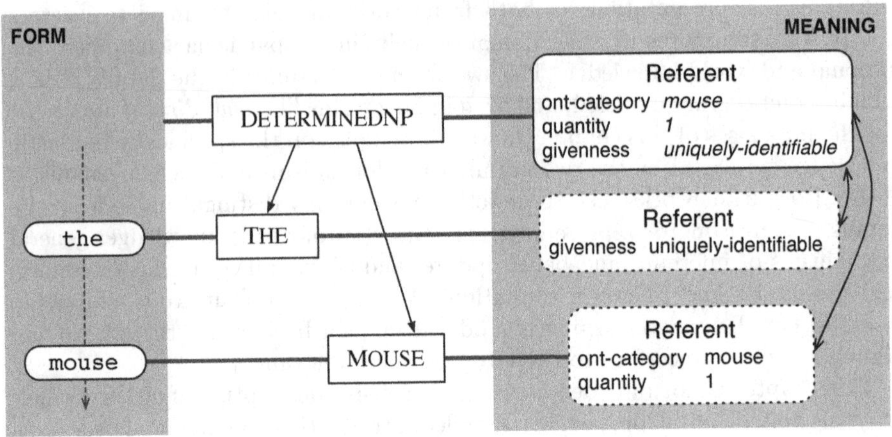

Fig. 1. A graphical depiction of one analysis of example phrase. Constructions (in the center) link the domains of form (left) and meaning (right). Each of the constructions shown here (the DETERMINEDNP construction and its two constituents, the THE and MOUSE constructions) contributes to and constrains the particular referent specified by the phrase.

referent constrained by the two constituents. Here, the relevant constraints do not conflict; in general, such compatibility or *agreement* in features must be met between determiners and nouns (hence **a mice*, **these mouse*).

The constructions in the middle of the Figure 1 reflect the phrase's constituent structure, mirroring that of a traditional syntactic parse tree (based on a phrase structure analysis). (See Section 5.3 for an alternative dependency analysis.) However, since these are not just syntactic symbols but constructions, each construction also has a link (shown by horizontal bars) to form (on the left) and meaning (on the right). The form domain contains the relevant word forms, where the dotted arrow indicates the time line (and therefore word order).

The meaning domain contains several structures labeled Referent, each listing features constrained to particular values (where ont-category is an abbreviation for ontological category). Essentially, this structure summarizes any information that is important for determining the actual referent of an expression in the current context. (Determination in both formalisms is further discussed in section 3.3.) The double-headed arrows between the Referents indicate that their values are shared (with values that originate non-locally, i.e. through such a binding, shown in italics). The dashed border of the two Referent structures contributed by the lexical constructions indicates a slightly different relationship than that between the DETERMINEDNP construction and its Referent; we return to this point below.

As should be apparent, even a noun phrase as simple as *the mouse* involves many representational choices, with reasonable alternatives varying in both the complexity of the structures defined and the generality of the phenomena they account for. Our goal here is not to argue for the particular analysis adopted here as the best or most general one possible; rather, we focus on the basic representational toolkit involved for expressing a variety of concepts and relations and compare those available in the ECG and FCG formalisms.

3 Formalizing Lexical Constructions

Diving now into the formal constructional analysis, we consider in this section how the lexical constructions for our example are defined in each of the two formalisms. We begin with the *mouse* construction shown in Figure 2. Both structures capture a relatively straightforward pairing of form (the orthographic string "mouse") and meaning (the mouse ontological category associated with a referent, whose quantity is additionally specified as 1). They also include grammatical information (e.g., that *mouse* is a singular noun), though they differ in precisely how this information is expressed.[2]

```
;; "mouse" in FCG (template-based)
(def-lex-cxn Mouse-Cxn
  (def-lex-cat Mouse-Cxn
    :sem-cat ((schema ?ref [ReferentDescriptor])
              (quantity ?ref 1))
    :syn-cat ((schema ?w [WordDescriptor])
              (type Noun)
              (number singular)))
  (def-lex-skeleton Mouse-Cxn
    :meaning (== (ont-category ?ref [mouse]))
    :form (== (orth ?w "mouse"))))
```

```
// "mouse" in ECG
construction Mouse-Cxn
  subcase of Noun
  constructional
    self.number ← singular
  form : Word
    self.f.orth ← "mouse"
  meaning
    evokes ReferentDescriptor as ref
    ref.ont-category ← @mouse
    ref.quantity ← 1
```

Fig. 2. Lexical constructions for *mouse* in FCG (left) and ECG (right)

A few differences in basic format are apparent even at first glance. Roughly speaking, the format of FCG reflects the influence of the Lisp programming language: internal structure is indicated with parenthesized lists employing prefix-list notation, and variable names are marked with a leading question mark. In contrast, the format of ECG reflects the influence of constraint programming languages and inheritance-based ontologies: special keywords (in boldface) are used to indicate internal structure and express inheritance relations and other constraints, and dotted slot chains are used to refer to non-local structures.

[2] Both distinguish a language-specific *number* categorization (in English, nouns can be either singular or plural) from a more general concept of number, which for clarity will be called *quantity* in the notation.

The sections below take a closer look at the two constructions in Figure 2. To ease comparison, we focus on how each captures the informal linguistic analysis described in the previous section, deferring until Section 6 the details of how constructions are used during language processing.

3.1 Nominal Constructions in FCG

The FCG definition for *mouse* shown on the left in Figure 2 uses the `def-lex-cxn` template for defining lexical units (described in [20]). This notation organizes the various elements of the informal analysis in two parts. First, the `def-lex-cat` clause specifies the linguistic categories (both semantic and syntactic) associated with *mouse*: a variable `?ref` is associated with the schema `ReferentDescriptor` and the quantity 1, and a variable `?w` is associated with the schema `Word`, the type `Noun` and the number `singular`. Second, the `def-lex-skeleton` clause specifies the ontological category (where square brackets on `[mouse]` denote reference to an ontology item) and orthographic string.

In fact, this template is an abbreviation for a more elaborate "native" FCG definition; we show the expanded version in Figure 3. Both styles of FCG definition contain the same information, but the template-based construction omits details shared with other lexical constructions, allowing a more concise definition. As should become apparent, the template-based version is closer to the level of abstraction used in the corresponding ECG definition, but we describe the expanded version here to shed some light on how these structures are used.

The full lexical definition consists of two main sections (or *poles*) separated by a double-headed arrow (`<->`), corresponding to the meaning (or semantic) and form (or syntactic) domains. Each pole includes two *units*, one named `?top-unit` and one named `?mouse-unit` (where the leading question mark indicates that these are variable names); this latter unit is a *J-unit* (as indicated by the operator `J`). These units specify the constraints and categorizations relevant to each domain, but they differ in the kinds of information they typically contain. J-units generally contain specifically linguistic information, typically expressed using semantic and syntactic categories (in the `sem-cat` and `syn-cat` lists, respectively). Other ("regular") units, like `?top-unit` here) tend to be based on perceptual or cognitive categorizations (here, the ontological category and the perceived word string).[3]

3.2 Nominal Constructions in ECG

We now turn to the right side of Figure 2, which shows a simple ECG construction for *mouse*. The high-level structure of the construction includes three blocks, where keywords (in boldface) indicate special terms and structures. The constructional block contains information relevant to the construction as a whole,

[3] Regular units and J-units also behave differently during language processing, where the J-operator and other notations (such as the `TAG` and `footprints`) notations play a special role. Language processing will be discussed in more detail in Section 6.1.

```
(def-cxn Mouse-Cxn
  ((?top-unit (TAG ?meaning
                   (meaning (== (ont-category ?ref [mouse]))))
              (footprints (==0 Mouse-Cxn)))
   ((J ?mouse-unit ?top-unit)
              ?meaning
              (sem-cat ((schema ?ref [ReferentDescriptor])
                        (quantity ?ref 1)))
              (footprints (Mouse-Cxn))))
  <-->
  ((?top-unit (TAG ?form
                   (form (== (orth ?w "mouse"))))
              (footprints (==0 Mouse-Cxn)))
   ((J ?mouse-unit ?top-unit)
              ?form
              (syn-cat ((schema ?wd [WordDescriptor])
                        (type Noun)
                        (number Singular)))
              (footprints (Mouse-Cxn))))))
```

Fig. 3. Lexical construction for *mouse* in FCG, expanded form

while the form and meaning blocks (or *poles*) contain information relevant to each domain. These poles are themselves structured, and can be referenced and constrained within the construction. The term self allows reference to the construction being defined, and self.f and self.m refer to the construction's form and meaning poles, respectively.

The MOUSE construction is defined as a *subcase*, i.e. a more specific instance, of the NOUN construction. In fact, ECG constructions are all defined in a multiple inheritance lattice, and a separate lattice defines represent schematic form and meaning categories, or *schemas*. (Both inheritance and schemas will be discussed further in Section 4.) Accessible structures can be constrained to instantiate particular schema categories. Each block contains various constraints that apply to the relevant domain, drawn from a fixed set of possibilities. We highlight a few of the notations that express these constraints:

- Category constraints are indicated with a colon (e.g., the form pole must be a Word), and role-filler constraints of the form x ⟵ y indicate that role (or feature) x is filled by the (atomic) value y (e.g., the form pole is associated with the orthographic string shown).
- The **evokes** ReferentDescriptor **as** ref declaration indicates that there is an instance of category ReferentDescriptor present, accessible using its local name ref. Subsequent constraints specify that its feature ont-category be filled by @mouse and its quantity set to 1. (Like the square brackets in the FCG definition, the @ symbol indicates reference to an external conceptual ontology.)

In short, the construction indicates that the MOUSE-CXN is a kind of NOUN; asserts constraints on the constructional (or grammatical) number feature and the particular orthographic form; and evokes a ReferentDescriptor of a specified ontological category and quantity.

For comparison, it may be useful to see how the ECG construction definition is expanded during processing. Figure 4 shows the corresponding feature structure representation. Note that the feature structure for Mouse-Cxn also contains two subsidiary feature structures for the Word and ReferentDescriptor categories mentioned in the definition. As discussed in Section 4.2 and illustrated in Figure 6 below, these additional schematic structures are also defined as part of the ECG formalism.

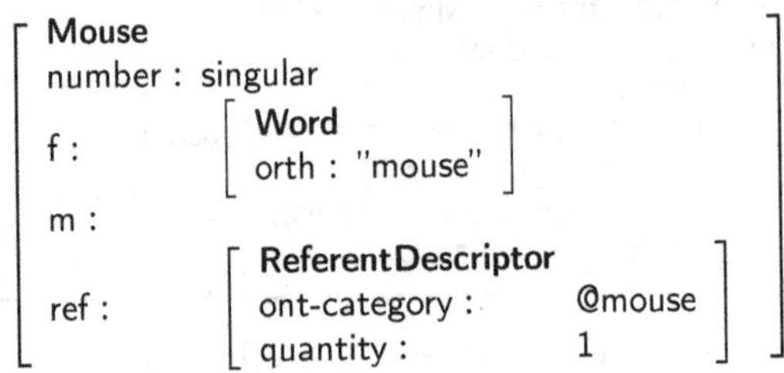

Fig. 4. Feature structure corresponding to the ECG *mouse* construction

3.3 Determiners in ECG and FCG

The basic lexical constructions just defined are easily modified for the determiner *the*. In accord with earlier accounts (e.g. [1]), we assume that determiners provide cues that help a hearer identify a referent in the discourse context. Thus, like the *mouse* construction, they constrain a referent, but instead of specifying its ontological category, they typically constrain features like number, gender and proximity. In the case of *the*, the referent is asserted to be uniquely identifiable.

The constructions in Figure 5 are structurally similar to the *mouse* constructions defined above. Each specifies that *the* is a Determiner (as the syntactic category `(type Determiner)` in FCG and the **subcase of** Determiner constraint in ECG); each specifies the relevant orthographic string; and each specifies a value for the referent's givenness feature (in FCG using the predicate `(givenness ?ref uniquely-identifiable)`, and in ECG with the constraint ref.givenness ⟵ uniquely-identifiable).

The two formalisms differ slightly in how they handle the feature of number. The FCG definition adds a number category to its list of syntactic categories, whose value remains underspecified (as indicated by the variable `?number`). The ECG definition does not mention number explicity. Note that ECG definitions for determiners like the plural *some* or singular *a*) would include a constructional block with a constraint on the number feature, thus more closely resembling the *mouse* construction.

;; "the" in FCG (template-based) (def-lex-cxn The-Cxn (def-lex-cat The-Cxn :sem-cat ((schema ?ref [ReferentDescriptor])) :syn-cat ((schema ?w [WordDescriptor]) (type Determiner) (number ?number))) (def-lex-skeleton The-Cxn :meaning (== (givenness ?ref uniquely-identifiable)) :form (== (orth ?w "the"))))	// "the" in ECG **construction** The-Cxn **subcase of** Determiner **form** : Word self.f.orth ← "the" **meaning** **evokes** ReferentDescriptor **as** ref ref.givenness ← uniquely-identifiable

Fig. 5. Lexical constructions for *'the'* in FCG (left) and ECG (right)

4 A First Comparison

The parallel definitions of lexical constructions in FCG and ECG given in Section 3 are based on the same linguistic analysis and designed to maximize similarity across the two formalisms. It is not entirely surprising, then, that they have much in common: each represents the basic forms and meanings involved, as well as additional grammatical information associated with reference, as expressed by common nouns (like *mouse*) and determiners (like *the*).

But these examples also exhibit some striking differences. Perhaps the most important distinction between the formalisms is the treatment of categories and inheritance. ECG structures are all defined within *inheritance lattices* specifying constructional and other relationships. Many ECG notations thus allow reference to other existing structures, for example to inherit features and values, or to assert values or bindings on connected structures. FCG constructions, on the other hand, rely on category lists associated with each domains; each construction is thus relatively stand-alone, and defined independently of other structures that may contain similar information. In the sections below we discuss several representational consequences of this fundamental difference.

4.1 Inheritance and Categorization

Categories play a prominent role in most linguistic theories: they capture generalizations about shared structure and behavior across different linguistic units. Part of speech categories, semantic (or thematic) roles, lexical subcategorization types, speech act types, and phonological categories are all well-established ways of carving up various linguistic domains into groups exhibiting similar properties. Both ECG and FCG allow such categories to be expressed, but they differ in the approaches taken, as well as the degree to which the relationships among categories is made explicit.

Inheritance hierarchies in ECG. The ECG approach to categories is based on inheritance networks, where shared properties are expressed at the highest level of generalization possible and inherited by subsidiary categories and instances.

That is, ECG constructions are defined (using the **subcase of** relation) within a multiple inheritance hierarchy (or lattice); structures and constraints defined in a *base* (or *parent*) construction are inherited by and accessible to their subcases, and thus need not be explicitly specified. The subcase can impose additional constraints, or refine existing ones.

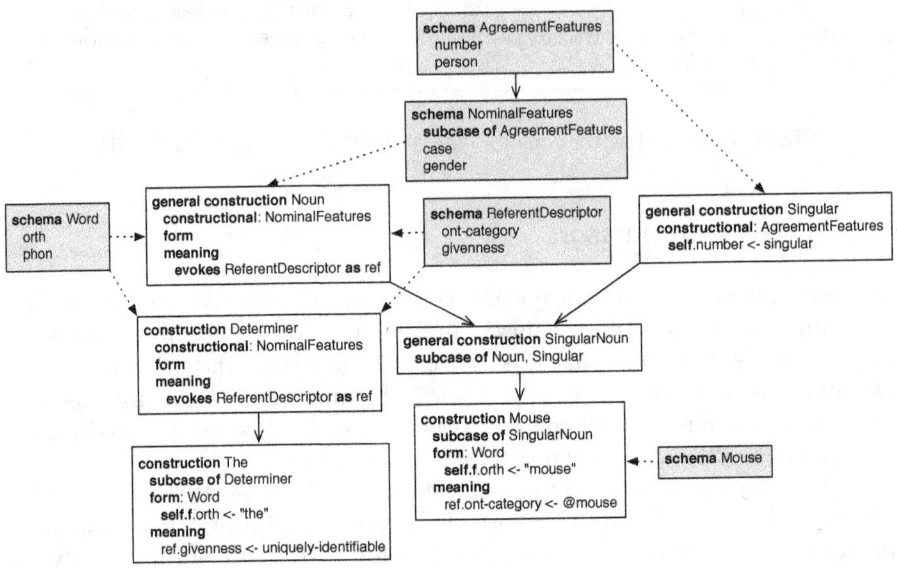

Fig. 6. A portion of the ECG construction lattice for the lexical items in the example, showing both constructions (white boxes) and schemas (shaded boxes). (Solid arrows indicate subcase (or inheritance) relations, while dotted lines indicate other links through the constructional, form or meaning domains.)

A fragment of the constructional lattice relevant to the lexical constructions in our example is shown in Figure 6, where both the MOUSE and THE constructions have been redefined to exploit inheritance. Focusing on the white construction boxes, we can see that this version of the MOUSE construction is defined as a subcase of the SINGULARNOUN construction, which in turn is a subcase of both NOUN and SINGULAR. These abstract ancestral constructions—marked **general** to indicate their lack of concrete form constraints—contain some constraints shared across noun constructions (the **evokes** statement and number ⟵ singular constraint), leaving only the most specific constraints for the MOUSE construction.

These examples illustrate how certain linguistic generalizations can be concisely captured through inheritance. Though not shown, the construction for the irregular plural *mice* inherits from the PLURAL and PLURALNOUN constructions, which are analogous to SINGULAR and SINGULARNOUN, respectively. Similarly, determiners that specify number (such as *these* or *a*) are defined as subcases of both DETERMINER and the appropriate number-specifying construction.[4]

Categories in FCG. Categories are a fundamental notion in FCG, expressed as predicates in the `sem-cat` and `syn-cat` lists. Constructions that have such predicates in common implicitly form a category: hence both *mouse* and *the* are associated with the syntactic category `schema`, which is further specified to be a `WordDescriptor`, and they also both include the syntactic category `number`.

Inheritance networks like those of ECG have not yet been much explored in FCG: there is no explicit notion of inheritance for constructions, meaning or form components, or semantic and syntactic categories. Recent developments, however—such as the use of templates [20] and distinctive feature matrices [22]—can be seen as moving in this direction.[5] Templates, for example, provide a means of capturing similarities across constructions, allowing a more concise, uniform declaration of constructions (as illustrated by the alternate definitions for *mouse* above). Note, however, that templates currently serve mainly as an abbreviation: they do not specify inheritance *relationships*. That is, there is no mechanism for allowing one construction to refer to or inherit from another, and more general lexical categories like `Noun` are not themselves defined as structures that can inherit features.

Of course, the use of templates in FCG is relatively recent and their precise form is still under development. Thus it may be possible to extend the template approach (as proposed in Section 5) to exploit the benefits of inheritance and type hierarchies. These benefits become especially important as grammars grow larger: keeping track of the various dependencies between constructions for any non-trivial language phenomenon is a tedious undertaking. Adopting approaches based on inheritance would enable more concise grammars that reduce errors.

4.2 Form and Meaning Representations

The lexical examples we have seen also illustrate different approaches to representing the domains of form and meaning. Organizationally, FCG distinguishes specifically linguistic categorizations (as listed in `sem-cat` and `syn-cat`) from the concrete forms and meanings taken to be based on perceptual or cognitive categorizations (associated with the `meaning` and `form` parameters. ECG constructions do not explicitly represent this difference in the notation itself (except for the use of `@` to denote ontological categories).

---

[4] Inheritance is only one way of capturing complex category structure of the kind described by [11], and the particular multiple inheritance lattices used by ECG are intended only as an approximation. While current versions of ECG allow overriding of inherited constraints and the incorporation of some probabilistic information, further refinements would be needed to handle categories including scalar and continuous quantitative values, prototype structures and other aspects of human categorization.

[5] See also [5], which describes FCGlight (a core subset of FCG that uses of lattices of constructions); and [2].

A more important difference lies in how these categories are represented. As noted before, all categorizations (linguistically specific or not) in FCG are expressed in predicate-argument format, and are independently defined as part of each relevant consruction. The particular style of semantic representation can vary; though the examples shown in this section have a declarative flavor (following the informal analysis presented in Section 2), other studies show how it is also possible to adopt procedural semantics [19] or frame semantics [15].

In ECG, both forms and meanings are represented using a special-purpose *schema* formalism, similar to that used for constructions and also defined within an inheritance lattice (see Figure 6 for some examples, shown in shaded boxes). ECG schemas resemble depictions of *semantic frames* [8] and *image schemas* in the literature, and are similarly used to bring together a set of associated and interdefined *roles* or *features* comprising a complex concept. The roles defined in a schema can be referred to and constrained by other schemas and constructions. Hence, both lexical constructions assert form constraints on the orth role of the Word schema, as well as meaning constraints on the roles of the ReferentDescriptor.

As with constructions, we see that ECG emphasizes the interdefined nature of constructions and their associated forms and meanings. Separately defined schemas capture various linguistic generalizations and expectations, allowing brevity in definitions and enforcing some consistency across constructions. FCG constructions, meanwhile, each independently define their relevant predicates, which are therefore less constrained. This tradeoff—between explicit representation of generalizations on the one hand, and freedom of expression on the other—will manifest itself in several other ways to be discussed.

4.3 Constructional Features and Grammatical Categories

The two formalisms differ, finally, in how certain kinds of grammatical information are treated. Specifically, while all categories and constraints in FCG must be in either the meaning or form pole, ECG allows some information to be expressed in the constructional lattice:

- Constructional inheritance: Lexical and grammatical categories (like noun and verb) can themselves be represented as constructions and associated with specific roles and values. Thus, the MOUSE construction can be defined as a subcase of the SINGULARNOUN construction, inheriting relevant properties it may share with other singular nouns.
- Constructional features: The constructional domain itself can be defined as having particular features, often inherited from ancestral types. In Figure 6, AgreementFeatures and NominalFeatures are schemas in the constructional domain that list various grammatical features. These are not strictly about either the form or meaning domain; rather, they are associated with the constructional connection between the two.

In both cases above, the equivalent information can be expressed in FCG but must be explicitly included in every constructional definition (unless the template system could be extended to do this, though this would be a non-trivial modification).

In each formalism, it remains largely at the discretion of the grammar writer how to decide precisely which features ought to be defined and what domain they belong in.

5 Constituent Structure and Agreement

We now turn our attention to the DETERMINEDNP construction. This construction combines a determiner and a noun into a larger phrasal unit. Combining smaller units into larger chunks and phrases and thus exhibiting hierarchical *constituent structure* is a defining feature of grammatical constructions. Like lexical constructions, such constructions can impose constraints in both the form and meaning domains, such as word order (form) or role-filler bindings (meaning). They may also enforce compatibilities, or *agreement*, across constituents. Both ECG and FCG have ways of introducing constituents, specifying relational constraints and enforcing agreement.

5.1 Determined NPs in ECG

The DETERMINEDNP construction in Figure 7 shows how determined noun phrases with constituent structure might be defined in ECG. The intuition behind the analysis is that such phrases draw on both determiners and nouns to provide crucial information for constraining an act of reference, resulting in a single larger unit (as in our informal analysis). Like lexical constructions, phrasal constructions have a form and meaning pole; they also, however, have a **constructional** block within which constructional **constituents** as well as additional **constraints**—for example, to enforce agreement—are specified.

Here, the two constituents have local variable names det and nom, and they are typed respectively as DETERMINER and NOUN. These constituent names allow simple access to their respective form and meaning poles. In the form block, their form poles (det.f and nom.f) are specified as coming in a particular order (expressed using the before relation). The meaning of the overall expression is itself constrained to be a ReferentDescriptor—which, recall, is also the type of the ref argument evoked in the meanings of each of the two constituents. That is, all three (the composite structure and each of the two constituents) have accessible ReferentDescriptors. Thus, the last two constraints simply identify the evoked referents of the constituents with the meaning of the overall phrasal construction. Note that these constraints enforce all the roles defined within the ReferentDescriptor structures to have the same value, including the ont-category, givenness, and quantity roles. This can be seen as a kind of semantic agreement: the referent that all of these constructions describes is the same, and therefore the constraints that apply to it as also the same.

```
construction DeterminedNP
  constructional
    constituents
      det : Determiner
      nom : Noun
    constraints
      self.number ⟷ det.number
      self.number ⟷ nom.number
  form
    det.f before nom.f
  meaning : ReferentDescriptor
    self.m ⟷ det.ref
    self.m ⟷ nom.ref
```

Fig. 7. A complex DeterminedNP construction

Turning to the constructional domain, we see another kind of agreement enforced by the constraints in the constructional block. These simultaneously encode agreement between the two constituents' number features (notated here as det.number and n.number) and ensure that this value is shared by the noun phrase (**self**.number). All of these require that these constructions are typed so that they have an accessible number feature (in our analysis, their constructional poles are all constrained to be of type NominalFeatures). This agreement might be seen as the more prototypical grammatical agreement, based on explicitly grammatical features like *number* that may not have any basis in the meaning domain alone.[6]

5.2 Determined NPs in FCG

An account of how determined noun phrases might be handled in FCG using phrasal construction templates is given in [20]. This section provides an alternative analysis that is as close as possible to the one given for ECG, while remaining within the limits of what is currently possible in FCG. Besides enabling a more detailed comparison, this variation is also intended to add another perspective to the relatively recent development of FCG templates that may help shed light on the benefits and drawbacks of different approaches.

Concretely, we define a phrasal construction for determined noun phrases in Figure 8, where the first definition expands (using the appropriate template code for `def-phrasal-cxn`) to the second. Like the lexical constructions, the `DeterminedNP` construction has both meaning and form components, each including both regular units (`?top-unit`, `?determiner`, and `?noun`) and a J-unit. The basic idea of constituency is captured by the specification that the

[6] Of course, it is not always possible to draw a neat boundary between the semantic and constructional domains, especially with respect to a linguistically oriented schema like ReferentDescriptor.

`?top-unit` lists the other two regular units in its `subunits`, corresponding respectively to a determiner and a noun (again, in both the meaning and form domains).

On the syntactic side, the construction furthermore specifies the constraint `(before ?det ?N)` on the word order of its constituents. On the semantic side it requires that the `ReferentDescriptor` schemas of both constituents are the same (through a variable equality). Agreement in number is also achieved through variable equalities.

```
;; DeterminedNP (template-based definition)
(def-phrasal-cxn DeterminedNP
   :syn-cat ((type DeterminedNP) (number ?number))
   :sem-cat ((schema ?ref [ReferentDescriptor]))
   :constituents
   ((lex-cxn ?Determiner
     :syn-cat ((type Determiner) (number ?number))
     :sem-cat ((schema ?ref [ReferentDescriptor]))
     :meaning ((givenness ?ref ?givenness))
     :form ((orth ?det ?orth-det)))
    (lex-cxn ?Noun
     :syn-cat ((type Noun) (number ?number))
     :sem-cat ((schema ?ref [ReferentDescriptor]))
     :meaning ((ont-category ?ref ?ont-cat))
     :form ((orth ?N ?orth-N))))
   :form ((before ?det ?N)))

;; DeterminedNP (expanded definition)
(def-cxn DeterminedNP
   ((?top-unit (footprints (==0 DeterminedNP))
               (sem-subunits (?Determiner ?Noun)))
    (?Determiner
      (meaning (== (giveness ?ref ?giveness)))
      (sem-cat (==1 (schema ?ref [ReferentDescriptor]))))
    (?Noun
      (meaning (== (ont-category ?ref ?ont-cat)))
      (sem-cat (==1 (schema ?ref [ReferentDescriptor]))))
    ((J ?DeterminedNP ?top-unit (?Determiner ?Noun))
      (sem-cat ((schema ?ref [ReferentDescriptor])))))
   <-->
   ((?top-unit
      (TAG ?form (form (== (before ?det ?N))))
      (footprints (==0 DeterminedNP))
      (syn-subunits (?Determiner ?Noun)))
    (?Determiner
      (form (== (orth ?det ?orth-det)))
      (syn-cat (==1 (type Determiner)
                    (number ?number))))
    (?Noun
      (form (== (orth ?N ?orth-det)))
      (syn-cat (==1 (type Noun) (number ?number))))
    ((J ?DeterminedNP ?top-unit (?Determiner ?Noun))
     ?form
     (syn-cat ((type DeterminedNP) (number ?number))))))
```

Fig. 8. DeterminedNP construction in FCG, both template and expanded versions

5.3 Comparing Complex Constructions

The two approaches to representing complex constructions demonstrated in the preceding sections are both capable of expressing constituency, word order and agreement. They differ, however, in several key respects.

First, as elsewhere, the ECG formalism avails itself of type lattices for both constructions and schemas. Thus, various constraints require that relevant features are defined and accessible for a given structure (i.e., a slot chain like det.number implies that det is defined as having inherited a number role). This stands in sharp contrast with FCG, which does not require typing of this kind: previously unspecified features are added during processing if not already defined, and only if it is explicitly indicated that this should be the case.

The less type-constrained approach of FCG may be seen as a double-edged sword: while it leaves more freedom of choice, it also requires that the grammar writer maintain the soundness of his or her grammars and ensure that the relevant semantic and syntactic categories of constituent units are percolated properly to newly created units. For instance, although the `?DeterminedNP` in the DeterminedNP construction unit is specified as an instance of the `ReferentDescriptor` schema, neither its `givenness` or `ont-category` values are specified. These could be inferred from its constituents, and the template could perhaps be changed to do this automatically, but again, doing so would be far from trivial. In contrast, ECG makes some structural assumptions that allow certain constraints to be succinctly stated, though possibly at the cost of flexibility. Thus the identification of the various ReferentDescriptors allows all their roles to be bound with one constraint, both across constituents and with the overall resulting construction.

Second, the two formalisms allow somewhat different options with respect to how particular kinds of features are expressed. As noted earlier, grammatical features and categories are typically expressed in the constructional domain in ECG (though as demonstrated above, agreement can also be enforced just in the form or meaning domain). As with the lexical constructions, FCG tends to express such grammatical information by including it as a syntactic category. This difference may not ultimately affect expressive power, but it does reflect different theoretical views of particular linguistic concepts.

6 Processing

Both frameworks under comparison are committed to the idea that grammatical formalisms should do more than just describe language: they should also support processes of language use. In this section we compare how processes of language use interact with the linguistic representations encoded by the two grammatical formalisms we have described.

6.1 Parsing and Production in FCG

The FCG formalism was designed to support processes of both parsing (mapping from form to meaning) and production (mapping from meaning to form). These processes have been described in detail elsewhere; we review them briefly here.

The internal structure of the FCG construction reflects a number of symmetries in how the different components are used during language processing, depending on whether parsing or production is performed. In particular:

- Each pole corresponds to the input to one process and to the output of the other: an utterance representation in the form pole is the input to parsing and the output of production, and vice versa for meaning representations in the meaning pole.
- The regular units and J-units together specify constraints and categorizations relevant to each domain, but they behave differently with respect to the *match* and *merge* operations at the core of language processing in FCG. Briefly, matching is used to test whether a transient structure fits (i.e., matches) a given construction; it thus acts as a filter on applicable constructions; merging then effects the construction's application and contributes additional information. Regular units in the input pole are matched, and thus are typically used to select which constructions to apply. J-units and regular units in the output pole are merged and thus provide additional constraints and categorizations.

In both processes, constructions operate on a *transient linguistic structure*. Before processing starts, the transient structure is initialized with the meaning that needs to be verbalized (production), or with the form that needs to be parsed (parsing); this structure is then gradually transformed to the desired output structure. We describe both processes for our example below.

Parsing. The aim of the parsing process is start from an empty meaning and gradually add content until a full meaning specification (and a complete parse) is achieved. The initial transient structure for parsing *the mouse* is as follows:

```
((top))
<-->
((top (form ((orth W1 "the") (orth W2 "mouse")
             (before W1 W2)))))
```

The form side of the linguistic structure specifies a single constituent named `top`, containing three predicates that together fully specifying the string "the mouse". These predicates include the constants `W1` and `W2` representing the actual words.

The application of the `mouse-cxn` to this structure is licensed through the *match* and *merge* operations mentioned above. The syntactic side of the construction is matched against the syntactic side of the transient structure (excluding J-units), resulting in a set of bindings for the variables in the construction.

The features marked by the special `TAG` operator (e.g., the meaning and form features in the MOUSE-CXN of Figure 2) cause the tag-variable (e.g., `?meaning` and `?form`) to be bound to the matched set of feature values.

In the example, the MOUSE-CXN is triggered by the predicate `(== (orth ?word "mouse"))` in its top unit, where the includes operator `==` indicates that other components besides the specified meaning are also allowed. The construction therefore matches the initial structure with the following bindings: '[?top-unit/top, ?form/(form ((orth W1 "mouse"))),?w/W1].[7]

The merge operation then results in a new, modified transient linguistic structure that is the union of the matched structure with the additional constraints specified in the construction. Merging in FCG thus roughly corresponds to unification in ECG and other unification- or constraint-based formalisms. Given the match-bindings obtained earlier, both sides of the MOUSE-CXN also merge with the transient linguistic structure.

In parsing, the resulting structure is as below:

```
((top (subunits (mouse-unit)))
 (mouse-unit
      (meaning  ((ont-category ?ref-1 [mouse])))
      (sem-cat  ((schema ?ref-1 [ReferentDescriptor])
                 (quantity ?ref-1 1)))))
<-->
((top (form ((orth W1 "the") (before P1 W1 W2)))
      (subunits (mouse-unit)))
 (mouse-unit
      (form     ((orth W2 "mouse")))
      (syn-cat  ((schema W2 [WordDescriptor])
                 (type Noun)
                 (number singular)))))
```

Note that the transient structure now includes a new unit named `mouse-unit` on each side, corresponding to the constructional J-unit. This new unit includes the tagged form predicate matched by the `mouse-cxn`, and its meanings have additional semantic categories as specified by the `mouse-cxn`)

Production. Production in FCG is entirely analogous to parsing, but with the role of the poles reversed. The initial structure for producing our example is as follows:

```
((top (meaning
       ((ont-category Ref [mouse])
        (giveness Ref uniquely-identifiable)))))
<-->
((top))
```

[7] If variable '$?x_1$' is bound to value X_1, and variable '$?x_2$' to X_2 etc., this is denoted as $[?x_1/X_1, ?x_2/X_2, ...]$.

Similar to the parsing situation, the semantic side of the MOUSE-CXN matches the semantic side of the initial transient linguistic structure above because the construction requires only that there is a unit, with variable name (`?top-unit`), which contains a `meaning` feature including the component `(ony-category ?ref [mouse])`. Matching results in the bindings: '[?top/top, ?meaning/(meaning ((ont-category Ref [mouse]))), ?ref/Ref]'.

Merging then results in the following modified structure:

```
((top (meaning ((giveness R uniquely-identifiable]))
      (subunits (mouse-unit)))
 (mouse-unit
      (meaning  ((ont-category R [mouse])))
      (sem-cat  ((schema R [ReferentDescriptor])
                 (quantity R 1)))))
<-->
((top (subunits (mouse-unit))
 (mouse-unit
      (form     ((orth ?word-1 "mouse")))
      (syn-cat  ((schema ?word-1 [WordDescriptor])
                 (type Noun)
                 (number singular))))))
```

As in parsing, all constraints in the construction missing in the initial transient structure have been added, and the new `mouse-unit` includes in its meaning the tagged component corresponding to the matched meaning of `mouse-cxn`.

Although not an issue for our simple example, many problems can arise in the search for matching constructions during processing and the selection of the best set of constructions to apply. FCG provides several mechanisms for coping with these challenges. These include the use of different goal tests (such as reentrance, in which a produced utterance is re-parsed using the current grammar to test for interpretability); the option of continuing processing if an analysis is insufficient; and the possibility of associating conventionality and preference scores with constructions as heuristics for guiding search. These strategies are explained in more detail elsewhere [20].

6.2 Constructional Analysis in ECG

In this section we briefly summarize how ECG constructions support language comprehension, as implemented by the construction analyzer described by [3]. The term *constructional analysis* as used here is analogous to *parsing* in FCG: it is the constructional analogue to syntactic parsing—that is, the identification of which linguistic structures are instantiated in a particular utterance—where the structures crucially include semantic information.

Overview. The input to constructional analysis is an ECG grammar (including both schema and construction lattices), along with the utterance to be analyzed, and (optionally) a situation description. All schemas and constructions are first translated into a feature structure representation, ensuring that all inherited roles, constituents and constraints are included. Earlier we showed the feature structure for *mouse* in Figure 4; Figure 9 shows a feature structure version of the DETERMINEDNP construction.

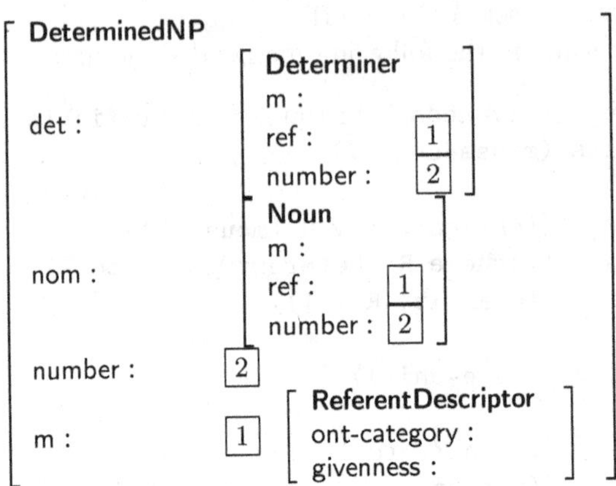

Fig. 9. Translation of the DETERMINEDNP construction into a feature structure. The features shown correspond to the two constituents (det and nom), the number constructions feature and the meaning pole m. Identification bindings are represented using boxed index numbers, where indices with the same number are bound to the same value.

The analyzer processes utterances from left to right, incrementally building up an *analysis graph* (a set of constructional instances or *constructs* linked by constituency relations) and a *semantic specification*, or *semspec* (a graph of the meaning schemas associated with all constructs in the analysis). In the broader research context for which ECG was developed, this semspec is an intermediate structure whose purpose is to support two connected language understanding processes: (1) contextual *resolution*, which grounds this interpretation in the situational context; and (2) embodied *simulation*, which draws on richer embodied structures to yield further context-sensitive inferences [1]. Here we focus on how the semspec is built up during analysis.

The construction analyzer described by Bryant (2008) uses unification as the basic mechanism for composing constructions and verifying that their constraints are consistent, where both constructions and schemas are represented as typed feature structures with unification constraints as specified by the ECG formalism. But the search for the best analysis also exploits many heuristics to improve efficiency, limit search and approximate aspects of human language processing, including:

- Incremental interpretation: the analyzer allows incremental left-to-right interpretation of the utterance. To do this, it employs left-corner parsing techniques [13] to keep track of competing analyses and update their scores, where partially matched subportions of complex constructions provide top-down expectations about which constructions may next be encountered.

- Best-fit interpretation: the analyzer defines a quantitative heuristic for combining information from disparate domains, ranking candidate interpretations, and guiding parsing decisions. The implementation is a Bayesian probabilistic model that integrates information affecting the likelihood of the analysis (e.g., lexical and constructional frequencies; the likelihood that one construction has another as a constituent; and the likelihood that a schema has a particular kind of filler in a given role).
- Partial interpretation: the analyzer produces partial analyses even when the input utterance is not covered by the grammar or is missing constituents. An extension to the analyzer permits analyses with omitted constituents (as often encountered in, for example, Mandarin) by integrating the score of an interpretation with the results of the contextual resolution process.

In sum, the analyzer is consistent with the constructional view, drawing on all available information at every step to ensure that syntactic, semantic and constructional constraints are satisfied. Crucially, the early incorporation of semantic, pragmatic and statistical constraints can dramatically reduce the search space that may result from purely syntactic approaches.

Example. We consider the simple case of analyzing the input sentence string "the mouse" given a grammar containing just the constructions defined earlier. Following the left-corner parsing algorithm, the analyzer maintains a stack of all the constructs (instances of constructions) recognized so far, all labeled as incomplete or complete; incomplete constructs are also annotated with which constituents still remain to complete it. Processing unfolds in several steps:

- The analyzer reads in the first word "the" and retrieves the THE construction based on the orthographic form and adds it to the current stack of available constructs. Since it has no constituents remaining, it is recorded as complete.
- All constructions of which THE is a subcase (here, just the DETERMINER construction) are added to the stack as complete.
- Because the first constituent of the DETERMINEDNOUN construction is typed as a DETERMINER, it is placed on the stack and a constituent binding (between the THE construction and its first constituent) is attempted. The binding is successful, resulting in a partial semspec consisting of the DETERMINER construction's evoked ReferentDescriptor being bound with the ReferentDescriptor of the DETERMINEDNOUN construction; this structure is also specified having a givenness status of uniquely-identifiable. The DETERMINEDNOUN construction has now scanned past the DETERMINER constituent.
- The analyzer reads in the second word "mouse" and retrieves the MOUSE construction. Similar to before, it places MOUSE as well its parent construction type NOUN on the stack as complete.
- The DETERMINEDNOUN construction placed on the stack earlier successfully scans its next unfulfilled constituent, adding the constituent binding to its nom constituent and updating the semspec with the relevant bindings.

– The DETERMINEDNOUN is now marked as complete; since the utterance string has been exhausted, it has been successfully parsed.

Figure 10 shows the output of the ECG constructional analyzer on our simple example of *the mouse*. In fact, this structure shows both (a portion of) the analysis graph and its associated semspec. (The form domain is not shown.) In brief, each large box corresponds to an instantiated construction or schema, shown with its constituents or roles. Thus, the box labeled DeterminedNP has as top-level features its two constituents det and nom, its constructional number feature, its meaning pole m and the evoked ReferentDescriptor ref. The boxed numbers indicate shared values, many referring to structures not shown in this reduced figure, but note that the boxed 2 indicates that ReferentDescriptor is shared in several places: the overall meaning of the DeterminedNoun construction, its ref slot as well as those of its two constituents.

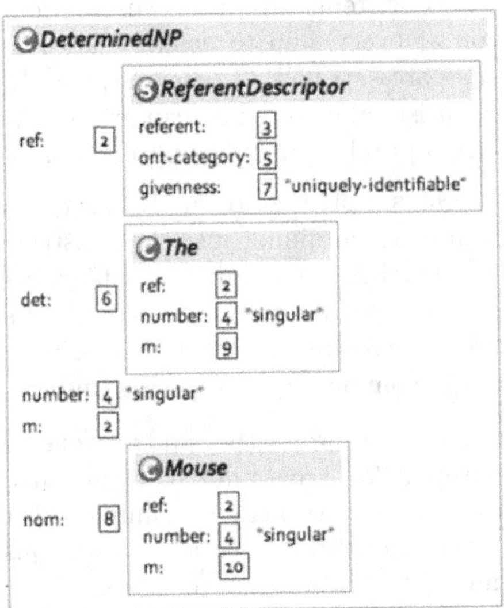

Fig. 10. The semantic specification resulting from analyzing "the mouse"

Though beyond the scope of the example, it may be illuminating to take the analysis above a few steps further. Once the DETERMINEDNP has been successfully matched, various constructions with an initial constituent matching that construction would be added to the stack for consideration. These include constructions corresponding to a variety of possible completions, including *The mouse ran, The mouse ran past, The mouse ran past the barn* and even *The mouse ran past the barn fell.* Depending on the actual input, these constructions would differ in, for example, how much of the form they account for, the semantic likelihood of the associated semspec, and the constructional likelihood. The combined scores is used to prune the set of candidate parser actions and select the best one.

The constructional analyzer has been applied to a variety of linguistic phenomena, including modeling families of related argument structure constructions [6], early Mandarin constructions [16] and Hebrew morphological constructions [18]. Besides serving as a platform for linguistic analysis, it has also been applied as a psycholinguistic model of reading time data [3], and versions of the analyzer have been integrated in models of child language acquisition [4, 16]. Ongoing research has integrated ECG representations of mental spaces and metaphor into the constructional analysis process (Feldman & Gilardi, In prep.), similar to earlier proposals [1, 17].

6.3 Two Processing Models

Major differences between FCG and ECG can be seen in their processing models. Although in some ways not surprising, given their different goals, it is nevertheless interesting to compare how the two frameworks handle essentially the same input. The comparison is most direct for the comprehension models: the two formalisms are subject to the same high-level requirements that they must select candidate constructions, check whether they fit with the current transient structure (in FCG) or partial analysis (in ECG), and choose the overall best set of such constructions. Where they differ is in what kinds of information are available for each of these steps, and what criteria they use for making decisions and prioritizing their respective searches. We discuss these differences below.

Bidirectionality. The most obvious difference between the two formalisms is defined by an absence: ECG currently lacks an implemented model of processing, and cannot thus be said to provide a full model of both sides of the usage coin. This asymmetry is due in part to the focus in ECG on building cognitively plausible models, since the preponderance of psycholinguistic evidence is in comprehension. In principle, however, ECG grammars are declarative sets of constraints that state relationships between form and meaning that should hold in production just as in comprehension. Thus, it is possible that production in ECG would draw on similar data structures and processes as used in comprehension (best-fit combination of evidence, prioritization based on semantic and cognitive heuristics, etc.). One hypothesis is that production may employ the same grammar structures (i.e., construction and schema definitions) as in comprehension, but with different usage statistics.

As noted earlier, the structural components of FCG constructions are used differently in parsing and production: in parsing, regular syntactic units are matched and J-units are merged, whereas in production the regular semantic units are matched, and J-units are merged. FCG thus makes a more specific claim about the relation between parsing and production than ECG can yet make—and it may well be that a working production model for ECG would make quite different kinds of claims, especially if (as conjectured above) the declarative structures of ECG are able to support both kinds of processes.

Matching, Merging and Unification. Both parsing and production in FCG rely on the distinction between matching and merging: the match performs the check or filter on candidate constructions, and the merge causes additional constraints from applicable constructions to be unified into the transient structure. Comprehension in ECG similarly involves determining which constructions out of the whole grammar apply, and then using unification to produce the interim semantic specification. The first step employs some heuristics to reduce the set of possible constructions: specific forms (typically orthographic strings) observed in the utterance are directly associated with constructions including those forms; and (as described earlier) the combination of left-corner parsing with constructional types restricts the set of candidate constructions at any given stage of processing. Constructions passing through this initial filter must still be tested for whether they can be unified with the analysis in progress; successful unification at this stage acts as both a filter on candidate constructions and the mechanism for combining all relevant constructional constraints. It thus corresponds to both matching and merging in FCG.

Essentially, both frameworks have devised different strategies to cope with the computational expense of unification. In FCG, the split between simpler matching heuristics and more expensive merging operations allows some degree of pre-optimization. In ECG, costly unification is part of the matching process, but the availability of a lattice of constructional types helps to compensate for that expense by supplying useful heuristics that restrict the search space of constructions.

Note, however, that the increased efficiency afforded by the use of inheritance in ECG may come at a price: changes to the grammar have potentially wide-ranging effects, and may necessitate costly measures to ensure consistency in the inheritance network. While such changes can be restricted to those that have minimal impact on the network, in general the cost of maintaining consistency may make inheritance impractical for situations in which grammars are liable to undergo frequent changes. But it is precisely situations involving dynamically changing grammars that are the overriding (and titular) concern in FCG.

It should also be mentioned that it is possible in FCG to skip the matching and directly apply merging. Although this strategy has not yet been fully investigated, initial results indicate that it indeed leads to an explosion of the search space. But it also facilitates less restricted and hence more creative usages of constructions, which may be useful both for learning and for achieving robust handling of unfamiliar input.

Structural Flexibility. At first glance the two formalisms differ in the surface impressions they make. In both content and appearance, ECG is heavily influenced by work in frame semantics and cognitive linguistics. The notation itself, though integrated with processes of language learning and use, is expressed in a constraint language that avoids explicitly procedural information. ECG's schema and construction definitions act as data structures that are created, used and altered by the language learning and comprehension models. FCG, on the other hand, stems more directly from work in artificial intelligence and symbolic programming. Though FCG constructions include many declarative constraints, they also have operations that are closely tied to aspects of processing (especially when shown in their expanded form). In a way, FCG constructions act like programs that transform a transient linguistic structure as data.

It is difficult, however, to draw too fine a line between declarative and procedural aspects of each formalism. Both formalisms are, of course, data in the sense that a separate processing engine ultimately controls their execution, verifying that the constraints they specify hold or performing the actions they entail. By the same token, the various notations employed by each formalism have direct effects on processing and thus include procedural information in that sense. Hence, despite the surface differences, most of the constraints expressed in each language can be seen in both lights.

One possible way in which FCG may exhibit a more procedural orientation is provided by TAGs and J-units. With TAGs, a construction can explicitly instruct the match process to remember a binding for a tag variable. Such a variable acts as a local variable in standard programs, and serves to temporarily store a value until it is needed again later, e.g. in a J-unit. J-units in turn serve to provide explicit instructions to the merge process. They specify how to change constituent structure and, in combination with tags, and how to move information between constituents.

Again, however, such effects could be viewed in terms of a set of constraints on the intermediate and final structures involved. The crucial observation here might center not on how these effects are described, but instead on what they do—in particular, the fact that they change constituent structure in this manner. As noted earlier, each FCG constructions specifies precisely the effects (agreement, categories, etc.) that apply to the resulting transient structure, which means that they are relatively free to change the internal structure. As a result, the constituent structure at the end of processing may be difficult to infer directly from constructional definitions. In ECG, on the other hand, constituent structure generally follows that declared in the constructional domain; while the semantic structure need not mirror this structure, the final constructional structure is related relatively directly to that specified in construction definitions. This difference reflects yet again the tendency toward flexibility and freedom in FCG, versus the importance of motivated constraints in ECG.

Cognitively Motivated Processing. Last, but not least, the two processing models differ markedly in the phenomena they target. FCG models are designed to be *functional*: they are intended to satisfy the input and output constraints of communication systems, often those exemplified by particular human linguistic phenomena. The particular processing mechanisms involved are not, however, intended to reflect the implementations of language processing in the human brain. In contrast, ECG's language comprehension model is specifically designed to be cognitively plausible: not only does it fulfill the basic task of identifying constructions instantiated by an utterance and producing the corresponding interpretations, but it does so in a way that reflects the robust, incremental and best-fit nature of human language processing. It thus exploits many efficiencies that come from psycholinguistic evidence about online sentence processing.

Recent work by Wellens (this volume) explores how usage-based networks of FCG constructions can be used to facilitate processing. Such work takes a step in the direction of cognitively motivated processing. Heuristics used to guide search during language processing may also capture some cognitively motivated factors, but thus far little work has been done to fully exploit the potential for learning from the constraints of human language processing in FCG.

7 Discussion and Outlook

The preceding sections describe two computational formalisms that implement ideas from construction-based approaches to grammar. Relative to the range of approaches in the literature, the similarities between the two formalisms and their associated research frameworks far outnumber their differences. Both include notational means of expressing constructional mappings between form and meaning, and both provide the basic representational toolkit for representing categories, agreement and constituent structure.

In addition to these theoretically inspired commitments, the two frameworks also share many methodological assumptions. Both formalisms aim to build working systems that not only describe but in fact instantiate the structures and processes proposed. Unlike many other approaches, they do not stop at describing linguistic knowledge in formal notation but rather offer models of how they are actually used in communication. Processing considerations have thus shaped both formalisms.

The many shared qualities discussed in the preceding sections might be seen as independent requirements for any computational construction grammar formalism. Their differences are perhaps even more revealing of the specific issues that computational implementations of construction-based grammar must face; we summarize some of these below.

7.1 Freedom of Expression

Perhaps the main recurring theme in this comparison has involved the relatively restricted nature of ECG as compared to FCG: in general, ECG allows a more restricted set of notational possibilities, as exemplified by its inclusion of a schema formalism for expressing constructional form and meaning; its limited set of expressible constraints; its stronger assumptions about (some) structural parallels between the form and meaning domains; and the relative monotonicity of the internal structures built up during processing.

By contrast, FCG has been designed to be as open-ended as possible, allowing grammar-writers (and, not coincidentally, evolving agents) a free hand in exploring different styles of representation and strategies for achieving successful communication. This freedom is apparent not only in the broad array of representational devices allowed in form and meaning, but also in the choice of syntactic and semantic categories; the flexible independence of units in the form and meaning domains; and the possibility of fundamental alterations of constituent structure allowed during processing.

These fundamental differences beg the question: how much freedom of expression is enough, and can you have too much? These questions must, of course, be posed relative to the kinds of phenomena the respective formalisms are intended to account for. While ECG is a simpler formalism, it has thus far proven sufficiently expressive for its purposes—to wit, capturing linguistic insights, accounting for psycholinguistic evidence, and being learnable in a developmentally plausible way. It has not, of course, been deployed in the context of language evolution experiments, so it is as yet unclear whether its restricted set of possibilities would give rise to the same unbounded range of communicative creativity, or allow the degree of representational fluidity, fostered by FCG. On the other hand, to the extent that FCG has interest in the specific questions of human communication, it would be worthwhile to find concrete, realistic cases in natural language that demand the amount of freedom and corresponding complexity afforded by FCG.

7.2 Structure and Process

A related issue concerns the directness of the connection between the structures appearing in the formalism and the particular procedures employed during processing. The structure of ECG definitions specifies constraints on the function of processing, but it does not specify precisely how the analyzer proceeds. This affords it a certain amount of stability across particular implementations of processing. The same structures are also intended to be useful for both language comprehension and language production, though a concrete implementation of the latter will be necessary before this idea can be explored and validated.

FCG constructions are not only useful in both language production and comprehension, but their internal structure also reflects some more specific claims FCG makes about the relation between those two processes. In particular, the ways in which different kinds of constraints are expressed (e.g., whether used for matching or merging) correspond directly to the (symmetric) ways in which they are used in these both processing modes.

These differences raise the question of whether and how directly the declarative constraints relevant to each construction can be abstracted from processes of use. A related question is how and whether such construction content must change in order to satisfy the constraints of both kinds of processing. Perhaps FCG's experience in this area could lead to predictions about how these questions would be answered for ECG.

7.3 Benefits and Drawbacks of Inheritance

The organization of FCG and ECG grammars reflects a major representational difference between the two formalisms. ECG makes explicit use of constructional and schematic inheritance relationships, as expressed by type lattices. Such relations capture various linguistic generalizations and naturally lead to more concise and coherent grammars. Not coincidentally, they are also more reminiscent of the kinds of linguistic structures typically proposed by cognitive linguists (and hence perhaps easier for them to understand), and exploit object-oriented design principles from computer science.

FCG grammars have mechanisms for achieving some of the effects of inheritance, such as the templates to notate shared structure. Some FCG grammars also employ frame-based ontologies that are comparable to the schema hierarchies of ECG (see for instance [14]). And, as mentioned, some relations implicit from the use and interaction of constructions during processing may be captured in constructional dependency networks, thus making constructional relations a directly usage-based matter. On the whole, however, FCG has not yet employed explicit notions of inheritance.

As noted earlier, this difference is consistent with FCG's emphasis on the independence of constructions, and the need for making small, local changes: it is relatively easy to change the flow of processing by modifying existing constructions or by adding new constructions to the constructicon (though it may be difficult to predict their consequences). By contrast, in grammars like ECG that employ extensive inheritance relations, small changes may affect a large number of constructions, necessitating more complicated measures for maintaining consistency or re-initializing to reflect updates. The effects of these differences on processing depend, of course, on particular implementational choices, and how much change and fluidity is necessary. The arena of language learning, though not discussed in the current chapter, may offer the best domain for exploring these questions: both formalisms have associated models of learning, though ECG's is developmental while FCG's is evolutionary; the parallels and differences between these endeavors should reward further investigation.

7.4 Different Formalisms for Different Goals

Many of the differences between FCG and ECG reflect their respective backgrounds and priorities. ECG was intended from the start as a theory of human cognition, embracing the foundational ideas of cognitive linguistics. Its goal has been to capture patterns of human categorization and processing, while expressing linguistic and conceptual generalizations. The roots of FCG in artifical language evolution have given it a more dynamic and fluid view of linguistic representations, which crucially requires a certain amount of independence among representations. The developmental path of each formalism reflects these biases and accounts for many of the phenomena we have illustrated here.

But stepping back, it should be clear that these different approaches provide complementary perspectives on the same underlying phenomena of embodied, situated communication. Though they ask different versions of the question—emphasizing, respectively, the constraints imposed by human cognition, versus the freedom to evolve diverse communicative strategies—they nevertheless both provide important ways of framing any complete approach to modeling language structure, use and acquisition. Perhaps most significantly, the fact that both formalisms have concrete implementations of their various structures and processes gives them an additional dimension of considerations not typically available for non-implemented grammatical theories and permits a much more nuanced comparison of approaches than would otherwise be possible. Only when such computationally precise descriptions are available can issues like those raised here be recognized and explored across the broader field of constructional approaches to grammar.

References

[1] Bergen, B., Chang, N.: Embodied Construction Grammar in simulation-based language understanding. In: Östman, J.O., Fried, M. (eds.) Construction Grammar(s): Cognitive and Cross-Language Dimensions. Johns Benjamins (2005)

[2] Bleys, J., Stadler, K., De Beule, J.: Search in linguistic processing. In: Steels, L. (ed.) Design Patterns in Fluid Construction Grammar. John Benjamins, Amsterdam (2011)

[3] Bryant, J.: Best-fit Constructional Analysis. Ph.D. thesis, UC Berkeley (2008)

[4] Chang, N.: Constructing grammar: A computational model of the emergence of early constructions. Ph.D. thesis, Computer Science Department, University of California, Berkeley (2008)

[5] Ciortuz, L., Saveluc, V.: Fluid Construction Grammar and Feature Constraint Logics. In: Steels, L. (ed.) Computational Issues in FCG. LNCS (LNAI), vol. 7249, pp. 289–311. Springer, Heidelberg (2012)

[6] Dodge, E.: Conceptual and constructional composition. Ph.D. thesis, Computer Science Department, University of California, Berkeley (2010)

[7] Feldman, J.: From Molecule to Metaphor: A Neural Theory of Language. MIT Press, Cambridge (2006)

[8] Fillmore, C.J.: Frame semantics. In: Linguistics in the Morning Calm, Seoul, pp. 111–137 (1982)

[9] Goldberg, A.E.: Constructions: A Construction Grammar Approach to Argument Structure. University of Chicago Press, Chicago (1995)

[10] Kay, P., Fillmore, C.: Grammatical constructions and linguistic generalizations: the whats x doing y? construction. Language 75(1) (1999)

[11] Lakoff, G.: Women, Fire, and Dangerous Things: What Categories Reveal about the Mind. University of Chicago Press, Chicago (1987)

[12] Langacker, R.W.: Foundations of Cognitive Grammar. Theoretical Prerequisites, vol. I. Stanford University Press, Stanford (1987)

[13] Manning, C., Carpenter, B.: Probabilistic parsing using left-corner language models. In: Proceedings of the 5th International Workshop on Parsing Technology (1997)

[14] Micelli, V.: Field Topology and Information Structure: A Case Study for German Constituent Order. In: Steels, L. (ed.) Computational Issues in FCG. LNCS (LNAI), vol. 7249, pp. 178–211. Springer, Heidelberg (2012)

[15] Micelli, V., Van Trijp, R., De Beule, J.: Framing fluid construction grammar. In: Proceedings of the 2009 Annual Meeting of the Cognitive Science Society, COGSCI (2009), http://www.csl.sony.fr/downloads/papers/2009/micelli-09a.pdf
[16] Mok, E.H.: Contextual Bootstrapping for Grammar Learning. Ph.D. thesis, Computer Science Department, University of California, Berkeley (2008)
[17] Mok, E.H., Bryant, J., Feldman, J.: Scaling understanding up to mental spaces. In: Proceedings of the 2nd International Workshop on Scalable Natural Language Understanding (ScaNaLU 2004), Boston, MA (2004)
[18] Schneider, N.: Computational cognitive morphosemantics: modeling morphological compositionality in hebrew verbs with embodied construction grammar. In: Proc. of the 36th Annual Meeting of the Berkeley Linguistics Society, Berkeley, CA (2010)
[19] Spranger, M., Loetzsch, M.: Syntactic indeterminacy and semantic ambiguity: A case study for German spatial phrases. In: Steels, L. (ed.) Design Patterns in Fluid Construction Grammar. John Benjamins, Amsterdam (2011)
[20] Steels, L. (ed.): Design Patterns in Fluid Construction Grammar. John Benjamins, Amsterdam (2011)
[21] Steels, L.: A first encounter with Fluid Construction Grammar. In: Steels, L. (ed.) Design Patterns in Fluid Construction Grammar. John Benjamins, Amsterdam (2011)
[22] van Trijp, R.: Feature matrices and agreement: A case study for German case. In: Steels, L. (ed.) Design Patterns in Fluid Construction Grammar. John Benjamins, Amsterdam (2011)

Fluid Construction Grammar and Feature Constraint Logics

Liviu Ciortuz and Vlad Saveluc

Department of Computer Science, "Al.I. Cuza" University, Iaşi, Romania

Abstract. Fluid Construction Grammars (FCGs) are a flavor of Construction Grammars, which are themselves unification-based grammars. The FCG syntax is similar to that of other unification-based grammars only to a small extent. Additionally, up until now, FCG has lacked a comprehensively-defined declarative semantics, whereas its procedural semantics is truly particular compared to other unification-based grammar formalisms.

Here we propose the re-definition of a core subset of the FCG formalism (henceforth called FCG light) within the framework of order-sorted feature constraint logics (OSF-logic) that would assign FCG a rigorous semantics, both declarative and procedural, that is suitable for both parsing, production and grammar learning.

This new framework allows us to clearly compare FCG to other unification-based grammars. We will also have the advantage of associating FCG with another classical paradigm for learning ("evolving") new grammars, namely learning in hierarchies (lattices) of concepts. This learning technique exploits the natural partial order relation of generalization/ specialization between grammars. The learning method currently used by FCG, is (inspired by) reinforcement learning. We claim that learning in a hierarchy of grammar versions enables us to establish a rather natural link with linguistic background knowledge when devising the grammar repair strategies. It also sets a stage on which we may compare different grammars that could be learned by an agent at each step during the grammar evolution process.

1 Introduction

Here we present FCG light, a core subset of Fluid Construction Grammars introduced by [33] [15] [34] which is currently implemented on a simplified version of the LIGHT platform [9].

The LIGHT system was developed with the explicit aim of doing efficient processing of HPSG-like unification grammars[25], but it is by no means restricted to working with HPSGs.[1] LIGHT comprises several feature structure (FS) unifiers[2]

[1] HPSG stands for Head-driven Phrase Structure Grammars.

[2] More exactly, LIGHT currently has 6 unifiers, of both typed and un-typed kinds: *a.* non-compiled (lazy) typed unification, *b.* compiled (eager) typed unification, *c.* compiled (eager) typed unification specialized for active, bottom-up, chart-based parsing and their un-typed counterparts (a', b', c'). For technical details, the interested reader should consult [12].

L. Steels (Ed.): Computational Issues in FCG, LNAI 7249, pp. 289–311, 2012.

and a control level (actually performing active bottom-up chart-based parsing) upon the unification level. An important number of optimizations were incorporated into the LIGHT system. In the past these optimizations were fine-tuned so as to achieve efficient parsing with ERG [17], the large-scale HPSG grammar for English developed at CSLI, Stanford University.

The present work leads to defining FCG light as a new flavor of unification grammars, which is derived from the FCG formalism and is transposed into the LIGHT setup, thus benefitting from a rigorous semantics (both a declarative and a procedural one) based on OSF-logic, which was introduced in [3] and [1].[3]

We argue that by using this logic-based semantics we are able to:

- redefine the procedural semantics of the chosen subset of FCG and associate it with a declarative semantics which we claim is not clearly visible in the FCG setup;
- gain certain benefits through this framework arising from the natural partial order relation between grammars defined via generalization/specialization;
- replace grammar learning, as a consequence of the above issue, in FCG (which is based on the reinforcement learning paradigm) through learning in a lattice of grammars. We argue that the latter paradigm is more naturally suitable for integrating linguistic background knowledge, and it leads to more efficient learning because it enables us to define certain *heuristics* that are very helpful for guiding the search for appropriate (rule) candidates in the grammar lattice;
- in certain conditions,[4] define parsing and production in FCG light in a declarative manner (as it is the case of unification grammars, in particular head-driven grammars).

This paper is organized as follows: Section 2 makes a review of the (core) FCG formalism from the feature constraint point of view. Section 3 goes through the details of FCG light language's definition, at both syntactic and semantic levels. Section 4 is concerned with grammar learning aspects in FCG light. Section 5 scrutinizes several tasks that we have planned, demonstrating further usefulness of FCG light.

[3] OSF-logic is closely related to Carpenter's logic of typed feature structures [5]. It has been associated with an abstract machine for compilation of FS unification [2], which was further extended by [10] to compiled typed FS unification. OSF is not concerned with appropriateness constraints; however, we have shown that in certain conditions one could automatically infer these constraints from the given input grammar [7]. For a good introduction to feature constraint logics, the reader should consult [31].

[4] When constraint reduction actions (see Section 3.1) are performed in "soft" mode, they do not affect logical entailment. This is why in FCG light the reduction operation is replaced (at unification level) by constraint marking for deletion (to be cared of by the parser/producer).

```
((?top-unit
  (tag ?meaning (meaning (== (read ?event)
                             (reader ?event ?agent)))))
((J ?verb-unit ?top-unit)
 ?meaning
 (referent ?event)
 (sem-cat (==1 (base-type ?event event)))))
<-->
((?top-unit
  (tag ?form (form (== (string ?verb-unit "cita")))))
 ((J ?verb-unit ?top-unit)
  ?form
  (syn-cat (==1 (pos verb)
                (gender ?agent ?agent-gender)
                (case ?object accusative)))))
```

Fig. 1. An FCG construction that acts as lexical entry for the Russian verb "cita", similar to the verb "risova" presented by [18], Chapter 3

2 FCG Revisited: A Feature Constraint-Based Perspective

Here we summarize the basic notions in the FCG formalism, relative to both its syntax and procedural semantics.

An FCG grammar is a set of structures called *constructions*, which are written in the FCG format, as exemplified in Figure 1. Unlike FCG authors [32] [14], here we give a *constraint*-based view on the definition of construction structures. To this aim, we need some basic notions of feature constraint logics. We briefly describe them here, yet without going into formal details. *Elementary constraints* considered here are of three kinds: sort constraints, feature constraints and equality constraints.[5]

It is useful to make the following *preliminary remark:*

In HPSG/LIGHT rules are expressed simply as FSs, enabling the user to employ a unique formalism for both the grammar rules and the structures to which they apply. However, in FCG formalisms, the *constructions* that express rules differ from the structures to which they are applied, namely the *coupled feature structures*. This *difference* is due to the fact that certain operations — beyond the level of deductive parsing and production — that have to be performed by the parser/producer are specified in the constructions representing rules.

[5] In FCG light, like in other formalisms, the equality constraints are not explicitly used at the syntax level. Instead they are automatically derived while building certain variable substitutions, i.e. during operations manipulating the FSs: subsumption, unification (computation of the GLB for two FSs), and generalization (LUB computation).

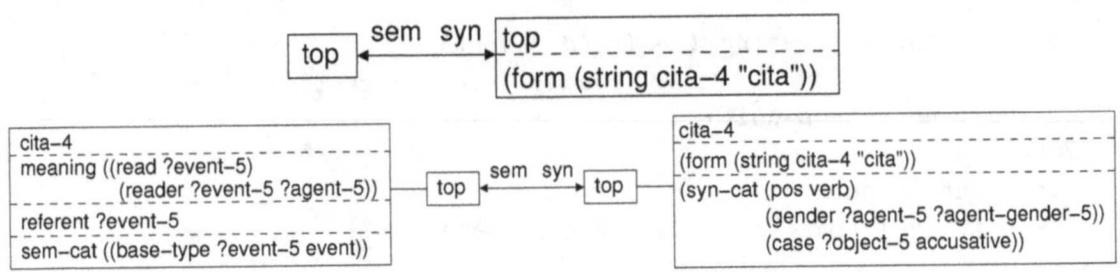

Fig. 2. Two simple couple feature structures. The lower CFS is obtained from the upper one by application of the construction given in Figure 1 in parsing mode.

This fact unfortunately leads to the disruption in FCG of the really nice correspondence between declarative and procedural semantics and also the orthogonality between the unifier level and the parser/producer level that characterize main-stream unification grammars, in particular HPSGs. This disruption seems to be the price to be paid by FCG for the benefit of offering the grammar writer the capacity to play with subtleties in the learning (evolvable) grammars.

Similar to HPSG/LIGHT, in defining FCG light we aim to reduce to a minimum (and, in certain conditions, even eliminate) the difference between the form of rules and the CFSs to which they apply, thus enabling our parser/producer to work very smoothly.

At this point, we can provide a set of informal *definitions* that can be seen as constraint-based alternatives to the ones that have been introduced in [34]:

A *coupled feature structure* (CFS) can be seen as a set of elementary constraints, partitioned into two disjoint subsets named *poles*. These poles are usually referred to as the *syntactic* pole and the *semantic* pole (more generally: the *left* pole and the *right* pole) of the given CFS. Each of the two poles further partitions its set of elementary constraints into several *units*. The units in a CFS are explicitly linked into a graph (usually a tree) using the multi-valued *features* `syn-subunits` (in the syntactic pole) and `sem-subunits` (in the semantic pole). Further on, each unit partitions its set of elementary constraints under several *slots*.

To illustrate the above notions, consider the CFS shown in the lower part of Figure 2, in which the `top-unit` has as sub-unit the `verb-unit`, and examples of slots in the latter unit are `syn-cat` and `sem-cat`.[6] The FCG constraints `(read ?event-5)` and `(base-type ?event-5 event)` correspond in OSF-logic to the elementary sort constraint #*event-5:read* and respectively the feature constraint #*event-5.base-type* ⇒ *event*.

CFSs and constructions in FCG are characterized by a certain, de facto user-specified correspondence between syntax and semantics. This correspondence starts with the `meaning` and `form` constraints in a top-unit and is down-propagated to the other units via parsing and production.

[6] The reader will see that this CFS can be obtained from the very simple CFS shown in the upper part of Figure 2 by the application of the FCG construction in Figure 1 in parsing mode.

Basically, the set of elementary constraints that constitute a CFS can be treated in either *match*/subsumption mode or *merge*/unification mode. The actual way in which the elementary constraints are processed is dependent on the parsing or production process (not detailed here) carried by the application of construction rules [14] [4].

The notion of *construction* extends the definition given above for CFS by adding the following:

- two *operators*, namely:
  the *J operator* that (indirectly) indicates `syn/sem-subunits` constraints and also separates the merge zone from the match zone in a pole;
  the *tag operator* that indicates a substructure (set of elementary constraints) to be deleted and eventually moved elsewhere;
- several *restrictors* ('==1','==0', etc.), which can be seen as meta-constraints to be checked while the match and merge operations are performed. For further details, the reader should consult [34].

In FCG, the scope of the match and merge operations is limited to slots. In FCG light we replace slots with features, whose values are implicitly $\top$-sorted, where $\top$ is the top sort in the sort hierarchy.[7] In FCG light the constraints associated with a slot must represent a rooted feature structure.

Similar to the LIGHT system, in FCG light we make no use of negation ((0==) in FCG), whereas the single-valued restriction ((1==) in FCG) is considered implicit for feature constraints.[8] Multi-valued features (designated using the =>> symbol) are restricted to SYN-SUBUNITS and SEM-SUBUNITS.[9] The treatment of these two features is reserved for the parser and the producer. In FCG light, features names are always capitalized.

Two additional features SYN and SEM, corresponding to the two poles in a CFS are introduced.[10] A syntactico-semantic graph, henceforth abbreviated as *syn-sem graph*, can be derived from each CFS. The notion of syn-sem graph is used in the sequel as an alternative/replacement for the notion of CFS.

From the restrictions and syntactic transformations listed above, it follows that a CFS in FCG can be naturally written as a FS in OSF/LIGHT.

3 FCG light Language Definition

Here we formally introduce in Subsection 3.1 the syntax of the FCG light subset of FCG, basically showing how constructions in FCG get translated into the OSF/LIGHT syntax (which in the past also supported HPSG grammars).

---

[7] For these slot-derived features, appropriateness constraints [5] with corresponding new sort values can be further added.

[8] Therefore, the symbol $\Rightarrow$ in OSF functional constraints is dropped.

[9] Multi-valued features are found, for instance, in F-logic [21]. OSF-logic can be naturally extended so as to accommodate such features.

[10] These features are not (necessarily) shown in the sequel, if the sets of syntactic slots and semantic slots are disjoint.

production

precond.	*♮top-unit.MEANING* = *♮event*, *♮event:read*, *♮event.READER* = *♮agent*
reduction	*♮top-unit.MEANING* = *♮event*, *♮event:read*, *♮event.READER* = *♮agent*
main	*♮top-unit.SEM-SUBUNITS* ∋ *♮verb-unit*, *♮verb-unit.MEANING*=*♮event*, *♮event:read*, *♮event.READER* = *♮agent*, *♮verb-unit.REFERENT* = *♮event*, *♮verb-unit.SEM-CAT* = *♮1*, *♮1.BASE-TYPE(♮event)* = *♮2*, *♮2:event*

parsing

precond.	*♮top-unit.FORM* ∋ *♮verb-unit*, *♮verb-unit.STRING* = *♮1*, *♮1:"cita"*
reduction	*♮top-unit.FORM* ∋ *♮verb-unit*, *♮verb-unit.STRING* = *♮1*, *♮1:"cita"*
main	*♮top-unit.SYN-SUBUNITS* ∋ *♮verb-unit*, *♮verb-unit.STRING* = *♮1*, *♮1:"cita"*, *♮verb-unit.SYN-CAT* = *♮2*, *♮2:verb*, *verb:pos*, *♮2.GENDER(♮agent)* = *♮agent-gender*, *♮2.CASE(♮object)* = *♮3*, *♮3:accusative*

Fig. 3. The sets of elementary constraints used in production and respectively parsing with the "cita" lexical entry given in Figure 1. The hash symbol (#) introduces variables, while the colon (:) precedes the sort of a variable (or a supersort of a sort). The symbols = and ∋ designate values for single-valued features and respectively multi-valued features. Feature names are written in upper case.

Then, in Subsection 3.2, we introduce the two basic aspects of FCG light semantics — the declarative one and the procedural one —, that further support the FS subsumption and FS unification operations used in parsing, production and grammar learning.

3.1 FCG light Syntax

Now we will (re)define for FCG light the notion of construction by getting it as close as possible to the notion of FS in OSF/LIGHT. (Re)defining the notion of construction for FCG light requires getting it as close as possible to the notion of FS in OSF/LIGHT.

Definition: In FCG light, a *construction* is a set of elementary (i.e. atomic) constraints which is divided into the following two (not necessarily disjoint) triplets of sets:

- a set of *precondition* constraints, a set of constraints marked for *reduction* actions and the set of *main* constraints used for parsing,
- a set of *precondition* constraints, a set of constraints marked for *reduction* actions and the set of *main* constraints used for production.

production

<table>
<tr><td>precond.</td><td><pre>#top-unit[MEANING =>> #event:read
                           [READER #agent]]</pre></td></tr>
<tr><td>reduction</td><td><pre>#top-unit[MEANING =>> #event:read
                           [READER #agent[TO-BE-REDUCED +],
                             TO-BE-REDUCED +]]</pre></td></tr>
<tr><td>main</td><td><pre>#top-unit
[SEM-SUBUNITS =>> #verb-unit
                     [MEANING #event:read
                                  [READER #agent],
                       REFERENT #event,
                       SEM-CAT top
                                  [BASE-TYPE(#event) event]]]</pre></td></tr>
</table>

parsing

<table>
<tr><td>precond.</td><td><pre>#top-unit[FORM =>> #verb-unit[STRING "cita"]]</pre></td></tr>
<tr><td>reduction</td><td><pre>#top-unit[FORM =>> #verb-unit[STRING "cita"
                                   [TO-BE-REDUCED +],
                               TO-BE-REDUCED +]]</pre></td></tr>
<tr><td>main</td><td><pre>#top-unit
[SYN-SUBUNITS =>> #verb-unit
                     [STRING "cita",
                       SYN-CAT verb:pos
                                 [GENDER(#agent) #agent-gender,
                                   CASE(#object) accusative]]]</pre></td></tr>
</table>

Fig. 4. The OSF rooted terms (FSs) corresponding to the sets of elementary constraints identified for the "cita" lexical entry (Figure 1), that have been shown in Figure 3. Compared to Figure 3, here above we did not show OSF variables that occur only once. Also, multi-valued feature constraints corresponding to the J operator were added; see the `SYN-SUBUNITS` and `SEM-SUBUNITS` features.

In FCG light we explicitly impose the following *restrictions:*[11] For both parsing and production, the constraints to be reduced must constitute a subset of the precondition set of constraints, and the set of main constraints must be disjoint from the precondition set.

In order to give an *exemplification* of the above definition of construction in FCG light, the sets of elementary constraints that build up the "cita" construction — which was given in FCG format in Figure 1 — are presented in Figure 3. Further on, Figure 4 shows these sets of constraints represented as rooted FSs in OSF/LIGHT format.[12]

[11] These demands are generally met by FCG grammar writers.

[12] The correspondence between sets of elementary constraints and (multi-rooted) feature structures should be familiar to the reader acquainted with feature constraints logics.

```
/* cita ; production */
#top-unit
[ SEM-SUBUNITS =>> #verb-unit
                    [ REFERENT #event,
                      MEANING #event:read
                                [ READER #agent ],
                      SEM-CAT top[ BASE-TYPE < #event, event > ],
                      STRING <! "cita" !>,
                      SYN-CAT verb
                                [ GENDER < #agent, #agent-gender >,
                                  CASE < #object, accusative > ] ],
  SYN-SUBUNITS =>> #verb-unit,
  ARGS < #top-unit[ MEANING #event:read
                               [ READER #agent ] ] > ]

/* cita ; parsing */
#top-unit
[ SYN-SUBUNITS =>> #verb-unit
                    [ SYN-CAT verb
                                [ GENDER < #agent, #agent-gender >,
                                  CASE < #object, accusative > ],
                      REFERENT #event,
                      MEANING #event:read
                                [ READER #agent ],
                      SEM-CAT top[ BASE-TYPE < #event, event > ] ],
  SEM-SUBUNITS =>> #verb-unit,
  ARGS < #top-unit[ FORM =>> #verb-unit[ STRING <! "cita" !> ] ] > ]
```

Fig. 5. The two FCG light rules that are associated to the construction "cita" given in Figure 1. The ARGS feature designates the right hand side (RHS) of the rule. The syntax <! !! > is a "sugar-ed" notation for difference lists. Using such a special structure is a very convenient way to replace the (interpretable) constraint `meets` used in FCG.

In many cases, it is possible to actually get rid of constraint reduction, which is why in the current implementation of FCG light we opted for a "soft" treatment of reduction. In other words, the set of constraints designated for reduction are *marked* at unification and/or subsumption level by using the reserved feature TO-BE-REDUCED that takes boolean values. The parser and the producer subsequently analyze these markings. Such treatment in FCG light is absolutely sufficient for reproducing a quite elaborate example of learning in FCG, such as the one described in Gerasymova's MS thesis [18].

Instead of having one construction/form treated in two different ways during parsing and respectively production (as it is done in FCG), in FCG light we explicitly associate each construction with two rules that are treated in exactly the same manner — the subsumption, reduction and unification sequence — in both parsing and production. The *general form* of a parsing or production rule that corresponds to an FCG light construction is

$$\mu : - \psi ; \alpha .$$

where μ is the main set of constraints, ψ is the precondition, and α is a set of to-be-reduced constrains. Here, μ, ψ and α should be seen as rooted FSs.

If the reduction actions are implemented in soft mode, and α' is the marked FS (using the TO-BE-REDUCED feature) that corresponds to α, then the rule $\mu : - \psi, \alpha$ becomes $\mu, \alpha' : - \psi$.

The latter can be even written as

$$\mu' : - \psi .$$

where μ' is the unification result for μ and α'.

The *algorithm* responsible for getting these two FCG light rules is presented in Figure 6. It has three main steps, each step translating/transforming in a certain way the output of its preceding step. Before we will comment on them, we show via an *example* what these steps are supposed to do. When applied on the "cita" construction given in Figure 1 the 'initial' translation step in this algorithm builds the sets of elementary constraints shown in Figure 3. In the 'intermediate' translation step, these sets of constraints are put under the form of (single-)rooted FSs, as shown in Figure 4. These FSs will be subject to a number of simple operations in the 'final' translation step, and their ultimate form (for this example) is given in Figure 5.

The idea behind the first part of the 'initial' translation step of our FCG-into-LIGHT algorithm is the following: Consider an arbitrary FCG construct and assume that we want to obtain an OSF/LIGHT rule that corresponds to the application of this construct in parsing mode. Among all the elementary constraints in which this construction is decomposed, those which are subject to (FCG) matching will be placed in the *precondition* part of the to-be-created LIGHT rule for parsing. Similarly, the constraints used for (FCG) merging will be put into the rule's *main* part. The (FCG) tag-ed constraints will be placed firstly into the rule's *reduction* part and secondly wherever the tag re-appears. The remaining part of the 'initial' translation step is concerned with building the two (parsing and production) rules out of the sets of elementary constraints that have just been built. As formalized above, each rule is of the form RHS :– LHS.

Something important is to be explained here: The application of the J operator in FCG will correspond in FCG light to (checking and enforcing) certain elementary constraints. These constraints will be expressed using the reserved features SYN-SUBUNITS for parsing, and respectively SEM-SUBUNITS for production. For instance, the FCG code `(J ?verb-unit ?top-unit)` in the left/semantic pole of the "cita" construction given in Figure 1 will be translated as the constraint `?top-unit.SEM-SUBUNITS` ∋`?verb-unit`.[13]

The 'intermediate' step of our algorithm puts sets/conjunctions of constraints under the form of rooted FSs. FCG light, which is oriented toward efficiency of

[13] In FCG light, where the use of multi-valued feature constraints is limited to the reserved SYN-/SEM-SUBUNITS features, the parser/producer will fully take care of them. In this way, the unification/subsumption procedure is exempted from this (inefficiency causing!) overhead.

Input: a construction given in FCG format
1. The *initial* translation step
   - by following the guidelines for construction application in FCG,
     build the sets of elementary OSF constraints corresponding to
       precondition, *reduction* and *main* body,
     for parsing and respectively production
   - then, for parsing do the following:
     place the parsing *precondition* and *reduction* constraints
       into the RHS of the newly to-be-created (parsing) rule
     the rest, i.e. the constraints corresponding to the parser's J actions, and
         all stuff in the left/semantic pole,
           including the producer's J constraints
           but not its *reduction* constraints
       is placed into the LHS part of the new (parsing) rule
   - for production: proceed similarly.
2. The *intermediate* translation step:
   for each rule of the two rules resulted from the 'initial' step,
   - in the LHS unify the FSs having the same root identifier
   - check whether the FSs in the *precondition*
       is a connex tree, i.e. single-rooted FS
   - do the same for the LHS part
   - do the same for the *reduction* part if necessary.
3. The *final* translation step:
   for each rule of the two rules resulted from the 'intermediate' step,
   - put *reduction* actions unto soft form
     i.e. mark constraints for reduction, using the TO-BE-REDUCED feature
   - replace the ("interpretable") feature MEETS with difference lists;
       constrain accordingly the variables in the difference lists
   - transform features whose names are non-atomic terms
   - extract sort (s1:s2) declarations
   - use the reserved feature ARGS to designate the rule's RHS.

Output: the two LIGHT rules obtained above.

Fig. 6. The FCG-into-LIGHT translation algorithm which, starting from a construction given in FCG format, obtains the two rules to be used in FCG light for parsing and respectively production. For instance, for the "cita" construction which was given in Figure 1, the two FCG light rules produced by this algorithm are those shown in Figure 5. The sets of elementary constraints (represented as FSs) into which that construction was de-composed (see Step 1 from above), were previously presented in Figure 3. They were further down translated as FSs, and the result of Step 2 was shown in Figure 4.

unification and subsumption, imposes that these (*precondition*, *reduction* and *main*) FSs be single-rooted.

The 'final' translation step is concerned with a. soften-ing the constrain reduction, i.e. marking the constraints which must be reduced; b. replacing "interpretable", i.e. procedurally defined FCG predicates like MEETS with non-procedural ones; c. transforming non-atomic feature names, and d. extracting is-a relationships between sorts (unary predicates in FCG).

We think it is useful to show how we transform constraint features identified by non-atomic terms (see Step 3 in Figure 6). For instance, the constraint

```
CASE( #object ) accusative
```

becomes:

```
CASE <#object, accusative>.
```

One final remark: The reader will note that in those two FCG light rules in Figure 5 we purposely omitted the (markings responsible for) constraint reduction. This is due to the fact that in FCG light the parser/producer itself (and not the unifier) takes care of constraint reduction. We should also add that in FCG light constraint reduction is restricted to the scope of `form` and `meaning`.

To summarize this section, we say that a *grammar* in FCG is a set of constructions (written in FCG format), each one of which is automatically translated using the algorithm in Figure 6 into a pair of rules (in OSF/LIGHT format), one for parsing and the other for production.

3.2 FCG light Semantics

The OSF-logic provided the *declarative semantics* to the LIGHT system. It does the same for FCG light — if reduction actions are implemented in soft mode — both at the FS unification and FS subsumption levels and at the deductive control level over FSs, i.e. parsing and production [28] [30].[14]

In FCG light all rules are unary rules, unlike the LIGHT system which supports both binary and unary rules. However, the argument — or the pre-condition, or the right hand side (RHS) — of each rule is not necessarily a phrase structure. Instead, it is the description of a rooted subgraph in the syn-sem graph created during parsing and production. The same is true about the rule's left hand side (LHS). More precisely, one of the *restrictions* that we impose on FCG light grammars is the following: all units specified in a construction should constitute a rooted graph, where edges are defined via the SYN-SUBUNITS and SEM-SUBUNITS features.

Concerning the *procedural semantics*, as outlined in Section 3.1, each construction in FCG light is associated with two *rules*, one for parsing and the other for

[14] We mention that unlike LIGHT when used for the HPSG ERG grammar, FCG light works with the un-typed counterpart of OSF-logic, since FCG does not impose appropriateness constraints on FSs.

production. Unlike LIGHT, for which the application of rules is fully unification-based, in FCG light the unique argument of a rule is checked for compatibility (with a syn-sem graph) by using FS *subsumption* (match, in the FCG formulation). The rule's LHS is treated via FS *unification*.[15]

In FCG light, the parsing and production can be partial. For parsing, this means that we drop off the usual requests that *i.* all lexical entries should be defined in the given grammar, and *ii.* a syntactic tree should be built so as to span the whole input sentence and to be subsumed by the grammar's start symbol. Just as for HPSG, there is usually no designated start symbol in FCG grammars. The function of such a symbol is taken by the *top-unit*, to which all the other units (morphological, lexical, syntactic or semantic) get linked in one way or another.

Given τ, the syn-sem graph whose root is the *top-unit* and whose arcs are given by the features SYN-SUBUNITS and SEM-SUBUNITS, an FCG light rule of the form $\mu : -\psi, \alpha$ is applied as follows:

> if subsume(τ', ψ), and σ is the corresponding most general substitution, then
>
> perform the reduction of the constraints $\alpha\sigma$ and
> unify($\mu\sigma, \tau''$)

where τ' is an arbitrary (single-rooted, maximally connected) subgraph of τ, and τ'' is the subgraph of $\tau\sigma$ whose root is identified by the root of $\tau'\sigma$.

It should be noted that a rule application has not necessarily a unique outcome, since τ' is not always unique. Here above, the unification operation is seen as a constraint satisfaction problem in OSF-logic. Such a problem is solved using for instance the so-called clause normalization procedure. If $\mu\sigma$ and τ'' are trees, then the usual FS unification algorithm can be used and the result is unique (up to variable renaming). Subsumption is also regarded in the classical way.

The following simple algorithm formalizes the way *parsing* is done in FCG light:

> *Input:*
> a grammar G, and
> τ the (initial) syn-sem graph corresponding to
> the FORM of a given input sentence.
>
> *Procedure:*
> as long as parsing rules in G apply successfully on τ,
> build up the corresponding new syn-sem graph(s).

Concerning the parsing *output:* syn-sem graphs that span the whole input are (eligible for) the output; the user may impose additional constraints on them. If there is no graph that satisfies these constraints, then other (partial) graphs may be considered.

Similarly one can formalize production in FCG light.

---

[15] For other perspectives on the unification and merge operations in FCG, the reader may consult [29] and [16].

4 Grammar Learning in FCG light

In FCG, the learning process is reinforcement-based, i.e. each construct receives a weight which is a real number between 0 and 1, and it is increased whenever the construction is used in successful parsing/production. If unsuccessful, the weight is decreased. One of our *objectives* has been to explore in FCG light a different paradigm for defining strategies for construction learning (as used, for instance, in grammar repairing), compared to the paradigm that is currently used by FCG.

In FCG light, learning is based on searching in a lattice of grammar versions, i.e. it amounts to searching in a *version space* which is partially ordered by means of a generalization/specialization (actually subsumption-based) relation between grammars, as illustrated in Figure 7 [22]. The version space is meant to induce a certain discipline while searching for new grammars (and, at lower level, new rules) during the learning process.[16] For a discussion on using lattices for learning in Embodied Construction Grammars (ECG) and comparison with FCG, the reader is referred to [6].

Learning in the FCG light system is performed in *on-line* (i.e. interactive) mode, via language games played by 2 agents, as in FCG. For a schematic view on the functional architecture used by FCG light for learning, the reader should see Figure 8.

In order to be able to go into more detail when explaining the learning strategy used by FCG light, we give in Figure 9 the pseudo-code of the procedure that implements in FCG lightthe language game presented by Gerasymova in Chapter 4 of her MS thesis [18]. This language game strategy supports the learning of an FCG grammar for the Russian verb aspects. During the language game played by the two agents, a number of *holophrasis* constructions are learned (see Step 1 in Figure 9). The generalization procedure which is called (see Step 2 in Figure 9) to elaborate new rules based on the previously produced holophrases is given also in pseudo-code in Figure 10.

Gerasymova's *target grammar*, which was translated in FCG light following the guidelines that have been presented in Section 3, is able to parse and produce sentences like "Misha pocital", "Masha narisoval lico", "kto pocital?".[17] In the beginning of the language game, from the target grammar — which is used as such by the 'teacher' agent —, the syntactic construction 'po-', and the associated 'mapping' rule and 'semantic' rule were eliminated in order to get the *start grammar*, which is to be used (in the beginning of the language game)

[16] One could merge the two learning paradigms by associating each rule (of each grammar) in the version space a weight and then updating it, as done in FCG. As a consequence, this new, composed paradigm would be a generalization of the two previous ones. One could think of the rule weights in the current implementation of FCG light as being initially set to 1; removing a rule from a grammar amounts to setting its weight to 0. As for FCG, in the new, compound paradigm one would have to keep track of the generalization/specialization relationships between newly created rules and the previously existing ones, and similarly between different grammar versions.

[17] These sentences translate into English as "Michael read for a while", "Masha has drown the face", and "Who read for a while?" respectively.

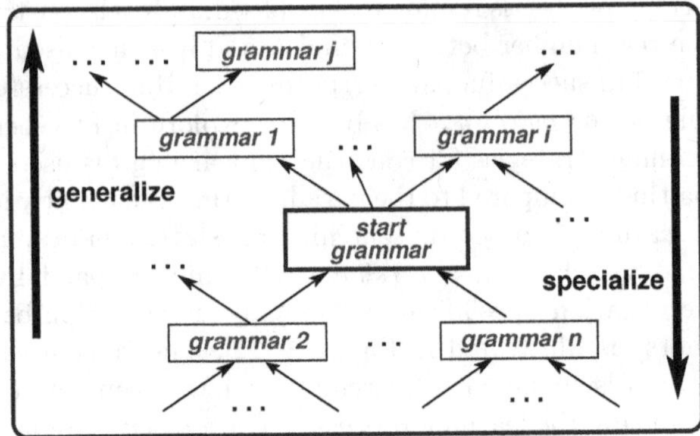

Fig. 7. Illustrating the notion of version space for the process of learning grammars in in the FCG light system. Upward arrows signify the generalization relation between grammars. Conversely we have the specialization relation. During the grammar learning process, the 'start grammar' can be generalized for instance to 'grammar 1' (which in turn can be generalized to 'grammar j'), or can be specialized to 'grammar 2' or 'grammar n'.

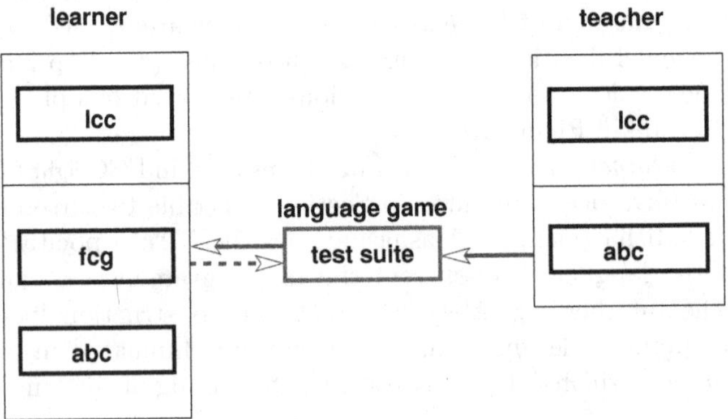

Fig. 8. Schematic view on the learning architecture in FCG light. Here **lcc** (a name which is an abbreviation for: LIGHT into C Compiler) designates the module in the LIGHT system that is in charge with the pre-processing and compilation of the input grammar; **abc** is the parser's name (abbreviation for: Active, Bottom-up Chart-based), while **fcg** is the learner module of FCG light. The dotted arrow corresponds to questions that the learner may ask the teacher in order to guide his or her search for better inferred rules/grammars.

Target grammar: ;
the given given in Chapter 3 of Gerasymova's MS thesis [18];
Input/start grammar: ;
obtained from the target grammar by deleting for instance the lexical construction for "po-" and the associated 'mapping rule' and 'semantic' rule.
Language game: ;
1. choose a *setup*, for inst. Misha read for-a-while; Masha read ongoing;
teacher: generate a question, for instance "kto pocital?"
learner:
parse the question,
get the corresponding *meaning*,
try to disambiguate it wrt the given *setup*,
if disambiguation is successful, then go to Step 1,
otherwise (since in this case 'po-' is unknown to him/her),
send to the teacher the *failure* message;
teacher: reveal the correct answer to the above question ("Misha");
learner:
after correlating the CFS previously obtained by parsing
with the meaning pointed to by the teacher's answer,
induce a *holophrasis* construction (corresponding to 'pocita');
2. after performing a number of times the Step 1,
use the procedure given in Figure 10 to
generalize over the learned holophrases, and then
extract new construction rules
by *decomposing* the generalized holophrasis.

Fig. 9. The pseudo-code for the language game strategy which was designed for learning for Russian verb aspects as presented inGerasymova's MS thesis [18], Chapter 4. The teacher agent uses the 'target' grammar, while the learner agent starts the game with an altered version of it, called the 'start' grammar.

and later on improved by the 'learner' agent. Skimming through the execution of the procedures given in Figures 9 and 10 during this language game allows us to make a couple of *remarks:*[18]

First, concerning Step 1 in the procedure given in Figure 9:

In FCG light a holophrasis (like 'pocita') is obtained by generalizing the CFSs obtained during parsing. More specifically, this holophrasis construction is obtained by:

- applying the LUB operation on the syn-sem CFSs that have been obtained after parsing slightly similar parsed sentences like "Misha pocital" and "Masha pocitala"; the LUB operation *generalizes* them with respect to the subject (Misha, Masha, kto) and the endings (-l/-la) indicating the perfect tense;[19]

[18] The reader may find useful to follow the explanations below by taking also a look at the whole picture of the learning process, as shown in Figure 13.

[19] [18] does not explicitly call this a generalization. Nor does it explicitly names the LUB operation.

Input: a set of holophrases produced (or, even the CFSs from which they originated) during the application of Step 1 of a series of language games played according to the strategy presented in Figure 9;
Output: a set of pair of constructions (each one made of a lexical entry and a lexical rule) corresponding to each prefix and its associated event-type;
Procedure: • Group (the CFSs that correspond to) all holophrases that have
- the same prefix (for example 'po-'),
- the same value for the EVENT-TYPE feature for the event which is associated to the respective verb's occurrence (for example, 'pocita', 'porisova' etc. correspond to the event-type 'for-a-while');

• for each such group g

generalize: apply the *least upper bound* (LUB) operation on the CFSs (representing the holophrases) in the group g; let's denote it LUB(g);

decompose: split the *generalized holophrasis* construction corresponding to LUB(g) into a *lexical construction* and a *lexical rule*;

to get this done, it is necessary to introduce a new ('AKTIONSART') feature; this feature makes the link between the prefix and the verb's EVENT-TYPE value. For example:

SYN-CAT top[AKTIONSART delimitative];
SEM-CAT top[AKTIONSART(#event) delimitative];

replace g in the current grammar with the above created rules.

Fig. 10. The procedure for generalizing over (CFSs corresponding to) the holophrases learned during a series of language games for acquiring the Russian verb aspects.

- then *inducing* a rule construction from the generalized (via LUB) CFSs obtained above, this is a construction which when starting from the FORM ('pocita') gets the associated MEANING (read for-a-while) and vice-versa.

Here above it became evident an *advantage* that FCG light has over the FCG approach, due to the fact that we use a feature constraint logics as support: the LUB operation is a well known operation defined on feature structures with a well defined correspondent in feature logics.

Second, concerning Step 2 in the language game strategy outlined in Figure 9: Here we do not stick (strictly) to the 3-step learning scheme used by Gerasymova, inspired by [35], so to produce a syntactic rule, a mapping rule and a semantic rule. We use instead a two-step strategy for building a lexical entry *and* a lexical rule. This is common practice for the HPSGs that have been implemented in the LIGHT system. We mention that the lexical construction and the lexical rule produced in the *decompose* step in Figure 10 correspond respectively to the syntactic rule and (a slightly simplified version of) the composition result of the mapping rule and the semantic rule in [18].[20]

[20] We are not interested here in maintaining the relationship between what we automatically learn in FCG light and the learning schemata discussed in Tomasello's work, as it was done in Gerasymova's thesis for the following reason: while being useful for didactic presentation purposes, we consider it a rather too difficult and complex endeavor to be conveniently followed (as such) by autonomous learning robots.

A. By simply analyzing the association of *(prefix, event-type)* pairs associated to verbs during the language game, it can be inferred that:

not all verbs can get prefixed (with 'po'-like prepositions), therefore:

- to distinguish between those verbs that accept prefixes and those that don't, introduce a *new sort*, 'perfective', and
- add (it as the value of) a *new feature*, 'ASPECT' at the verb's SYN-CAT level:

  SYN-CAT top[ASPECT perfective];

B. By simply analyzing the values of the EVENT-TYPE feature for events corresponding to the verbs whose ASPECT is 'perfective' it follows that:

only events whose EVENT-TYPE value is different from 'ongoing' are associated (as meaning) to those verbs, therefore:

- invent a *new sort*, name it for instance 'non-ongoing', and
- add (it as the value of) a *new feature*, 'VIEW' at the verb's SEM-CAT level, for all perfective verbs, i.e. those that can be prefixed:

  SEM-CAT top[VIEW(#event) non-ongoing].

Fig. 11. The procedure for specializing over verbs while learning in FCG light the Russian verb aspects. Like in the generalization procedure, our approach is slightly different from the one presented in [18]. A couple of remarks could be added here, namely 1. for step *A*: the complementary sort to 'perfective' would be 'non-perfective', and 2. for step *B*: in the FCG light's sort hierarchy, the 'non-ongoing' sort will be the parent sort for all values taken by the EVENT-TYPE feature which are different from 'ongoing', as graphically illustrated in Figure 12.

The generalization procedure given in Figure 10 is a significantly revised version of the one in [18]. Concerning its application in the afore mentioned language game, the reader should note that due to the one-step rule decomposition (producing a 'syntactic' construction and a 'combined' rule), it is enough to use the AKTIONSART feature at the verb's SYN-CAT level. Further rule splitting/decomposition of the 'combined' rule is possible, and so a 'mapping' rule and a 'semantic' rule can be obtained (à la Tomasello).

After the work performed by the generalization procedure in Figure 10, a specialization task can be performed on constructions for prefixed verbs, as presented in Gerasymova's MS thesis [18].[21] This task, which consists of two steps, namely *A* and *B* in Figure 11, can be performed by alternative means compared to those used in [18]. We claim that in FCG light these means are simpler, more diverse and more naturally fitted into the framework.

Indeed, in OSF-logics it is easy to consider/introduce new sorts by generalizing/grouping some already existing sorts. This is for instance the case of 'non-ongoing' when learning Russian verb aspects, as implemented at Step *B* in Figure 11 and illustrated in Figure 12. Also, instead of introducing new features

[21] Alternatively, this specialization can be applied before generalization. In such a case it would work on syn-sem CFSs directly, not on the rules created afterwards based on these CFSs.

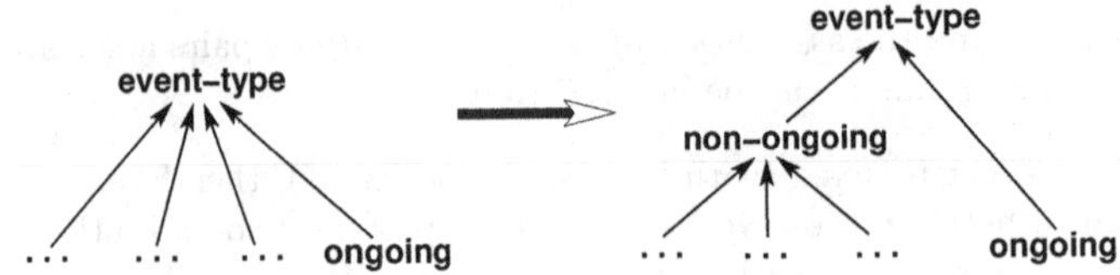

Fig. 12. Example of sort signature refinement in FCG light. Such a refinement can be commanded during the specialization procedure, see Figure 11

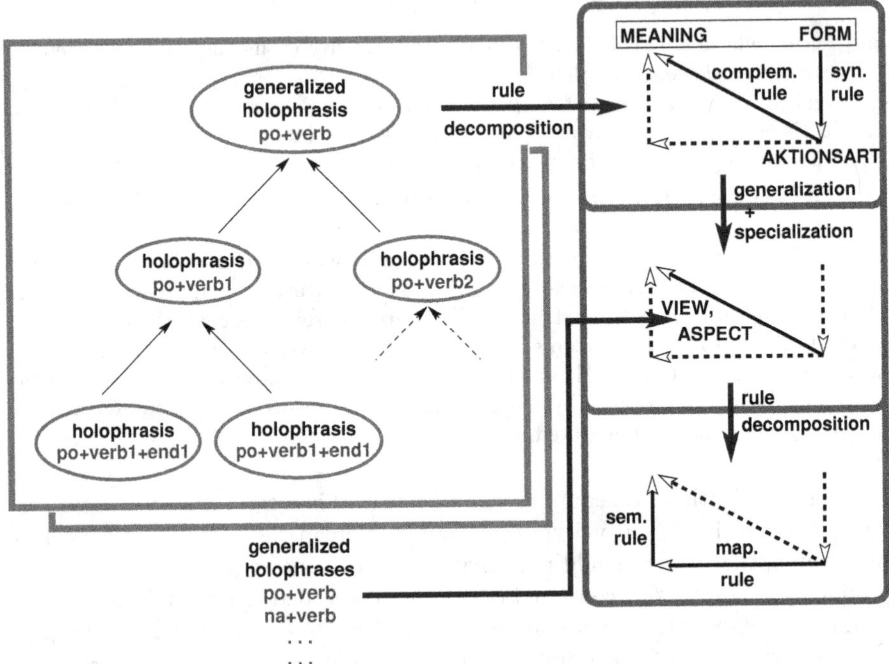

Fig. 13. An overview on grammar repairing, i.e. rule learning in FCG light, as done during the language game for acquiring the Russian verb aspects. For the rule composition scheme (acting on syntactic, mapping and semantic rules) please refer to [19].

— like ASPECT, at Step *A* in Figure 11 —, one could opt for redefining the sort hierarchy. In our example, we mean introducing the sort 'perfective-verb' as a subsort to the sort 'verb'.

After having presented the procedures that support the learning process (Figures 9-11), we add the *remark* that they make explicit a *heuristics* responsible for guiding the learning agent — based on *background* linguistics *knowledge* — to rightly choose a (certain) construction among the (possibly many) different ones which are situated in the lattice of rule versions between the *most specific* and the *most general* constructions that are compatible with the sentences to be learned in the current language game.

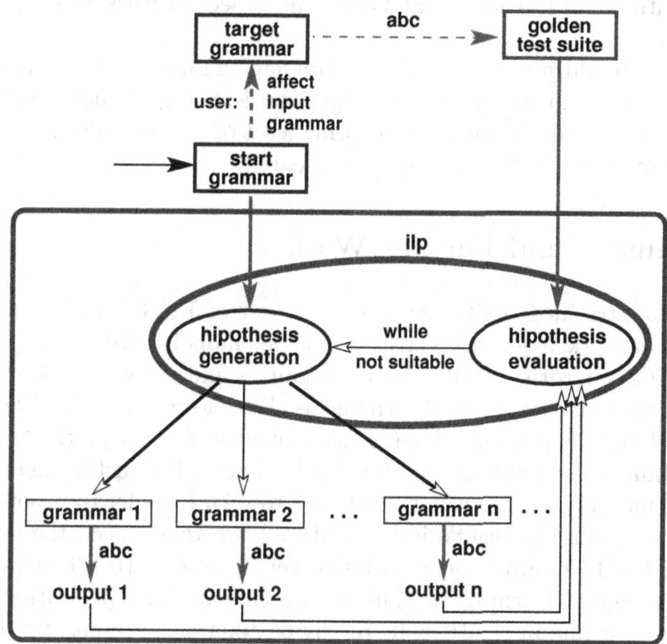

Fig. 14. The learning architecture of the ilpLIGHT extension/configuration of the LIGHTsystem. The **abc** and **ilp** modules are the parser and respectively the ILP-based learner components of LIGHT.

For Gerasymova's example, we could be formulate as follows the simple linguistic reason that supports the learning of the construction for the 'po-' lexical entry and the corresponding lexical rule via generalization on the 'pocital'-like holophrases (see Step 2 in Figure 9):

> Because 'po-' is a prefix morpheme inside the word 'pocital', the grammar learning process should concentrate on elaborating the relationship between the newly learned holophrasis and the already existing constructions or CFSs for the other two morphemes that compose that word, namely the verb root ('cita') and the ending ('-l'/'-la').

It turns out that this specific *relationship* can be identified by a *heuristics* that generalizes twice on the CFSs corresponding to learned holophrases, namely: firstly generalizing on the ending '-l'/'-la' (by simply using the LUB operation, see Step 1 in Figure 9), and secondly generalizing on the verb (followed by application of the rule decomposition procedure, see Figure 11). The "invention" of holophrasis constructions — starting from CFSs relating morphemes/words unknown to the learner to the meaning that the teacher points to — followed by rule creation is the essence of the grammar learning process during this language game. A synthesis of learning in FCG light the aspect of Russian verbs is shown in Figure 13.

Finally we should note that different language games in FCG and FCG light require different language strategies. Therefore learning in such a setup is not general-purpose. Defining and implementing a set of useful, wider-range learning strategies should be the focus of further research.

5 Conclusion and Further Work

This chapter introduces FCG light, a core subset of FCG, which is (re)defined using as framework a feature constraint logic, namely OSF-logic. The latter provides FCG light with a well-defined semantics and allows its clear comparison with other unification-based formalisms. We showed how FCG light can be implemented by using a simplified version of LIGHT — a platform on which HPSG grammars have previously been implemented. For further details on the actual implementation, the reader is referred to [27]. In order to proof-check the functionality of our FCG light's implementation we reproduced the experiment for learning the FCG grammar of Russian verb's aspects [18]. Instead of using reinforcement-based learning as done in the current implementation of FCG, we opted for learning in a lattice/hierarchy of different grammar versions. This lattice is naturally provided by the OSF-logic setup by exploiting the specialization/generalization relationship among grammars. Building on this experiment, in our recent paper [13] we have shown how to model in FCG a Slavic-based phenomenon present in a regional dialect of the Romanian language (more exactly, a certain verbal aspect), and how to model in FCG the transformation that presumably takes place in a child's brain when "learning over" that Slavic construction a Latin-rooted phrasal construction in modern Romanian.

Apart from our experiment and that of Gerasymova's, both using FCG for learning phenomena related to Slavic languages, there is already another one done for Polish [20].

We intend to apply such, and other, learning strategies to learn the clitic pronouns in the Romanian language, which is a rather difficult issue for non-native speakers. The result of the Romanian clitics' formation in FCG light could then be compared, for instance, to the HPSG description of these clitics as done in the Paola Monachesi's PhD thesis [23].

Also, inspired by the FCG approach to grammar learning, we are now able to suggest new ways for learning grammars in other unification-based formalisms. In particular, we aim to test these ideas on ilpLIGHT [8]. This is an extension/configuration of the LIGHT system which adapted the learning paradigm of Inductive Logic Programming (ILP, [24]) so as to work with HPSG-like unification grammars.

In ilpLIGHT, the learning process — also based on searching in a lattice of grammar versions, as in FCG light — is done in *off-line*/batch mode, by using a "golden" test suite given to the learner by the supervisor/teacher.[22] For the learning architecture of ilpLIGHT, the reader is referred to Figure 14. [11] has demonstrated that it is possible to induce each of three basic HPSG principles — the head principle, the subcategorization principle and the saturation principle, as presented by [25] — given that the grammar contains the other two principles and a simply annotated test suite is provided.

We suggest that ilpLIGHT can be substantially improved by using certain ideas borrowed from FCG:

- instead of using a given "golden" test suite (on which parsing is performed and against which the progress of grammar learning is checked), this test suite can be dynamically produced during the language game played by two agents;
- the grammar learning process can be "grounded", something which, up to our knowledge, was not considered before for HPSGs;
- new rules can be learned by generalizing upon several already learned rules, instead of simply modifying one or at most two rules, as is currently done in ilpLIGHT, thus constituting a significant step forward.

Upgrading the ilpLIGHT system so to do parsing and production with SBCG grammars [26] would further enhance the possibilities to compare FCG with other construction-based systems.

Acknowledgements. This work has been done in the framework of the European FP7 research project "ALEAR" and its sister project "ALEAR 37EU" funded by the Romanian Ministry of Education and Research". The authors wish to thank Joachim De Beule and Kateryna Gerasymova for their useful comments on an earlier draft of this chapter.

References

[1] Aït-Kaci, H., Podelski, A., Goldstein, S.: Order-sorted feature theory unification. Journal of Logic, Language and Information 30, 99–124 (1997)

[2] Aït-Kaci, H., Di Cosmo, R.: Compiling order-sorted feature term unification. Tech. rep., Digital Paris Research Laboratory (1993), pRL Technical Note 7

[3] Aït-Kaci, H., Podelski, A.: Towards a meaning of LIFE. Journal of Logic Programming 16, 195–234 (1993)

[4] Bleys, J., Stadler, K., De Beule, J.: Search in linguistic processing. In: Steels, L. (ed.) Design Patterns in Fluid Construction Grammar. John Benjamins, Amsterdam (2011)

[5] Carpenter, B.: The Logic of Typed Feature Structures – with applications to unification grammars, logic programs and constraint resolution. Cambridge University Press (1992)

[22] The test suite is a set of sentences with associated parsing trees and eventually other informations.

[6] Chang, N., De Beule, J., Micelli, V.: Computational Construction Grammar: Comparing ECG and FCG. In: Steels, L. (ed.) Computational Issues in FCG. LNCS (LNAI), vol. 7249, pp. 259–288. Springer, Heidelberg (2012)
[7] Ciortuz, L.: Expanding feature-based constraint grammars: Experience on a large-scale HPSG grammar for English. In: Proceedings of the IJCAI 2001 co-located Workshop on Modelling and Solving Problems with Constraints, Seattle, USA (2001)
[8] Ciortuz, L.: A Framework for Inductive Learning of Typed-Unification Grammars. In: Adriaans, P.W., Fernau, H., van Zaanen, M. (eds.) ICGI 2002. LNCS (LNAI), vol. 2484, pp. 299–301. Springer, Heidelberg (2002)
[9] Ciortuz, L.: LIGHT — A Constraint Language and Compiler System for Typed-Unification Grammars. In: Jarke, M., Koehler, J., Lakemeyer, G. (eds.) KI 2002. LNCS (LNAI), vol. 2479, pp. 3–17. Springer, Heidelberg (2002)
[10] Ciortuz, L.: LIGHT AM – Another abstract machine for feature structure unification. In: Oepen, S., Flickinger, D., Tsujii, J., Uszkoreit, H. (eds.) Efficiency in Unification-based Processing, pp. 167–194. CSLI Publications, The Center for the Study of Language and Information, Stanford University (2002)
[11] Ciortuz, L.: Inductive learning of attribute path values in typed-unification grammars. Scientific Annals of the "Al.I. Cuza", University of Iasi, Romania. Computer Science Series, pp. 105–125 (2003)
[12] Ciortuz, L.: Parsing with Unification-Based Grammars — The LIGHT Compiler. EditDan Press, Iasi (2004)
[13] Ciortuz, L., Saveluc, V.: Learning to unlearn in lattices of concepts: A case study in Fluid Construction Grammars. In: Proceedings of SYNASC 2011, pp. 160–167. IEEE Computer Society, Timişoara (2011)
[14] De Beule, J.: A Formal Deconstruction of Fluid Construction Grammar. In: Steels, L. (ed.) Computational Issues in FCG. LNCS (LNAI), vol. 7249, pp. 215–238. Springer, Heidelberg (2012)
[15] De Beule, J., Steels, L.: Hierarchy in Fluid Construction Grammars. In: Furbach, U. (ed.) KI 2005. LNCS (LNAI), vol. 3698, pp. 1–15. Springer, Heidelberg (2005)
[16] Fernando, C.: Fluid Construction Grammar in the Brain. In: Steels, L. (ed.) Computational Issues in FCG. LNCS (LNAI), vol. 7249, pp. 312–330. Springer, Heidelberg (2012)
[17] Flickinger, D., Copestake, A., Sag, I.A.: HPSG analysis of English. In: Wahlster, W. (ed.) Verbmobil: Foundations of Speech-to-Speech Translation. Artificial Intelligence, pp. 254–263. Springer (2000)
[18] Gerasymova, K.: Acquisition of aspectual grammar in artificial systems through language games, Humboldt Universitaet zu Berlin, Germany, MS thesis (2009)
[19] Gerasymova, K.: Expressing Grammatical Meaning with Morphology: A Case Study for Russian Aspect. In: Steels, L. (ed.) Computational Issues in FCG. LNCS (LNAI), vol. 7249, pp. 91–122. Springer, Heidelberg (2012)
[20] Höfer, S.: Complex Declension Systems and Morphology in Fluid Construction Grammar: A Case Study of Polish. In: Steels, L. (ed.) Computational Issues in FCG. LNCS (LNAI), vol. 7249, pp. 143–177. Springer, Heidelberg (2012)
[21] Kifer, M., Lausen, G., Wu, J.: A logical foundation of object-oriented and frame-based languages. Journal of the ACM 42(4), 741–843 (1995)
[22] Mitchell, T.M.: Machine Learning. McGraw-Hill, New York (1997)
[23] Monachesi, P.: A grammar of Italian clitics. Ph.D. thesis, Tilburg University, iTK Dissertation Series 1995-3 and TILDIL Dissertation Series 1995-3 (1995)
[24] Muggleton, S., De Raedt, L.: Inductive logic programming: Theory and methods. Journal of Logic Programming 19(20), 629–679 (1994)

[25] Pollard, C., Sag, I.A.: Head-driven Phrase Structure Grammar. CSLI Publications, Stanford (1994)

[26] Sag, I.A.: Sign-Based Construction Grammar: An informal synopsis. In: Boas, H., Sag, I.A. (eds.) Sign-Based Construction Grammar. CSLI Publications, The Center for the Study of Language and Information, Stanford University (2010) (Version of August 23, 2010)

[27] Saveluc, V., Ciortuz, L.: FCGlight, a system for studying the evolution of natural language. In: Proceedings of SYNASC 2010, pp. 188–193. IEEE Computer Society, Timişoara (2010)

[28] Shieber, S.M., Schabes, Y., Pereira, F.: Principles and implementation of deductive parsing. Journal of Logic Programming, 3–36 (1995)

[29] Santibáñez, J.S.: A Logic Programming Approach to Parsing and Production in Fluid Construction Grammar. In: Steels, L. (ed.) Computational Issues in FCG. LNCS (LNAI), vol. 7249, pp. 239–255. Springer, Heidelberg (2012)

[30] Sikkel, K.: Parsing Schemata. Springer (1997)

[31] Smolka, G.: Feature-constraint logics for unification grammars. Journal of Logic Programming 12, 51–87 (1992)

[32] Steels, L.: A first encounter with Fluid Construction Grammar. In: Steels, L. (ed.) Design Patterns in Fluid Construction Grammar. John Benjamins, Amsterdam (2011)

[33] Steels, L., De Beule, J.: A (very) brief introduction to Fluid Construction Grammar. In: ScaNaLU 2006: Proceedings of the Third Workshop on Scalable Natural Language Understanding, pp. 73–80. Association for Computational Linguistics, Morristown (2006)

[34] Steels, L., De Beule, J.: Unify and Merge in Fluid Construction Grammar. In: Vogt, P., Sugita, Y., Tuci, E., Nehaniv, C.L. (eds.) EELC 2006. LNCS (LNAI), vol. 4211, pp. 197–223. Springer, Heidelberg (2006)

[35] Tomasello, M.: Construction grammar for kids. Constructions (2007)

Fluid Construction Grammar in the Brain

Chrisantha Fernando[1,2]

[1] School of Electronic Engineering and Computer Science, Queen Mary University of London, UK

[2] Department of Informatics, University of Sussex, Falmer, Brighton, UK

Abstract. I propose how symbols in the brain could be implemented as spatiotemporal patterns of spikes. A neuron implements a re-write rule; firing when it observes a particular symbol and writing a particular symbol back to the neuronal circuit. Then I show how an input/output function mapped by a neuron can be copied. This permits a population of neuron-based rules to evolve in the brain. We are still very far from understanding how FCG could be implemented in the brain; however, understanding how a basic physical symbol system could be instantiated is a foundation for further work.

1 Introduction

Fluid Construction Grammar is a formalism for defining and operationalizing the highly complex symbolic operations that occur in language processing [11, 53, 55, 57]. The implementations of FCG made so far are all carried out through symbolic programming languages, mostly in LISP but also in PROLOG (as discussed in other chapters of this volume [54]). How can the brain do Fluid Construction Grammar (FCG)? Constructions are rules that act on structured symbolic representations. To implement FCG the brain would need to implement a physical symbol system (PSS) [21]. Therefore my aim is to discuss the validity or otherwise of a PSS and how it can be implemented. So far I have not been able to propose any plausible neuronal mechanisms capable of the more complex matching and merging operations required by FCG. However, I am able to hypothesize neuronal implementations of symbolic re-write rules [16], to show at an algorithmic level how these rules could be evolved in the brain to develop syntactic conventions [15], and to then show at an implementation level how such rules could replicate in neuronal tissue.

My approach rests on two novelties. The first is the recent formulation of polychronous computing [31, 34], i.e. computing on the basis of spike patterns. This suggests a neural substrate for symbol structures [16]. The second is the neural replicator hypothesis proposed by Eörs Szathmáry and myself that suggests that rules operating on such symbols could be units of evolution in the brain [43]. We hypothesise that constructions of FCG replicate in the brain and evolve using a kind of neurally implemented learning classifier system [15].

Historically, purely symbolic architectures whilst in principle endlessly expressive, in practice have been hard to train, e.g. SOAR [24]. The FCG is no

L. Steels (Ed.): Computational Issues in FCG, LNAI 7249, pp. 312–330, 2012.

exception. Why is this? I suggest that it is because a grounding of FCG in lower level perceptual mechanisms is needed. This would allow local synaptic learning rules to become available to the symbolic learning system. For example, it is conceivable that a symbolic system would be able to exapt (re-use for a different function) visual and auditory shift-invariant pattern recognition mechanisms for the matching operation of FCG [37, 58]. Alternatively, it is possible that hierarchical predictive model building mechanisms originally formulated in visual perception could be re-used to construct conceptual categories [49], or that mechanisms for causal learning could be used to learn causal dependencies between symbol tokens, e.g syntactic regularities [44]. So far, such links have been poorly explored. To some extent this is because of a sociological divide between the symbolic and the connectionist factions in cognitive science [21, 23]. To help to bridge this divide it is useful to consider how chemical information is symbolic in a sense, and to realize that symbolic computation takes place in the biochemical systems of cells.

2 A Chemical Symbol System

Chemical machines, or in other words fluid automata [22] are constructed from interacting chemicals. Chemistry can be usefully thought of as containing a kind of physical symbol system. These chemical machines are very far from serial Turing machines at the implementation level, although they may well be Turing complete at the computational level [39]. An archetypical example of such a chemical machine is a cell.

What are molecules? They are objects composed of atoms that have specific structural relationships between them. A molecule is assembled according to a combinatorial syntax, i.e. a set of chemical structural constraints such as valance, charge, etc... that determine how atoms can legally join together to make the molecule. Combinatorial semantics determine how a molecule with a particular structure will react or behave in a given environment. So, semantic content in the case of the chemical symbol structure equates to chemical function, or in other words reactivity. The function of a molecule is itself a function of the semantic content of its parts, e.g. the reactivity of a benzene ring is modified by side-groups such as methyl groups. The physical symbols and their structural properties cause the system behaviour.

Note that a chemical system, whilst consisting of molecules that are symbol structures, operates in parallel (rather than in series). It is constrained by kinetic and other dynamic aspects. It is subject to non-encoded (implicit) influences such as temperature. All these aspects were not aspects which naturally came into the picture when thinking about physical symbol systems, but they do enter when considering chemical symbol systems. For good example of a symbolically specified computation in chemistry is a chemical clock. The two coupled autocatalytic cycles of the BZ reaction constitute a fluid automaton that implements a chemical clock [2, 22]. Whilst it is the symbolic (as defined above) organization of its molecules that specifies the reaction network topology, it is by the analog operation of the assembled reaction network that the clock like phenomena of the BZ reaction arises.

The properties of atoms and molecules described above give chemistry a very special set of macroscopic characteristics. For example, chemistry is **productive**. The capacity for chemical reactivity is unlimited, i.e. there are many more possible reactions than could be implemented in any realistically sized system. Indefinitely many molecules can be produced allowing indefinitely many reactions. This is possible with only a finite set of distinct atomic types. Therefore, an unbounded set of chemical structures must be composite molecules. In the same way, an indefinite number of propositions can be entertained, or sentences spoken. This is known as the productivity of thought and language, Therefore if neural symbols exist, they must have the same capacity for being combined in unlimited ways. This is not merely a crude analogy. No non-human animal has the capacity for productive thought [45].

Secondly, chemistry is **systematic**; the capacity for atoms to be combined in certain ways to produce some molecules is intrinsically connected to their ability to produce others. Consider how a chemist might learn chemistry. There are rules of thumb that help a chemist to guess how a molecule will react based on its structure. A chemist does not learn just a list of valid reactions. In the same way, there is systematicity in language, e.g. the ability to produce or understand a sentence is intrinsically connected with the ability to produce and understand other sentences. Languages aren't learned by learning a phrasebook. Languages have syntax.

Thirdly, the same atom makes approximately the same contribution to each molecule in which it occurs. For example, the contribution of hydrogen to a water molecule is to affect all sorts of properties of the reactivity of that molecule. For example, hydrogen atoms have reducing power (i.e. they suck electrons) wherever they bind in a molecule and this effect is a property of the hydrogen atom itself. This means that there is systematicity in reactivity (semantics) as well as in structure (syntax). This is known as **compositionality**. In the same way, lexical items in sentences have approximately the same contribution to each expression in which they occur. This approximate nature suggests that there is a more fundamental set of 'atoms' in language than words themselves.

Let us also consider briefly why the idea of a chemical symbol system was entertained in chemistry, that is, why scientists first came to believe in discrete atoms coming together systematically to form molecules. The crucial discoveries were of the *systematic* nature of chemistry. In Hudson's "The History of Chemistry" he describes the following discoveries [28]. Lavoisier discovered a systematic relationship in chemical reactions, i.e. the conservation of mass. Proust discovered the law of definite proportions, i.e. that compounds when broken down, produce constituents in fixed proportions. Dalton extended this to the law of multiple proportions that explained that when two elements came together to form different compounds (notably the oxides of metals), they would come together in different small integer proportions [28]. These results could elegantly be explained by an atomic theory. We see that there are analogous reasons to believe in symbols in the brain, based on an examination of the properties of human thought and language.

However, there are *extra* properties required of the PSS in cognition compared to the PSS in chemistry. Cognition includes the capacity to *learn* an appropriate PSS, not just to implement a PSS. Children can learn and manipulate explicit rules [10, 36] which implies the existence of a neural physical symbol system capable of forming structured representations and learning rules for operating on these representations [41][1].

The following is a concise definition of a symbol system adapted from Harnad to emphasize the chemical aspects [26]. A symbol system contains a set of arbitrary **atoms (or physical tokens)** that are manipulated on the basis of "**explicit rules**" that are likewise physical tokens or strings (or more complex structures, e.g. graphs or trees) consisting of such physical tokens. The explicit rules of chemistry generate reactions from the structure of atoms and molecules (plus some implicit effects, e.g. temperature). The rule-governed symbol-token manipulation is based purely on the shape of the symbol tokens (not their "meaning"), i.e., it is **purely syntactic**, and consists of "rulefully combining" and recombining symbol tokens, in chemical reactions. There are primitive atomic symbol tokens and **composite symbol-token strings (molecules)**. The entire system and all its parts – the atomic tokens, the composite tokens, the syntactic manipulations both actual and possible and the rules – are all "**semantically interpretable**:" The syntax can be systematically assigned a meaning e.g., as standing for objects or as describing states of affairs [26]. For example, semantic interpretation in chemistry means that the chemical system exhibits chemical reactivity, and in biochemistry it means that the intra-cellular chemical system stands for states of affairs in the environment outside the cell, for example the conformation of a signaling molecule may *represent* the glucose concentration

[1] Gary Marcus has shown that 7 month old infants can distinguish between sound patterns of the form ABA versus ABB, where A and B can consist of different sounds e.g. "foo", "baa" etc. Crucially, these children can generalize this discrimination capacity to new sounds that they have never heard before, as long as they are of the form ABA or ABB. Marcus claims that performance in this task requires that the child must extract "abstract algebra-like rules that represent relationships between placeholders (variables), such as "the first item X is the same as the third item Y", or more generally that "item I is the same as item J" [42]. Several attempts have been made to explain the performance of these children without a PSS (e.g. using connectionist models) [50] but Marcus has criticized these as smuggling in symbolic rules in one way or another by design [41, p.70]. For Marcus it seems that the system *itself* must discover the general rule. In summary, the problem with a large set of connectionist learning devices is that a regularity learned in one component of the solution representation is not applied/generalized effectively to another part [41]. Marcus calls this the problem of *training independence* [42]. Marcus considers this one of the fundamental requirements for a learning system to be described as symbolic or rule based, and I agree.

outside the cell. In the same way a neural symbol system exhibits behavior such as the child's capacity to distinguish ABA from ABB in grammar learning tasks. This chemical formulation may not seem of benefit, and may even be confusing to linguists, but it certainly helps me to link these two domains of computation, the biochemical and the cognitive, and this allows one to consider a new range of computations.

3 A Neural Physical Symbol System

In this section I present the outline of a neural framework for arbitrary physical tokens (atoms) arranged into molecules or symbol structures. I show how they can undergo explicit rule-governed symbol-token manipulation (reactions). Finally I show how these explicit rule sets can be learned.

In a recent paper [16] we simulated a network of cortical spiking neurons [30, 32] with synaptic weight dynamics governed by spike-time-dependent plasticity (STDP). STDP is an empirically observed process by which synaptic weights change as a function of the timing of pre- and post-synaptic spike activity. If a pre-synaptic spike reaches the post-synaptic neuron *before* the post-synaptic neuron fires, then the strength of that synapse will increase. However, if a pre-synaptic spike reaches a post-synaptic neuron *after* that post-synaptic neuron fires, then the synaptic strength will decrease. This implements a kind of causality detector. If the pre-synaptic neuron *caused* the post-synaptic neuron to fire, the synaptic strength will increase. When the extent of STDP is modulated by a reward molecule such as dopamine, it is possible to solve reinforcement learning tasks [32].

Consider first a possible neural representation of an atomic symbol token, see Figure 1. At the top we see four examples of symbol-tokens consisting of spatiotemporal patterns of spikes. The y-axis indicates which neuron the spike will stimulate, and the x-axis indicates the axons down which the spikes are passing from left to right. Thus, the depiction of the (purple) spatiotemporal pattern on the left indicates that the middle neuron is stimulated 10ms later than the top and bottom neurons (because the spikes have travelled further to the right in the top and bottom axons than the spike on the middle axon). The remainder of the figure shows the consequences of stimulating a chain of neural connections with this spike pattern in the top left box. Each chain consists of three synapses in series. There are three chains. The chain is activated by asynchronously stimulating the first three neurons on the left of the chain. That is, the top and bottom neurons are stimulated first, and then 10ms later the middle neuron is simulated. The spikes will then flow down the axons of the chain (from left to right) asynchronously activating the second and third layer neurons. It is this spatiotemporal pattern of spikes that we define as an atomic neural symbol-token. The diagram shows that detector neurons at various locations along the chain can detect this spatiotemporal spike pattern if the axonal delays from the pre-synaptic neuron to the detector neuron are properly matched to the spatiotemporal pattern such that depolarization reaches the detector neuron body

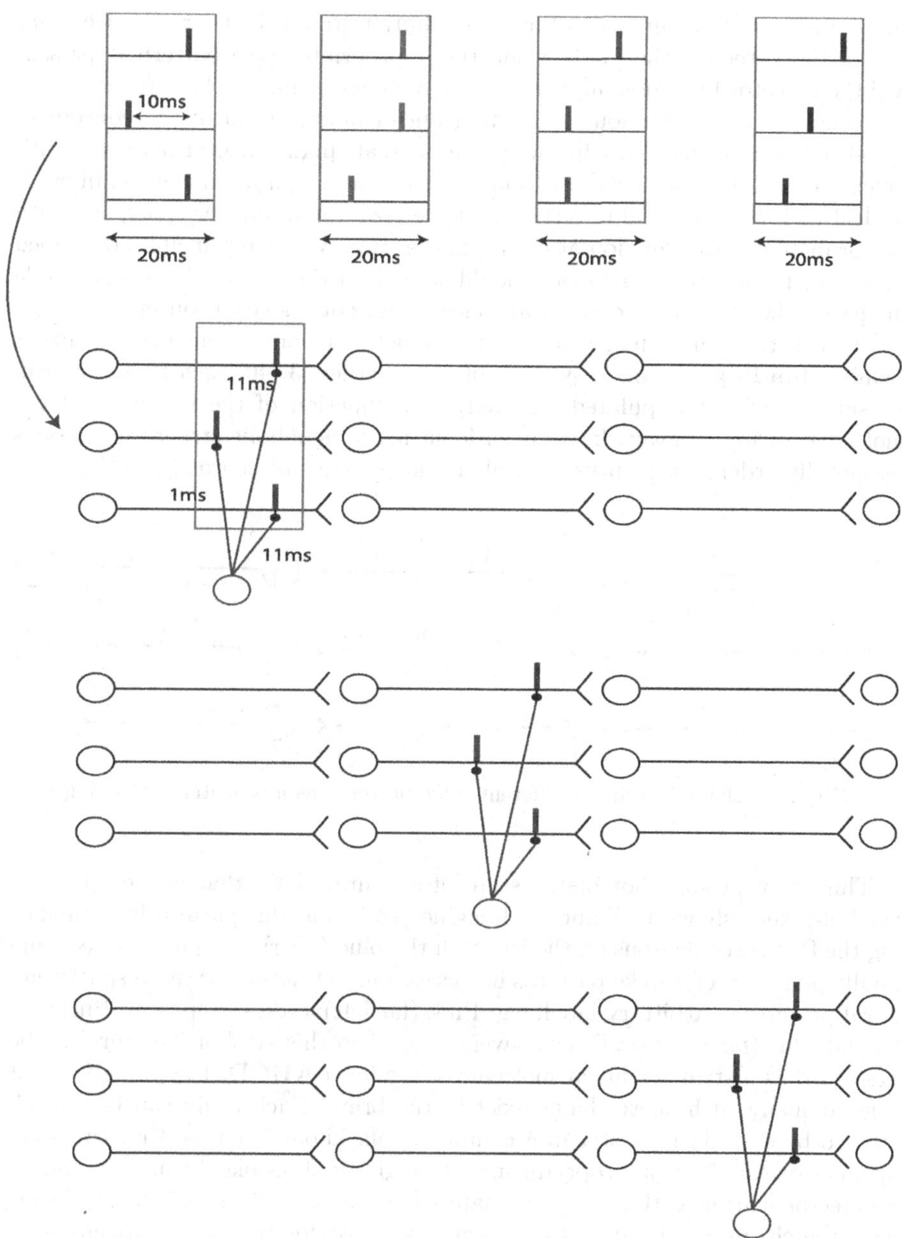

Fig. 1. Four possible spatiotemporal spike pattern based symbol-tokens are shown at the top. Below one of these spike patterns is injected into a chain of neurons running from left to right (three synaptic layers are shown). From top to bottom we see three snapshots over time as this injected symbol-tokens passes from left to right along a chain of parallel axons. Three possible detector neuron sites are shown in purple. The detector neurons inputs are arranged with a set of delays such that all three spikes reach the body of the detector neuron at the same time.

simultaneously. If a summed voltage contribution from each neuron is necessary to fire the detector, then only when the appropriate spike pattern is present will the detector fire. This implementation of neural symbol-tokens (atoms) uses the concept of polychronous computing and a modification of the concept of wavefront computing [33, 34]. Of course, in real spiking neural networks with much noise, it may be necessary to use a much larger spatial dimension in order to deal with the temporal uncertainty of the position of any one spike, and with low probability transmission at each synapse. However, the principles described here remain unchanged. Also, one should not expect the chain to be neatly visible in space. The chain is a topological concept and not a spatial concept.

The construction of molecular symbol structures from atomic symbol-tokens requires **binding** of atomic symbol-tokens together [3, 40] such that they can be subsequently manipulated (reacted) as a function of the structure of the molecule. In my framework, compositional neural symbolic structures exist as temporally ordered sequences of symbols along chains of neurons, see Figure 2.

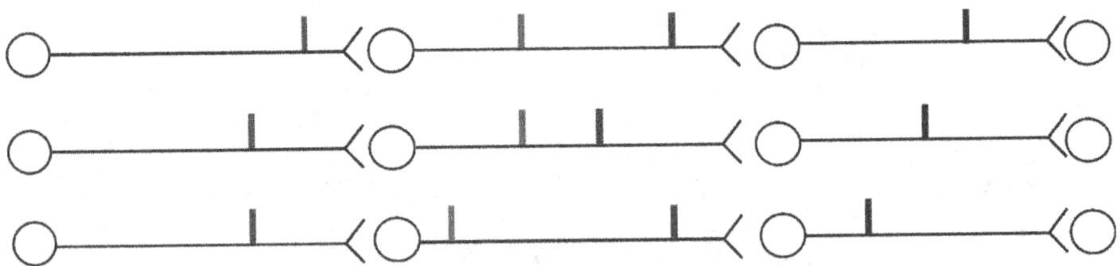

Fig. 2. A chain carrying 4 different spike patterns as a concatenated string

This shows a snapshot of the state of a neural chain that carries the four symbol-tokens shown in Figure 1. Imagine producing this pattern by stimulating the first three neurons on the left with the blue (far right), purple, green and finally pink (far left) spike patterns in succession. Let us allocate each spatiotemporal pattern an arbitrary label, e.g. Pink (far left) = A, Green = B, Purple = C, and Blue (far right) = D for convenience. Then this symbol-structure can be described as a string or linear molecule of the form **ABCD**. I hypothesize that a great many such short chains exist in the brain. Each chain can be considered to be a kind of register in a computer, blackboard or tape that can store symbol-tokens of the appropriate size. A single symbol-token could be read by a detector neuron with the appropriate axonal delay pattern when interfacing with the chain. Similar detector neurons can exist for the symbol-tokens A, B and D and as many others as the spatial width of the chain and the temporal resolution of the neuronal detector allows.

Thus, I envisage a potentially large parallel symbol system in the brain consisting of a *population* of such chains, each capable of storing a set of symbol-token strings and operating on these strings in parallel. Interaction between (and within) such chains constitutes the operations of symbol-manipulation. Returning to the chemical metaphor, such interactions can be thought of as chemical reactions between molecules contained on separate chains, and rearrangements within a molecule expressed on the same chain. Whilst in a sense a chain can be thought of as a tape in a Turing machine (due to the serial nature of the strings), it also can be thought of as a single molecule in a chemical system (due to the existence of multiple parallel chains). This constitutes the core representational substrate on which symbol manipulation will act. The reactivity of symbol structures on these chains is described in the next Section.

A fundamental operation on a symbol token is to replace it with another symbol-token, or simply to transform it in some way, see Figure 3. The network figure shows a chain, again of three neurons width. Receiving input from the chain and writing activity back into the chain is done by a detector neuron with specific input and output delays in relation to the chain. A detector neuron (blue, bottom) only fires when the correct pattern of input is detected (as described above). In this case, the neuron's input delays are set so that it recognizes (fires for) patterns only of type D.

In the experiment the pattern of stimulation was given shown in Figure 3B. The spike raster plot and the voltage plot (Figure 3C) show two spatiotemporal patterns input to the input neurons, input pattern 1 and input pattern 2. These both fail to make the classifier neuron fire. It can be seen that in this case where the classifier fails to fire, the same pattern enters the chain as leaves the chain. This is because the spatiotemporal organization of these patterns does not match the spatiotemporal tuning curve of the detector neuron. Only when the third spatiotemporal spike pattern is input does the detector neuron fire. Once fired, the output of the detector neuron is injected back to the neurons of the chain. If the output of the detector neuron slightly precedes the normal passage of the untransformed pattern through the chain, then the refractory period of the output neurons of the chain prevents interference by the original untransformed pattern, which is thereby replaced by the new pattern specified by the detector neuron. Such a detector neuron we will now call a classifier neuron because it is a simple context free re-write rule with a condition (detection) *and* an action pole of the type seen in Learning Classifier Systems (LCS) [27].

It can be seen that such classifier neurons are selective filters, i.e. the classifier neuron is only activated if the spatiotemporal pattern is sufficiently **matched** with the axonel delays afferent upon the neuron. The above classifier implements an implicit rule. An implicit rule is a rule that operates on atomic or molecular symbol structures *without* being specified (encoded/determined/controlled) by a symbol structure itself. There is no way that a change in the symbol system, i.e. the set of symbols in the population of chains, could modify this implicit matching rule. The implicit rule is specified external to the symbol system. Whenever the symbol D passes along this chain, it will be replaced by the new symbol, irrespective of the presence of other symbols in the system.

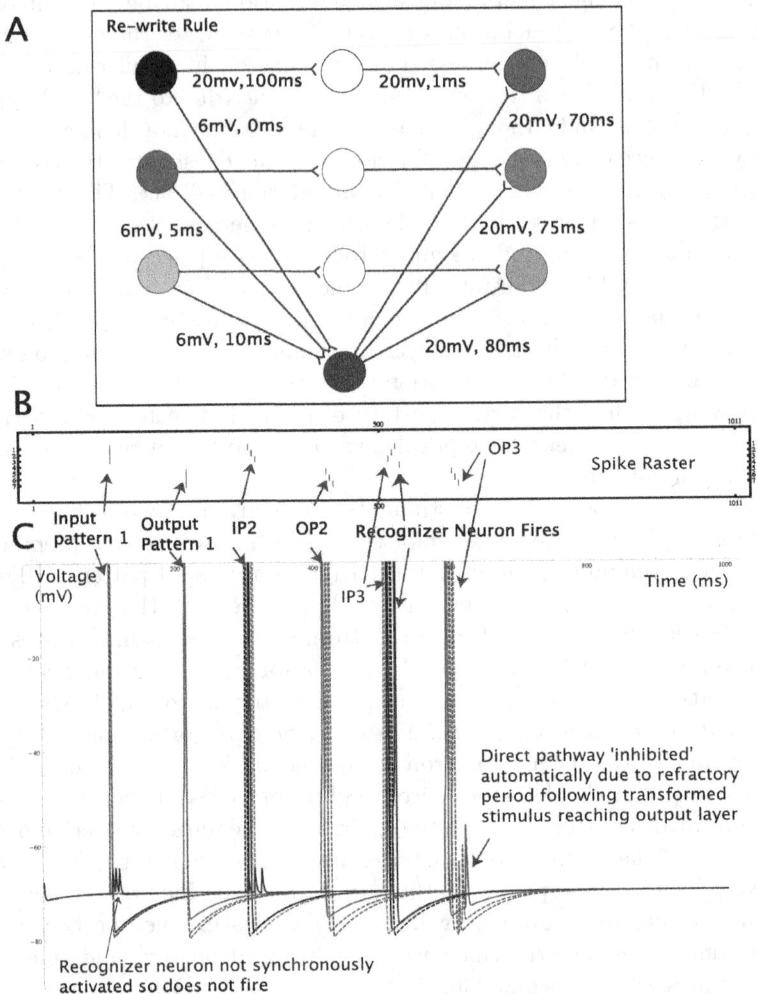

Fig. 3. The above circuit implements a context-free re-write rule. There are three input channels in this case, although it is trivial to add more. The direct pathway is by a delay line via an intermediate layer. The indirect pathway to the outputs is via a classifier neuron (blue, bottom). Only if the delays match the inter-spike interval of the input spike ensemble does the recognizer fire. Once fired, it sends signals down outputs with delays that are set so that the desired output pattern is produced. **Part B.** A spike raster showing the 3 input patterns and 3 output patterns produced in an experiment. Patterns that do not match the re-write rule pass through the classifier neuron, but those that do match the re-write rule are converted, and the passage through by the original pattern is inhibited due to the refractory period of the output neurons (see **Part C** which shows the voltages of input, output and classifier neuron). Also it is possible to explicitly inhibit the passage of the original input, but this is not needed here.

In a symbol system (as in chemistry), symbols are manipulated (partly) on the basis of "**explicit rules**" [2]. This means that the operations or reactivity of symbols depends on/is controlled by/is causally influenced by their syntactic and semantic relationship to other symbols within the symbol-structure and between symbol structures. Figure 3 above showed a classifier neuron implementing an implicit rule. This rule was not controlled by any symbols in the system; it merely operated on symbols in the system. Figure 4 below shows a classifier neuron and an inhibitory gating neuron can implement an explicit rule within our framework.

The classifier and chain shown in Figure 3 is simply modified to include an inhibitory gating unit that must receive a particular pattern of spikes (T for trigger) in order for it to become active. The simplest relation is where T immediately precedes X. Only when this is the case will the classifier neuron be disinhibited. Only when the classifier neuron is disinhibited will X be converted to Y. Otherwise X will pass through an inactive classifier (as will all other symbols). This is formally a context-sensitive re-write rule. The rule is called context sensitive because the conversion of X to Y depends on the relation of X to another contextual symbol T. A set of context-sensitive re-write rules is capable of generating a grammar of spike-patterns. Consider starting the system off with a single symbol-token S. Probabalistic application of the rules to the initial symbol S would result in the systematic production of spike patterns consisting of grammatically correct context-sensitive spike pattern based sentences. A major implementation issue in real neuronal tissue would be the fidelity of transmission of spatiotemporal spike patterns. The information capacity of such a channel may fall off with decreasing fidelity of copying in that channel in a manner analogous to Eigen's error catastrophe in genetic evolution [14].

However, the system so far described could not easily implement the kind of rule that Marcus wishes a symbol-manipulation system to learn, namely to extract "abstract algebra-like rules that represent relationships between placeholders (variables), such as 'the first item X is the same as the third item Y', or more generally that 'item I is the same as item J"' [42]. This kind of rule requires hash symbols which implement the concept of same and different, namely, If $\#_1\#\#_1$ then S, Else If $\#_2\#\#_1$ then D. That is, if the first and last string are the same,

[2] Quoting [26, p.335]: "Wittgenstein (1953) emphasized the difference between explicit and implicit rules: It is not the same thing to 'follow' a rule (explicitly) and merely to behave 'in accordance with' a rule (implicitly). The critical difference [between an implicit and explicit rule] is in the **compositeness** (7) and **systematicity** (8) criteria. The explicitly represented symbolic rule is part of a formal system, it is decomposable (unless primitive), its application and manipulation is purely formal (syntactic, shape-dependent), and the entire system must be semantically interpretable, not just the chunk in question. An isolated ('modular') chunk cannot be symbolic; being symbolic is a systematic property... For systematicity it must be possible to combine and recombine entities rulefully into propositions that can be semantically interpreted... It is possible to devise machines whose function is the transformation of symbols, and whose operation are sensitive to the syntactical structure of the symbols that they operate upon."

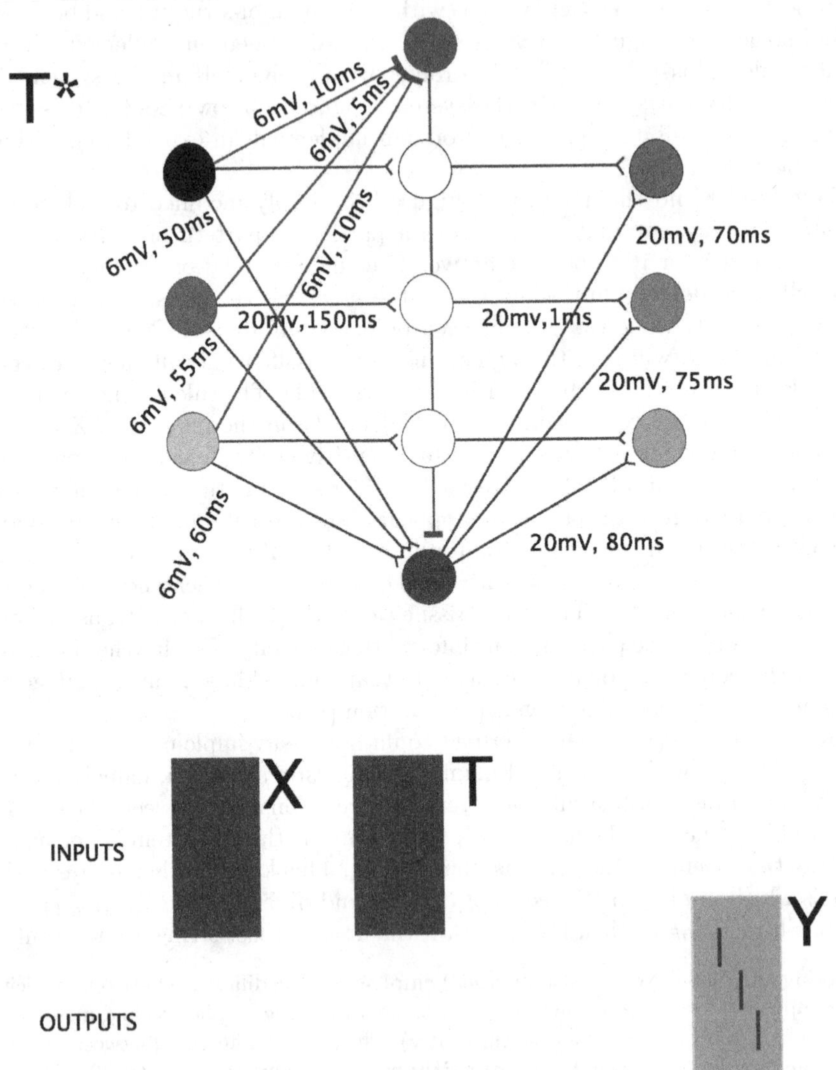

Fig. 4. An explicit rule implemented by a classifier neuron and an inhibitory gating neuron. The classifier neuron (blue, bottom) only fires if it is disinhibited by the neuron at the top (red). This occurs only if T preceeds X as these spike patterns pass down the chain from left to right. If T preceeds X, then X is converted into Y.

write S = same, and if the first and last strings are different write D = different. In the absence of hash symbols of this type, a classifier system would have to learn all the explicit rules for each possible pair of symbols at the first and last position, instead of learning the general rule. Both systems would be systematic, however, the system with hashes would allow a more concise specification of the same level of systematicity, and may be easier to learn. But how can such hashes be implemented within my framework? One method for obtaining hashes is that a classifier neuron contains many delay lines from one channel so that it fires for a range of spike delays along that channel. Another is that it is sufficient for a classifier to be activated by only a subset of the spatiotemporal components of a symbol-token. Another possibility for implementing a same/different rule is shown in Figure 5.

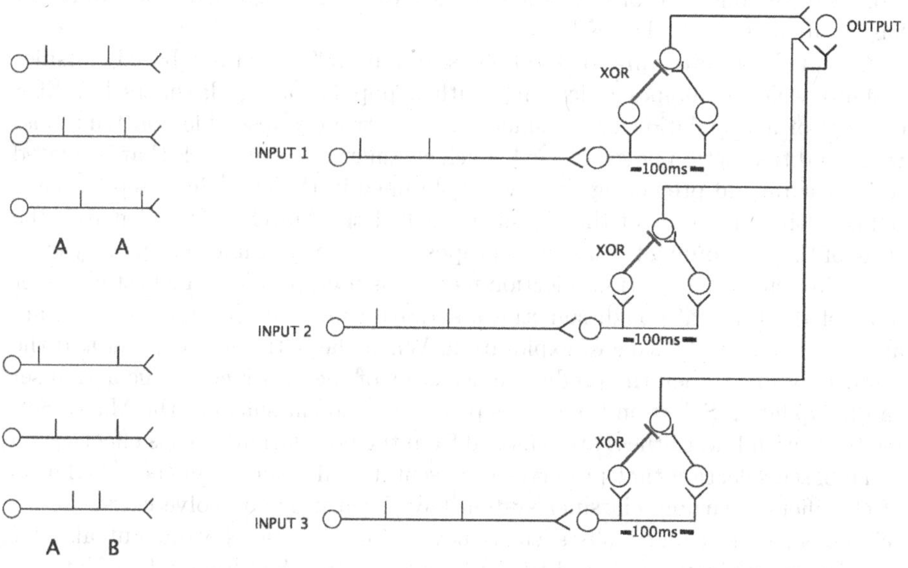

Fig. 5. A method for detecting whether successive symbol-tokens are the same or different (Left) Two pairs of sequentially presented symbols, AA and AB are shown (Right). A device that is capable of identifying consecutive symbol pairs that are different, using three XOR circuits in parallel.

On the left, the figure shows two pairs of sequentially presented symbols flowing down two reaction chains, in this case, AA on the top chain and AB on the bottom chain. On the right we see that the symbols AA from the top chain have been sent to a chain that is capable of recognizing same/different. This circuit is very simple and consists only of three XOR gates implemented by spiking neurons. The XOR function is at the heart of same/different classification because it fires 1 for the inputs 01 and 10, but fires 0 for the inputs 00 and 11. In this case, if two spikes are separated by 100ms along each channel then they will cancel each other out. However, if only one spike is present then it will be capable of activating the XOR gate. By setting the threshold of the output neuron it is possible to detect adjacent symbol tokens that differ by some specified number of spikes. The output neuron can write to the channel in the same way as described for the implicit rule action, e.g. implementing the rule, If $\#_1\#\#_1$ then S.

It seems that the neural capacity for detection of same and different is a significant departure from what can easily be achieved in chemistry! A neural physical symbol system is capable of exploiting generalization mechanisms unavailable to chemistry. In chemistry there is no known molecular mechanism by which one molecule can determine whether two other molecules are the same or different, for any more than *one* pair of such molecules. The above mechanism of detecting same and different is a neural basis for simple **matching**. We now address the more difficult question of how a symbol system can be learned, and later how hash matching can be learned.

A powerful architecture for symbolic search is XCS (accuracy based classifier system) which combines Q-learning with a population of classifiers [7]. XCS consists of a population of classifiers (which strongly resemble constructions) with condition-action poles, $C \rightarrow A$. Each classifier has a fitness F that is related to its accuracy in predicting the reward obtained in the next time step. At each point in time a subset of the classifiers (called the Match Set) will match the state of the environment. Classifiers proposing several possible actions may exist in the Match Set. An action selection method is used to select the best classifier most of the time, although sometimes actions using sub-optimal classifiers are also executed for the sake of exploration. When the action is executed and the reward obtained, then the prediction accuracy of the classifiers in the action set can be updated. Selection then takes place between classifiers in the Match Set, i.e. those with lower fitness are removed from the population. This is effectively a niche-based selection that preserves representational diversity in the population of classifiers. Learning classifier system have been used to evolve classifiers for reinforcement learning tasks such as navigation, robotic control, but also for function approximation [6] and the systematic approach used may be of interest in FCG algorithmics.

The FCG and XCS both are algorithms that require replication of classifiers (constructions). The neuronal replicator hypothesis states that replicators exist in the brain and can undergo natural selection [17–20, 56].

In order for the argument that an FCG or XCS is implemented in the brain to be plausible, and if such spatiotemporal symbols do actually exist, then it is a fundamental prior question to explain how it is possible to replicate classifiers of the type shown in Figure 3 (implicit) and Figure 4 (explicit). There are several steps to obtain replication of classifiers. The first is to understand how a single classifier can be trained. Here we return to STDP. Using the STDP based synaptic plasticity rules described previously it is possible to train a classifier neuron to fire only when exposed to a particular spatio-temporal pattern of spikes. If we wish to train the output neuron to fire only for a particular interspike interval between two input neurons, it can be done as follows. We assume that each input neuron has many pathways for communicating with the output neuron. For example dendrites form the post-synaptic neuron may connect with the axon of the pre-synaptic neuron at many locations, a not unreasonable assumption [8]. Alternatively, it may be the case that several neurons are involved in the path from input to output neuron. In the model I assume delays of 5ms, 10ms, 15ms, and 20ms each. Each weight from input to output neuron is initially sub-threshold, i.e. insufficient to allow an action potential from an input neuron to an output neuron to produce another action potential. In fact 3 input neurons must fire for the output neuron to fire. Because only two pre-synaptic neurons can contribute to a synchronous pulse, the output neuron should therefore never fire! Indeed, only if a sub-threshold depolarization is provided by an external teacher *to* the output neuron, will it fire, if at that same time it is sufficiently stimulated by pre-synaptic neurons. In our experiments, sub-threshold (training) depolarization of the post-synaptic output neuron was given 20ms after the desired condition-spike-pattern was presented to the input neurons. Due to STDP the appropriate weights from the input neurons to the output neuron increased. The tuning curve of the output neuron was entrained, confirm it was possible to train a classifier neuron to recognize particular interspike intervals [15]. The second step was to train a classifier capable of reading *and* writing a spatiotemporal spike pattern. During the training period the spike pattern to be recognized entered along the 3 input channels with spikes at 0, 50ms and 100ms latency. This pattern was presented 9 times. A short fixed time period after each input pattern was presented to the input neurons, a pattern of sub-threshold depolarization was presented to the output neurons. This output pattern was the desired output pattern, which in this case is an inversion of the original pattern (although any pattern can be trained). A set of alternative possible delay lines from each input neuron to the classifier neuron, and another alternative possible set of delay lines from the classifier neuron to each output neuron, was trained. In addition, the classifier neuron was linked to a neuromodulatory inhibitory system blocked the passage of the original spike-pattern if it was recognized. If it was not recognized then the original pattern passed through to the outputs with a delay of 120ms, unchanged in form, see [15] for a full description of the experiment.

This training procedure is sufficient for the classifier neuron to learn both the input required to activate it, and the desired output. It should be clear that the above supervised training regime for entraining the input-output function mapped by one classifier can be trivially extended to allow replication of input-output functions. This is because once a single classifier neuron has been trained, this classifier neuron can train *other* classifier neurons in the following manner. The plasticity of the first (trained) classifier neuron is held fixed. The input-spike-pattern passes now to both classifiers, and the output of the first classifier is used to produce sub-threshold output neuron depolarization in the second classifier.

Systems that are capable of being trained by supervised learning, are typically also capable of training other such systems. The mechanism of copying by supervised training/learning is exhibited in the mechanism of "didactic transfer" of receptive fields that occurs by horizontal STDP and synaptic gain modification during deafferentation of visual cortex [59]. It is also exhibited in the mechanism of copying of connection topology shown previously [18]. Recent experiments show that such temporal specific training is indeed possible [35].

4 FCG Specific Operations

Matching and merging is critical for FCG. Matching means comparison for equivalence of two symbol structures X and Y [12][9][52]. In the simplest case, X and Y are atomic symbols and there is a match if the atoms are identical. This can trivially be done by writing X and Y to a chain. They should be separated by the transformation interval; in the case of Figure 5 this is 100ms. If X and Y atoms are identical then the classifier fires. We admit the fact that this delay imposes a very severe constraint on the number of possible matches, and it is necessary to think carefully about how faster matching could be done. Let us assume that matching requires sending the two patterns to a location in the brain that can do the matching. The process by which such flexible transport can be achieved is highly non-trivial and as yet we have no explanation for this. One possibility is that matching occurs in one of the sub-cortical structures that receive many incoming connections from a wide range of cortex, e.g. the cerebellum or the basal ganglia. Indeed the striatum of the basal ganglia is responsible for matching in Anderson's ACT-R cognitive architecture, although he does not give an explanation of how it should occur there [1].

The introduction alluded to how perceptual mechanisms could be exapted for symbolic operations. An example is now given for the case of matching in FCG. The experiments in [37] use rapid reversible synaptic plasticity (dynamic link matching) to learn classes of visual transformation, e.g. reflection, rotation etc. The same mechanism can be applied to the unsupervised learning of the concept of same and different in a symbol system. The power of the method is that it can generalize, i.e. it is only necessary to show a subset of possible instances of same and different symbols for the system to be able to extend this same/different classification to novel symbols or symbol structures. The dynamic link matching algorithm has recently been applied to spiking neural networks [46]. Related algorithms are used for auditory scene analysis [5]. It is conceivable that the same perceptual mechanisms used for interpreting sensory input are also used for interpreting internally generated symbolic inputs that are similarly encoded.

A more complex case of matching occurs where X and Y are not atomic but consist of an unordered list of elements. Here X and Y are equivalent if the list contains the same elements, e.g. match('(a b c)', '(a b c)') = true but also ('(a b c)', '(b a c)') = true. The next level of matching complexity occurs when X and Y are trees. Matching can either ignore or take into consideration the order of branching, e.g. if ignored a(bc) = a(cb) but in both cases a(b(c)) != a(bc).

The next step is partial tree matching, which is when some elements of X are in Y, but there are no elements in X that are not in Y: e.g. (a (d (e g))) partially matches with (a (b c) (d (e f g))).

Following matching of two symbol structures there can be merging. Merge takes already constructed objects and constructs from them a new object. Merge assumes that there has been a partial match and then adds everything of Y that is not in X to X. So when X = (a (d (e g))) partially matches with Y = (a (b c) (d (e f g))), then X becomes X' = (a (b c) (d (e f g))). Note that Y is left unchanged and can undergo further matches with other structures. The merge operation involves the copying of a symbol on the basis of the result of a match comparison. Therefore it is a type of explicit re-write rule. It is special because it requires hash based re-write, i.e. the rule does not just say if XT write TX, it says for example, if $\#_1\#_2$ write $\#_2\#_1$. That is, the re-write must work for a *range* of symbols. Whether this is plausible within our framework is not yet known. We are not yet able to provide plausible neuronal mechanisms capable of dealing with the more complex merge operations described above.

5 Discussion

There are several alternative connectionist type theories for the implementation of 'mental representations' or symbol-structures in the brain, but these are not considered in detail here [4, 38, 41, 47, 51]. I believe that it is more straightforward to face the problem head on. That is, to acknowledge that we need a full physical symbol system in the brain, and then to relax our biases about how such a physical symbol system could in fact be implemented. Thinking about a chemical symbol system helps me to do this.

There is some weak neurophysiological evidence for spatiotemporal spikes as symbol-tokens. The discovery of "cortical songs" is suggestive that discrete unique tokens such as symbols can be encoded as spatiotemporal patterns of spikes. Cortical songs are higher-order sequences of spike patterns repeated in the *same sequential order* observed in neocortical brain slices, of the form [A,C,D,E,F][A,C,D,E,F] for example where each letter represents a stereotyped polychronous pattern of activity [29]. Furthermore, there is evidence for the training methods we used to train classifiers, for example, synaptic inputs at distal dendrites can act as supervisory signals in the Hippocampus [13]. This maps to the sub-threshold depolarization we used to train classifier and output neurons. Several other papers also demonstrate methods for supervised training of spike classifiers, and so our classifier replication mechanism is by no means out of the blue. For example, the "Tempotron" is an example of learning to classify specific spatiotemporal patterns of spikes using a gradient-descent type rule to adjust weights on the basis of how rapidly a pattern results in firing of a classifier leaky-integrator neuron [25], see also [48]. Therefore, there is a growing body of work showing how replication of spatiotemporal spike pattern classifiers is possible.

In short, first I presented a plausible implementation of symbol-tokens in a brain. I then presented the core operation of an algorithm for learning symbol manipulation rules, i.e. replication of the input/output function of a classifier neuron. I have described elsewhere the details of a cognitive architecture based on a learning classifier system to learn simple syntactic rules [15]. These three components serve may provide a core for further work on understanding the neuronal basis of fluid construction grammar.

References

[1] Anderson, J.: How Can the Human Mind Occur in the Physical Universe. Oxford University Press (2007)
[2] Belousov, B.P.: A periodic reaction and its mechanism. Compilation of Abstracts on Radiation Medicine 147, 145 (1959)
[3] Biederman, I.: Recognition-by-components: A theory of human image understanding. Phychological Review 94(2), 115–147 (1987)
[4] Bienenstock, E., Geman, S.: Compositionality in Neural Systems. MIT/Bradford Books, Elsevier (1995)
[5] Bregman, A.S.: Auditory scene analysis. MIT Press, Cambridge (1990)
[6] Bull, L., Kovacs, T.: Foundations of Learning Classifier Systems. STUDFUZZ, vol. 183. Springer, Heidelberg (2005)
[7] Butz, M.: Rule-Based Evolutionary Online Learning Systems: A Principled Approach to LCS Analysis and Design. STUDFUZZ, vol. 191. Springer, Heidelberg (2006)
[8] Chklovskii, D., Mel, B., Svoboda, K.: Cortical rewiring and information storage. Nature 431, 782–788 (2004)
[9] Ciortuz, L., Saveluc, V.: Fluid Construction Grammar and Feature Constraint Logics. In: Steels, L. (ed.) Computational Issues in FCG. LNCS (LNAI), vol. 7249, pp. 289–311. Springer, Heidelberg (2012)
[10] Clark, A.: In defense of explicit rules. In: Ramsey, W., Stich, S.P., Rumelhart, D. (eds.) Philosophy and Connectionist Theory. Lawrence Erlbaum (1991)
[11] De Beule, J., Steels, L.: Hierarchy in Fluid Construction Grammars. In: Furbach, U. (ed.) KI 2005. LNCS (LNAI), vol. 3698, pp. 1–15. Springer, Heidelberg (2005)
[12] De Beule, J.: A Formal Deconstruction of Fluid Construction Grammar. In: Steels, L. (ed.) Computational Issues in FCG. LNCS (LNAI), vol. 7249, pp. 215–238. Springer, Heidelberg (2012)
[13] Dudman, J., Tsay, D., Siegelbaum, S.: A role for synaptic inputs at distal dendrites: Instructive signals for hippocampal long-term plasticity. Neuron 56, 866–879 (2007)
[14] Eigen, M.: Selforganization of matter and the evolution of biological macromolecules. Naturwissenschaften 58(10), 465–523 (1971)
[15] Fernando, C.: Co-evolution of lexical and syntactic classifiers during a language game. Evolutionary Intelligence 4(3), 165–182 (2011)
[16] Fernando, C.: Symbol manipulation and rule learning in spiking neuronal networks. Journal of Theoretical Biology 275, 29–41 (2011)
[17] Fernando, C., Goldstein, R., Szathmáry, E.: The neuronal replicator hypothesis. Neural Computation 22(11), 2809–2857 (2010)
[18] Fernando, C., Karishma, K., Szathmáry, E.: Copying and evolution of neuronal topology. PLoS ONE 3(11), e3775 (2008)

[19] Fernando, C., Szathmáry, E.: Chemical, neuronal and linguistic replicators. In: Pigliucci, M., Müller, G. (eds.) Towards an Extended Evolutionary Synthesis, pp. 209–249. MIT Press, Cambridge (2009)
[20] Fernando, C., Szathmáry, E.: Natural selection in the brain. In: Glatzeder, B., Goel, V., von Müller, A. (eds.) Toward a Theory of Thinking, pp. 291–340. Springer, Berlin (2009)
[21] Fodor, J., Pylyshyn, Z.: Connectionism and cognitive architecture: A critical analysis. Cognition 28, 3–71 (1988)
[22] Gáanti, T.: The Principles of Life. Oxford University Press, Oxford (2003)
[23] Gallistel, C., King, P.: Memory and the Computational Brain: Why Cognitive Science Will Transform Neuroscience. Wiley-Blackwell (2010)
[24] Goertzel, B., Lian, R., Arel, I., de Garis, H., Chen, S.: World survey of artificial brains, part ii: Biologically inspired cognitive architectures. Neurocomputing 74, 30–49 (2010)
[25] Gutig, F., Sompolinsky, H.: The tempotron: a neuron that learns spike timing-based decisions. Nature Neuroscience 9(3), 420–428 (2006)
[26] Harnad, S.: The symbol grounding problem. Physica D 42, 335–346 (1990)
[27] Holland, J., Reitman, J.: Cognitive systems based on adaptive algorithms. ACM SIGART Bulletin 63, 43–49 (1977)
[28] Hudson, J.: The History of Chemistry. MacMillan (1992)
[29] Ikegaya, Y., et al.: Synfire chains and cortical songs: Temporal modules of cortical activity. Science 304, 559–564 (2004)
[30] Izhikevich, E.M.: Simple model of spiking neurons. IEEE Transactions on Neural Networks 14, 1539–1572 (2003)
[31] Izhikevich, E.M.: Polychronization: computation with spikes. Neural Computation 18(2), 245–282 (2006)
[32] Izhikevich, E.M.: Solving the distal reward problem through linkage of stdp and dopamine signaling. Cerebral Cortex 17, 2443–2452 (2007)
[33] Izhikevich, E.M., Gally, J.A., Edelman, G.M.: Spike-timing dynamics of neuronal groups. Cereb. Cortex 14(8), 933–944 (2004)
[34] Izhikevich, E.M., Hoppensteadt, F.: Polychronous wavefront computations. International Journal of Bifurcation and Chaos 19, 1733–1739 (2009)
[35] Johnson, H., Goel, A., Buonomano, D.: Neural dynamics of in vitro cortical networks reflects experienced temporal patterns. Nature Neurosci. 13(8), 917–919 (2010)
[36] Karmiloff-Smith, A.: Beyond Modularity: A Developmental Perspective on Cognitive Science. MIT Press, Cambridge (1996)
[37] Konen, W., von der Malsburg, C.: Learning to generalize from single examples in the dynamic link architecture. Neural Computation 5(5), 719–735 (1993)
[38] Love, B.: Utilizing time: Asynchronous binding. In: Advances in Neural Information Processing Systems, vol. 11, pp. 38–44 (1999)
[39] Magnasco, M.: Chemical kinetics is turing universal. Physical Review Letters 78, 1190–1193 (1997)
[40] von der Malsburg, C.: The what and why of binding: The modeler's perspective. Neuron 24, 95–104 (1999)
[41] Marcus, G.: The Algebraic Mind: Integrating Connectionism and Cognitive Science. MIT Press (2001)
[42] Marcus, G., Vijayan, S., Bandi Rao, S., Vishton, P.: Rule learning by seven-month-old infants. Science 283(5398), 77–80 (1999)
[43] Maynard Smith, J.: The problems of biology. Oxford University Press, Oxford (1986)

[44] Nessler, B., Pfeiffer, M., Maass, W.: Bayesian computation emerges in generic cortical microcircuits through spike-timing-dependent plasticity. Theoretical Computer Science, 1–40 (2010)
[45] Penn, D., Holyoak, K., Povinelli, D.: Darwin's mistake: Explaining the discontinuity between human and nonhuman minds. Behavioral and Brain Sciences 31(2), 109–130 (2008)
[46] Pichevar, R., Rouat, J., Tai, L.: The oscillatory dynamic link matcher for spiking-neuron-based pattern recognition. Neurocomputing 69 (2006)
[47] Pollack, J.B.: Recursive distributed representations. Artificial Intelligence 46(1), 77–105 (1990)
[48] Ponulak, F., Kasinski, A.: Supervised learning in spiking neural networks with resume: Sequence learning, classification and spike-shifting. Neural Computation (2009)
[49] Rao, R., Ballard, D.: Predictive coding in the visual cortex: A functional interpretation of some extra-classical receptive-field effects. Nature Neuroscience 2(1), 79–87 (1999)
[50] Seidenberg, M., Elman, J.: Networks are not 'hidden rules'. Trends in Cognitive Sciences 3, 288–289 (1999)
[51] Shastri, L., Ajjanagadde, V.: From simple associations to systematic reasoning: A connectionist representation of rules, variables and dynamic bindings. Behavioural and Brain Sciences 16, 417–494 (1993)
[52] Santibáñez, J.S.: A Logic Programming Approach to Parsing and Production in Fluid Construction Grammar. In: Steels, L. (ed.) Computational Issues in FCG. LNCS (LNAI), vol. 7249, pp. 239–255. Springer, Heidelberg (2012)
[53] Steels, L. (ed.): Design Patterns in Fluid Construction Grammar, Constructional Approaches to Language, vol. 11. John Benjamins, Amsterdam (2011)
[54] Steels, L. (ed.): Computational Issues in FCG. LNCS (LNAI), vol. 7249. Springer, Heidelberg (2012)
[55] Steels, L., De Beule, J., Neubauer, N.: Linking in Fluid Construction Grammars. In: Proceedings of BNAIC, pp. 11–18. Transactions of the Belgian Royal Society of Arts and Sciences, Brussels (2005)
[56] Szathmáry, E., Fernando, C.: Concluding remarks. In: Calcott, B., Sterelny, K. (eds.) The Major Transitions in Evolution Revisited, pp. 301–310. MIT Press (2011)
[57] van Trijp, R., Steels, L., Beuls, K., Wellens, P.: Fluid construction grammar: The new kid on the block. In: Proceedings of the 13th Conference of the European Chapter of the Association for Computational Linguistics. ACL, Avignon (2012)
[58] Wiskott, L., von der Malsburg, C.: Recognizing faces by dynamic link matching. In: Proceedings of ICANN 1995, pp. 347–352 (1995)
[59] Young, J., Waleszczyk, W., Wang, C., Calford, M., Dreher, B., Obermayer, K.: Cortical reorganization consistent with spike timeing but not correlation-dependent plasticity. Nature Neuroscience 10(7), 887–895 (2007)

Author Index

Beuls, Katrien 123

Chang, Nancy 259
Ciortuz, Liviu 289

De Beule, Joachim 215, 259

Fernando, Chrisantha 312

Gerasymova, Kateryna 91

Höfer, Sebastian 143

Loetzsch, Martin 37

Micelli, Vanessa 178, 259

Saveluc, Vlad 289
Sierra-Santibáñez, Josefina 239
Stadler, Kevin 75
Steels, Luc 3

van Trijp, Remi 51